Collecting
Qualitative
Data

Collecting Qualitative Data

A Field Manual for Applied Research

Greg Guest
FHI 360, Social Research Solutions

Emily E. Namey
FHI 360, Social Research Solutions

Marilyn L. Mitchell
Gray Insight/Insightlink Communications

Los Angeles | London | New Delhi
Singapore | Washington DC

Los Angeles | London | New Delhi
Singapore | Washington DC

FOR INFORMATION:

SAGE Publications, Inc.

2455 Teller Road

Thousand Oaks, California 91320

E-mail: order@sagepub.com

SAGE Publications Ltd.

1 Oliver's Yard

55 City Road

London, EC1Y 1SP

United Kingdom

SAGE Publications India Pvt. Ltd.

B 1/I 1 Mohan Cooperative Industrial Area

Mathura Road, New Delhi 110 044

India

SAGE Publications Asia-Pacific Pte. Ltd.

3 Church Street

#10-04 Samsung Hub

Singapore 049483

Publisher: Vicki Knight

Associate Editor: Lauren Habib

Editorial Assistant: Kalie Koscielak

Production Editor: Brittany Bauhaus

Copy Editor: Patrice Sutton

Typesetter: C&M Digitals (P) Ltd.

Proofreader: Jennifer Gritt

Indexer: Diggs Publication Services, Inc.

Cover Designer: Anupama Krishnan

Marketing Manager: Nicole Elliott

Permissions Editor: Adele Hutchinson

Printed in the United States of America

Library of Congress Cataloging-in-Publication Data

Guest, Greg, 1963-
Collecting qualitative data : a field manual for applied research / Greg
Guest, Emily E. Namey, Marilyn L. Mitchell.

p. cm.
Includes bibliographical references and index.

ISBN 978-1-4129-8684-7 (pbk.)

1. Qualitative research. 2. Social sciences—Research. I. Namey, Emily E. II. Mitchell, Marilyn L. III. Title.

H62.G829 2013
001.4'2—dc23   2012009523

This book is printed on acid-free paper.

16 17 18 19 20 10 9 8 7 6 5 4 3 2

Brief Contents

Detailed Contents

Preface

Researchers (and nonresearchers) around the world are increasingly utilizing qualitative data collection methods. Participant observation, focus groups, and in-depth interviews are now commonly practiced across a diverse range of research-oriented fields including marketing, behavioral and social sciences, public health, international development, public policy, and program evaluation. Surprisingly, few resources exist to provide researchers and, perhaps more importantly, up-and-coming researchers, with practical, step-by-step instruction on how to prepare for, implement, and manage qualitative data collection activities in the field.

The three of us have designed, managed, and conducted qualitative research in each of the major research sectors—academic, nonprofit, corporate, and government. Our combined research experience also spans dozens of countries, where we have both taught qualitative data collection methods and overseen their implementation. Based on this experience, we have found that most applied researchers are concerned with learning and improving the skills necessary for executing a credible and effective qualitative study. It is these skills, developed over the years through academic study and practical trial and error in varied contexts, that we impart in this book.

Many existing qualitative methods books focus on ongoing epistemological debates that divide certain sectors of academia. Admittedly, there are interesting philosophical questions associated with these debates that constitute an integral part of the academic experience for students in research-oriented disciplines. However, books that focus primarily on these questions do little to provide instruction on how to actually carry out research, particularly research with an applied focus. Our primary purpose in writing this book is to fill this "practicality gap" by providing a pragmatically driven manual that researchers of all types can use to enhance the design and conduct of qualitative research projects. Each chapter provides instructions on how to implement the methods outlined. We walk readers through each data collection method, with explanations, cautionary notes, examples, and templates along the way.

So what exactly makes this approach unique? The distinct features of this book that we feel set it apart from other texts include the following:

- **A cross-disciplinary approach**—This book is written for audiences across the entire spectrum of qualitative research; it is not specific to a particular discipline or research sector.
- **A how-to format**—The book provides practical (field-tested) information on the logistics of planning and conducting qualitative data collection. For each topic covered, we include illustrative examples, step-by-step instructions, and concrete tools and templates.
- **An accessible style**—We minimize theoretical or discipline-specific jargon and provide real-world examples, drawn from our diverse research experience, wherever possible.
- **A well-balanced scope**—This book covers the three most common forms of qualitative data collection used worldwide—participant observation, in-depth interviews, and focus groups—in one text. It also includes instruction on additional qualitative data collection methods, such as free-listing, pile sorts, ethnographic decision modeling, document analysis, and projective techniques.
- **A current perspective**—All three authors are active applied researchers. The book references many of the technological advancements relevant to the qualitative research world (e.g., digital recording, Livescribe, remote interviewing).
- **Focused coverage of research ethics**—We devote an entire chapter to research ethics, both the general aspects and those that relate specifically to qualitative research.
- **A practical guide to data management**—Chapter 7 describes the main principles behind good data management and includes practical guidance, tools and templates for readers to use and adapt to their own research situation.
- **Explicit inclusion of an international perspective**—We draw upon our international and cross-cultural experience to provide readers with essential considerations for working in foreign cultures.

HOW THIS BOOK IS ORGANIZED

The book begins with an introductory chapter on qualitative research. It outlines the diversity of perspectives in the field and positions the book's contents relative to those perspectives. Chapter 1 also contains a section on research design and includes guidance on establishing research objectives, determining project scope, and choosing data collection methods. Chapter 2 is dedicated to sampling in qualitative research, an often neglected topic in many qualitative research books. Chapters 3, 4, and 5 cover the three most commonly employed qualitative data collection methods—participant observation, in-depth interviews, and focus groups, respectively. In addition to instructions for executing each of these methods, these chapters also include discussions on some of the recent technological advancements in the field and their implications for data collection (e.g., Internet and/or phone interviews and focus groups, digital recording, and note-taking).

The data collection methods outlined in Chapters 3 to 5 are time-tested techniques that work, which is why each has its own chapter in this book. But each can benefit from supplemental activities that go beyond the traditional usage of the methods, such as listing, categorizing, drawing, decision-modeling, and projective techniques. We cover these activities in Chapter 6, as well as document analysis. Unlike the other methods covered in this book, document analysis is not a form of data *generation*, but it is considered by many to be a constituent component of qualitative research so we have opted for its inclusion.

Data management is probably one of the most neglected topics in the qualitative methods literature. And those sources that do cover it tend to conflate data management with data analysis or treat it as a synonym for qualitative data analysis software. In Chapter 7, we discuss data management as an organizational process and provide multiple templates and examples along with procedural guidance to this end. Chapter 8, the final chapter, details research ethics in qualitative research. In contrast to other books, which tend to place ethical discussions nearer to the front, we have chosen to include a summary of ethical research practices as a concluding chapter, based on our belief that in order for readers to relate research ethics principles to qualitative research, they first need to be familiar with what qualitative research entails.

We have done our best in this book to balance comprehensive coverage with concision; an exhaustive treatment for each method and approach discussed is not possible within the confines of one book, so we have focused on the necessary steps to design and conduct good qualitative research using these techniques. For those individuals who wish to read more about a particular method or issue, we include a list of additional readings at the end of each chapter. These lists are themselves not exhaustive but they provide a good place to begin further exploration.

For those readers who conduct, or plan to conduct, research in a foreign country or culture, we include a section at the end of each chapter outlining the unique issues associated with working internationally and/or cross-culturally. The three of us have spent a good portion of our research careers in international and cross-cultural settings and convey some of the lessons we have learned (often the hard way), as they relate to the specific material in each chapter.

We have chosen not to include data analysis in this text (although we touch upon it in some of the chapters). Qualitative data analysis is a diverse and complex process, and we feel that the topic deserves more coverage than a book chapter can accommodate. In addition, several excellent data analysis texts already exist (see Chapter 1 for references); we didn't feel the need to duplicate these efforts. This book is about qualitative data collection and management, and so we focus our complete attention on this part of the research process.

Acknowledgments

This book is based on our combined experience with planning, implementing, executing, and managing qualitative research studies. Without those experiences, this book would not exist. We are therefore thankful to the various clients and funders who have supported our research over the decades. We are also grateful to our colleagues, from whom we have learned, and continue to learn, a great deal. Additionally, we would like to express our deepest gratitude to all of the students we have had the pleasure of teaching over the years. They have made us better researchers and instructors. Their insights and questions are implicitly embedded throughout this book.

On a more personal level, Greg wishes to thank his wife, Gretel and their two sons, Hunter and Aaron, for putting up with his evening and weekend absences to write his portion of the book. Greg is also indebted to his many mentors over the years who have taught him about the various facets of the research process, including the methodological, the political, the ethical, and the managerial. Of particular note in this regard are Kate MacQueen, Jeff Johnson, Larry Severy, Susan Newcomer, Russ Bernard, and Bob Rhoades.

Emily is extremely grateful to her husband, Jason, for making her contributions to this project possible. She would also like to thank JoAnn (Plantz), Zola (Amig), George (Labecki), and Stephen (King) for teaching her how to write; Drs. Bryan Page and Bob Trotter for introducing her to qualitative methods; Drs. Annie Lyerly and Laura Beskow for providing opportunities to refine her data collection skills; and her colleagues at Duke University, FHI 360, and Social Research Solutions for their continual mentorship and support.

Marilyn wishes first and foremost to thank Jerome Kirk for combining the best of mentor, life partner, and critic in one very lovable package. Additionally, from a very large group of colleagues, clients and students who have been key to her development as a researcher, she would like to recognize Robert Gray of Gray Insight/Insightlink Communications, Bob Mueller of the Kern Mueller Group/Kaplan Research, and Gery Ryan of the RAND Corporation for the many hours of productive and enjoyable discussion of research methods, analysis, and the meaning of life.

Finally, we'd like to thank everyone at Sage, particularly Vicki Knight, for putting their full support behind this book. Once again, Sage has proven to be a first rate publisher.

SAGE Publications and the authors would also like to express their gratitude to the following reviewers for their thoughtful and constructive comments:

Laura S. Abrams, *University of California, Los Angeles*

Roni Berger, *Adelphi University*

Maenette Benham, *University of Hawaii, Manoa*

Christopher Brkich, *Georgia Southern University*

Paula C. Carder, *Portland State University*

Dawn Comeau, *Emory University*

Daniel Dohan, *University of California, San Francisco*

Debra S. Emmelman, *Southern Connecticut State University*

Caren J. Frost, *University of Utah*

Roberta E. Goldman, *Harvard School of Public Health*

Etsuko Kinefuchi, *University of North Carolina at Greensboro*

Sarah A. Mathews, *Florida International University*

Diane B. Monsivais, *The University of Texas at El Paso*

Andrea Leverentz, *University of Massachusetts Boston*

Deborah K. Padgett, *New York University*

Terry M. Pollack, *San Jose State University*

Yuping Zhang, *Lehigh University*

About the Authors

Greg Guest received an MA in anthropology from the University of Calgary and a PhD in anthropology from the University of Georgia. Over the past 15 years, he has carried out research in academia (Duke University, East Carolina University, the University of Georgia), the private sector (Sapient Corporation), government (Centers for Disease Control and Prevention), and in the nonprofit sector (FHI 360). Guest has implemented and managed multidisciplinary projects in various fields of applied research, including human ecology, agricultural development, human-computer interaction, consumer experience, and international health. Greg is currently a social-behavioral scientist at FHI 360, where he manages multisite, qualitative, and mixed methods research projects related to reproductive health, HIV prevention, and other infectious diseases. Guest's other books include two edited volumes—*Globalization, Health and the Environment: An Integrated Perspective* (AltaMira, 2005) and *Handbook for Team-Based Qualitative Research* (AltaMira, 2008)—as well as the co-authored book, *Applied Thematic Analysis* (Sage, 2012). He's published articles in journals such as *Field Methods, American Journal of Public Health, JAIDS, AIDS Care, AIDS Education and Prevention, African Journal of AIDS Research, AIDS and Behavior, Journal of Family Planning and Reproductive Health Care, Human Ecology,* and *Culture and Agriculture*. Guest is also owner of the research consulting firm Social Research Solutions, which specializes in methodological training and consultation (www.socialresearchsolutions.com).

Emily E. Namey recently rejoined FHI 360, where she manages several international qualitative and mixed methods projects related to global health and HIV prevention. Prior to her work at FHI 360, she spent over 5 years at Duke University, splitting time among the Institute for Genome Sciences and Policy, the Department of Obstetrics and Gynecology, and the Trent Center for Bioethics. At Duke, Namey implemented qualitative research on subjects ranging from maternity care to vaccine trial participation to ethical approaches to genomic research recruitment to the use and understanding of Certificates of Confidentiality. She has experience in the private sector as well, having completed projects at Intel Corporation and Nike, Inc. She also currently serves as a qualitative research consultant for Social Research Solutions, conducting trainings on qualitative research methods, analysis, and software. Her publications include contributions to the *Handbook for Team-Based Qualitative Research* (AltaMira,

2008) and *Applied Thematic Analysis* (Sage, 2012) as well as articles in *Social Science & Medicine, Fertility and Sterility, AIDS Care, IRB,* and the *Journal of Empirical Research on Human Research Ethics.* Namey received her MA in applied anthropology from Northern Arizona University.

Marilyn L. Mitchell is a cultural anthropologist with extensive experience in quantitative and qualitative research design, interviewing techniques, cultural analysis, survey development, sampling, and forecasting. She works as an independent researcher and as an associate of Gray Insight, for clients that have included dozens of Fortune 500 companies, educational institutions, government agencies, and nonprofit organizations in the United States and nearly 100 other countries. She has lectured on social science research and related topics at University of California, Los Angeles, University of Southern California, San Francisco State University, the Nissan Summer Institute for Instructors at Historically Black Colleges, Chapman University, the U.S. Army's Human Terrain Systems, and the Centers for Disease Control and Prevention. Marilyn earned her BA, MA, and PhD in cultural anthropology and BS in biology from the University of California at Irvine and conducted her dissertation research at the National Museum of Ethnology in Osaka, Japan. She is also the author of *Employing Qualitative Methods in the Private Sector* (Sage, 1998).

1

Qualitative Research

Defining and Designing

The qualitative research methods introduced in this book are often employed to answer the *whys* and *hows* of human behavior, opinion, and experience— information that is difficult to obtain through more quantitatively-oriented methods of data collection. Researchers and practitioners in fields as diverse as anthropology, education, nursing, psychology, sociology, and marketing regularly use qualitative methods to address questions about people's ways of organizing, relating to, and interacting with the world. Despite the interdisciplinary recognition of the value of "qualitative research" (or perhaps because of it), qualitative research is not a unified field of theory and practice. On the contrary, a plethora of viewpoints, sometimes diametrically opposed to one another, exist on the subject. Scholars regularly debate about what qualitative research is, how and why it should be conducted, how it should be analyzed, and in what form it should be presented. In fact, fundamental and often heated disagreements about philosophical assumptions and the nature of data exist among qualitative researchers. We don't pretend to be able to solve any of these controversies. Nor do we suggest one approach or viewpoint is superior to another in the grand scheme of things. How one approaches qualitative research, and research in general, depends on a variety of personal, professional, political, and contextual factors. Ultimately, there is no right or wrong way of conducting a qualitative research project. Nevertheless, some approaches and methods are more conducive to certain types of qualitative inquiry than are others. A key distinction in this regard is the difference between *pure* and *applied* research. It is the latter of these—applied research—for which the contents of this book will be most (though certainly not exclusively) relevant.

Applied research "strives to improve our understanding of a problem, with the intent of contributing to the solution of that problem" (Bickman & Rog, 2009, p. x). It is generally grounded in systematic and scientific methodology and is highly pragmatic in nature. Applied research can, and often does, generate new knowledge and contribute to theory, but its primary focus is on collecting and generating data to further our understanding of real-world problems. It is through this lens that this book is written, with the intent of providing researchers with practical procedures and tools to collect and manage qualitative data in a rigorous and transparent manner.

We begin this chapter by providing a definition of qualitative research that serves to frame the content and scope of the chapters that follow. We then provide a brief overview of one of the main epistemological debates in the field—that between positivist and interpretivist perspectives. Despite the practical timbre of this book, we feel it would be a disservice to readers if we omitted this discussion.

We then discuss some of the prevailing traditions in qualitative inquiry—phenomenology, ethnography, inductive thematic analysis and grounded theory, case study approaches, discourse-conversation analysis, and narrative analysis—as they relate to qualitative data collection. We cover these because they are related to data collection efforts and analytic strategies, both of which are key factors in research design.

The second half of the chapter addresses qualitative research design. In this section, we provide guidance on when to use and, equally importantly, when not to use qualitative methods. Following this, we break the research design process down into smaller components to help readers consider more thoughtfully the parameters of a research project, such as units of analysis, research scope, and the degree of structure in research design and data collection methods and instruments.

WHAT IS QUALITATIVE RESEARCH?

There are about as many definitions of qualitative research as there are books on the subject. Some authors highlight the research purpose and focus:

> Qualitative researchers are interested in understanding the meaning people have constructed, that is, how people make sense of their world and the experiences they have in the world. (Merriam, 2009, p. 13)

Others emphasize an epistemological stance:

> [Qualitative research is] research using methods such as participant observation or case studies which result in a narrative, descriptive account of a setting or practice. Sociologists using these methods typically reject positivism and adopt a form of interpretive sociology. (Parkinson & Drislane, 2011)

Still other definitions focus on the process and context of data collection:

> Qualitative research is a situated activity that locates the observer in the world. It consists of a set of interpretive, material practices that makes the world visible. These practices transform the world. They turn the world into a series of representations, including field notes, interviews, conversations, photographs, recordings, and memos to the self. At this level, qualitative research involves an interpretive, naturalistic approach to the world. This means that qualitative researchers study things in their natural settings, attempting to make sense of, or to interpret, phenomena in terms of the meanings people bring to them. (Denzin & Lincoln, 2005, p. 3)

While we don't disagree with the above definitions, we don't find them particularly useful in an applied research context. We prefer the simpler and more functional definition offered by Nkwi, Nyamongo, and Ryan (2001, p. 1): "Qualitative research involves any research that uses data that do not indicate ordinal values." For these authors, the defining criterion is the type of data generated and/or used. In short, qualitative research involves collecting and/or working with text, images, or sounds. An outcome-oriented definition such as that proposed by Nkwi et al. avoids (typically inaccurate) generalizations and the unnecessary (and, for the most part, inaccurate) dichotomous positioning of qualitative research with respect to its quantitative counterpart. It allows for the inclusion of many different kinds of data collection and analysis techniques, as well as the diversity of theoretical and epistemological frameworks that are associated with qualitative research.

Qualitative Data Types

Given our working definition of qualitative research, you can begin to imagine the range of possible data types that qualitative research might generate. At one extreme, we may have a single-word answer in response to an open-ended question on a survey (e.g., In what city were you born? _____). At the other end of the spectrum, a researcher could be dealing with a 50-page narrative of a participant's life history, produced from an in-depth interview. In order to narrow the range of data types for this book's focus, we look to Ryan and Bernard's (2000) typology of qualitative research that divides qualitative data into its three main forms—text, images, and sounds (Figure 1.1). Analysis of text is further subdivided into two primary components—text as an object of analysis (e.g., linguistic type approaches, such as structural linguistics) and text as a proxy for experience.

This book focuses mainly on data collection methods that produce textual and visual data as a proxy for experience and as a means to understand the social, cultural,

Figure 1.1   Typology of Qualitative Research

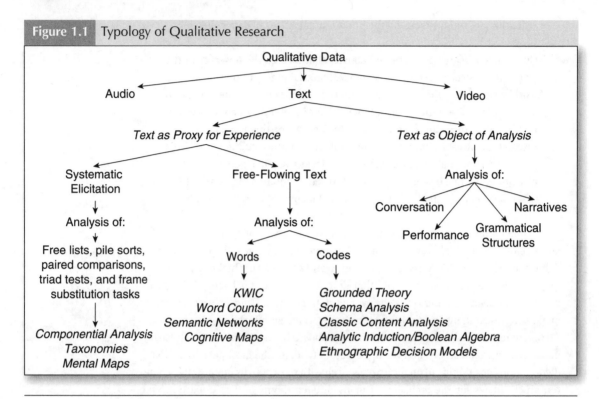

Source: Ryan and Bernard (2000).

and physical context in which behavior occurs. The methods covered here—participant observation, in-depth interviews, and focus groups—are the most commonly used methods in applied qualitative inquiry. We do, however, cover other methods such as systematic elicitation and document analysis in Chapter 6, since these are also important, often-used methods in applied qualitative inquiry.

A common thread throughout almost all forms of qualitative research is an inductive and flexible nature. Though there are certainly a few qualitative data collection and analysis techniques that are more structured and deductively oriented than others (e.g., content analysis), most research initiatives in the qualitative vein take an iterative approach. Flexibility can be built into the research design itself by employing a theoretical sampling strategy in which a researcher adjusts the sampling procedures during the data collection process based on incoming data (see Chapter 2).

Another defining attribute of qualitative research is the open-ended and inductive style of questioning and observation. The quintessential feature of both in-depth interviews and focus groups is the use of open-ended (though not necessarily unscripted) questions, which are followed up with probes in response to participants' answers. In fact, inductive probing is the sine qua non of these methods and is why we devote a significant amount of attention to it in Chapters 4 and 5. Likewise, participant observation is much more inductive and flexible compared to its quantitative cousin, direct observation. While participant observation can benefit from semi-structured data collection templates and other types of tools for focusing attention (covered in Chapter 3), in applied research, it is almost always used in an exploratory capacity, to help develop research focus and set the parameters for subsequent data collection activities.

EPISTEMOLOGICAL PERSPECTIVES

The epistemological landscape in qualitative research is as diverse and complex as the various disciplines that employ qualitative methods. We don't attempt to recreate it here. Given the practical orientation of the book, we focus mostly on methodological procedures and offer actionable suggestions for carrying out qualitative research in a rigorous manner. At the same time, we feel that researchers (and future researchers) need at least to be aware of the ongoing debates in social and behavioral science pertaining to the philosophy of knowledge and the scientific method. Below, we briefly address the two most commonly referred to approaches—interpretivism and positivism or post-positivism. We briefly touch upon a relatively new epistemological viewpoint that has emerged from theoretical physics—model-dependent realism—which, in our view, may provide a useful philosophical framework for qualitative research and the social and behavioral sciences in general.

Interpretivism

Though there are various definitions of *interpretivism*, for brevity we like Walsham's (1993) description, which posits that

> interpretive methods of research start from the position that our knowledge of reality, including the domain of human action, is a social construction by human actors and that this applies equally to researchers. Thus there is no objective reality which can be discovered by researchers and replicated by others, in contrast to the assumptions of positivist science. (p. 5)

Proponents of the interpretive school, popularized by scholars such as Clifford Geertz (1973), argue that the scientific method is reductionist and often misses the point of qualitative research. Instead, this approach, stemming from a hermeneutic tradition,[1] is more interested in interpreting deeper meaning in discourse that is represented in a collection of personal narratives or observed behaviors and activities. As Geertz (1973, p. 29) explains,

---

[1]Hermenuetics was originally the practice of interpreting meaning within biblical text. Usage of the term has expanded to include interpretation of nonreligious texts as well, in search of underlying sociopolitical meaning.

To look at the symbolic dimensions of social action—art, religion, ideology, science, law, morality, common sense—is not to turn away from the existential dilemmas of life for some empyrean realm of deemotionalized forms; it is to plunge into the midst of them. The essential vocation of interpretive anthropology is not to answer our deepest questions, but to make available to us answers that others, guarding other sheep in other valleys, have given, and thus to include them in the consultable record of what man has said.

As such, an interpretive perspective is based on the idea that qualitative research efforts should be concerned with revealing multiple realities as opposed to searching for one *objective* reality. In Denzin's words, "Objective reality will never be captured. In depth understanding, the use of multiple validities, not a single validity, a commitment to dialogue is sought in any interpretive study" (Denzin, 2010, p. 271).

We recognize that the interpretive field is much more diverse than we portray here and includes different perspectives such as post-structuralism, experimentalism (not to be confused with experimental design), and critical theory. For readers who wish to read more about these perspectives and the ongoing epistemological debates, we suggest looking at Denzin and Lincoln (2011) and Alvesson and Skoldberg (2009).

Positivism, Post-Positivism and Model-Dependent Realism

Positivism, at least within social and behavioral science, views knowledge differently from interpretivism. Traditional positivism as envisioned by Compte (i.e., "logical" or "rigid" positivism) assumes that there is an objective reality independent of the observer and that, given the right methods and research design, one can accurately capture that reality. Nowadays, there are few supporters of rigid or logical positivism in the social sciences. Rather, as Patton asserts, most contemporary social scientists who adhere to the scientific method are really post-positivists (Patton, 2002, pp. 91–96), and

> are prepared to admit and deal with imperfections in a phenomenologically messy and methodologically imperfect world, but [sic] still believe that objectivity is worth striving for. (Patton, 2002, p. 93)

A post-positivist approach is based on the fundamental ideas that (a) interpretations should be derived directly from data observed and (b) data collection and analysis methods should, in some way, be systematic and transparent. Post-positivism is, therefore, closely associated with the scientific method. It distances itself, however, from the strict epistemological position that a truly objective reality can be assessed and represented.

Indeed, from a theoretical and philosophical perspective, the notion of being able to observe and document one true objective reality is a dubious concept, particularly for social and behavioral phenomena, which are extremely complex, dynamic, and unbounded entities. Compounding this is the fact that every part of any research process is influenced by, and filtered through, the researchers' own cognitive predilections. Identifying and operationalizing the research question, data collection and analysis, and report writing are all subject to decisions a researcher or research team make. Post-positivism recognizes these limitations.

Post-positivists accept the premise that a completely objective reality is impossible to apprehend but assume that research accounts can approximate, or at least attempt to approximate, an objective truth. As Denzin and Lincoln (2005, p. 27) observe, "post-positivism holds that only partially objective accounts of the world can be produced, for all methods examining such accounts are flawed." Post-positivists still rely on scientific methods to gather and interpret data but view their findings as evidence-based probabilities rather than absolute truths. The end goal is to generate a reasonable *approximation* of reality that is tied closely to what is observed (e.g., participants' responses, observations).

The interpretive–positivist debate affects the data analysis process more so than the data collection process, but the epistemological approach a researcher holds still influences how she goes about data collection. For a post-positivist, standard data collection procedures are systematic (in as much as they can be in qualitative inquiry) and transparent. Interpretations are grounded in the data collected and are intended to be as accurate a representation of the subject as possible. In contrast, from an interpretive view, the focus is more on depth of inquiry—particularly personal and shared meaning—and more leeway is given for how data are interpreted and presented.

A good number of the world's scientists, across many fields of research, agree with the philosophical tenet that an observer-independent view of the world is an unachievable goal. Two of the world's most notable physicists, Stephen Hawking and Leonard Mlodinow, argue that "[t]here is no picture- or theory-independent concept of reality." Hawking and Mlodinow (2010) adopt a position they call model-dependent realism. In their words,

> Model-dependent realism is based on the idea that our brains interpret the input from our sensory organs by making a model of the world. When such a model is successful at explaining events, we tend to attribute to it, and to the elements and concepts that constitute it, the quality of reality or absolute truth (p. 7). . . . According to model-dependent realism, it is pointless to ask whether a model is real, only whether it agrees with observation. If there are two models that both agree with observation . . . then one cannot say that one is more real than another. (p. 46)

While model-dependent realism is new and has not yet been adopted in the behavioral and social sciences, the concept is certainly applicable and compatible with a post-positivist approach. Both perspectives emphasize data (observations) and the degree to which they can explain one's assertions and interpretations of the world (models). Both approaches strive to support interpretations of the world we present with the best supporting data possible. In our view, this is what applied research is all about.

Most applied research is founded on a post-positivist approach (and perhaps in the future, model-dependent realism). One reason has to do with the purpose of applied research, which is to understand and provide recommendations for real-world issues and problems. As Miles and Huberman (1994) note, a well-told story can still be wrong. Applied researchers can't afford to get the story wrong. And although most would readily admit that it's impossible to convey a complete and entirely accurate account of things, their goal is to try to tell the most accurate and comprehensive story their data and research constraints permit. It is this perspective that forms the epistemological foundation of this book.

BASIC APPROACHES IN QUALITATIVE RESEARCH

In this section, we briefly describe some of the more common approaches to collecting and using qualitative data. There is certainly overlap between them; the distinctions are not always readily evident. To help make sense of the complexity, we include a summary of each approach and the implications they have for data collection in Table 1.1 below. For those interested in reading more on these approaches, we provide references in the Additional Reading section.

Table 1.1	Research Approaches and Implications for Data Collection	
Type of Approach	**Defining Features**	**Data Collection Implications**
Phenomenology	• Focuses on individual experiences, beliefs, and perceptions. • Text used as a proxy for human experience.	• Questions and observations are aimed at drawing out individual experiences and perceptions. • In focus groups, group experiences and normative perceptions are typically sought out. • In-depth interviews and focus groups are ideal methods for collecting phenomenological data.
Ethnography	• Oriented toward studying shared meanings and practices (i.e., culture).	• Questions and observations are generally related to social and cultural processes and shared meanings within a given group of people.

Type of Approach	Defining Features	Data Collection Implications
	• Emphasizes the emic perspective. • Can have a contemporary or historical focus.	• Traditionally, it is associated with long-term fieldwork, but some aspects are employed in applied settings. • Participant observation is well suited to ethnographic inquiry.
Inductive Thematic Analysis	• Draws on inductive analytic methods (this would be same for Grounded Theory below as well). • Involves identifying and coding emergent themes within data. • Most common analytic approach used in qualitative inquiry.	• ITA requires generation of free-flowing data. • In-depth interviews and focus groups are the most common data collection techniques associated with ITA. • Notes from participant observation activities can be analyzed using ITA, but interview/focus group data are better.
Grounded Theory	• Inductive data collection and analytic methods. • Uses systematic and exhaustive comparison of text segments to build thematic structure and theory from a body of text. • Common analytic approach in qualitative studies.	• As above, in-depth interviews and focus groups are the most common data collection techniques associated with GT. • Sample sizes for grounded theory are more limited than for ITA because the analytic process is more intensive and time consuming. **Note:** Many researchers incorrectly label all inductive thematic analyses "grounded theory," as a default. Technically, they are not the same thing.
Case Study	• Analysis of one to several cases that are unique with respect to the research topic • Analysis primarily focused on exploring the unique quality.	• Cases are selected based on a unique (often rarely observed) quality. • Questions and observations should focus on, and delve deeply into, the unique feature of interest.

Discourse/ Conversation Analysis	• Study of "naturally occurring" discourse
	  ○ Can range from conversation to public events to existing documents.
	  ○ Text and structures within discourse used as objects of analysis.
		• These linguistically focused methods often use existing documents as data.
		• Conversations between individuals that spontaneously emerge within group interviews or focus groups may be studied but are not preferred.
		• Participant observation is conducive to discourse analysis if narratives from public events can be recorded.

(Continued)

Table 1.1 (Continued)		
Type of Approach	**Defining Features**	**Data Collection Implications**
Narrative Analysis	• Narratives (storytelling) used as source of data. • Narratives from one or more sources (e.g., interviews, literature, letters, diaries).	• If generating narratives (through in-depth interviews), then questions/tasks need to be aimed at eliciting stories and the importance those stories, hold for participants, as well as larger cultural meaning.
Mixed Methods	• Defined as integrating quantitative and qualitative research methods in one study. • Two most common designs are sequential and concurrent.	• Collection of qualitative data in a mixed methods study can be informed from a wide range of theoretical perspectives and analytic approaches. • Researchers must specify up front, and in detail, how, when, and why qualitative and quantitative datasets will be integrated.

Phenomenology

Phenomenology, the study of conscious experience, can be traced back to early 20th-century philosophers such as Husserl, Sartre, and Merleau-Ponty. Many of the ideas embodied in the works of these early phenomenologists were later adopted in the behavioral and social sciences by notable scholars such as psychologist Amedeo Giorgi (1970) and social scientist Alfred Schütz, (1967). In contemporary social science, the term is used more broadly to denote the study of individuals' perceptions, feelings, and lived experiences. Smith, Flowers, and Larkin (2009), for example, define *phenomenology* as

> a philosophical approach to the study of experience . . . [that] shares a particular interest in thinking about what the experience of being human is *like*, in all of its various aspects, but especially in terms of the things that matter to us, and which constitute our lived world. (p. 11)

Phenomenology is a commonly employed approach in clinical psychology, and in this context it is associated with a unique set of methods and procedures (Moustakas, 1994).

Many of the ideas within the phenomenological field are embedded within qualitative inquiry in general; much qualitative research is phenomenological in nature in that it attempts to understand individuals' lived experiences and the behavioral, emotive, and social meanings that these experiences have for them. For instance, the notion of open-ended questions and conversational inquiry, so typical in qualitative research, allows research participants to talk about a topic in their own words, free of the constraints imposed by fixed-response questions that are generally seen in quantitative studies. Similarly, market researchers don't test products, they test peoples' *experiences* of products.

Of course not all qualitative research has phenomenological underpinnings. In some cases, the topic of study might be social structures or cultural processes that transcend individual experience, such as we might find in ethnographic research. But even so, data on such topics are often collected through interviews with individuals and hence through their experiential lens.

Ethnography

Ethnography literally means "to write about a group of people." Its roots are grounded in the field of anthropology and the practice of in situ research, where a researcher is immersed within the community he/she is studying for extended periods of time. Early 20th-century anthropologists such as Bronislaw Malinowksi and Franz Boas pioneered traditional ethnography, which historically has focused on the cultural dimensions of life and behavior, such as shared practices and belief systems. A hallmark feature of the ethnographic approach is a holistic perspective, based on the premise that human behavior and culture are complicated phenomena and are composed of, and influenced by, a multitude of factors. These might include historical precedents, the physical context in which people live and work, the social structures in which individuals are embedded, and the symbolic environment in which they act (e.g., language, shared meanings).

Traditionally, ethnographic research has involved a researcher's total and prolonged immersion within a study community, often for a year or longer. With the luxury of time, proximity to the field site, and the ability to coordinate data collection in an integrated and inductive manner, research can be more fluid.

Another strength of the ethnographic approach is the naturalistic, in situ manner in which it is carried out and its emphasis on understanding the *emic* (insider/local) perspective. Observing individual and group behavior in its natural context and participating in that context can generate insights that other forms of research cannot. Not surprisingly, participant observation has historically been an integral component of ethnographic inquiry.

Ethnography has evolved significantly since its formal emergence in the early 20th century. Many disciplines outside of anthropology now utilize an ethnographic approach, and its adoption in applied research has grown as well. But commensurate with these changes is a dilution of the method. Contemporary use of ethnography outside of anthropology, particularly in applied research, is generally not as immersive as traditional ethnography. Most researchers cannot afford—in time or funds—to spend a year or more in the field. Extended fieldwork is still considered by many anthropology departments a rite of passage for doctoral students, but outside of this context, modern ethnography is much shorter in duration than its traditional predecessor.[2]

Another change, at least in applied research fields, is the move toward team research. Ethnography used to be a lonely enterprise. An ethnographer would travel by himself or herself to some exotic and remote place and live with the local people for a year or more. In such a research context, the entire research process—design, data collection, analysis, and write-up—was embodied within one individual. Nowadays, field research is often a collaborative enterprise, with teams consisting of multiple members from professional disciplines who represent various organizations. We provide key references on ethnography in the Additional Readings section for those with an interest in delving deeper into the method and its history.

Clarifying Terms

In our day-to-day interactions with colleagues, funders, and clients, we regularly encounter incorrect usage of research terms when discussing qualitative inquiry. One of the more common transgressions is the use of inappropriate terms as synonyms for qualitative research. So for the record:

Ethnography—Ethnography stems from the Greek root *ethnos*, meaning "an ethnic group," and *graphy*, denoting "a form of writing, drawing or representation." Ethnography can involve all types of data collection methods, including structured quantitative approaches, so it is therefore not interchangeable with qualitative research.

Formative Research—Formative research refers to research that precedes and informs a larger research component. While in many cases qualitative methods are used in such a capacity, they are just as often employed as independent methods in and of themselves. Further, quantitative methods can also have a formative purpose. In other words, formative research may or may not be qualitative, and qualitative research may or may not be formative.

---

[2]Professional anthropologists tend to compensate for this by doing fieldwork during summer breaks and sabbaticals, or, by getting research grants to cover their salaries in place of teaching commitments.

Inductive Thematic Analysis and Grounded Theory

Inductive thematic analysis is probably the most common qualitative data analysis method employed in the social, behavioral, and health sciences. The process consists of reading through textual data, identifying themes in the data, coding those themes, and then interpreting the structure and content of the themes (see Guest, MacQueen, & Namey, 2012).

Grounded theory is a type of inductive thematic analysis. Developed by Glaser and Strauss (1967), grounded theory is a set of iterative techniques designed to identify categories and concepts within text that are then linked into formal theoretical models (Corbin & Strauss, 2008). Charmaz (2006, p. 2) describes grounded theory as a set of methods that "consist of systematic, yet flexible guidelines for collecting and analyzing qualitative data to construct theories 'grounded' in the data themselves." The process entails systematically reviewing units of text (often line-by-line, but units can be words, paragraphs, or larger units of text) as they are collected, creating emergent codes for those units, and writing memos that expand on created codes and the relationships between codes. This process is repeated until data collection is completed.

A defining feature of grounded theory is the "constant comparison method." Done properly, grounded theory requires that all segments of text are systematically compared and contrasted with each other. Theoretical models are created and continuously revised as data are progressively collected and analyzed. The exhaustive comparison between small units of text, such as lines or words, is often not a part of many applied inductive thematic analyses because it is extremely time consuming, especially for larger datasets. Guest and colleagues characterize applied inductive thematic analysis as:

> a rigorous, yet inductive, set of procedures designed to identify and examine themes from textual data in a way that is transparent and credible. Our method draws from a broad range of several theoretical and methodological perspectives, but in the end, its primary concern is with presenting the stories and experiences voiced by study participants as accurately and comprehensively as possible. (Guest et al., 2012, p. 15–16)

Another difference is that the output of an applied thematic analysis is not necessarily a theoretical model but often recommendations for program and policy. In terms of data collection, one of the primary distinctions between general inductive thematic analyses and grounded theory is that the latter *requires* an iterative research design in which data collection and analysis are merged and sample sizes are not predetermined. Sampling and data collection procedures in an applied thematic analysis context can be iterative, but these can also be predetermined and temporally separate from analysis.

Case Study Approaches

A qualitative case study examines a phenomenon within its real-life context. Data are collected on or about a single individual, group, or event. In some cases, several cases or events may be studied. The primary purpose of a case study is to understand something that is unique to the case(s). Knowledge from the study is then used to apply to other cases and contexts. Qualitative case study methods often involve several in-depth interviews over a period of time with each case. Interviews explore the unique aspects of the case in great detail, more so than would be typical for a phenomenological interview. Implications of a case study approach for qualitative data collection and analysis are several. First, participants and/or cases, by definition, should be selected for their unique properties. Because it is the case's special attributes that are of interest, sample sizes are generally small, usually one to several cases. Inquiry in these types of studies focuses largely on their defining case features and the differences they exhibit from other individuals/events in the larger population. The overall idea is to tease out what makes them so different and why. Often, knowledge gained from case studies is applied to a larger population.

A poignant case study example can be found in the education literature, in which the educational experience of a gifted African American boy living in an impoverished community is described (Hebert & Beardsley, 2001). Combining interviews with the young boy, a university researcher, and a classroom teacher, the authors document the boy's struggles within the educational system and beyond. As a result of the study, the authors provide recommendations for identifying and addressing the educational needs of gifted children in impoverished communities.

Discourse and Conversation Analysis

Both discourse and conversation analysis approaches stem from the ethnomethodological tradition (e.g., Garfinkel 1967, 2002), which is the study of the ways in which people produce recognizable social orders and processes. Thus, ethnomethodology and its subgenres view text as a window into broader social and cultural processes. Referring back to Ryan and Bernard's typology (Figure 1.1), both of these approaches tend to examine text as an "object of analysis." Analysis can be quite detailed, looking at the specific structure of discourse and interaction between two or more speakers to understand how shared meanings are socially constructed.

Both approaches study (usually recorded) "naturally" occurring language, as opposed to text resulting from more "artificial" contexts, such as formal interviews, and aim to extract social and cultural meanings and phenomena from the discourse studied. An illustrative example of discourse analysis from the anthropological literature is found in Edwin Hutchin's *Culture and Inference* (1980). Hutchins employed discourse analysis to study the indigenous land tenure system in the Trobriand Islands. Using recorded text from local land tenure disputes presented at village courts as a basis, Hutchins went through the transcripts, line by line, and examined patterns of reasoning. What he found—and contrary to the prevailing views at the time—was that the Trobriand Islanders exhibited a rational system of reasoning, but for an outsider to understand this system, they would first have to know the basic tenets upon which the Trobriand land tenure system is based (which most outsiders did not).

While conversation and discourse analysis are similar in a number of ways, there are some key differences. Discourse analysis (DA) is generally broader in what it studies, utilizing pretty much any naturally occurring text, including (existing) written texts, lectures, documents, and so forth. Conversation analysis (CA) is a subset of discourse analysis. Its scope is narrower and confined to natural conversations between two or more people. Another difference is that discourse analysis emphasizes how humans construct meaning through speech and text, and its object of analysis typically goes beyond individual sentences. Conversation analysis, on the other hand, tends to be more granular, looking at elements such as grammatical structures and concentrating on smaller units of text, such as phrases and sentences.

The implications of discourse and conversation analyses for data collection and sampling are twofold. The first pertains to sample sizes and the amount of time and effort that go into text analysis at such a fine level of detail, relative to a thematic analysis. In a standard thematic analysis, the item of analysis may be a few sentences of text, and the analytic action would be to identify themes within that text segment. In contrast, linguistic-oriented approaches, such as conversation and discourse analysis, require intricate dissection of words, phrases, sentences, and interaction among speakers. In some cases, tonal inflection is included in the analysis. In short, linguistic types of analysis require much more analytic time and effort per page of text, so sample sizes are on the smaller end of the spectrum.

Another consideration is the source of data. Since both DA and CA are most interested with naturally occurring language, in-depth interviews and focus groups are not ideal data collection methods for these types of analyses. One exception to this might be conversation between individuals in the context of group interviews and focus groups (as opposed to responses aimed at the interviewer), but purists would still argue that both the environment and group dynamic in a focus group context are artificial, thereby, contaminating the purity of the discourse.

Existing documents are an excellent source of public discourse for DA or CA. In terms of field research, participant observation is ideal for capturing "naturally occurring" discourse, as Hutchins did in the Trobriands. Many meetings, public events, and public discourses are easily recorded. During participant observation, one can also record naturally occurring conversations between individuals within the study population—for example, two fishermen deciding where to set a net, a husband and wife discussing contraceptive options, or three government officials talking about a civic policy. Note, however, if the event is not clearly in the public domain (and the above three cases are clearly not) informed consent and explicit permission to record need to be obtained (see Chapter 8 for more on research ethics).

Narrative Analysis

As with all of the above techniques, narrative analysis is based on the study of discourse and the textual representation of discourse. What distinguishes it from CA or DA is the *type* of discourse or text it deals with—narratives. Narratives, in this context, refer to stories that represent a sequence of events. They can be generated during the data collection process, such as through in-depth interviews or focus groups; they can be incidentally captured during participant observation; or, they can be embedded in written forms, including diaries, letters, the Internet, or literary works. Narratives are analyzed in numerous ways and narrative analysis itself is represented within a broad range of academic traditions—sociology, anthropology, literature, psychology, health sciences, and cultural studies. Narrative analysis can be used for a wide range of purposes. Some of the more common include formative research for a subsequent study, comparative analysis between groups, understanding social or historical phenomena, or diagnosing psychological or medical conditions. The underlying principle of a narrative inquiry is that narratives are the source of data used, and their analysis opens a gateway to better understanding of a given research topic. Researchers used narrative analysis, for example, in a study on tuberculosis (TB) in Delhi slums (Khan, 2012). Using data from personal narratives of women living with TB, the authors examined the "genderization" of TB and the related consequences for women. Their findings indicate how gender, in conjunction with other social forces, influences disease outcomes and stigmatizes women, as well as how women strategize to reduce such burdens.

Mixed Methods Approaches

Research studies are becoming increasingly diverse and inclusive of both qualitative and quantitative methods—that is, they are mixing methods to address specific objectives. The basic premise behind using a mixed methods research design is that the combination of both approaches provides a better understanding of a research problem than either approach could alone. Creswell and Plano Clark (2011) argue that integrating methodological approaches strengthens the overall research design, as the strengths of one approach offset the weaknesses of the other, and can provide more comprehensive and convincing evidence than mono-method studies. Another more practical benefit is that mixed method research can encourage interdisciplinary collaboration and the use of multiple paradigms.

The overarching premise is that the integration of two or more approaches should provide some added benefit with regard to research objectives that a single approach could not offer. Note that many research questions can be adequately answered with a mono-method approach. In such cases, creating a larger and more complicated design is not justified. The decision of whether or not to integrate multiple approaches depends on a combination of the research objectives, the resources and time available, and the audience for the study's findings.

There are more than a dozen (constantly evolving) mixed methods research typologies in the literature, each emphasizing different aspects of methodological integration and looking at the research process from different angles. For the most part, however, typologies include at the very least two basic dimensions— timing of data integration and purpose of integration (see Guest et al., 2012, chap. 8). Timing of integration refers to how qualitative and quantitative datasets are used chronologically and analytically with respect to each other. The two most commonly used terms in this regard are *sequential* and *concurrent* designs (Creswell & Plano Clark, 2007; Morgan, 1998; Morse, 1991). Sequential designs are those in which integration occurs across chronological phases of a study and where data analysis procedures for one dataset type inform another type of dataset. In a sequential design, for example, qualitative data can be used either to inform a subsequent quantitative dataset or data collection procedure, or to explain and provide further insight to findings generated from quantitative inquiry. In contrast, in a concurrent design, datasets are not dependent on one another and are integrated at the same time within an analysis. In concurrent designs, the idea is to compare qualitative and quantitative datasets *during* data analysis and determine whether findings between the datasets converge, diverge, or are contradictory. If you are thinking about using a mixed methods research design, we offer the following two suggestions:

- Try to explicitly justify why you're using a mixed methods design and why each component is necessary. If you can't come up with some good reasons, then a mixed methods study is probably not necessary.
- If you're convinced that an integrated design is best (and have the resources to carry one out), plan in detail how and when datasets will be integrated. For each methodological component of the study, think about how, specifically, each dataset will be analyzed and subsequently linked to other datasets. Draw a schematic of your study, depicting how and when each component is related to all the others.

FINDING YOUR FOCUS: RESEARCH DESIGN CONSIDERATIONS

The intent of this section is not to explain in detail how to develop a research question, since that process can vary substantially from one field to the next and from one context to another. In academic settings, for example, the primary source of research questions is either a gap in the literature and/or a need to build and develop theory. In business, the topic of research is often determined by one's boss or a client. In nonprofit settings, it can derive from a real-world problem that needs to be better understood, any of the aforementioned sources, or some variant combination thereof. Moreover, the source of a research question may vary from one project to the next within the same working environment. Because of this variability, we recommend that readers who are interested in learning more about how to develop effective research questions consult the literature relevant to their particular field and circumstance. What we have done instead is identify and discuss below certain research parameters that any researcher needs to think about and decide upon in order to properly operationalize and carry out a qualitative research initiative.

Establishing Research Objectives

Everything begins with the research objectives. A study's objectives, if properly conceptualized and documented, determine everything that follows, including selection of data collection methods, sampling approach(es), instrument development, analysis, and dissemination format and strategy. While establishing objectives is probably the hardest part of a research initiative, the process is critical to ensuring data are collected in such a way as to be useful. Use Table 1.2 below as a jumping off point from which to begin building your research strategy.

Table 1.2 Some Basic Research Design Considerations

Decision Point	Some Options (options are not mutually exclusive)	Some Considerations
Primary Purpose of Study	**Understand a Real-World Problem.** Research that is *primarily* guided by the need to understand or help resolve problems in the real world; these research problems may be investigator driven or passed on to researchers by funders, clients, and other stakeholders.	Findings should lead to actionable and evidence-based recommendations.
	Build Knowledge/Theory. Research that is *primarily* guided by existing theories and literature.	Findings should inform existing theories and bodies of literature.
	Develop Intervention/Program. Research intended to inform the development of a program, product, or intervention.	Findings should directly inform the development and/or proof of concept of an intervention or program.

Decision Point	Some Options (options are not mutually exclusive)		Some Considerations
	Evaluate something. Research intended to evaluate a program, product, or intervention.		Study is highly focused. Study results comprise the evaluation.
	Inform a Larger Study. Research whose primary purpose is to provide information for the conduct of a larger study; the smaller component could be considered a formative study to, or an embedded component of, a larger study.		Study is highly focused. Findings should directly inform another study component or feed into the overall study findings.
Primary Audience of the Findings	Scholars Researchers Academicians Funders Clients	Community Stakeholders Dissertation Committee	Appraisal criteria often vary by the audience/end user of study findings. Be sure to know what those criteria are BEFORE you begin collecting data.
What Is Already Known About Topic	• Nothing documented on topic • Some qualitative research has been done on the topic but not among study population • Some qualitative research has been done on the topic and among your study population • A good deal of qualitative and quantitative research has been carried out on your topic with the target population for your study		The less that is known about a topic, the more exploratory (and typically qualitative) research is generally required. Always start with existing secondary data (if available) and work forward from there. If a lot of good data (QL and QT) already exist for a topic and within the context of your study population, your study should be very precise and important in scope to warrant moving forward.
Study's Focus	• Deep understanding of the topic • Somewhat deep—but also want an idea of range of perspectives • Broad—variation exhibited across study population		The deeper you wish to delve into a topic, the fewer resources you will have to explore its breadth. You can have some sort of mix, but unless you have unlimited time and resources available, you will need to moderate one aspect for the other. Generally speaking, depth of topic is best served with qualitative methods and breadth of topic with quantitative.

(Continued)

Table 1.2	(Continued)	
Decision Point	**Some Options (options are not mutually exclusive)**	**Some Considerations**
Study Objective(s)	• Identify • Explore • Describe • Explain • Assess/Evaluate	Although there is considerable overlap among these objectives, subtle differences exist. Your interview/focus group questions and framing of observations will vary by objective. Choose other verbs that make the most sense for your study, but make sure that your objectives are appropriate for qualitative inquiry. If they include words and phrases such as "measure," "test," or "how many," you're headed in a quantitative direction (which is not a bad thing—it just means you have to change your objectives or your data collection methods).
Time Parameters	• Immediate need for data • Reasonable deadline • No deadline	Time available invariably determines the size and scope of a study. The faster data are needed, the smaller and more refined the research should be. Longitudinal studies, by their very nature, require more time.
Resources Available	• Solo effort • Small team • Large team • Infrastructure at Data Collection Site(s)	As with time, human resources play a big role in the scope of study that can be achieved. The more colleagues that are available to collect and analyze data, the faster you can get a research study done. However, working in teams requires additional procedures to enhance consistency of data collection and analysis activities. Roads, communication, electricity, and other types of infrastructure in some areas of the world are not always reliably available. Be sure to become familiar with infrastructural conditions on the ground prior to finalizing your research design. And always have a Plan B in your pocket.

From here, think about formulating your research objectives. When we conduct research design trainings, we encourage students to use the word *to*, followed by a verb. The verb you choose is extremely important. It defines not only what it is you're actually trying to do, but also it defines whether or not your objectives are best served by qualitative methods, quantitative methods, or a combination of both. Some of the more commonly used verbs when describing qualitative research objectives are identify, explore, describe, understand, and explain. If you're thinking of using words like *test* or *measure* or *compare* in your objectives, you should be thinking about quantitative methods, as they are better suited to these types of aims. Some verbs, such as *evaluate*, fall somewhere in the middle and can be construed as being qualitative or quantitative. Note, though, that one study can have multiple objectives that may require both qualitative and quantitative approaches.

When to Use Qualitative Methods

The inductive and flexible nature of qualitative data collection methods offers unique advantages in relation to quantitative inquiry. Probably the biggest advantage is the ability to probe into responses or observations as needed and obtain more detailed descriptions and explanations of experiences, behaviors, and beliefs—this is how we answer the *why* and *how* questions mentioned at the beginning of this chapter. If, for example, we wanted to describe readers' assessments of this book, we might ask them an opening question, such as "What is your overall impression of this book?" Less verbose readers might offer a two-word answer, such as "It's great" or "It's boring." In qualitative inquiry we have the ability to follow up with a subsequent probe, perhaps, "Why do you think so?" or "What in particular did you [not] like?" As we proceed with our line of questioning, we can obtain more and more details about the readers' perceptions of the book and delve further into specifics such as particularly helpful or problematic chapters, perceptions of writing style, and so on. In collaboration with the participant, the interviewer helps create a narrative that is rich, has depth, and informs the overall study objective. Contrast this with a set of survey questions in which response categories are fixed (e.g., check the box) and interval (e.g., fill in the number) and probing is absent. Surveys will yield useful information regarding prevalence and variation of certain variables within a population, but they are not well suited to building a deep, more personal knowledge of a given topic.

Another advantage of using open-ended questions is that one can get information not anticipated the researcher. How many times have you encountered a question on a structured survey that does not list your answer as a response choice? Researchers can provide only fixed responses based on their own perspective and experience with a particular topic. Any response that falls outside of this range is either lost, or it falls into the "Other" category. The former does not provide useful information beyond how valid (or not) the response categories are. The latter transforms the response into a qualitative format, which can be coded, but the response is typically so brief that any potential depth and richness is lost.

Qualitative research can also directly document causal relationships. Everyone knows from Statistics 101 that "correlation does not equal causation." We've been to many presentations and have read countless articles in which a researcher presents quantitative findings from a correlational analysis with an excitingly low p value, which then leads into a speculative discussion about what the correlation means. A qualitative researcher may be equally fascinated with the correlation but would look for, or plan to collect, qualitative data to *explain* the association. We may know from certain metrics, for example, that a particular intervention, program, or advertisement is effective (i.e., it elicits the desired outcome), but without qualitative data, we won't know what particular aspect(s) of the intervention was effective, or why.

The process of collecting qualitative data provides an additional advantage when it comes to face validity. For one, a researcher isn't artificially constraining the responses and trying to fit them into predetermined buckets. Survey questioning is almost always an immutable scripted process, in which data collectors are explicitly instructed to repeat the question verbatim if a participant does not understand it, to ensure reliability across interviewers. Qualitative questioning allows for more flexibility, and an interviewer is typically permitted to ask questions in a different way, to make sure the participant has understood it well. In fact, in a less structured in-depth interview, specific questions may not even be formulated. Such a lack of structure decreases reliability, at least as it is traditionally defined, but it does enhance overall face validity.

Related to the issue of validity is the nature of the data generated. Questioning in qualitative inquiry is open-ended, so responses are provided in the participants' own vernacular. This is helpful if the goal of a research study is to develop some form of communication plan or messaging strategy; you can do so in a way that is salient for, and will resonate with, your target population.

With the above in mind, one can see how qualitative research is better suited for some objectives rather than others. Below, we examine three general (and conceptually overlapping) types of qualitatively-oriented objectives—identifying and exploring, describing, and explaining. Note, however, that these are by no means exhaustive, or exclusive of quantitative forms of inquiry.

Identifying and Exploring

Identifying items in a conceptual domain is probably one of the most basic, yet important, elements of research. If, for example, we want to know what the water-related issues are in a particular community, we must begin by generating some type of "issues" list. In marketing, we might want to know all of the features of a product that consumers view positively, versus those they don't like. Similarly, if we're trying, for example, to get more men to undergo vasectomy, we might start by having participants identify all of the perceived barriers and facilitators to having the procedure. This process is about establishing range. Various methods can be used in this capacity, but regardless of the method, identification of the range of items in a conceptual domain is often the first stage of establishing inquiry validity. The open-ended nature of qualitative questioning is ideal for such a purpose.

Related to the process of identifying is "exploring." It can involve generating lists of items, but it is not limited to just this task, and may go beyond simple list creation. A research initiative can explore water issues in a community, for example, to find out how problematic or fixable each might be. A marketing team may be interested in exploring *why* certain product features are desired whereas others are not. Exploring might also entail investigating topics or issues among the study population that are investigator (rather than population) initiated. A key feature of exploration is the degree of flexibility it connotes, which is why it is a common objective in qualitative inquiry. Qualitative research is very much inductively oriented and is conducive to achieving an exploratory goal.

Describing

Having lists can be quite useful, and the process of exploration allows a researcher to probe into topical areas that researchers might otherwise have missed, again enhancing inquiry validity. But once you have a good sense of the range of issues and perspectives surrounding a particular topic within a given population, you will likely want to know more about each item or thing. Often, the next logical step in qualitative research is to describe these items in as much depth as possible. Once the list of vasectomy barriers has been generated, for example, we can ask participants to describe each in detail (the who, what, where, why, and how), and to discuss possible ways to overcome them. Within this description, we would likely try to capture various dimensions associated with each barrier—psychological, familial, political-economic, cultural, and so forth—to provide a more holistic perspective on vasectomy acceptance.

Qualitative methods are especially effective at describing complex processes. Whether the process is planting maize, buying a car, or deciding whether or not to get vaccinated, the open-ended and inductive style of questioning that is a hallmark of qualitative research can readily capture the inherent complexity of process. It may take as few as a handful of knowledgeable individuals or may require a somewhat larger sample—depending on the individual variability exhibited with respect to experiencing the process (see Chapter 2)—but the end result either way will be a pretty good understanding of the process in question.

Explaining

Social and behavioral researchers are often interested in explaining why or how individuals do (or don't do) certain things, how social systems function, or the relationship between two or more processes. The inductive and flexible nature of qualitative data collection is particularly useful for delving deep into internal psychological processes such as motives, values, and causes of behavior. Refer back to our vasectomy example. The list of reasons for not getting the procedure might include things such as fear of physical pain or of being emasculated. We could dig deeper into these reasons to see precisely how they affect motivation to undergo the procedure. It may be that men are intimidated by the thought of a needle or scalpel in the nether regions, as opposed to the primary procedure of severing the *vasa deferentia.* This is, in fact, what many studies have found, and in most developed countries, no-needle and no-scalpel vasectomies are now available.

Through qualitative inquiry, a researcher can more directly document why individuals behave in a certain way, because the participants themselves can make that causal connection explicit. A simple example is why people choose one ice cream flavor over another. We can just simply ask, "Why do you prefer this flavor?", and then probe inductively. We can explore deeper into why a particular flavor tastes good. If the answer is something like, "This flavor reminds me of my childhood", then we know that nostalgia enters into the equation and can probe as to why and how the chosen flavor triggers this sentimental feeling, and so on. In contrast, young children often choose ice cream based solely on color, another easily documented relationship. The bottom line is if nine out of your 10 in-depth interviewees tell you they did X because of Y, that's a fairly good indicator of causation that you can then examine in more detail.

Evaluating/Assessing

You can certainly use quantitative methods and experimental or quasi-experimental designs to evaluate a product, intervention, or program. In many cases, these highly structured approaches are justified, and the resources to carry them out are available. But generating quantitative data or implementing randomized controlled trials (RCT) is not always necessary or the only approach to evaluation (see Smith & Pell [2003] for a humorous take on the use of RCTs). As Patton (2002) observes, "[e]valuative research, quite broadly, can include any effort to judge or enhance human effectiveness through systematic data-based inquiry" (p. 10). Qualitative methods are an important part of evaluative efforts because "they tell the *program's story* by capturing and communicating the *participants' stories*" (p. 10, italics in original). It's no accident that focus groups are so widely used in product design research. They can provide detailed insights into preferences and thought processes of potential consumers. The same can be said for program evaluation. Qualitative assessments are directed at understanding participants' experiences of being part of a program and their perceptions of what worked and what did not. Qualitative evaluation research usually comprises one or more of the aforementioned objectives—to identify (e.g., problems), explore (e.g., likes/dislikes), and explain (e.g., decisions)—but its overarching goal of evaluating a specific entity is what makes it unique.

When Not to Use Qualitative Methods

The benefits and advantages of qualitative research are many, and we've discussed many of them above. We'd be remiss, however, if we did not also discuss some of the weaknesses and disadvantages associated with qualitative methodology. One limitation is that proper analysis of text is time consuming. It involves not only collecting the data but also transcribing, coding, and interpreting the data. If research is done in a foreign language, add the extra step of translation to the analysis process. All of these processes take time. For an average hour-long in-depth interview, it will take a minimum of 4 hours just to transcribe from the audio (if recording the event), another couple of hours to read through the text and make notes, several days to create an initial codebook, and then at least another hour to actually code the one transcript. Coding then needs to be summarized somehow and interpreted for the intended audience. Because free-flowing text for any given study can reach into the thousands of pages, much consideration must be given to how much time and resources can be allocated to the analysis. The good news is that in most cases, large samples are not needed for qualitative inquiry. In fact, carrying out a large number of data collection events is often an exercise in diminishing returns (more on this in Chapter 2). And not all qualitative analyses need to be so rigorously executed. In some cases, a "quick and targeted" analysis (Guest et al., 2012) is all that is warranted or possible within exigent time constraints.

Because samples in qualitative research are usually (though not always) small and non-probabilistic, the ability to claim a representative sample is often diminished, and statistical generalization is impossible. Related to this is the inability to *measure* variation of responses in any meaningful way. True, we can talk about how half of our study sample mentioned X theme, but this is only a very crude indicator of prevalence. If your main objective is to describe variation across a population, you should be thinking about a structured instrument and a probabilistic sample. In this situation, qualitative methods are not your best option. They can indeed identify the range of responses and help inform a structured instrument but are not suited to measuring variability.

Because qualitative questioning is open-ended and inductive, it is also not an ideal choice for reliably comparing groups. This includes objectives that involve the verb *test*, since testing usually involves some form of direct comparison (pre-post, control-intervention). Some forms of quantitatively-oriented content analysis are more amenable to systematic comparison, but inductive thematic approaches are less so. And while comparison of thematic expression across groups can and does take place, it's an underdeveloped field, and extra care must be taken to maximize the ability to meaningfully compare. We refer interested readers to Chapter 7 of Guest et al. (2012), which is dedicated to analytically comparing thematic data.

What Aspect(s) of Human Experience Do I Wish to Examine?

To help operationalize data collection procedures and tools, it's necessary to establish which dimension(s) of the human experience will comprise the core element(s) of your research problem. As you can imagine, each of these elements requires different approaches and procedures. It is important, therefore, to clarify in the early stages of designing your research which aspect(s) you are most interested in examining. In many studies, it is often a combination of two or more of the following:

- Behaviors
- Attitudes/Opinions/Perceptions
- Knowledge
- Emotions and Values
- Culturally Shared Meaning
- Social Structures and Relationships
- Processes and Systems
- Environmental Context

A second dimension to this question is temporal. Are you interested in looking at something at one point in time (i.e., a cross-sectional design), or does your research topic have a time dimension that you wish to explore (i.e., a longitudinal study)? If the latter, then deciding upon the duration of data collection activities and the number of data collection points within that period is a key step in the process, as is determining how you will sample over time. Will you include the same participants each time (i.e., a cohort study), or will you choose different samples from the same population? If the former, how will you keep track of participants and minimize attrition? How many time points will you include in your study? All of these questions, among others, need to be considered when choosing a longitudinal design.

What Is My Unit of Analysis?

The unit of analysis in a study is the level of abstraction at which you look for variability. The most commonly used unit in social-behavioral research is the individual. This is the level at which we often synthesize and compare data. That said, analysis of qualitative data can be carried out at higher levels of abstraction, such as groups (as is the case with focus groups), households, or even communities. A classic example of the latter is Edmund Leech's (1954) ethnography of the Kachin people of Burma (Myanmar), in which he compares political systems among three different ethnic groups.

In some cases, the unit can be an event, such as we might see in participant observation or in an interview designed to generate data about events. Bernard and Ryan (2010, p. 129) created a simple but useful diagram depicting levels of analysis (Figure 1.2). Theoretically, a study can collect and compare data at a level ranging from a specific isolated behavior (episode) to an entire country and its attributes. In real life, of course, levels of abstraction are not always as neatly defined as depicted in the graphic. There are many levels at which you can collect and organize data that are not represented (e.g., dyadic, institutional, etc.).

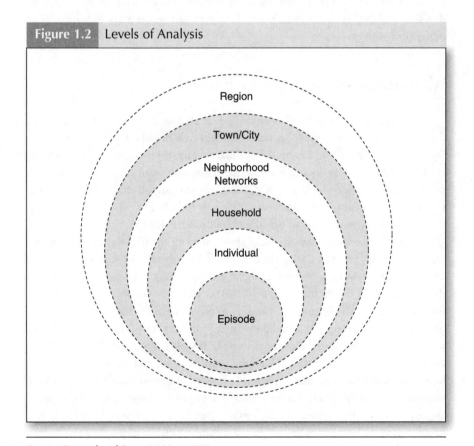

Figure 1.2   Levels of Analysis

Region

Town/City

Neighborhood Networks

Household

Individual

Episode

Source: Bernard and Ryan (2010, p. 129).

Note that the unit of analysis is not the same thing as the unit of observation. The former refers to the level at which data will be analyzed, the latter at which it is collected. They are often, but not always, the same thing. For example, a study may have a unit of observation at the individual level but may have the unit of analysis at the community level, comparing data across two or more communities, as in Leech's ethnographic study.

For in-depth interviews, the unit of observation is always the individual. In focus groups, the observational unit is both the individual and the interactions among individuals within the group. For participant observation, units of observation vary with the research context and can include individual or group behavior, specific events or activities, or contextual factors such as physical environments.

We can also turn the diagram on its head and examine how all of these factors (which Bernard and Ryan collectively call "context") influence individual behavior, thoughts, and experiences. How does the town in which one lives constrain or enable certain choices? How are household dynamics involved in individual decision making? How do one's peers determine an individual's experiences or behaviors?

What Is the Scope of My Research Topic?

Research design in general is typically funnel shaped, as are most qualitative data collection events. Inquiry begins with a relatively broad topical scope and narrows as data collection continues. The primary reason for this narrowing breadth is to enhance inquiry validity. We want to make sure that we're asking questions that make sense and are relevant to our participants and overall study objectives. It is easy to gain momentum on a track of inquiry, only to find out near the end of the line that the track is destined for, or has already ended at, a dead end.

A focus group experience of one of the authors exemplifies this propensity and how it might be dealt with during the data collection process. Mitchell was hired by a copper mining company to conduct focus groups among employees to document their perceptions about the company's 401(k) plan. As per standard qualitative research practice, she opened with a general question, to set the tone and get the participants warmed up. She asked the seemingly innocuous question, "What's it like working here?" In unison, the group answered, "It sucks!" She couldn't very well proceed with questions about the 401(k) plan until she probed into what were much larger issues, at least from the participants' perspective. The 401(k) plan had very little salience (i.e., inquiry validity) for the employees, despite the importance it held for the employer. We see this time and time again, when clients or researchers think they know what the salient issues are, only to be surprised by incoming data. This is not to say that all research needs to be exploratory and broad in scope, but one should have at least some knowledge of the topic and study population's perspective as a basis for formulating a research plan and subsequent data collection procedures.

Balancing Research Scope, Time, and Resources

We all want to do the perfect study. Clients and funders do too, but they additionally want it done quickly and cheaply. The triangle below is a useful graphic to conceptualize the balance between research scope with time and resources. Increasing one element almost always means that you'll have to adjust at least one other element.

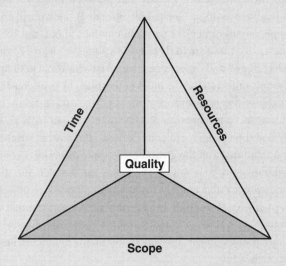

To strike a balance, the element of time must be carefully calculated and captured in a realistic schedule. Resources—financial, human, and material—must be identified. Scope is reflected in your research objectives, and it is the most ambiguous of the three elements. The larger the scope, the more time and resources (labor and cost) it will require to execute.

Let's say you are planning to conduct a study with in-depth interviews and have one month for data collection. Based on your budget, you've calculated that you are able to conduct 30 interviews within a 1-month period using two interviewers. Your client, funder, and/or boss, however, tells you that they want 45 in-depth interviews in the same amount of time. To accommodate this, and generate the same quality of data, you'll either need more time or have to hire an additional interviewer.

If funders and/or clients expect too much for too little, it's up to the researcher to educate them on the effects such demands will have on the quality of the end product. Provide them with outcome scenarios based on different decision routes. Easier said than done, but it's still easier than explaining, ex post facto, why your data are substandard, why the project is behind schedule, or why you went over budget.

Another dimension of scope pertains to how widely shared the knowledge, beliefs, and/or behaviors of interest are across a population. Ask yourself, How widely shared and variable are responses and behaviors likely to be within my study population vis-à-vis my topic? Topics at a more general level include shared cultural knowledge: e.g., what time the market opens, activities and rituals involved in a local wedding, how many types of goats are raised in the village, or the local voting process. We would expect minimal variation in responses and outcomes on such widely shared topics. Contrast these with more specific and personal topics of inquiry such as unique events (e.g., a meeting a few people attended), individual experiences (an individual's personal bankruptcy), or personal opinions about, say, the government. Domains of inquiry like these are likely to exhibit a greater degree of variability than those more widely shared and experienced (we revisit this topic in Chapter 2).

Research scope, unfortunately, is often determined by time constraints and the resources available—that is, people and money. You can certainly conduct a lot more interviews or focus groups with $50,000 than you can with $5,000. Likewise, the more funds and time you have at your disposal, the greater number of perspectives (i.e., subpopulations) and the greater geographic diversity (i.e., research sites) you can incorporate into your study. The same can be said for the number of research methods you are able employ. Granted, not all research objectives warrant large samples, inclusion of multiple groups and sites, or mixed methods designs, but knowing your budget and deadlines (if any) up front will help you negotiate and balance the scope triangle in the above text box titled "Balancing Research Scope, Time, and Resources."

How Much Structure Do I Need?

The degree of structure in a research project overall, and in data collection processes more specifically, are probably two of the most important decisions that a qualitative researcher will have to make. In an ideal world, the process of scientific inquiry follows a funnel pattern, starting off with broader and more general types of questioning and moving to more specific and structured types of inquiry as more about a topic is learned (Figure 1.3). As such, the early stages of research are likely to be exploratory, and the selection of data collection methods and development of instruments should reflect this. The early stages in the overall research process are where qualitative methods are often (though not always!) employed. As discussed earlier, the primary reason for using less structured forms of inquiry in the incipient stages of research is to improve inquiry validity—that is, to make sure that we're asking the right questions and in the right way.

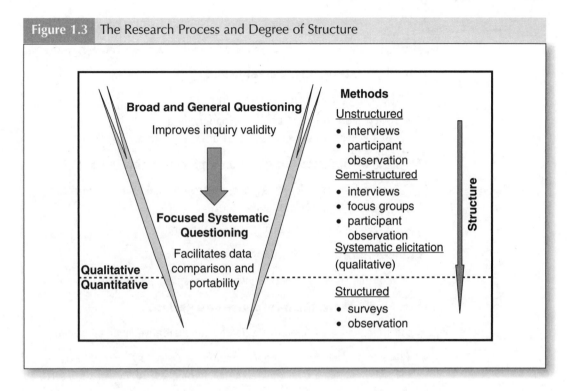

Figure 1.3   The Research Process and Degree of Structure

Not surprisingly, the advantages of a less structured approach come with some trade-offs. More general and unstructured forms of inquiry are great at generating valid data, identifying locally relevant issues, and gaining a deeper understanding of a given research topic. They are not, however, as well suited to comparative analyses. The less structure one incorporates into the research process—whether it be at the instrument level (structured vs. semi-structured vs. unstructured) or the degree of topical specificity (shared cultural processes vs. individual experiences)—the lesser is one's ability to carry out a valid comparative analysis. It is, for example, difficult to meaningfully compare responses between participants if using an unstructured form of questioning during in-depth interviews. There is no way to tell if differences observed between participants' responses are due to actual variability in how participants feel and think or if they are due to the fact that participants are responding to different questions, or, different variations of a question. It's the proverbial apples versus oranges scenario. Structured and semi-structured forms of inquiry help minimize this problem and are much better suited to comparative analyses. The next text box, Structure and Selection of Methods, provides some basic guidance in this regard.

Structure and Selection of Methods

If topic of interest isn't established . . .

NOT enough focus yet for fieldwork. Instead:

- Review more literature and/or secondary data
- Talk to client, funder, colleagues, local experts/stakeholders

If topic is established but question topics/domains are not . . .

NOT enough structure for focus groups or semi-structured interviews. Instead:

- Engage in (more) participant observation, and/or
- Review more literature and/or secondary data

If question topics/domains are established . . .

- Your study is ready for focus groups or semi-structured in-depth interviews

If leaning toward fixed-response categories . . .

Too structured. NOT appropriate for general qualitative inquiry. Instead:

- Create and implement a survey, and/or
- Employ systematic qualitative elicitation techniques (e.g., free lists, pile sorts)

The bottom line is that if you're planning to do some sort of comparative analysis and still wish to base it on qualitative data, we suggest adding a certain amount of structure to the inquiry process. Ask participants the same verbatim questions (though still open-ended and followed by inductive probing), use some sort of semi-structured template to focus observation activities, or employ more systematic elicitation methods described in Chapter 6. If a team project, make sure that all data collectors are conceptually on the same page and doing things in a similar way. We cover these topics in more detail in the chapters that follow.

We should note here that it is common for many topics to already have a good deal of existing research. Depending on the extent of existing data specific to your context, qualitative research may not even be needed. Nothing prevents a researcher from entering the research process at the narrower end of the funnel, so long as enough data and knowledge exist to justify forgoing more exploratory research. This is a judgment call that requires a sound knowledge of the research topic and study population. This doesn't mean that all researchers make the right call. We've observed and experienced numerous situations in which the researcher thought he or she knew what the issues and range of responses were for a particular topic and group of people and decided to skip doing qualitative research, only to find out the resulting data were not very valid or meaningful. If in doubt, err on the side of caution, and do some exploratory data collection to get it right.

SUMMING UP

In this chapter, we covered the basic principles of research design, with the exception of sampling, which is the topic of the following chapter. We presented questions for consideration and suggestions to help provide guidance with respect to making decisions about research design and data collection methods (additional information about how and why specific qualitative data collection methods are used can be found in Chapters 3 through 6). To help organize this abundance of information, we've condensed and summarized most of the key decision points in research design in Table 1.3. We have written the steps in a rough chronological order—that is, the order in which they are often considered during research design. But this order is by no means based on any fixed or immutable rules. Research design is a messy, iterative process and often involves considering multiple factors simultaneously and constant adjusting and revising of components (note the last step!). The same caveats apply to the options and considerations presented in Table 1.3. Despite the authors' best efforts, these are not exhaustive lists of options. The options are also not mutually exclusive. Any one study can embody, for example, multiple objectives, populations, sampling strategies, data collection methods, and so on. And these elements can be combined in countless numbers of ways. Table 1.3 is intended as an organizational and didactic tool, not as a fixed procedural map to a successful research design.

Table 1.3	Research Design Steps and Options
Step	**Options/Considerations**
Determine Study's Primary Purpose	• Understand a Real-World Problem • Build Knowledge/Theory • Develop an Intervention/Program • Evaluate Something • Inform a Larger Study
Determine Study's Primary Audience	• Scholars, Researchers, Academicians, Funders, Clients, Stakeholders, Dissertation Committee
Define the Study Population(s) and Geographic Parameters	• Number of Sites • Study Population(s) Boundaries and Eligibility Criteria
Decide if and What Comparative Elements to Include (See Chapter 2)	• Between Groups Comparison • Within Groups Comparison
Determine Temporal Orientation of Design	• Cross-Section vs. Longitudinal
Choose Your Research Objective Verb(s)	• Identify, Explore, Describe, Explain, Evaluate, Other

(Continued)

Table 1.3 (Continued)	
Step	**Options/Considerations**
Choose Your Qualitative Approach(es)	• Phenomenology • Ethnography • Inductive Thematic Analysis • Grounded Theory • Case Study • Discourse/Conversation Analysis • Narrative Analysis • Mixed Methods
Select Attribute(s) of Human Experience to Examine (for EACH population in your study)	• Behavior • Attitudes/Opinions/Perceptions • Values and Emotions • Knowledge • Culturally Shared Meaning • Social Structure and Relationships • Processes and Systems • Environmental Context
Select Data Collection Methods (for EACH population in your study)	• Participant Observation (Ch 3) • In-Depth Interviews (Ch 4) • Focus Groups (Ch 5) • Document Analysis (Ch 6)
Determine If/How Additional Activities/ Procedures Will Inform Study (Chapter 6)	• Listing • Categorizing • Timelines • Drawing/Mapping • Visual Elicitation (projective) • Rating/Ranking • Post-Event Reflection • Delphi Technique • Collages • Building a Campaign • Laddering • Ethnographic Decision Modeling
Establish Sampling Procedures (Chapter 2) (for EACH population and data collection method in your study) *Determine Sampling Flexibility*	 • Inductive versus A Priori Sampling

Step	Options/Considerations
Determine Sampling Strategy(ies) *Determine/Estimate Sample Size(s)*	• Census • Purposive (choose type. Table 2.1) • Quota • Convenience • Simple random • Systematic • Other
Determine Recruitment Method(s) (for EACH population and data collection method in your study). See Table 2.2.	• Media-Based • Investigator Initiated • Socially Based • Panel/List-Based
Time and Resource Constraints	• Consider what, if any, the scheduling expectations are for the study. • Know what your budget's bottom line is. • Balance the research scope with the time and budget parameters. • Manage client/funder/stakeholder expectations as required.
Review, Revise, and Repeat	Include collaborators (client, funder, stakeholders) and colleagues in review process.

About This Book

Although we have written this book as a compendium, with each chapter logically connected to the others, the chapters are intended to stand on their own. In each of the eight chapters, we incorporate examples, as well as practical tools such as checklists, templates, and actionable tips (learned through trial and error), to help data collectors efficiently go about their job. This book is, therefore, written primarily for the practitioner of qualitative research, in both applied and academic settings and across a wide range of disciplines. As a consequence, we have incorporated a broad range of examples, from a diversity of research fields such as marketing, public health, and anthropology. The connecting thread throughout is the "how to" instructional focus. As the book's title suggests, it is intended as a manual that data collectors can use prior to, during, and after conducting field research, to build and enhance qualitative data collection skills and practices.

We would also like to explicitly point out what this book does *not* cover, so as to not raise false expectations. To start, we do not discuss participatory or participatory action research (PAR), which is an exciting trend in field research. Based in a democratic philosophy toward research, PAR makes concerted efforts to include local communities in various (and often all) stages of the research process. While PAR often uses the same qualitative methods we cover in this book, the political and social processes involved in designing and implementing data collection and analysis are quite unique. We recommend that those researchers specifically interested in PAR consult books devoted to the topic (e.g., McIntyre, 2008; Pillsbury-Pavlish & Dexheimer-Pharris, 2011). Our book should be seen as complementary to PAR, as an instructional manual that research managers can use to train others, such as lay community members, novice researchers, or anyone involved in research design and data collection activities.

We also do not cover data analysis, for two primary reasons. Other books cover the topic of qualitative data analysis well and in detail (e.g., Bernard & Ryan, 2010; Charmaz, 2006; Grbich, 2007; Guest et al., 2012; Miles & Huberman, 1994). To include a thorough description of data analysis, in our opinion, would be to create a tome that would be counter-productive to the intended use of this book—a portable field manual for qualitative data collection. We recognize that designing research and carrying out data collection requires analytic forethought, which is why we include descriptions of the analytic traditions in this chapter. It would require at least another entire book to do justice to the diversity and complexity involved in the various analytic traditions described above.

REFERENCES

Alvesson, M., & Skoldberg, K. (2009). *Reflexive methodology: New vistas for qualitative research* (2nd ed.). Thousand Oaks, CA: Sage.

Bernard, H. R., & Ryan, G. (2010). *Qualitative data analysis: Systematic approaches.* Thousand Oaks, CA: Sage.

Bickman, L., & Rog, D. (2009). Applied research design: A practical approach. In L. Bickman & D. Rog (Eds.), *Handbook of applied social research methods* (2nd ed., pp. 3–43). Thousand Oaks, CA: Sage.

Charmaz, K. (2006). *Grounded theory: A practical guide through qualitative analysis.* Thousand Oaks, CA: Sage.

Corbin, J., & Strauss, A. (2008). *Basics of qualitative research: Techniques and procedures for developing grounded theory.* Thousand Oaks, CA: Sage.

Creswell, J., & Plano Clark, V. (2007). *Designing and conducting mixed methods research.* Thousand Oaks, CA: Sage.

Denzin, N. (2010). On elephants and gold standards. *Qualitative Research, 10,* 269–272.

Denzin, N., & Lincoln, Y. (Eds.). (2005). *Handbook of qualitative research* (3rd ed.). Thousand Oaks, CA: Sage.

Denzin, N., & Lincoln, Y. (Eds.). (2011). *Handbook of qualitative research* (4th ed.). Thousand Oaks, CA: Sage.

Garfinkel, H. (1967). *Studies in ethnomethodology.* Englewood Cliffs, NJ: Prentice-Hall.

Garfinkel, H. (2002). *Ethnomethodology's program: Working out Durkheim's aphorism.* Lanham, MD: Rowman & Littlefield.

Geertz, C. (1973). *The interpretation of cultures: Selected essays.* New York, NY: Basic Books.

Giorgi, A. (1970). *Psychology as a human science.* New York, NY: Harper & Row.

Glaser, B., & Strauss, A. (1967). *The discovery of grounded theory: Strategies for qualitative research.* New Brunswick, NJ: Aldine Transaction.

Grbich, C. (2007). *Qualitative data analysis: An introduction.* Thousand Oaks, CA: Sage.

Guest, G., MacQueen, K., & Namey, E. (2012). *Applied thematic analysis.* Thousand Oaks, CA: Sage.

Hawking, S., & Mlodinow, L. (2010). *The grand design.* New York, NY: Bantam.

Hebert, T., & Beardsley, T. (2001). Jermaine: A critical case study of a gifted Black child living in rural poverty. *Gifted Child Quarterly, 45,* 85–103.

Hutchins, E. (1980). *Culture and inference: A Trobriand case study.* Cambridge, MA: Harvard University Press.

Khan, K. (2012). Understanding the gender aspects of tuberculosis: a narrative analysis of the lived experiences of women with TB in slums of Delhi, India. *Health Care Women International, 33*(1), 3–18.

Leech, E. (1954). *Political systems of highland Burma: A study of Kachin social structure.* Cambridge, MA: Harvard University Press.

McIntyre, A. (2008). *Participatory action research.* Thousand Oaks, CA: Sage.

Merriam, S. (2009). *Qualitative research: A guide to design and implementation.* San Francisco, CA: Jossey-Bass.

Miles, M., & Huberman, M. (1994). *Qualitative data analysis: An expanded sourcebook* (2nd ed.). Thousand Oaks, CA: Sage.

Morgan, D. (1998). Practical strategies for combining qualitative and quantitative methods: Applications to health research. *Qualitative Health Research, 8,* 362–376.

Morse, J. (1991). Approaches to qualitative-quantitative methodological triangulation. *Nursing Research, 40,* 120–123.

Moustakas, C. (1994). *Phenomenological research methods.* Thousand Oaks, CA: Sage.

Nkwi, P., Nyamongo, I., & Ryan, G. (2001). *Field research into socio-cultural issues: Methodological guidelines.* Yaounde, Cameroon, Africa: International Center for Applied Social Sciences, Research, and Training/UNFPA.

Parkinson, G., & Drislane, R. (2011). Qualitative research. In *Online dictionary of the social sciences.* Retrieved from http://bitbucket.icaap.org/dict.pl

Patton, M. (2002). *Qualitative research and evaluation methods* (3rd ed.). Thousand Oaks, CA: Sage.

Pillsbury-Pavlish, C., & Dexheimer-Pharris, M. (2011). *Community-based collaborative action research.* Sudbury, MA: Jones & Bartlett Learning.

Ryan, G., & Bernard, R. (2000). Data management and analysis methods. In N. Denzin & Y. Lincoln (Eds.), *Handbook of Qualitative Research* (pp. 769–802). Thousand Oaks, CA: Sage.

Schütz, A. (1967). *Phenomenology of the social world.* Evanston, Il: Northwestern University Press.

Smith, G., & Pell, J. (2003). Parachute use to prevent death and major trauma related to gravitational challenge: Systematic review of randomised controlled trials. *British Medical Journal, 327,* 1459–1461.

Smith, J., Flowers, P., & Larkin, M. (2009). *Interpretive phenomenological analysis: Theory, method and research.* Thousand Oaks, CA: Sage.

Walsham, G. (1993). *Interpreting information systems in organizations.* Chichester, NH: Wiley.

ADDITIONAL READING

Case Studies

Ellet, W. (2007). *The case study handbook: How to read, discuss, and write persuasively about cases.* Cambridge, MA: Harvard Business Press.

Swanborn, P. (2010). *Case study research: What, why and how?* Thousand Oaks, CA. Sage.

Yin, R. (Ed.). (2008). *Case study research: Design and methods.* Thousand Oaks, CA. Sage.

Discourse/Conversation Analysis

Gee, J. (2010). *An introduction to discourse analysis: Theory and method.* New York, NY: Routledge.

Hutchby, I., & Wooffitt, R. (2008). *Conversation analysis.* Boston, MA: Polity.

Epistemological Theory and Debate

Bernard, H. R. (2000). About social science. In H. R. Bernard (Ed.), *Social research methods: Qualitative and quantitative approaches* (Chapter 1, pp. 3–28). Thousand Oaks, CA: Sage.

Delanty, G., & Strydom, P. (Eds.). (2003). *Philosophies of social science.* Maidenhead, UK: Open University Press.

Denzin, N. (2009). The elephant in the living room: Or extending the conversation about the politics of evidence. *Qualitative Research, 9,* 139–160.

Kuznar, L. (2008). *Reclaiming a scientific anthropology* (2nd ed.). Lanham, MD: AltaMira Press.

Romney, A. K. (1989). Quantitative models, science and cumulative knowledge. *Journal of Quantitative Anthropology, 1*(1), 153–223.

Ethnography

Agar, M. (1996). *The professional stranger: An informal introduction to ethnography* (2nd ed.). Emerald Group.

Fetterman, D. (2009). *Ethnography: Step-by-step* (3rd ed.). Thousand Oaks, CA: Sage.

Handwerker, W. (2001). *Quick ethnography*. Lanham, MD: AltaMira.

Grounded Theory

Charmaz, K. (2006). *Grounded theory: A practical guide through qualitative analysis*. Thousand Oaks, CA: Sage.

Corbin, J., & Strauss, A. (2008). *Basics of qualitative research: Techniques and procedures for developing grounded theory*. Thousand Oaks, CA: Sage.

Glaser, B., & Strauss, A. (1967). *The discovery of grounded theory: Strategies for qualitative research*. New Brunswick, NJ: Aldine Transaction.

Mixed Methods

Creswell, J., & Plano Clark, V. (2011). *Designing and conducting mixed methods research* (2nd ed.). Thousand Oaks, CA: Sage.

Teddlie, C., & Tashakkori, A. (2009). *Foundations of mixed methods research: Integrating quantitative and qualitative approaches in the social and behavioral sciences*. Thousand Oaks, CA: Sage.

Narrative Analysis

Holstein, J., & Gubrium, J. (Eds.). (2011). *Varieties of narrative analysis*. Thousand Oaks, CA: Sage.

Lieblich, A., R. Tuval-Mashiach, R., & Zilber, T. (1998). *Narrative research: Reading, analysis, and interpretation*. Thousand Oaks, CA: Sage.

Reissman, C. (2007). *Narrative methods for the human sciences*. Thousand Oaks, CA: Sage.

Phenomenology

Giorgi, A. (1970). *Psychology as a human science*. New York, NY: Harper & Row.

Giorgi, A. (2009). *The descriptive phenomenological method in psychology*. Pittsburgh, PA: Duquesne University Press.

Moustakas, C. (1994). *Phenomenological research methods*. Thousand Oaks, CA: Sage.

Polkinghorne, D. E. (1989). Phenomenological research methods. In R. S. Valle, & S. Halling (Eds.), *Existential-phenomenological perspectives in psychology* (pp. 41–60). New York, NY: Plenum.

Smith, J., Flowers, P., & Larkin, M. (2009). *Interpretive phenomenological analysis: Theory, method and research*. Thousand Oaks, CA: Sage.

Sokolowski, R. (1999). *Introduction to phenomenology*. Cambridge, MA: Cambridge University Press.

Research Design

Bickman, L., & Rog, D. (2009). Applied research design: A practical approach. In L. Bickman & D. Rog (Eds.), *Handbook of applied social research methods* (2nd ed., pp. 3–43). Thousand Oaks, CA: Sage.

Flick, U. (2007). *Designing qualitative research.* Thousand Oaks, CA: Sage.

Merriam, S. (2009). *Qualitative research: A guide to design and implementation.* San Francisco, CA: Jossey-Bass.

Thematic Analysis

Guest, G., MacQueen, K., & Namey, E. (2012). *Applied thematic analysis.* Thousand Oaks, CA: Sage.

Saldana, J. (2009). *The coding manual for qualitative researchers.* Thousand Oaks, CA: Sage.

2

Sampling in Qualitative Research

Sampling is one of the most important aspects of research design. In a research context, sampling refers to the process of selecting a subset of items from a defined population for inclusion into a study. We say *items* because the subset of things to include in your study may not always be people. Individuals are certainly the most common sampling unit in social and behavioral research, but sampling units can also be groups, events, places, and points in or periods of time. Whatever your sampling unit, you'll need to consider carefully *how* items are to be chosen.

The degree of generalizability (or not) of findings and their representativeness relative to the larger population (or not) are dependent on (or constrained by) one's sampling strategy. Likewise, the validity of study findings is related to sampling. If, for example, the "key informants" selected for a study are not very knowledgeable about the topic being investigated, the resulting data will not be particularly informative. Because sampling is so important, we devote an entire chapter to the subject. The chapter is divided into the three major components of selecting participants for a research study—deciding whom to include, choosing how to include them (i.e., sampling strategy), and determining how to bring them into your study (recruiting techniques).

Defining Key Terms

Study Population

The entire group of elements that you would like to study. This is often a group of individuals (e.g., firefighters in New York City, migrant workers in North Carolina, female sex workers in Bangkok), but it can also be composed of larger units such as families, institutions, communities, cities, and so on. The study population is entirely defined by the researcher, based on the study objectives. Note that a single study can include multiple populations, depending on how your research problem is defined.

Sampling Frame

A sampling frame is a list of all the elements in a study population. It is always defined by your study population. If, for example, your study population is vendors in market X, then your frame would be a list of all vendors in that market. Note that the sampling frame is the largest possible sample of a study population. It is often not easy to obtain in field research.

Sampling Unit

This is the thing (person, place, event, etc.) that is selected for inclusion in the study. For example, if you are sampling high school students, your sampling unit would be one student.

Study Sample

The group of sampling units chosen from the larger population for inclusion in the study becomes your study sample. Note that any given sample can be part of more than one population.

SELECTING WHOM TO SAMPLE

For highly targeted research studies, selecting whom to sample may not be a difficult task. Your study population may be precisely defined by your research objectives. If, for example, your research objective is to explore the personal experiences of women who participated in a particular clinical trial or programmatic intervention, your primary inclusion criterion is already determined by your research objective. But not all research questions are this precise, especially in qualitative research, which is often exploratory in design and purpose. For most research initiatives, you will need to think carefully about whom to include in your research as you design your study, and, in some cases, as data collection progresses.

Whom you include in your study will be based on several criteria, but first and foremost, the rationale behind your design should directly reflect your research objective(s) or question(s). Ask yourself: What specific individuals or types of individuals (i.e., roles, occupations) might know a lot about my research topic in the study site(s)? This is the basis of the key informant concept. Some individuals are simply more knowledgeable than others about certain subjects. If you are investigating medicinal plant use within an indigenous community, for example, traditional healers would likely be at the top of your list of whom to include.

One of the hallmarks of qualitative research is the ability to account for context and gain a more holistic picture of a research topic. Including the most knowledgeable individuals in a qualitative study is essential, but it is often not enough to fully understand the social, cultural, and contextual complexities associated with a research question, particularly if it's on the complicated end of the spectrum. Seeking and documenting multiple viewpoints is part of any good research study, even more so for qualitative inquiry. To this end, think about who else in your study community has knowledge about the subject and who may have a different perspective. Referring back to the medicinal plant use example, you might decide to also sample adult women if they use medicinal plants in the home, or local pharmacists if they sell herbal remedies in their shops. Each of these groups will likely have different types of knowledge and use plants in different ways. Capturing this range of opinions and experiences would be essential if your interest is at the community level.

Perhaps your research is intended to inform policy. If this is the case, you'll need to consider including (a) individuals who would be most affected by any policy change to emerge from your study findings and (b) individuals who have control over policy pertaining to your research topic and study site(s). In other words, identify the key stakeholders. Including stakeholders in your sample provides not only important information, but also it can facilitate their cooperation if and when recommendations are developed.

Unless you have unlimited funding and time (i.e., you're independently wealthy and have nothing else to do), you will need to prioritize whom you include in your study. Talking to everyone in your study community and documenting every voice is usually not possible. But defining inclusion criteria and narrowing the scope of your study is not an easy task. In fact, when we teach research methods, the most common type of questions we receive pertains to choosing participants. Students often ask questions such as, Do I need to include both men and women or both wealthy and impoverished individuals in my study? or If I have focus groups with patients, do I need to do focus groups with doctors too? We have two general responses to these types of sampling questions:

It is always a good idea to elicit multiple perspectives on a given research question. Men and women, for example, often have different experiences and take on different social roles in many cultures, so including both in research studies is common practice. But think beyond gender. How would you expect knowledge, behavior, beliefs, and experience regarding your research topic to vary within your study population? Would you expect, for example, older individuals to have different or more knowledge than younger individuals, or wealthy people to have different perceptions than those more impoverished? Is there a group of individuals that share has a unique experience who might view the topic differently? You would ask the same types of questions if sampling events or places. Places and events often have temporal variability associated with them. Do the activities or locations you wish to sample vary by season? by day of the week? time of day? or some other temporal parameter?

Answering these types of questions in an informed manner requires a certain degree of knowledge about your research topic and study community. If you've never been to the study site(s) or worked within the study communities, consult other researchers or local residents who are knowledgeable about the area of study.

The decision to include or exclude particular groups or strata also depends on how your research question is framed and how your study population is defined. When conceptualizing your research question, you should have at least a sense of the study's scope, which is partially determined by budget and time available. Investigating an entire community's perspective on something is different (and much more difficult) than focusing your study on a very specific and targeted group of individuals (e.g., 2012 high school students in X county, or religious leaders in Baghdad). Another factor bearing on sampling decisions is the degree to which you want to explicitly compare data between groups. If comparison is a key element in your study design, you need to think about which groups you wish to compare. For each comparative group you add, the total sample size for your study will at least double (more so if your groups are segmented into more than two categories), so be mindful of budgetary and time constraints when making your selection.

It's often helpful to take an open, brainstorming approach to designing your sampling parameters. List all of the groups, people, events, or places that could provide relevant information on your research topic; then, rank or prioritize the list based on the salience of the information that you would expect to obtain from each. Let budgetary and timing issues help you reduce your sample(s) from the ideal to the feasible. Creating a title for a research study is another incredibly useful exercise in defining the boundaries of your research. It forces you to think about who you really want to include in your study and why. A good title should tell your audience who your study population is. Referring back to the example of medicinal plant usage, think how different your sampling strategy would be for each of the following three study titles:

Title 1: "Medicinal Plant Usage in Village X"

Title 2: "Medicinal Plant Usage Among Traditional Healers in Village X"

Title 3: "Medicinal Plant Usage Among Traditional Healers and Mothers in Village X"

In Title 1, your study population is defined as everyone in community X. This, at least theoretically, includes men, women, children, young, old, traditional healers, merchants, and so forth. With such a long list of subpopulations, you will likely need to refine your question to exclude less relevant groups, or stratify your sample so that at least a few members of key groups are represented in your sample. Title 1 suggests a large study and will require a relatively complicated sampling strategy for an in-depth qualitative study. In contrast, Title 2 requires that you identify traditional healers in the community and include at least some of them in your study, a much easier proposition than Title 1. Finally, Title 3 suggests a comparative design, in which usage is compared between traditional healers and mothers. In terms of complexity, this study design falls between Title 1 and Title 2. The title suggests inclusion of two subpopulations within the village, both of which should be relatively easy to identify.

Inductive Sampling

Much applied research is relatively focused in scope, with clear objectives from the outset. The range of stakeholders is known up front, as are the cultural and social contexts in which the study is embedded. But a good deal of qualitative research is inductive and exploratory in nature. Sometimes you may not know who the stakeholders are when you begin your research, or who in the study community is the most knowledgeable about your research topic. In this case you would gather as much information as you could from existing resources. If you still don't have enough information to make an informed decision, your research design will be, by necessity, exploratory in design. You will likely need to employ an inductive sampling strategy.

Inductive, or emergent, sampling allows for the inclusion of groups and types of cases not originally specified or included in the study design. The flexibility to follow new leads during fieldwork and to take advantage of new information as it is collected and reviewed is a major strength of inductive sampling, and of qualitative research in general. Consider one of the author's studies on contraceptive decision making in India. The original sampling design included married women, married men, and health care providers. After a few interviews it was apparent that mothers and mothers-in-law play an important role in contraceptive decisions of their children in Indian culture. These two groups were subsequently incorporated into the sampling plan.

Inductive sampling—also called "theoretical sampling" in the grounded theory literature (Charmaz, 2006; Glaser & Strauss, 1967)—is more commonly employed in longer-term research such as ethnographic studies. The iterative and inductive process of collecting data, analyzing them, and formulating new sampling and recruiting procedures takes time. In applied research, which generally has more targeted research questions and shorter time horizons, inductive sampling methods are logistically more difficult (though the study of Indian contraceptive use just cited was an applied project, so it is possible).

Inductive sampling can also be problematic at the regulatory level. You may have been required in a funding proposal and/or ethics review application to state how many individuals you will sample from which populations, as well as your sampling strategy and method of recruitment for each (in applied research this is typically the case). If sampling procedures or characteristics of your sample are altered significantly, most ethical oversight bodies require a protocol amendment and subsequent review. So if you know up front you will be sampling inductively, it's best to incorporate that flexibility into your proposal and protocol from the beginning.

SAMPLING APPROACHES

In the previous section, we talked about choosing whom to include or not include in your study. Once this has been figured out (or at least partially so), the next step is to think about *how* you will sample the units (usually people) in your study population(s). Essentially, there are three general sampling approaches to choose from—censuses, non-probability sampling, and probability sampling—each with its own unique strengths and limitations.

Census

A census is the process of collecting information from or about *every item* in a study population. It is technically not a sampling method since no selective process is involved; i.e., you include everyone in your sampling frame. Censuses are often associated with large quantitative data collection efforts, such as the U.S. Census, but they can also be employed in qualitative research. Theoretically, a census is always preferable to any kind of sample. It obviates the need to make inferences from the sample to a larger population, and avoids criticisms about the representativeness of your "sample." Unfortunately, censuses are rarely employed in qualitative field research due to logistical constraints. Most study populations are large, and including everyone from a population in a research study is usually prohibitively time consuming and costly. Moreover, once you reach a large enough sample size—in either qualitative or quantitative research—the law of diminishing returns kicks in, and the effort-to-information ratio becomes lopsided; each new item in your sample adds very little information to the data that has already been collected.

Nonetheless, there are certainly situations in which the population of interest is small enough to permit a census. Some examples might include all of the senior executives in a large company, every caregiver in a public health clinic, or all elders in a small village. We recommend using a census if possible, as it eliminates the potential for criticisms pertaining to generalizability of findings (at least relative to your study population). In most cases, some sort of strategy will be required to select a sample from a larger study population.

Non-Probability Sampling

Non-probability sampling is typically defined in relation to its probability-based counterpart. There are two main points to this comparison:

- Non-probability sampling does not involve random selection.
- Relatedly, since non-probabilistic samples cannot depend upon probability theory, we can't know the odds or probability with which the chosen sample represents the population.

This does not necessarily mean that non-probability samples are not representative of the larger study population or that we can't conceptually generalize from our sample to a larger population in some cases. It does mean, though, that we can't statistically extend our findings to a larger population or place confidence intervals around our findings. Fortunately, qualitative research is not intended, nor expected, to generate these metrics.

Non-probabilistic sampling is the norm in qualitative research, for several reasons:

- Statistical analyses (inferential)—most of which require probability-based samples—of qualitative data are not common.
- Qualitative inquiry is not intended or designed for statistical generalizability.
- Qualitative sample sizes are generally too small to be subject to probability theory.

Qualitative studies seek to generate rich, contextually laden, explanatory data and are therefore not concerned with generating population-based estimates and p-values. Probability samples provide little benefit to this end, and the effort needed to acquire a proper sampling frame, as is necessary for most probability samples, is not justified. And, in many cases, employing a probability sample in a qualitative research study can be fundamentally detrimental to the validity of one's findings because it may gloss over specific individuals who have unique attributes (e.g., knowledge, experiences, social position) relative to your research question(s).

The suitability of non-probability samples for qualitative research is also related to the types of objectives that drive much qualitative inquiry. In many cases, qualitative studies are designed to understand common processes, shared experiences and understandings, or to identify shared cultural knowledge and norms. It doesn't take a probabilistic sample to gain insight into these types of topics. In fact, as we discuss in more detail below, sample sizes as small as six individuals are often adequate in this regard. How many of your neighbors would you need to ask to find out what time the local supermarket opens? How many colleagues would you need to interview to get a general picture of what it's like to visit a dentist in your country? Much experience and knowledge is so widely shared or processes so standardized within a culture or community that only a few individuals are needed to address a research question. In cases where we are interested in variability—as opposed to commonalities and patterns— qualitative inquiry is extremely useful in establishing the *range of* attributes associated with the phenomena of interest. If it is a *measure* of variability you're after, however, don't bother with qualitative methods. Structured inquiry with a probabilistic sample is the way to go.

Purposive Sampling

The most commonly employed non-probabilistic sampling approach is purposive, or purposeful, sampling (also sometimes called "judgment" sampling). Perhaps the most intuitive way to think of purposive sampling is that you choose study participants based on the purpose of their involvement in the study. In Bernard's words, "you decide the purpose you want your informants (or communities) to serve, and you go out and find some" (Bernard, 2000, p. 176). The logic and power of purposive sampling, argues Patton, "lie in selecting information-rich cases for study in depth . . . those [cases] from which one can learn a great deal about issues of central importance to the purpose of the inquiry" (Patton, 2002, p. 230). Operationally, this means establishing one or more eligibility criteria for inclusion into a study. Your criteria could be as simple and broad as "adult males in community x." Or they may include multiple criteria exhibited by a specific group of people. If, for example, you wanted to understand how a niche market might react to the introduction of a new beer bottle shape, you might screen for sex (males), marital status (single), annual income (> $80K), and consumptive behavior (drink more than 12 bottles/week). Or perhaps your research is aimed at understanding a very specific experience, such as traveling through security checkpoints in a conflict zone. Your criterion might be individuals who have traveled through X number of checkpoints in the past month. Table 2.1, extracted and adapted from Patton's *Qualitative Research and Evaluation Methods* (2002) provides a framework from which to start thinking about the various dimensions of purposive sampling.

Table 2.1	Types of Purposive Sampling Approaches	
Sampling Type	**Characteristics**	**Example**
Homogeneous	• Sample is similar on one or more dimensions • Often used in focus group discussions • Useful if the population to which the results will be inferred is also homogeneous, as it simplifies analysis • One of the most common sampling approaches • Data are often collected from multiple homogeneous groups for a more holistic perspective and/or comparative purposes	For a U.S.-based marketing study of female motorcycle riders, you might sample female motorcycle owners from four different regions of the country: for example, Los Angeles, New York City, Atlanta, and Chicago. If you were interested in assessing the introduction of a new sex education curriculum in secondary schools, you would likely interview various homogeneous stakeholder groups: teachers, parents, students.
Extreme or Deviant Case	• Focus on unusual manifestations of the phenomenon of interest • Often used to find key factors associated with extreme behavior • Such cases are easily identified with quantitative data (e.g., the *nth* percentile)	You may use this approach if you want to identify outstanding successes or notable failures, such as the best or worst students in a class. In reproductive health studies, participants might be selected based on extreme (reported) condom usage (i.e., all the time versus never).
Intensity	• Information-rich cases that manifest the phenomenon of interest intensely, but not extremely • Differ from extreme/deviant cases in that they are in a normal range and not on the extreme end of the curve	You may be interested in sampling good students and poor students or individuals who are above average/below average on a given dimension (rather than the "extreme" cases of brilliance and abject failure).
Typical Case	• Illustrate or highlight what is typical, normal, average • If selected well, a few individuals can provide accurate insight into general patterns and processes across a larger population • Illustrative, not definitive • Particularly good for understanding phenomena that are widely shared across a culture or community	If your research objective is to understand the experience of purchasing a new vehicle from a GM dealership, you could simply interview individuals who recently purchased a new, average priced car from a GM dealership (i.e., not a Corvette or a Volt). The assumption is that if the process and experience are fairly typical across dealerships, relatively few participants need to be sampled.

(Continued)

Table 2.1 (Continued)

Sampling Type	Characteristics	Example
Critical Case	• Permits logical generalization and maximum application of information to other cases because if it is true of this one case, it's likely to be true of all other cases	If you interview highly educated health professionals and they have a problem understanding a health message, you can be fairly certain that lay people will also have problems.
Confirming and Disconfirming Cases	• Helpful for elaborating and deepening initial analysis, seeking exceptions, and testing variation • Often used to validate (confirming) or expand/negate (disconfirming) data-driven models • Often sought out near the end of a research project to establish boundaries around one's interpretation of a dataset	If your data reveal a widely shared theme, take a second look through the same dataset in search of data that diverge or contradict that theme. Imagine, for example, 28 out of 30 participants have positive views of a product or program you're evaluating. The deviant two cases are analyzed more closely to understand why they have such different views. Often these views can be highly informative. If your research is flexible in design and you have enough time, you can follow up with those participants who expressed these divergent or contradictory viewpoints to gain further insight.
Politically Important Cases	• Purposely eliminating or including politically sensitive cases • Sample individuals to attract attention to the study or to avoid attracting undesired attention	Local leaders or political activists, for example, are often included in a study to increase political cooperation.
Criterion	• Picking all cases that meet some predetermined criterion • Often used in quality assurance processes	You may use criterion sampling to identify cases that fail set standards, such as sampling all children abused in a treatment facility. Or on the positive side, you may wish to identify all substance abuse program graduates who stay clean for x amount of time.
Maximum Variation	• Purposely picking a wide range of cases for a sample to get variation on dimensions of interests • Document unique variations that have emerged in relation to different conditions	You're interested in documenting the diversity of opinions regarding a new product or program that is scheduled for roll out. Seek diversity within your target population and select accordingly. Common parameters

(Continued)

Sampling Type	Characteristics	Example
Maximum Variation (continued)	• Identify important common patterns that cut across variation (cut through the noise of variation) • Also useful for generating a wide range of responses • Used when time/resource constraints prohibit sampling multiple groups	include age, sex, ethnicity, education, income level, geographic location, and occupation.
Stratified Purposeful	• Study population is broken down into strata that have some theoretical importance to the study objectives • Typically based on illustrative characteristics of particular subgroups of interest • Frequently used strategy, facilitates comparisons	Examples of commonly used strata include gender, ethnicity, age, education, and income level. Or it can be much more specific such as the amount of experience using a product or degree of exposure to an intervention.
Quota	• Variation of a stratified sample • Relative size of substrata are proportional to their relative size in the larger population	A general quota sample of men and women with an n of 20 would break down to 10 men and 10 women, since the sex ratio in general populations is 50/50. If, however, your study population was injection drug users, your quota sample of 20 would be composed of 18 men and 2 women, if 90% of injection drug users are men.
Theory-Based	• Finding real-world manifestations of a theoretical construct of interest so as to elaborate and examine the construct and its variations • Cases are chosen based on their ability to inform parts of the theoretical model	Models can come from various sources: for example, literature, primary quantitative data, primary qualitative data. In one of the author's studies, for example, quantitative data showed a significant inverse correlation between pornography viewing and subsequent condom use. We specifically searched the qualitative data from the study for any references that would inform this association (i.e., our theory that was derived from the quantitative analysis).

(Continued)

Table 2.1	(Continued)	
Sampling Type	**Characteristics**	**Example**
Snowball or Chain Referral	• Utilizes participants' social networks to identify other participants • Ask existing participants to refer others based on certain criteria (often attributes similar to the referring participant) • Very useful for sampling hard-to-reach populations, but it is vulnerable to recruiting biases [Note: This is actually a recruiting technique, since chain referrals are used to *achieve* types of samples. However, since chain referral techniques are typically referred to as sampling methods in the literature (correct or not), we include them in this table.]	Chain referral techniques are often used with injection drug users since the activity is usually illicit, and users tend to have solid social connections based on the activity they share in common. Another example from marketing research comes from 3M. In their desire to better understand how surgical drapes are applied to the body, they initially contacted specialists they knew from various fields who used such devices, such as a veterinarian and a Broadway makeup artist. They then asked this initial group of experts to suggest other experts they knew who could offer more information.
Convenience or Haphazard	• Collect data from whatever cases present themselves • Convenience sampling has the lowest credibility of all sampling approaches—should be viewed as a last resort. Explicitly justify use of this technique when disseminating findings	Conducting research in conflict zones, for example, may permit only convenience samples due to security issues. In ethnographic research, initial interviews may be convenience based, until the researcher becomes more familiar with the study community.

Source: Adapted from Patton (2002, pp. 243–244).

Consider also what you intend to do and achieve with the data. Look at Table 2.1 again. Certainly, one's analytic aim would differ between, say, a homogeneous and a maximum variation sample. In the former, one is more likely looking for common themes across the group; in the latter, establishing the range of responses would be a more appropriate analytic aim. If, on the other hand, you're looking for unique individual attributes relative to your research question, extreme and critical case samples might be useful. Each of the variations of purposive sampling has a distinct function.

Probabilistic Sampling

As we mentioned earlier, non-probability sampling is the norm for qualitative inquiry, but this is not to the exclusion of probability sampling. A *probabilistic*, or *probability*, sample is derived using some form of *random selection.* Random selection means that the probability of each sampling unit being chosen is known. One of the defining features of probability sampling is that one can calculate the odds or probability that your sample represents the larger population well.

So when should a qualitative researcher use probability sampling? In our view, the main reason is that in some cases, it can enhance the representativeness of your sample. And, in cases where a probability sample may not actually enhance the representativeness of your sample, it can enhance the perception of such. As anyone in the research world is acutely aware, there is more to research than just data collection and analysis procedures. Logistics and political factors invariably play a role in determining how we carry out and report on our research. Even though one can't statistically generalize, say, from a small random sample of in-depth interviews to the larger study population—due to the small sample size and unstructured nature of the data—from a pragmatic perspective, it can often behoove a researcher to randomly choose a sample in qualitative research.

A personal experience from one of the authors' studies provides a poignant example. Guest was tasked with qualitatively assessing the procedures in a year-long clinical trial from the study participants' perspective. Twenty-four participants were selected from the study population of 400 (i.e., all participants enrolled in the clinical trial) using a simple random sampling procedure and were administered in-depth interviews. A thematic analysis of these data revealed several perceived shortcomings in the clinical trial procedures. When the data were presented to clinical trial staff, their immediate response was, "How do we know these data are representative of the larger clinical trial population?" The researcher's reply was simply, "Because the participants were chosen randomly." The criticism was curtailed right then and there. Whether or not a random sample of 24 open-ended interviews from a population of 400 is statistically generalizable is not the point here. Rather, the random sample was seen, at least theoretically, as being more representative of the population than a non-probabilistic sample. This example is not unique. The notion of a random sample is—rightly or wrongly—held in high esteem among many research audiences, whether corporate executives, funders, or other researchers.

The primary driver of your sampling strategy selection should be your study design and research objectives. For qualitative research, this often means some type of purposeful sampling strategy. Nonetheless, if you have a choice between choosing a homogeneous sample purposively or randomly from a larger population and you have a decent sampling frame, why not use a simple random sample? If it is possible to obtain a probabilistic sample (note that in the above example this was uncharacteristically easy), and if there are no reasons to the contrary (that is, your use of a probability method would not capture your intended population, such as in extreme case sampling), random sampling approaches in qualitative research are perfectly acceptable.

Below we cover only two of the more common probabilistic sampling techniques—simple random and systematic. We do not discuss other methods, such as cluster, stratified, time and space, or respondent-driven sampling, as they are rarely employed in qualitative research.

Simple Random Sample (SRS)

Probably the most common probability sample, an SRS is also one of the most robust. In an SRS, each sampling unit has the same probability of being selected relative to all other units in the sampling frame. The procedure is straightforward and based on three fundamental steps.

1. Assign a number from 1 to N to each element in the population, with N being the total number of known elements in the population.

2. Obtain a list of n different numbers (n being the number of elements you want in your sample) within the 1 to N range, each one obtained using a random process. In contemporary research, random number generation is invariably done with computer software (Excel or any statistical program) or via the Internet, although hard copy random number tables are still available and used occasionally.

3. Choose the elements in the population corresponding to these numbers.

One of the main advantages of an SRS, compared to other probability methods, is that it is conceptually the simplest probabilistic sampling method and thus easy to analyze. In fact, many statistical analysis packages and standard statistical methods assume this type of sampling.

One of the challenges associated with an SRS, however, is the requirement that all the sampling units in the entire population be identified and numbered prior to selection (i.e., are enumerated). In other words, you need a sampling frame. In many research contexts, this is simply not possible. But in some contexts a little creativity can go a long way. For example, with the widespread accessibility of information and maps on the Internet, it's relatively easy to obtain an SRS of houses in a small town or village. Pull up a satellite photo of your study site (which will need to be validated on the ground), number the houses on your map, and randomly choose your sample from there. With a little ingenuity, you may be able to create a sampling frame where no "official" enumeration exists.

Another drawback to an SRS is that it may not adequately capture subpopulations if they are hidden or small in number, relative to the larger population. If, for example, for analytic purposes we wanted roughly an equal number of men and women in our study and only 10% of the study population was female, an SRS wouldn't likely produce enough women in the sample. We would instead use some type of stratified approach. The same principle holds if we are interested in sampling unique individuals or key informants within our study population. Using an SRS, or any probability sample for that matter, would not be very useful in this instance.

Systematic Sample

A systematic sample involves the selection of every *nth* unit within a study population. For example, we might select every *nth* name in a phone book, visit every 8th house in a village, or interview every 20th person entering a market or attending a health clinic. While theoretically systematic sampling is not true random sampling (because once the first unit is selected, the odds of selection for every other unit have been predetermined), it is as robust as an SRS for the vast majority of research contexts that require a probability sample. There are four basic steps to the process:

1. Define the sampling population.
2. Determine the desired sample size.
3. Estimate the size of sampling population.
4. Determine the sampling interval. This is calculated by dividing the estimated population size by the desired sample size.

Defining your population is trickier, and more important, than it might seem at first. If, for example, you're interested in an activity that has temporal variability—for example, people who visit a car dealership—inferences from your study's findings are constrained by your sampling parameters. Sampling on weekends will limit inferences from your findings to weekend customers; if you want to make broader inferences, include weekdays as well.

One of the main advantages of a systematic sample is that its use does not require a sampling frame, which makes it more versatile in many cases than a SRS. There are some limitations to the method, however. The first is that you need to be able to estimate the population size fairly well. If you underestimate, you will reach your sample size prematurely. Conversely, overestimation will result in having run through the entire population before obtaining your desired sample size.

Systematic sampling also works best if your sampling units are configured in an orderly or defined manner. So if you want to sample, say, people attending a sporting event, it helps if there are either defined entrances from which to count and sample or orderly and fixed seating from which to count and select. If the sampling context is more fluid or less orderly, then systematic sampling becomes more difficult. Imagine, for example, trying to obtain a systematic sample at a large political rally in an open space, where people are milling about.

Work-arounds can be created for such amorphous contexts. One can, for example, create invisible transects through the crowd and, walking along a transect, select every *nth* person on that line. Multiple transects at different spatial orientations through an invisible center—for example, Corner A to Corner B, Corner C to Corner D, middle of Side A to middle of Side B, and so forth—can subsequently be created and followed if one transect is not enough to generate the desired sample size. In general, though, diffuse and mobile environments are not ideal for systematic sampling.

A less commonly encountered problem with systematic sampling is an order bias. If the list, event, or assemblage of units to be counted has some sort of regular patterning (e.g., people are seated in an alternating male, female configuration) this can introduce obvious, and significant, bias into a sample.

How Do I Choose a Sampling Strategy?

Above, we have described a number of sampling methods from which to choose. There are no prescriptive, mechanistic methods for selecting a sampling approach, but we can offer some criteria you can consider to help guide your efforts. The four steps below are intended as guidelines only. We cannot account for every possible permutation of contextual, theoretical, and logistical parameters of a given study. Every researcher will need to carefully consider ALL of the parameters of their particular research project to arrive at an informed decision.

1. Estimate the size of the population of interest. If it's small enough and ethically and logistically feasible to do, choose a census and proceed to Step 4. If a census is not possible or desirable, proceed to Step 2.

2. Consider (a) how much control you will have over your recruitment and sampling procedures and (b) how certain you are about *who, what, where* you need to sample for your study. If you have a good sense of what types of individuals (or events or places) will best inform your study and if you can access those individuals or places, a purposive sampling strategy is a good choice. Choose among the variations of purposive sample approaches outlined in Table 2.1 by identifying which variation best suits your research objectives and study population and which is feasible within your research context. If your population is "hidden" and socially connected somehow, consider augmenting your sampling strategy with a chain referral technique. Proceed to Step 4.

    If you have no or little control over who you can sample or if you are uncertain about who the most appropriate participants (or places and events) are for your study, carry on to Step 3.

3. If you're unsure of whom you should sample, do some more desk work (i.e., read more about your topic and the proposed study community). If you've exhausted this route, reach out to other researchers and local community members to help inform your research design and sampling strategy (this is good practice, even if you do have a well-informed and focused research design). If this doesn't provide enough information, you may have to initiate your study with a convenience sample, perhaps within a participant observation context. Proceed to Step 4.

   If you have no or little control over whom or what places you can access, a convenience sample is pretty much your only option.

4. Regardless of which sampling strategy you choose, consider how inductive and flexible your study procedures can be. The more room for iterative processes you have during data collection activities and the more time you have to carry out your study, the greater the consideration you can give to choosing an inductive sampling approach. If your sampling procedures have to be predetermined (due to funder or ethics committee requirements) or if you have substantial time constraints, inductive sampling is not your best option and may be logistically unfeasible. Unless you're employing a census, proceed to Step 5.

5. Once you have gone through Steps 1 through 4 and have selected a sampling method, determine whether or not adding a probability component to it would (a) enhance the representativeness of your sample and (b) not detract from the initial sampling strategy's purpose. If you answer in the affirmative to both these questions and it's logistically feasible to obtain an SRS or systematic sample, consider choosing one of these methods to enhance your study. Proceed to Step 6.

6. For each population and data collection method in your study, repeat Steps 1 through 5.

You likely will have noticed that sampling methods are not necessarily mutually exclusive. They also don't have to be employed in isolation relative to one another. You may, for example, use a convenience sample to identify people who are exceptionally knowledgeable about your study topic (i.e., *intensity* form of purposive sampling) and interview a sample of these key individuals. But imagine that you also want to make sure that you capture as diverse a range of viewpoints as possible from this population of knowledgeable individuals (*maximum variation* form of purposive sampling). As you complete the interviews with the initial sample of key informants, you ask them to refer others who are equally knowledgeable about the subject but who may have different perspectives (*chain referral* sampling). You've just utilized three sampling approaches to select one defined population (the convenience sample is, by its nature, undefined, although you would still record basic information about the individuals within the sample).

And if your study includes more than one population (which is common in field research), you may wish to sample one population using one method and another population using a different method. You may, for example, be able to get a census of one group of individuals because their population size is extremely small, whereas another much larger group might have to be sampled purposively. There are no hard and fast rules about combining and integrating sampling techniques. Do what makes the most sense for your research and that can most effectively (and ethically) help you achieve your research objectives.

CHOOSING SAMPLE SIZES

In-Depth Interviews

Estimating probabilistic sample sizes is a fairly straightforward enterprise. They are estimated mathematically based on preselected parameters and objectives (i.e., x statistical power with y confidence intervals).[1] Non-probability samples are entirely different when it comes to estimating necessary sample sizes. Several years ago, in preparation for a sampling article, Guest, Bunce, and Johnson (2006) searched through the social, behavioral, and health science literature to see what general recommendations existed regarding non-probability sample sizes. The authors reviewed 24 research methods books and seven databases. They found that although numerous works explained how to select participants (e.g., Johnson, 1990; Trotter, 1991) or provided readers with factors to consider when determining non-probabilistic sample sizes (Flick, 2009; LeCompte & Schensul, 2010; Miles & Huberman, 1994; Morse, 1995; Patton, 2002; Rubin & Rubin, 2004), only seven sources provided guidelines for actual sample sizes.

Bertaux (1981), for example, argues that an n of 15 is the smallest acceptable sample size in qualitative research, while Bernard (2000, p. 178) observes that most ethnographic studies are based on 30 to 60 interviews. Morse (1994, p. 225) outlines more detailed guidelines. She recommends at least six participants for phenomenological studies; approximately 30 to 50 participants for ethnographies, grounded theory studies, and ethnoscience studies; and 100 to 200 sampling units in qualitative ethology.

Creswell's (2006) ranges are somewhat different. He recommends between five and 25 interviews for a phenomenological study and 20 to 30 for a grounded theory

---

[1]Since the vast majority of inductive, qualitative field studies are not interested in statistical analyses of data, and subsequently probability sampling, we do not cover the subject of power analysis in this book. For those readers interested in pursuing the topic of probabilistic sample sizes in more detail, we suggest any basic statistical textbook, or the classic "Statistical Power Analysis for the Behavioral Sciences" (Cohen, 1988). Various sample size calculators are also available on the Internet. Though crude, they are simple to use and can provide ball park estimates (e.g., www.raosoft.com/samplesize.html).

study. Kuzel (1992, p. 41) ties his recommendations to sample heterogeneity and research objectives, recommending six to eight interviews for a homogeneous sample and 12 to 20 data sources "when looking for disconfirming evidence or trying to achieve maximum variation."

A key limitation of these recommendations is that, though derived from experience, none are based on empirical evidence (at least none of the authors cited above present evidence for their recommendations). During their review, Guest and colleagues (2006) observed that nearly all of the relevant literature recommended that purposive, non-probabilistic sample sizes be determined inductively: That is, sampling should continue until *theoretical saturation*—the point at which no or little new information is being extracted from the data—is reached (e.g., Bluff, 1997; Byrne, 2001; Fossey, Harvey, McDermott, & Davidson, 2002; Morse, 1995; Sandelowski, 1995). In fact, a good number of journals in the health sciences recognize theoretical saturation as the main criterion by which to justify adequate sample sizes in qualitative inquiry. Saturation is the status quo by which non-probability sample sizes should be determined in social and behavioral research, at least according to the methodological literature.

Guidelines and Qualitative Research

The issue of guidelines in qualitative research is a contentious one. Some scholars argue that we should not, or cannot, establish guidelines because practitioners of qualitative research do not agree about what these guidelines should be, or they disagree on the simple premise that qualitative research should follow guidelines at all (Chapple & Rogers, 1998; Sandelowski & Barroso, 2002). One argument is that guidelines are overly prescriptive and, in and of themselves, do not confer rigor (Barbour, 2001; Eakin & Mykhalovskiy, 2003). Another point critics make is that guidelines focus too much on procedure and methods and that their uncritical application "legitimize[s] substandard research" (Lambert & McKevitt, 2002). Some qualitative scholars posit that developing and/or adhering to predetermined structures or processes contradicts the inductive essence of qualitative inquiry (Denzin, 2009; Lambert & McKevitt, 2002).

For the most part, we don't disagree with the general intent behind any of these criticisms of guidelines. We do disagree, however, with the hyperbolic forms these arguments take. Using guidelines as templates to blindly design or evaluate qualitative research is indeed irresponsible. And, true, there will always be a disagreement over what constitutes best practice. Equally true, if one imposes *too much* structure on qualitative inquiry, it loses its inductive power. But "guidelines" are substantially different than "standards." As Guest and MacQueen (2008) point out, guidelines are suggestions. Standards are prescriptive assertions. In other words, guidelines provide direction, not absolute rules, and they need to be applied intelligently and with good judgment. The suggestions, procedures, and templates we provide in this book are designed to help researchers think through their sampling, data collection, and data management procedures, not dictate one particular way of doing things. The suggestions, however, are based on the applied methodological literature and the combined experience of three applied qualitative researchers.

Research, including qualitative research, in an applied context is intended to address real-world problems and, if we're lucky enough, to inform policy. We do our best to understand a research problem by employing the most appropriate sampling and data collection method we can find (which are not always qualitative). Guidelines and best practices are landmarks to help us navigate the journey to our destination.

Guest and colleagues' review also revealed that the same literature did a poor job of operationalizing the concept of saturation, providing no description of how saturation might be determined. Using theoretical saturation as a determinant of sample size is problematic from another practical standpoint as well. As mentioned earlier, reviewers of research proposals and protocols (e.g., funders, institutional review boards [IRBs]) typically require researchers to state planned sample sizes for a study *before* it begins (Cheek, 2000). This requirement is antithetical to the very principles and procedures inherent in grounded theory and other inductively-based research designs (Charmaz, 2006, p. 30). Waiting to reach saturation in the field is, therefore, not often an option. Researchers must follow the a priori sampling plan they outlined in their proposal or protocol, regardless of the emergent situation on the ground.

So how does one go about estimating when saturation will occur before data are collected? An empirical study conducted by one of the book's authors sought to answer this question in the context of in-depth interviews (Guest et al., 2006). Using data from a study involving 60 in-depth interviews with female sex workers in two West African cities, the authors systematically documented the degree of thematic saturation and variability in the data over the course of their analysis. Based on their analysis, they posited that the dataset was relatively "thematically saturated" after only 12 interviews. After analyzing 12 of the 60 interviews, 100 of the 114 (88%) total codes applied to the entire dataset had been identified and developed. Seventy percent of all codes were identified within the first six interviews (Figure 2.1).

The magic number of six interviews is consistent with one other empirically-based study (Morgan, Fischoff, Bostrom, & Atman, 2002) and Morse's (1994) (albeit

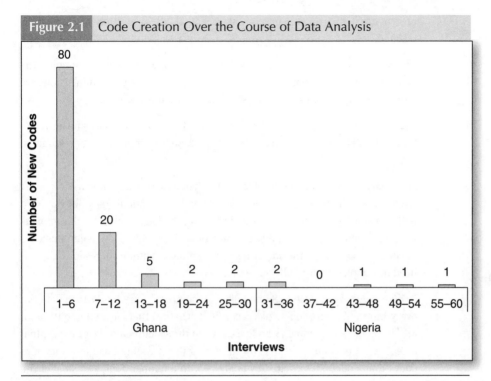

Figure 2.1 Code Creation Over the Course of Data Analysis

Source: Guest, Bunce, and Johnson (2006).

unsubstantiated) recommendation for phenomenological studies. Similar evidence-based recommendations can be found for qualitative research in technology usability. Nielsen and Landauer (1993) created a mathematical model based on results of six different projects and demonstrated that six evaluators (participants) can uncover 80% of the major usability problems within a system and that after about 12 evaluators, this diagnostic number tends to level off at around 90%. While helpful, be aware that the numbers above come with two important caveats:

Caveat 1—All Studies Are Different. The studies from which the saturation data above were derived have three important factors in common. Researchers for each of these studies (a) used a fairly homogenous sample, (b) used a semi-structured data collection approach, and (c) were interested in finding patterns across the sample. Not every qualitative study exhibits any one, let alone all, of these characteristics. In general, the rapidity at which saturation is reached is related to five factors.

The degree of instrument structure. The more structure embodied in the instrument, the sooner saturation will be reached. Note that for studies using an unstructured instrument, or no instrument at all, saturation may never be reached.

The degree of sample homogeneity. The more homogeneous the sample, the quicker saturation is achieved. Groups that are alike on various dimensions are more likely to think in similar ways and have similar experiences.

The complexity and focus of the study topic. For more complex and intricate topics, it will take longer to reach saturation than for simpler and more targeted topics.

Study purpose. Finding high-level common themes across a sample will generally require fewer sampling units than identifying the maximum range of variation within a sample. If you're interested in finding the big issues, a small sample is often sufficient. Conversely, if your study objectives require the comprehensive documentation of all the idiosyncrasies exhibited within your sample, you'll need to sample substantially more than six or even 12 units.

Analyst categorization style. Some folks are "splitters." They tend to see detail in everything and create codebooks accordingly. On the other end of the continuum are "lumpers"—individuals who like to group things into a few large conceptual categories. Codebooks created by splitters will invariably include a lot more codes than codebooks created by analysts with a lumper bent. The smaller the codebook being used to code the data, the quicker saturation will be achieved.

So, if you have a heterogeneous sample, a less-structured instrument, a highly complex topic, are interested in the range of variation, and your analysts are all splitters, you may never reach saturation. The magic numbers of six and 12 per subgroup would be meaningless. They are minimum estimates. Use your best judgment to estimate your sample sizes by building off of the few existing empirical studies and considering the five factors above, rather than viewing recommendations as the ultimate authoritative source.

Caveat 2—Your Audience May Have Different Standards. We point out above that evidence-based studies, as well as the collective experience of qualitative researchers around the world, suggest that a sample size of six to 12 individuals per group is sufficient for many (but not all!) types of qualitative studies. For many audiences, however, this number is perceived as too small, regardless of the empirical or anecdotal evidence. Rarely, for example, will a journal accept a qualitative manuscript with such small sample sizes. Most will want an *n* of 25 or more. Likewise, we know of PhD committees who have insisted on increasing the sample size beyond 15 for a dissertation research project, even though 15 participants would have been more than sufficient for the particular research context.

Even in the corporate sector, where the cost of a single interview can be as much as several thousand dollars, we've experienced this propensity for wanting larger samples. Clients will often insist on an *n* of 20 to 30 per target group, in spite of the added cost and contrary to researcher recommendations. In sum, our advice is that while increasing one's sample size may not be necessary from a scientific perspective, you need to consider your audience's predilections. In most cases, it doesn't hurt to increase your sample size, and doing so provides the appearance of extra diligence (real or perceived).

Every research context is unique. And sampling decisions will need to be made within the parameters of a specific context. Notwithstanding, some general guidelines in selecting non-probabilistic sample sizes can be posited. Padgett (2008, p. 56) outlines four rules of thumb that we find helpful:

> *The smaller the sample size, the more intense and deep are the data being collected.* This is why, for example, case study analyses typically involve relatively small sample sizes.

> *Larger samples are needed for heterogeneity, smaller sizes for homogeneity.* This rule applies to both your research objectives and your study population. Finding shared, high-level themes across a group of individuals, for example, will require smaller sample sizes than those for revealing a large range of responses.

> *Avoid sacrificing depth for breadth.* Ideally, you'll have enough resources to cover both the depth and breadth of a particular topic, at least to a certain degree. But be careful not to stretch your resources too thin by including too many stakeholder groups, having too broadly defined a study population, or having too many research objectives. In qualitative inquiry, depth is your primary methodological objective.

> Larger numbers are preferred, as long as rule 3 is honored.

Focus Groups

To our knowledge, no empirical studies have been published that provide evidence-based guidance on how many focus groups are needed for a given research study.[2] In the focus group literature, as with the in-depth interview literature, scholars often cite theoretical saturation as the primary method for determining sample sizes. But since there are no supporting data as to how many groups this might actually entail, researchers must rely on general recommendations based on anecdotal experience. The

---

[2] There are, however, more specific recommendations for individual focus group size. We present these in Chapter 5.

recommendations in the literature range from as few as three groups per study population (or subpopulation) to as many as 50 groups (Greenbaum, 1997; Kitzinger & Barbour, 2001; Krueger & Casey, 2009/2010; Morgan, 1996; Powell & Single, 1996; Vaughn, Schumm, & Sinagub, 1996). A commonly agreed upon guideline is that saturation requires conducting at least two groups for each defining demographic, which means that the greater the variety of participants, the more focus groups are required (Carey, 1995; Knodel, 1993; Krueger & Casey, 2009/2010; Ulin, Robinson, & Tolley, 2005).

Based on the experience of others, as well as our own, we would recommend carrying out at least three focus groups per population or subpopulation. Even if one focus group for some reason goes awry (which does happen), you still have data from two groups that should provide enough insight for most research objectives. Note that focus groups are typically conducted with homogenous groups. So if you want to, say, include employees and managers from the same company in your study, this would mean three groups of employees and three groups of managers, if you were to use our minimum recommendation. Another point to keep in mind is that when analyzing focus group data, each *group* is the unit of analysis. One of the implications of this analytic property regards publishing. Focus groups are not often used as stand-alone data in peer reviewed publications, for two general reasons. The first is that response-dependence exists between participants within a group, which in turn affects validity (Guest, MacQueen, & Namey, 2012). The second is that you may need to conduct 15 or more focus groups (at the very least) for acceptance into most peer-reviewed journals, which entails recruiting 90 to 180 participants, depending on the size of your focus groups). That said, there are plenty of applications of focus group methodology for which publication is not the aim; we describe focus groups and their strengths in more detail in Chapter 5. The point is that it can be difficult to accurately estimate (and defend) an appropriate sample for focus groups, regardless of their purpose in the research design. At the time this book went to press, however, Guest received a grant to empirically study data saturation and variability in focus groups. We hope the results will comprise the establishment of an evidence base for focus group sample sizes upon which others can build.

Participant Observation

Because participant observation is so varied in its practice, there really aren't any recommendations as to the number of places, events, or behaviors you should observe. We can, however, offer several factors to consider:

The degree of structure in your participant observation procedures. If you are in the early exploratory stages of a study and are conducting participant observation to get a general lay of the land, you will probably need to carry out several observation events to get a feel for what to focus on while observing and who to talk to. Conversely, the more you know about a community, its people, and your research topic, the more structure you can impose on observation activities. Templates and checklists might be used, for example, in the later stages of a research project. With more structure, you may need only one observation event to accomplish a particular data collection objective.

The degree of temporal variability inherent in your research topic. As a general rule, the more variability, the more participant observation events required. As mentioned earlier, you may need to observe at multiple times of the year, multiple days of the week, or multiple times during a day. It all depends on the activities, events, and behaviors in which you're interested. Imagine, for example, that you are interested in agricultural practices. These normally vary by season, so you would want to observe activities at different times of the year. Or maybe your research topic is drinking behavior. You would want to make sure you observe people and places during weekdays, weekends, and paydays, since you might expect drinking behavior to be different across these dimensions. If you can obtain some sort of census—that is, you or your research team is in the field every day for a particular event—even better.

The degree of spatial variability inherent in your research topic. The same principle for temporal variability holds for spatial variability. You want to make sure that you have as representative a set of observations as possible, within the logistical and budgetary constraints of your study. If you are observing behavior in shopping malls, for example, you might consider observing in malls within a range of geographic areas that are associated with different ethnic or socioeconomic groups. If there are few enough malls in your population, you can do even better and obtain a census of malls in your study area.

Being mindful of the above factors should help mitigate the possibility of missing a pivotally important and obvious piece of information in your observation activities. In addition to considering the three factors above, you can sample places, events, and times using any of the sampling methods discussed in this chapter. We mentioned a census, but you can choose observational venues randomly or based on specific criteria such as extreme cases. An example of the latter would be to observe drinking behavior on a specific holiday when certain locals are notoriously consumptive (think Carnival or Mardi Gras). In sum, as with sampling for other data collection methods, choosing what, when, and how to sample for participant observation activities should be guided by a combination of your research objectives, logistical parameters, and ethical considerations.

Sampling in Mixed Methods Research

Mixed methods research—defined as the integration of qualitative and quantitative methods in a single study—is becoming increasingly mainstream in social-behavioral studies. Commensurately, more is being written about sampling in mixed methods contexts (e.g., Collins, 2010; Teddlie & Yu, 2007). Of the various articles written, we find the work of Onwuegbuzie and Collins (2007) particularly insightful as it presents the mechanics of sample integration in a concise and practical way. They describe the combination of sampling efforts based on two underlying dimensions—timing of procedures and the type of relationship between sampling units in two or more samples. Onwuegbuzie and Collins (2007) combine these two dimensions with the various types of mixed methods designs to generate Figure 2.2.

Timing

Sequential. Samples are selected sequentially, at different times. A previous sample informs a subsequent sample. A subsequent sample is dependent in some way on a prior sample.

Concurrent. Samples are drawn at the same (or close in) time. Samples are independent of one another.

Relationship Between Samples

Identical. Sampling units and sample sizes are the same. Use if you want to directly compare qualitative to quantitative (QL/QT) responses at the level of measurement unit.

Parallel. Samples are drawn from the same population but are composed of different units. Use if there is no need to directly compare data at unit level or if identical sampling is too burdensome for participants.

Nested. A smaller sample is a subset of a larger sample. Use if you need to either directly compare between samples or infer from a smaller second sample to the larger sample.

Multilevel. Samples come from two or more different populations or two or more levels of analysis (definition depends on author). This feature is particularly useful if triangulating or comparing independent groups or levels of analysis.

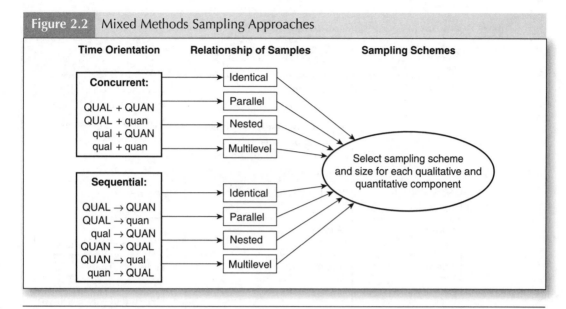

Figure 2.2 Mixed Methods Sampling Approaches

Source: Onwuegbuzie and Collins (2007, p. 294).

RECRUITING

Recruiting methods are related to sampling strategies, but they are not the same thing. Recruitment of study participants refers to the process by which participants are first informed about and, if eligible, asked to join a study. Recruitment is the means used to obtain a desired sample. It is often an overlooked subject in the research design literature, which is why we provide a description of the more common recruitment techniques and their characteristics in Table 2.2 (see pages 68 and 69). As with every other dimension in research design, your method of recruitment will be determined by a combination of research objectives, logistical constraints and contextual parameters, and ethical considerations. More details on implementing recruiting strategies are provided in Chapters 4 and 5, in the context of in-depth interviews and focus groups, respectively.

WORKING INTERNATIONALLY

On a conceptual level, political borders and cultural practices have no bearing on sampling strategies. Sampling methods should be chosen, first and foremost, based on their appropriateness with respect to the proposed data analysis, their ability to

Table 2.2	Recruitment Techniques and Characteristics		
Type	**Technique**	**Advantages**	**Disadvantages**
Media-based	Posters/ flyers	• Inexpensive • Targeted coverage • In many cases, the choice of venues acts as a prescreen for qualified interviewees.	• Dependent on visibility of the recruiting message • May miss many qualified interviewees
	Newspaper/ magazine	Relatively wide coverage	Expensive
	Radio/TV	Wide coverage	Expensive Coverage not highly targeted
	Internet	Inexpensive	• Little control over coverage • Dependent on visibility of the recruiting message • May miss many qualified interviewees
Investigator initiated	Door-to-door	Higher response rates (than approaches that are not face-to-face)	Labor intensive
	Facility-based	Good response rates	Generalizability limited to facility patrons
	Intercept	• If done at a venue relevant to the study topic or target interview population, can be an efficient way to locate qualified participants who might be hard to find through other methods. • May be linked to time/ space sampling.	• Involves approaching individuals in public places. • Subject to bias created by lack of representativeness of the intercept location(s) or by approach bias from the recruiter doing the intercepts
	E-mail	• Inexpensive • In many cases the choices of e-mail addresses acts as a prescreen for qualified interviewees	• Limits sample to Internet users • Potentially low response rate (dependent on population and topic) • Subject to self-selection bias

Type	Technique	Advantages	Disadvantages
	Phone	If randomly selected, useful for getting unbiased representation of residents of a particular area	• Limits sample to those with phones • Obtaining sampling frame may be difficult • Can be time consuming, especially if the screening criteria disqualify many from participation
	Mail	Inexpensive	Lower response rates
Socially-based	Chain referral (participants refer other participants)	Good for hard-to-reach populations	• Participants must have substantial social ties • Social connections between the interviewees may create bias in the research findings
	External referral (nonparticipants refer participants)	Can be effective, depending on who is referring (e.g., community leaders)	Possible ethical issues relating to participant volition
Panel/list-based	National panel	Prescreened lists, usually balanced to provide a nationally representative source of market research participants, can be easily screened to provide participants matching almost any set of demographic, behavioral, attitudinal, or other characteristics	• Expensive • Depending on how the panel is developed and maintained, panels may contain people who participate in studies simply to get the incentive money or who take on the personae of "professional respondents" causing skewed data • May miss particularly well-qualified interviewees who are not part of the database
	Research facility or professional/ affiliation-based panel	• Range in cost from free to expensive • Range in quality, depending on how the lists are developed and maintained	
		• Assuming the lists closely match the screening criteria, makes for fast, efficient recruiting of highly qualified interviewees • Useful for tough-to-locate categories of interviewees	• Dependent on the quality/ representativeness of the lists • Use of some lists may raise issues of privacy if those on the list have not preapproved being contacted by researchers

achieve the desired research objectives, and ethical considerations. But geography and culture can affect the logistics of implementing a particular sampling approach. As we discussed earlier, logistical issues can be a key factor, if not *the* primary determinant, of whom and how you sample. Reality has a way of impinging on the best of plans. Physical access to your study population, for example, can be impeded due to poor roads (whose conditions can be highly seasonal) or lack of transportation routes altogether. And helpful resources such as recruiting companies or reliable data to construct sampling frames are less likely to exist in developing countries. This is one of the areas where local collaborators and stakeholders can play a key role.

Involving local stakeholders (e.g., religious leaders, chiefs, politicians, institutional leaders) and/or local investigators before embarking on data collection is always good research practice and helps mitigate (though not eliminate) unwelcome surprises and barriers to implementation. It is especially critical when doing research in international settings. Not only is stakeholder cooperation necessary for the successful implementation of a study, but local experts can also tell you which recruitment techniques are most appropriate—and, more importantly, which ones are inappropriate—for your study population. For example, in one of the author's studies in Malawi, village chiefs helped the study team identify willing and eligible couples for the assessment of a family planning intervention (Shattuck, Kerner, Gilles, Hartmann, & Guest, 2011). Without the chiefs' help, recruitment would have taken twice as long at best, and may never have gotten off the ground at worst. Even experienced ethnographers, who may be very familiar with a particular community, rely on local community members to provide guidance for research processes and to gain entry into local communities. These same tenets hold true if conducting research among subpopulations within your own country, such as immigrant communities or socially isolated or deviant subpopulations.

SUMMING UP

The old adage that everything works well in theory is certainly true of sampling (and recruiting). A researcher may design *the* perfect sampling strategy for a study and have an airtight rationale for it. But the truth is, no matter how "perfect" a sampling strategy is, it can be quickly foiled by simple logistics on the ground. Reality has a way of keeping theory in check. Factors such as access to the study population and willingness of individuals to participate in research (or even to informally talk to field staff) are critical. Without either of these, there is no study. The study environment is another consideration. Working in conflict zones or other dangerous areas (e.g., high crime areas, red light districts) will seriously impede the ability to locate and talk freely with individuals.

The best defense against "reality" is to be as prepared as you can be. If you're not familiar with the study site or population, visit it before finalizing the research design and sampling strategy. If a personal visit isn't possible, consult local investigators or others familiar with the area and population. Get as much information as possible before deciding on a sampling plan.

Note that reality can occasionally be helpful and present an unexpected gift. In a recent study conducted by Guest in Kampala, Uganda, one of the populations in the study was female market vendors in a huge market (8,000 plus vendors, spread across a large area, much of which was undefined). When designing the study, Guest (the U.S. based investigator) developed an elaborate sampling plan—consisting of multiple integrated sampling approaches—in order to draw a probabilistic sample from the market's overwhelming chaos. On his first visit to the field site, Guest visited the market administrator with his local collaborator to get permission to conduct the study. During this brief conversation, the administrator mentioned that he had a list of all the market vendors and that the field team could copy it. Within minutes, the sampling strategy transformed from a cumbersome, multimethod approach to a simple random sample. The key is to be open to emergent possibilities when sampling. Be flexible when things don't work out as planned, and, always have a plan B in your back pocket.

REFERENCES

Barbour, R. S. (2001). Checklists for improving rigour in qualitative research: A case of the tail wagging the dog? *British Medical Journal, 322*, 1115–1117.

Bernard, H. (2000). *Social research methods: Qualitative and quantitative approaches.* Thousand Oaks, CA: Sage.

Bertaux, D. (1981). From the life-history approach to the transformation of sociological practice. In D. Bertaux (Ed.), *Biography and society: The life history approach in the social sciences* (pp. 29–45). London, UK: Sage.

Bluff, R. (1997). Evaluating qualitative research. *British Journal of Midwifery, 5*(4), 232–235.

Byrne, M. (2001). Evaluating the findings of qualitative research. *Association of Operating Room Nurses Journal, 73*(3), 703–706.

Carey, M. (1995). Comment: Concerns in the analysis of focus group data. *Qualitative Health Research, 5*(4), 487–495.

Chapple, A., & Rogers, A. (1998). Explicit guidelines for qualitative research: A step in the right direction, a defense of the "soft" option, or a form of sociological imperialism? *Family Practice, 15*(6), 556–561.

Charmaz, K. (2006). *Grounded theory: A practical guide through qualitative analysis.* Thousand Oaks, CA: Sage.

Cheek, J. (2000). An untold story: Doing funded qualitative research. In N. Denzin & Y. Lincoln (Eds.), *Handbook for qualitative research* (2nd ed., pp. 401–420). Thousand Oaks, CA: Sage.

Cohen, J. (1988). *Statistical power analysis for the behavioral sciences* (2nd ed.). New York, NY: Psychology Press.

Collins, K. (2010). Advanced sampling designs in mixed research: Current practices and emerging trends in the social and behavioral sciences. In A. Tashakkori & C. Teddlie (Eds.), *Handbook of mixed methods in social and behavioral research* (2nd ed., pp. 353–378). Thousand Oaks, CA: Sage.

Creswell, J. (2006). *Qualitative inquiry and research design: Choosing among five approaches* (2nd ed.). Thousand Oaks, CA: Sage.

Denzin, N. (2009). The elephant in the living room, or extending the conversation about the politics of evidence. *Qualitative Research, 9,* 139–160.

Eakin, J., & Mykhalovskiy, E. (2003). Reframing the evaluation of qualitative health research: Reflections on a review of appraisal guidelines in the health sciences. *Journal of Evaluation in Clinical Practice, 9*(2), 187–194.

Flick, U. (2009). *An introduction to qualitative research: Theory, method and applications* (4th ed.). Thousand Oaks, CA: Sage.

Fossey, E., Harvey, C., McDermott, F., & Davidson, L. (2002). Understanding and evaluating qualitative research. *Australian and New Zealand Journal of Psychiatry, 36,* 717–732.

Glaser, B., & Strauss, A. (1967). *The discovery of grounded theory: Strategies for qualitative research.* New Brunswick, NJ: Aldine Transaction.

Greenbaum, T. L. (1997). *The handbook for focus group research.* Thousand Oaks, CA: Sage.

Guest, G., Bunce, A., & Johnson, L. (2006). How many interviews are enough? An experiment with data saturation and variability. *Field Methods, 18,* 59–82.

Guest, G., & MacQueen, K. (2008). Reevaluating guidelines for qualitative research. In G. Guest & K. MacQueen (Eds.), *Handbook for team-based qualitative research* (pp. 205–226). Lanham, MD: AltaMira.

Guest, G., MacQueen, K., & Namey, E. (2012). *Applied thematic analysis.* Thousand Oaks, CA: Sage.

Johnson, J. (1990). *Selecting ethnographic informants.* Newbury Park, CA: Sage.

Kitzinger, J., & Barbour, R. S. (2001). Introduction: The challenge and promise of focus groups. In J. Kitzinger & R. S. Barbour (Eds.), *Developing focus group research: Politics, theory and practice* (pp. 1–20). London, UK: Sage.

Knodel, J. (1993). The design and analysis of focus group studies: A practical approach. In D. L. Morgan (Ed.), *Successful focus groups: Advancing the state of the art* (pp. 35–50). Thousand Oaks, CA: Sage.

Krueger, R., & Casey, M. A. (2010). *Focus groups: A practical guide for applied research* (4th ed.). Thousand Oaks, CA: Sage. (Original work published 2009)

Kuzel, A. (1992). Sampling in qualitative inquiry. In B. Crabtree & W. Miller (Eds.), *Doing qualitative research* (pp. 31–44). Newbury Park, CA: Sage.

Lambert, H., & McKevitt, C. (2002). Anthropology in health research: From qualitative methods to multidisciplinary. *British Medical Journal, 325,* 210–213.

LeCompte, M., & Schensulm J. (2010). *Designing and conducting ethnographic research: An introduction* (2nd ed.). Lanham, MD: AltaMira.

Miles, M., & Huberman, A. (1994). *Qualitative data analysis* (2nd ed.). Thousand Oaks, CA: Sage.

Morgan, D. L. (1996). Focus groups. *Annual Review of Sociology, 22,* 129–152.

Morgan, M., Fischoff, B., Bostrom, A., & Atman, C. (2002). *Risk communication: A mental models approach.* New York, NY: Cambridge University Press.

Morse, J. (1994). Designing funded qualitative research. In N. Denzin & Y. Lincoln (Eds.), *Handbook for qualitative research* (pp. 220–235). Thousand Oaks, CA: Sage.

Morse, J. (1995). The significance of saturation. *Qualitative Health Research, 5,* 147–149.

Nielsen, J., & Landauer, T. K. (1993). A mathematical model of the finding of usability problems. *Proceedings of InterCHI, 93,* 206–213.

Onwuegbuzie, A., & Collins, K. (2007). A typology of mixed methods sampling designs in social science research. *Qualitative Report, 12,* 281–316.

Padgett, D. (2008). *Qualitative methods in social work research* (2nd ed.). Thousand Oaks, CA: Sage.

Patton, M. (2002). *Qualitative research and evaluation methods* (3rd ed.). Thousand Oaks, CA: Sage.

Powell, R. A., & Single, H. M. (1996). Focus groups. *International Journal of Qualitative Health Care, 8,* 499–504.

Rubin, H., & Rubin, I. (2004). *Qualitative interviewing: The art of hearing data* (2nd ed.). Thousand Oaks, CA: Sage.

Sandelowski, M. (1995). Sample size in qualitative research. *Research in Nursing and Health, 18,* 179–183.

Sandelowski, M., & Barroso, J. (2002). Reading qualitative studies. *International Journal of Qualitative Methods, 1*(1), Article 5, 74–108.

Shattuck, D., Kerner, B., Gilles, K., Hartmann, M., & Guest, G. (2011). Encouraging contraceptive uptake by motivating men to communicate about family planning: The Malawi Male Motivator Project. *American Journal of Public Health, 101,* 1089–1095.

Teddlie, C., & Yu, F. (2007). Mixed methods sampling. *Journal of Mixed Methods Research, 1,* 77–100.

Trotter, R., II. (1991). Ethnographic research methods for applied medical anthropology. In C. Hill (Ed.), *Training manual in applied medical anthropology* (pp. 180–212). Washington, DC: American Anthropological Association.

Ulin, P. R., Robinson, E. T., & Tolley, E. E. (2005). *Qualitative methods in public health: A field guide for applied research.* San Franciso, CA: Jossey-Bass.

Vaughn, S., Schumm, J. S., & Sinagub, J. (1996). *Focus group interviews in education and psychology.* Thousand Oaks, CA: Sage.

ADDITIONAL READING

Bernard, H. (2000). Sampling. In H. R. Bernard (Ed.), *Social research methods: Qualitative and quantitative approaches* (chap. 5, pp. 143–185). Thousand Oaks, CA: Sage.

Daniel, J. (2011). Sampling essentials: Practical guidelines for making sampling choices. Thousand Oaks, CA: Sage.

Johnson, J. (1990). *Selecting ethnographic informants.* Newbury Park, CA: Sage.

Onwuegbuzie, A., & Collins, K. (2007). A typology of mixed methods sampling designs in social science research. *Qualitative Report, 12,* 281–316.

Ritchie, J., & Lewis, J. (2003). Designing and selecting samples. In *Qualitative research practice* (chap. 4). Thousand Oaks, CA: Sage.

EXERCISES

1. Under the heading *Caveat 1—All Studies Are Different,* we listed five factors that influence the speed at which saturation is reached. Think about, and jot down, other factors that can affect saturation.

2a. For a study you're planning, create a list of all the types of individuals or sampling units that would inform your research question(s). Can you include them all in your study? If not, how will you deal with their omission?

   b. Once you're comfortable with the type of groups to include (and it may be only one), select a sampling strategy for each group (or multiple strategies if appropriate).

   c. Next, estimate the required sample sizes for each group and mentally justify your numbers.

   d. For each group and strategy, choose a recruitment technique.

3. Review a qualitative article in a top journal in your field. Carefully review the sampling design. Is the sampling strategy (including sizes) appropriate? How could it have been improved, if at all?

3

Participant Observation

Participant observation is in some ways both the most natural and the most challenging of qualitative data collection methods. It connects the researcher to the most basic of human experiences, discovering through immersion and participation the hows and whys of human behavior in a particular context. Such discovery is natural in that all of us have done this repeatedly throughout our lives, learning what it means to be members of our own families, our ethnic and national cultures, our work groups, and our personal circles and associations. The challenge of harnessing this innate capability for participant observation is that when we are participant observers in a more formal sense, we must, at least a little, systematize and organize an inherently fluid process. This means not only being a player in a particular social milieu but also fulfilling the role of researcher—taking notes; recording voices, sounds, and images; and asking questions that are designed to uncover the meaning behind the behaviors. Additionally, in many cases, we are trying to discover and analyze aspects of social scenes that use rules and norms that the participants may experience without explicitly talking about, that operate on automatic or subconscious levels, or are even officially off limits for discussion or taboo. The result of this discovery and systemization is that we not only make ourselves into acceptable participants in some venue but also generate data that can meaningfully add to our collective understanding of human experience.

Participant observation is used across the social sciences, as well as in various forms of commercial, public policy, and nonprofit research. Anthropology and sociology, in particular, have relied on participant observation for many of their seminal insights, and for most anthropologists and many sociologists, doing a participant observation study at a field site is an important rite of passage into the discipline. Bronislaw Malinowski's (1922) work among the Trobriand Islanders is not only one of the foundational works of ethnography, but it is also one of the earliest to both exemplify and articulate the value of participant observation. Sociologists also conducted participant observation studies and discussed the use of the technique early on, including Beatrice Webb (1926) in the 1880s and the Chicago school of urban sociologists in the 1920s (Park, Burgess, & McKenzie, 1925).

For most people, these early studies create the iconic images of participant observation being performed by either an anthropologist—a somewhat field-worn character living in a remote village learning the ways of an exotic culture by deep and lengthy immersion in the day-to-day lives of the people—or an urban sociologist becoming wise in the ways of a gritty inner-city slum. (The anthropologist image has produced the old joke that a household in a native village consists of a married couple, their parents, their children, and the graduate student. When you retell this joke, feel free to insert your favorite study culture and locale for the native village.) While these images of participant observation focus on the sort of long-term research endeavor exemplified by ethnography, the technique is very flexible and can be employed to great benefit in addressing a range of research objectives. Many participant observation studies are not as lengthy in duration as ethnography, are less comprehensive in scope, and are conducted in relatively mundane locations. But even when it is used on a limited basis, there is no denying the power of this technique to produce penetrating insights and highly contextual understanding.

Almost any setting in which people have complex interactions with each other, with objects, or with their physical environment can be usefully examined through participant observation. Since doing participant observation means being embedded in the action and context of a social setting, we consider three key elements of a participant observation study:

1. *Getting into the location of whatever aspect of the human experience you wish to study.* This means going to where the action is—people's communities, homes, workplaces, recreational sites, places of commercial interaction, sacred sites, and the like. Participant observation is almost always conducted in situ.
2. *Building rapport with the participants.* The point of participant observation is that you wish to observe and learn about the things people do in the normal course of their lives. That means they have to accept you, to some extent, as someone they can "be themselves" in front of. While you don't necessarily have to be viewed as a complete insider, a successful participant observer has to inspire enough trust and acceptance to enable her research participants to act much as they would if the researcher were not present.

3. *Spending enough time interacting to get the needed data.* The informal, embedded nature of participant observation means that you cannot always just delve straight into all the topics that address your research issues and then leave. You must spend time both building rapport and observing or participating for a long enough period to have a sufficient range of experiences, conversations, and relatively unstructured interviews for your analysis. Depending on the scope of the project and your research questions, this may take anywhere from days to weeks, months, or even years, and it may involve multiple visits to the research site(s).

There is a reason that the phrase "you had to be there" is a cliché used by those who feel their verbal descriptions have not fully captured the essence of some scene or event. The phrase encapsulates a genuine truth—there are often important elements of human experience that are only visible to those who are actually there. Participant observation excels in capturing these elements, particularly:

- Rules and norms that are taken for granted by experienced participants or cultural insiders
  - For example, unspoken rules exist about who sits where at a meeting, what sort of encouragement listeners give to speakers to keep them talking (or deny to them in order to get them to shut up!), how many times a guest must refuse food before accepting it from a host, and so on.
  - While these rules can be elicited through interviews, it is often more efficient to learn them in situ and as they happen.

- Routine actions and social calculations that happen below the level of conscious thought
  - For example, things like the movements of parents when loading and unloading vehicles when both cargo and children are part of the scene or unconscious adjustments that salesmen make to their pitch in response to equally unconscious cues from potential buyers.
  - In these cases, interviews might miss the action entirely—a parent describing how they put the kids and the cargo in their car will not generally mention all the times they adjust the relative position of doors, kids, seatbelts, and objects so as to never leave a child or a precious object, such as a purse, exposed. A camera could capture all their movements but would not capture the reasons for them. Watching and talking to parents as they load their vehicles provides a much more complete view of this behavior and the rules that govern it.

- Actions and thoughts that are not generally recognized as part of the "story," such as personal rituals and routines, are sometimes missed or hard to uncover in conventional interviews because people may not think to mention them or may consider it silly to bring them up

  o For example, many business people have good luck rituals they engage in before setting off on an important trip or appointment. But their answers to questions about how they prepare for an important meeting will almost never reveal that, for example, they always kiss or touch their children's picture before heading to a key meeting or departing on a business trip.

For all these types of topics and many more, your research can benefit hugely from being there. And when you have to be there, participant observation is the method of choice.

DIRECT OBSERVATION VERSUS PARTICIPANT OBSERVATION

"An observer is under the bed. A participant observer is in it."

—spoken by John Whiting, age 80-something, to an undergraduate class when he was a guest lecturer at UC Irvine

The important distinction between direct observation and participant observation so pithily captured in Dr. Whiting's remark is critical to users of both observation methods. Direct observation is primarily a quantitative technique in which the observer is explicitly counting the frequency and/or intensity of specific behaviors or events or mapping the social composition and action of a particular scene. While most direct observation data collection is conducted by actual observers, many direct observation studies do not technically require a human data collector. The data captured in direct observation are, by definition, those that can be *observed* and do not inherently require any interaction between the observer and those being studied. In principle, an audio or video recording setup, if properly placed, could record the phenomena of interest without the researcher ever appearing on the scene. In actuality of course, most direct observation studies are far easier to conduct with a human observer—humans are often both cheaper and more comprehensive than video or audio recording—and it is common to conduct some form of interviews during direct observation. But the distinction is still there—direct observation is about observable behavior and is typically associated with research objectives that require some sort of ordinal data or purely factual description: how often, how many, how intensely, who was there, and the like. As such, direct observation is normally a fairly structured form of data collection.

In contrast, participant observation is inherently a qualitative and interactive experience and relatively unstructured. It is generally associated with exploratory and explanatory research objectives—why questions, causal explanations, uncovering the cognitive elements, rules, and norms that underlie the observable behaviors. The data generated are often free flowing and the analysis much more interpretive than in direct observation. And it is this aspect of participant observation that is the method's greatest strength as well as the source of critiques that sometimes surround participant observation studies.

Embedding into a scene as a participant inevitably means that the information collected is, in certain ways, unique to the individual collecting the data. While anyone living in a traditional village in India would become aware of the caste system and would learn its rules, the experience of that system would be very different for a male participant observer belonging to a high ranking caste than it would to a female participant observer of a lower ranking caste. We would expect these two different participant observers to notice different nuances of how the caste system operates, to have different experiences of the consequences of violating caste rules, and possibly to make different judgments of the benefits and costs of the caste system to its participants and to Indian society as a whole.

Indeed, one of the reasons for doing participant observations is that many aspects of some social milieus are only visible to insiders, and only certain people can get inside. For example, Liza Dalby's (1983) famous study of geisha culture could have been written only by someone who was female, fluent in Japanese, and willing to undergo at least some of the lengthy and rigorous training required to become a geisha. No matter how interested a male researcher might be in geisha culture, there is simply no way he could be apprenticed as a geisha. By the same token, we can assume that Dalby's status as a *gaikokujin*—a person not of Japanese ancestry—made her geisha experience somewhat different than that of someone of Japanese heritage. For some readers, her description is a compelling blend of outsider objectivity and insider knowledge, exemplifying both insider and outsider perspectives. Others doubt that any *gaijin* (the common, less respectful term for a non-Japanese) was ever allowed far enough inside geisha life to provide a "real" description of it. For both camps, the subjective and personal aspects of participant observation are central to the argument—either enabling a viewpoint that could be captured no other way or skewing that viewpoint so much that the findings are in question.

WHY USE PARTICIPANT OBSERVATION?

Almost anyone who has ever visited a foreign land, been a visitor to an unfamiliar social environment, or joined someone else's family as a spouse or even as a casual guest can understand some of the ways in which participant observation can be useful. Bernard (2006) identifies five reasons for conducting participant observation research. The reasons listed below are Bernard's, with explanatory comments from this book's authors.

1. *Opening up the areas of inquiry to collect a wider range of data.* Only those with the privileges accorded to participants can observe certain sorts of events. In most social groups, there are things that outsiders are simply not allowed to do, see, or know. You cannot collect data about these things if you aren't on the inside as a participant.

2. *Reducing the problem of reactivity.* People change their behavior around outsiders, and if you have an interest in "normal" behavior, you have to stop being someone around whom people make these adjustments. A successful participant observer fits into the scene well enough to be ignored, even if he is doing abnormal things such as interviewing, taking pictures, recording video or audio, or taking notes.

3. *Enabling researchers to know what questions to ask.* Being embedded in the social context helps researchers learn what questions are relevant and to ask them in terms that make sense to the "natives." The value of participant observation at the early stages of learning about an unfamiliar culture or social setting can be huge. One of the most common errors in designing survey questions or in-depth interview guides is asking questions that are not sensible to the research participants or that are asked in some form of "research speak" rather than the local vernacular. Participant observation teaches you what to ask about and how to ask it.

4. *Gaining intuitive understanding of the meaning of your data.* The interpretation of qualitative data is always a somewhat subjective activity, and those who question the validity of qualitative methods often point to examples of studies in which the researchers grossly misunderstood something that was obvious to knowledgeable insiders or members of the studied culture or social group. Participant observation gives you an intimate knowledge of your area of study that greatly reduces this type of validity error. As someone who has directly experienced the social phenomena of interest, you are capable of taking positions about the meaning of your data with confidence that you are "getting it right."

5. *Addressing problems that are simply unavailable to other data collection techniques.* For many types of human experience there are no books, official sets of rules, or formal training of children or newcomers. This is true for many of aspects of our private and public life—how our organizations and institutions work, how we make our living, how we grow and develop to be a member of our various social groups. We learn these things by doing them, and if you want to learn about them, there is often no substitute for doing them yourself, as a participant observer.

In addition to Bernard's five reasons for using participant observation, there are also some other benefits of using the technique. These include the following:

1. *To establish the topics of inquiry for later, more structured data collection.* If your knowledge of a social milieu is so minimal you aren't even sure what topics might exist to ask about—participant observation is an excellent starting point.
2. *To avoid suspect self-reported data.* There are some topics for which people cannot or will not accurately report their own behavior (petty criminality, violations of social norms, etc.). Participant observation can lessen this form of self-report bias and obtain a more valid understanding of these behaviors.
3. *To identify behaviors that might go unreported or be missed due to the limitations of procedural memory.* Highly routine or unconscious behaviors are notoriously easy to miss during interviews, focus groups, and surveys. Seeing these occur in a participant observation setting allows them to become part of the data.
4. *To lessen reporting biases.* Those without direct knowledge of a social scene may collect data that reflect their own points of view rather than the social reality of the people in it. Edmund Leach (1967) famously corrected an earlier study of land use in Sri Lanka when his participant observations in the area showed that the earlier study had used a definition of *household* that did not conform to local understanding and that skewed the data to a false conclusion about village disintegration.
5. *To integrate the observed behavior into its physical context.* If the location and setting of the behavior of interest are critical to understanding, participant observation allows you to see and experience how the setting and the behavior interact.
6. *To see the behavior you are interested in as it happens.* If your research questions are about observable behaviors, why settle for merely hearing about them secondhand? Seeing is believing, and seeing is often data collection, as well. Participant observation puts you in direct contact with the phenomena of interest in a way unrivaled by other data collection techniques.

One of the most compelling examples of the value of participant observation in gaining insights that would be hard to capture through any other research method is the work done by Stephen Koester (Koester & Hoffer, 1994) among injection drug users in Denver. In the early 1990s, public education and needle-exchange programs to lessen needle sharing and its associated disease risks were active. Considerable evidence existed that the messages had been heard and understood by injection drug users and that needle sharing had, indeed, been greatly reduced. Nevertheless, rates of disease transmission remained unacceptably high among this population. Having established rapport among a Denver community of IV drug injectors, Koester conducted participant observations at "shooting galleries" and came up with some extremely important information.

The injection drug users were, in fact, no longer sharing needles. But other forms of sharing—*things the original researchers and public health officials had not known to ask about*—were occurring. Drug injectors shared other equipment, such as cottons and cookers in which drugs were filtered and prepared. Also, some users practiced *back-filling*, opening the back of a syringe so that a friend could draw a specified amount of drugs from it. These sources of cross contamination, dubbed "indirect sharing," were potentially responsible for the continued transmission of HIV and hepatitis among the IV drug user population. Subsequent education campaigns added references to the dangers of indirect sharing, with an aim to reducing this disease transmission channel.

THE ROLE OF PARTICIPANT OBSERVATION IN THE RESEARCH PROCESS

The most traditional use of participant observation is at the exploratory stages of the research on a new topic, culture, venue, or behavior. In these situations, it is hard to beat participant observation for the sheer volume of insight and information that can be collected. Spending time working, playing, or living with people will produce data that would require dozens of interviews or focus groups to uncover. And, as indicated in the example of Koester's IV drug user research, there are often findings that might be completely missed using other methods.

But participant observation can also play an important role when examining topics where there is already a considerable body of knowledge. As with other qualitative methods, participant observation can often help explain quantitative findings by providing the contextual meaning behind other data. In these cases, the participant observation may occur after or at the same time as other forms of data collection, such as analysis of secondary data or a quantitative survey. The participant observation may be used to explain apparent contradictions in other data—as in Koester's work, to learn the causal relationship behind a numerically observed correlation—or to confirm or gain face validity (sometimes referred to as triangulation) for the findings produced by another research method.

The ability of participant observation to provide explanation, context, causation, and confirmation means that it is often a useful element to include in a mixed method study. As indicated above, the participant observation may occur at multiple stages of the research—either early on as an exploratory element or later as an explanatory or confirmatory element. The example below in Table 3.1 highlights the points in a multiyear, mixed methods study where participant observation played a role. In this research, a large manufacturer of customized adhesive labels was looking for opportunities among health care providers, such as doctors' offices and hospital and medical labs, in response to both concerns about avoiding medical care errors and new laws related to patient privacy and records handling.

Table 3.1	Using Participant Observation Across Multiple Phases of Research
Phase of Research	**Examples**
Phase 1—exploratory	On-site participant observation of labeling of medical records, lab samples, patients, equipment
Phase 2—questionnaire development	Focus groups with key audiences to decide content and wording for quantitative surveys
Phase 3—survey	Quantitative survey focused on labeling practices and spending
Phase 4—concept test	Product concepts developed and interest assessed through an online quantitative survey
Phase 5—in situ prototype use test	Working prototypes developed and placed for on-site use test. On-site participant observation of prototypes in actual use followed by in-depth interviews to determine prototype strengths, weaknesses, areas for re-design
Phase 6—large scale use test of final products	Final products tested in-use, with survey to finalize pricing and target marketing

When considering use of participant observation to address your research objectives, you must also consider the things it does *not* do well. The potential drawbacks of participant observation include these elements:

- *Potentially and unpredictably time consuming.* You may be in the field for a while before you learn much that addresses your research objectives, and it can be difficult to estimate in advance how long the study will take. If you are in a time-is-money situation, you may need to address your objectives through a quicker or more predictable approach.

- Highly "practitioner-sensitive." The results you get from participant observation may be idiosyncratic, difficult to compare with the findings of others, or simply biased.

- Sometimes difficult to generalize from. It can be hard to know if the findings seen in participant observation are typical of other sites, times, and circumstances, potentially limiting the value of the data or leaving the interpretation of the findings open to challenge.

- Your audience may not respect it. The very flexible, naturalistic nature of participant observation causes some research sponsors or data users to dismiss it as unscientific or as a form of tourism rather than data collection.

In considering a participant observation study, it is important to confront these issues head-on. Consider your research objectives and be realistic about what participant observation can and cannot do to help you address them. Is the participant observation going to be the primary focus of your findings, as it might be in a traditional ethnography? Or is it an exploratory exercise to pave the way for more structured sorts of data collection? Will more than one person take part in the participant observation? If so, how will the analysis address any differences in what they observe? Do you plan to confirm any of your participant observation findings with other types of data such as formal interviews (informal interviews are almost always part of participant observation), surveys, social network mapping, direct observation, cultural domain analysis, or text analysis? If so, how will these additional data fit into the data collection and analysis time line and budget? In short, draw on participant observation's strengths and have a plan for eliminating or addressing its weaknesses.

HOW TO CONDUCT PARTICIPANT OBSERVATION

The very flexible nature of participant observation means that the researcher has considerable leeway in how to design and conduct the data collection. As with any other qualitative research endeavor, the primary consideration that determines how you go about your participant observation is your research objectives. Accordingly, the details provided below, organized in roughly chronological order for most projects, are intended as guidelines rather than strict rules. The highly individualized nature of participant observation means that virtually every researcher will need to adapt these guidelines, at least in places, to his or her research situation, the objectives of the research project, and the individual's own personal style.

Choosing the Research Venue(s)

Most participant observation is conducted at field sites where the activity that is the topic of the study naturally occurs. For participant observation, your choice of venues determines your sample (who, where, what you will observe) and is therefore critical to how well your data address your research objectives and the generalizability (or lack thereof) of your findings.

If you know at least a little bit about the people, behavior, or events that you wish to study, you will probably have a pretty good idea of at least some of the places you can go to observe them. For example, if you are interested in child rearing, you will need to choose venues—homes, schools, family-oriented places and events—where adults interact with children and attempt to shape their behavior. Similarly, studies of professional behavior may take you to people's workplaces, while for projects involving political movements, you might include meetings and rallies among your research sites.

A very important consideration in choosing your venues is scale—the scale of your research objectives, the scale of your project in terms of funds, labor and other key resources, and even the geographical scale of the venue(s). For example, participant observation that is intended to be a primary data source for an ethnography of an entire tribal group will require a large scale effort in both time and, quite possibly, geography. In contrast, a study of how IRS (Internal Revenue Service) agents use their organization's website could be geographically restricted to a single IRS building and might take only a few days to provide the key insights. Be sure that your choice of venues matches the scale of your intended study. In choosing your participant observation venue(s) ask yourself a few key questions:

- Where does the activity of interest occur? Is it always in the same place(s), or does it move around?
- Is the phenomenon of interest time specific (such as a traditional festival or celebration), or is it always there (such as customer-server interactions in a bar)?
- If there is more than one possible location, is one more representative or more important than another?
- Will you need to visit multiple sites to understand the range of behavior (such as for participant observation of mortality and morbidity review committees at area hospitals), or are your objectives focused on a single, particular case (social networking at an Antarctic research station)?
- Are there ethical or practical issues with the proposed venue? Are there ways to avoid or mitigate these issues?

As you answer the questions above, remember that your final choice of venue(s) and the number and timing of your visits to the venue(s) will produce participant observation data reflective of that choice. Be sure that your chosen location(s) will meet the sampling requirements implicit in your research objectives and chosen topics of inquiry.

For some smaller scale participant observation studies, it is possible to create venues for participant observations rather than go to the venues where the action naturally occurs. This is sometimes done in commercial research, especially when the behavior naturally occurs only sporadically or unpredictably or at locations that are dispersed, hard to access, or dangerous. For example, a study done some years ago by one of the authors included participant observation of buyers who were considering the purchase of SUV type vehicles. The behavior of interest tends to occur at auto dealerships—locations that are common, physically accessible, and safe and where this sort of shopping activity is fairly frequent. But no dealership would consider the potential loss of a sale that might occur from the presence of participant observers—complete with audio and video recording devices—in the middle of such a lucrative transaction. To gather the needed data, the research team constructed a fake "dealer-ship" setting with an array of SUVs parked as they would be in an auto dealer's lot. Potential SUV buyers were invited to the location, and these research participants were instructed to act, as closely as possible, to the way they would when examining the vehicles at a real dealership. While this somewhat artificial setting was not ideal for participant observation, the "buyers" did fall quickly into their role and some interesting findings were obtained. The observed behavior, supplemented with semi-structured in-the-moment interviews as these buyers viewed and touched the cars, revealed some important differences in the ways men and women assess this cate-gory of vehicles. In particular, women were far more likely than men to assess the ability to reach into the back seat from the driving position—a feature that is impor-tant to them as a way of maintaining control over kids and cargo. Men were more likely to take at least one good view of the vehicle from a front, three-quarters position—making sure that the leading edge of the SUV was sufficiently vertical—a characteristic that allows men to refer to their SUVs as "my truck" rather than "my car," a more appealing image for many males.

There are, of course, substantial potential drawbacks to doing participant observation in a created venue. It is often difficult to recreate some elements of the real venue (the SUV research, for example, did not include the presence of a sleazy salesman backslapping the male buyers or addressing the females as "ma'am"—the research team did not feel this reduced the value of the findings). If you are at a very exploratory stage of the research, you may not know enough about the real venue to emulate it, and your failure to accurately recreate the real venue may totally invalidate your data—people may act so differently that you are doing participant observation in a fantasyland of no interest or value to anyone. In some cases, it would be unethical to create the venues or situations of interest—no matter how interested we might be in the immediate responses of victims of violent crime, we can't commit crimes in order to learn about them. But in cases where getting into the real venue is not practical and where the created venue can provide an acceptably accurate environment, created venues can be an element in your participant observation tool kit.

Preparing to Enter the Field

Despite the romantic traditions of intrepid social scientists arriving to do fieldwork with nothing more than natural curiosity and a blank journal, it is advisable to spend some time actually figuring out what you are going to do when you arrive at your participant observation venue(s). This is equally important for short-term, highly focused applied projects and for long-term research efforts such as ethnographies. With short-term projects, lack of good planning creates the risk of not getting the needed data. In long-term efforts, a lack of planning can mean that days or weeks are expended either with basic rapport building or with the researcher gaining lots of information and insight but in such a disorganized fashion that analysis is almost impossible. In these cases, the researcher may find herself having to go over the same ground again and again simply to bring coherence to the findings—a process that can be time consuming, frustrating, and costly. The section below details important considerations as you make your plans to enter the field.

Self-Presentation

In the forthcoming section on ethics and informed consent, we allude to some of the issues surrounding how you present yourself to the others who will be present in your research venue. In addition to raising questions about informed consent, confidentiality, and related matters, your choices about how to present yourself—and to whom—have important consequences about the types of data you can collect, how rapport develops with your research participants, and the limits of your analysis. Table 3.2 below details some of the issues regarding the extent to which other participants are aware of your role.

Data Collection Objectives

For a highly exploratory study at the earliest stages of learning about your research topic, you may meet your data collection objectives by doing little more than just appearing in the venue, hanging out, and asking casual questions. But in many cases, your objectives will be better met by a more planned and systematic approach.

Table 3.2	Degrees of Self-Revelation in Participant Observation
Degree of self-revelation	**Implications**
Presenting yourself as an observer–researcher to all participants in the research setting	If all participants know you are a researcher, ethical issues are less problematic, but rapport may take longer to develop. There may be limits on the types of social (inter)action you will be able to observe. In some cases, it may not be possible or practical to inform all the participants in a venue.
Presenting yourself as an observer–researcher to only some participants in the research setting	Informing some participants but not others of your role may be difficult to manage. It can create the risk of being "outed" by knowledgeable participants, or, having participants feel that you were dishonest with them if they learn your role is different than they originally understood. In some environments, there may be a risk of reprisal against the research effort or the researcher. Handling informed consent can be tricky if not all participants are treated the same way.
Presenting yourself as an observer–researcher to none of the participants in the research setting	Staying "incognito" can easily create ethical dilemmas in venues where participants have a reasonable expectation of privacy and confidentiality. In some venues, it may be extremely difficult to stay "in character." In many venues, useful additional data collection techniques (photos, audio and/or video recordings, free lists and pile sorts, and many others) cannot be done without revealing the research role.

Thinking in advance about the types of activities you will participate in at your field site will enable you to maximize your data collection. In Figure 3.1 are some common participant observation activities arranged along a two-axis grid in which the x-axis is the degree of participation relative to the degree of observation, while the y-axis is the degree of revelation or concealment of the researcher role.

It should be obvious that different types of data will be available depending on what role(s) you play. It should be equally obvious that some roles require knowledge, skill, or physical capability. For George Plimpton (1966) to write his famous book *Paper Lion*, he had to be capable of participating as a trainee in a National Football League (NFL) training camp—a form of participant observation that would be outside of many researchers' comfort zones. In addition to physical and mental preparation, you may also need to plan for moral issues that can arise in the field. If you are studying groups that engage in socially disapproved or criminal activity, then you should have a clear sense, in advance, of what you will or will not be comfortable

Figure 3.1   Participant Observation Continuums

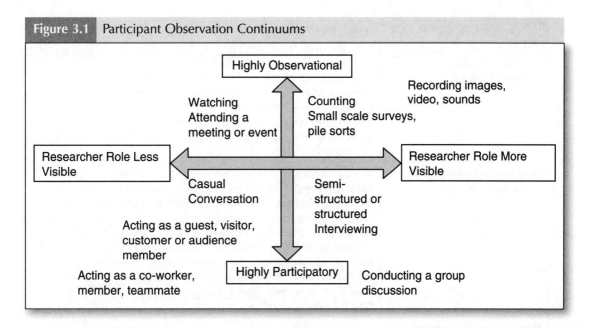

observing or participating in—and should adjust your informed consent and introduction to the field site accordingly.

Entering the Observation Venue

Once your planning is complete, you can enter your participant observation
venue. This may be as simple as just driving to your selected location and walking in,
or you may spend weeks or months getting permissions, invitations, visas, or safe passage into a challenging or restricted research environment. Once you have found a
way to get to your venue (and the funds and the physical and mental resources to
collect data and, for a long-term study, to survive there comfortably), you need to
make an effective entry into your fieldwork site. While stories of botched arrivals in
the field are a staple of cocktail party conversation among field researchers, they are
no fun when they are actually happening. Many projects have been severely limited by
poor entry into the field site, and some venues have had to be abandoned altogether
after the research effort went so awry that no meaningful data could be collected or
even because the researcher(s) was in danger. Table 3.3 lists some of the areas of
potential pitfalls in entering the field.

Table 3.3	Potential Pitfalls Entering the Field (and possible solutions)
Issue	**Discussion**
Self-introductions	Have a version of your self-introduction that is truthful, concise, and understandable in local terms and that does not set off alarms or cause offense among the people you are approaching. If possible, learn something about the local norms in advance, get someone to introduce you, or hang back and observe a bit until you know the rules.
Who you will approach and who approaches you	In some venues, an outsider is more likely to be approached by marginal members of the group than by more centrally placed individuals. In Japan, for example, Mitchell found that members of the *yakuza* (organized crime families) are often quite willing to talk to foreigners. But being seen with a *yakuza* can wreck your chances of talking to more respectable members of Japanese society. In societies with strict social classes, it may be very difficult to move outside of the class where you first enter. Be careful about becoming attached to or dependent on the first "insider" who welcomes you.
How you handle problems/ challenges	In almost any field setting, sooner or later, something will go wrong—loss of data, discovering that you have been lied to or misled, practical jokes or pranks, thefts, personal disputes. Be prepared to handle these in a way that allows you to continue your work. In general, your response should match that of locals who face the same challenges. Do not fly off the handle if you are in a high-tolerance, high-forgiveness culture. Similarly, do not be a wimp in a venue where people are expected to stand up for themselves and respond vigorously when they are wronged.
Personal style	Consider what aspects of your personal style will facilitate your data collection and which might get in your way. Think how you will take advantage of your strengths (i.e., empathy, good humor, the ability to drink others under the table) or suppress your weaknesses (low frustration level, impatience, overactive fear response). Think seriously about who you are and how you will be in a particular venue. If you are the type who melts into tears at the thought of children suffering, participant observation in a pediatric oncology ward may not be for you.

   If your study is one that has a big community involvement aspect, as is common in international development or community improvement projects, you must be careful to learn who the relevant stakeholders are and plan how you will make contact with them. The buy-in of stakeholders is an important part of these projects, and you need their goodwill to conduct your project successfully. Additionally, their insights, social networks, and insider knowledge can be extremely valuable in helping to make sure that your data collection and analysis are as comprehensive and valuable as possible. Depending on your research venue and the type of project the study is part of, the stakeholder groups you consider may include various types of social and political leaders, political parties, heads of clans or tribes, members of various social strata, elders, members of both sexes, members of various age cohorts, and those with specialized knowledge or interests (economic, social, or otherwise) in your research topic.

If your preparations have been successful, then you should be able to enter your field site comfortably (both physically and socially), effectively, and safely. Allow time to build rapport with your participants. In most cases, it is better to gradually build from a mostly observer role toward more active participation. Do not be overly anxious to instantly and precisely address your research objectives or to steer naturally occurring conversations toward your research objectives. The point of participant observation is to learn in context, and to do that you need to immerse yourself in the place, people, and action of your research location. Keep your objectives in mind, but have patience. If you have chosen a meaningful topic for your research, picked an appropriate location, and are prepared to watch and learn, you can have confidence that the insights you are seeking will emerge.

What to Observe

The list of things you might observe during participant observation is extremely varied and is limited only by your research objectives and your imagination. That said, there are some broad categories that are commonly observed, as detailed in the Table 3.4.

Table 3.4	General Things to Observe	
Category	**Includes**	**Researchers should note**
Appearance	Clothing, age, gender, physical appearance	Anything that might indicate membership in groups or in subpopulations of interest to the study, such as profession, social status, socioeconomic class, religion, or ethnicity

(Continued)

Table 3.4	(Continued)	
Category	Includes	Researchers should note
Verbal behavior and interactions	Who speaks to whom and for how long, who initiates interaction, languages or dialects spoken, tone of voice	Gender, age, ethnicity, profession
Physical behavior and gestures	What people do, who does what, who interacts with whom, who is not interacting	How people use their bodies and voices to communicate different emotions, what people's behaviors indicate about their feelings toward one another, their social rank, or their profession
Personal space	How close people stand to one another	What people's preferences concerning personal space suggest about their relationships
Human traffic	How and how many people enter, leave, and spend time at the observation site	Where people enter and exit, how long they stay, who they are (ethnicity, age, gender), whether they are alone or accompanied
People who stand out	Identification of people who receive a lot of attention from others	These people's characteristics, what differentiates them from others, whether people consult them or they approach other people, whether they seem to be strangers or well-known by others present Note that these individuals could be good people to approach for an informal interview or to serve as key informants

Source: Mack, Woodsong, MacQueen, Guest, and Namey (2005, p. 20).

While the table above lists some of the categories of observations you might make, it does not indicate what the data from these observations might actually look like. The flexibility of participant observation means that you have lots of leeway about how to actually record what happens during your research and that it can be as structured or unstructured as you wish. The degree of structure should align with your research objectives and the stage of learning the research is intended to illuminate—less structure is necessary for broad, exploratory, and early stage research and more structure for focused, applied studies that are intended to provide additional depth, new perspectives, or confirmation on topics where a lot is already known. That said, having some structure can greatly facilitate data collection and analysis. Table 3.5 lists some of the most common types of data collected during participant observation and the advantages and disadvantages of each.

Table 3.5	Types of Data Collection in Participant Observation	
Data Type	**Description**	**Pros and Cons**
Observation Notes/ audio/video	• The baseline for participant observation, notes, and recordings • Written/transcribed/digital record of what the researcher saw, heard, or felt during the observation period	• Very open to emergent data, little/no instrument bias • Can be difficult to capture in some venues, time consuming to analyze, subject to the bias of the researcher regarding what to note or record
Casual conversations/ informal interviews	• Notes or recordings of actual conversations	• Captures data in the vernacular and in context • May not be relevant to research objectives, can be hard to accurately record in some settings • May be highly idiosyncratic and difficult to analyze
Semistructured or structured interviews	• Interviews conducted using an interview guide	• Provides data relevant to the research objectives • Takes the encounter into a "research" mode that decreases some aspects of the natural context
Counts of specific observations	• Counts of the frequency/ intensity/source of specific behaviors of interest— usually collected with the aid of a template listing the types of things to be counted	• Provides data that can be used to identify norms or make comparisons between events/times/individuals, and so on. • Requires the development of a data collection instrument and the ability to accurately record the behavior of interest in the field setting
Process flows	• Visual or verbal records of common processes—often laid out in a flow chart or stepwise diagram	• Excellent for understanding sequenced events (work flows, manufacturing processes, decision processes) • Can be challenging to capture • Danger of capturing an idiosyncratic version
Lists and categories	• Lists of items, categories. and inclusion/exclusion rules	• Provide both list content and cultural meaning • Can be tedious to collect and may be difficult to extract "rules"

As mentioned above, having some degree of structure can facilitate data collection and structure can take myriad forms. On the following page are examples of five of the more common types of data collection aids that can help structure participant observation data collection.

1. *A general list of topics to be discussed or the types of things to be observed.* The example below shows a list that was used for a study of women who were high-frequency clothing shoppers. The participant observation portion of the study followed women through live shopping expeditions and used video recordings and casual questioning.

   1. What triggers the shopping? What need(s) is the shopper trying to fulfill?
   2. What stores are visited?
   3. What happens at each store (capture activity, duration, frequency, emotional valence, interactions with sales staff and other shoppers)?
   4. What interactions occur with the merchandise (viewing items on the rack/shelf, trying on, price comparisons, purchasing)?
   5. What is the aftermath of the shopping? Needs fulfilled? Emotional valence?

2. *A fill-in the blank template.* Figure 3.2 below below was used by Human Terrain Teams in Iraq and Afghanistan to make quick sociocultural assessments of communities visited by U.S. ground troops.
3. *A reporting summary template* can be used to summarize the key points from lengthy, free-flowing notes/recordings/transcripts. The example below is from a series of participant observations of enrollment visits made by potential vocational school students to a school they were considering.

Date and School: 10/8/09 - Long Beach

Program Considered: Massage Tech

Classroom visit: yes
Interaction with instructors: yes
Financial aid briefing: yes
Stated interest in enrolling: uncertain
Parent/guardian involved: no
Planned follow-up contact: yes, admissions rep to phone

Notes/Comments: prospect seemed overwhelmed/impressed by school, worried about cost relative to employment prospects in field. Excited about hands-on learning approach.

4. *A process model template* helps lay out sequenced or stepwise processes and decision pathways. Figure 3.3 on page 97 below is for a study focused on real-estate sales in a part of Baghdad. The goal of this study was to find out how extortion of buyers and sellers worked to funnel money into terrorist operations.
5. *A map,* accompanied by instructions on what to include, can be helpful in venues where the physical context is important to the observed action. Figure 3.4 on page 98 below is from a village level study involving economic and subsistence activities.

Figure 3.2   Village Assessment Form

Date:

Geographic Information

Province: District: Village:

MGRS: Latitude: Longitude:

Notes/Comments:

Demography

Est. Population:

Est. Number of Houses:

Avg. Family Size:

Ethnic Groups:

Tribes Present:

Notes/Comments:

Infrastructure & Services

Education:

Health:

Water Sources:

Type of Irrigation:

Government:

Electricity:

Communication:

Transportation:

Other Services & Infrastructure:

Infrastructure & Services Shared with Other Villages (schools, wells, clinics, etc.):

Notes/Comments:

(Continued)

Figure 3.2 (Village Assessment Form, Continued)

Landscape

General Description of Terrain:

Transportation Access to Village:

Connections to Other Villages (roads, wadis, passes, etc.):

Travel Time to Nearest Bazaar:

Travel Time to Nearest Clinic:

Travel Time to Nearest City:

Notes/Comments:

Economy

Shops:

Nearest Bazaar:

Main Sources of Income:

Industry:

Crops:

Livestock:

Threats to Local Economy:

Notes/Comments:

Government & Leadership

Elders:

Religious Officials:

Other Influential People:

Notes/Comments:

Figure 3.3

Figure 3.3 Iraq Real Estate Sales Procedure Map

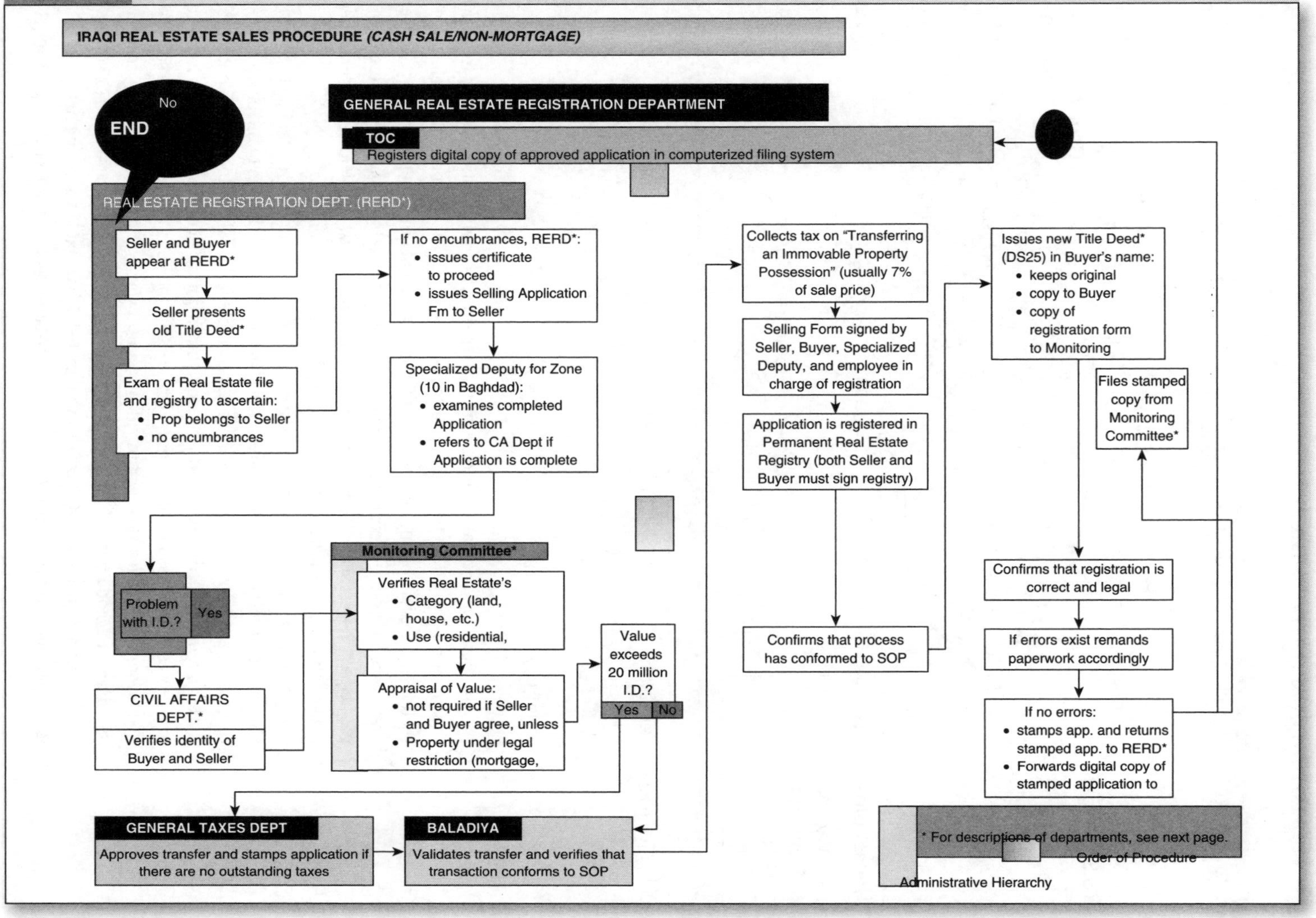

IRAQI REAL ESTATE SALES PROCEDURE *(CASH SALE/NON-MORTGAGE)*

GENERAL REAL ESTATE REGISTRATION DEPARTMENT

TOC
Registers digital copy of approved application in computerized filing system

REAL ESTATE REGISTRATION DEPT. (RERD*)

Seller and Buyer appear at RERD*

Seller presents old Title Deed*

Exam of Real Estate file and registry to ascertain:
- Prop belongs to Seller
- no encumbrances

If no encumbrances, RERD*:
- issues certificate to proceed
- issues Selling Application Fm to Seller

Specialized Deputy for Zone (10 in Baghdad):
- examines completed Application
- refers to CA Dept if Application is complete

Collects tax on "Transferring an Immovable Property Possession" (usually 7% of sale price)

Selling Form signed by Seller, Buyer, Specialized Deputy, and employee in charge of registration

Application is registered in Permanent Real Estate Registry (both Seller and Buyer must sign registry)

Confirms that process has conformed to SOP

Issues new 'Title Deed'* (DS25) in Buyer's name:
- keeps original
- copy to Buyer
- copy of registration form to Monitoring

Files stamped copy from Monitoring Committee*

Confirms that registration is correct and legal

If errors exist remands paperwork accordingly

If no errors:
- stamps app. and returns stamped app. to RERD*
- Forwards digital copy of stamped application to

Monitoring Committee*

Verifies Real Estate's
- Category (land, house, etc.)
- Use (residential,

Appraisal of Value:
- not required if Seller and Buyer agree, unless
- Property under legal restriction (mortgage,

Value exceeds 20 million I.D.?   Yes   No

CIVIL AFFAIRS DEPT.*
Verifies identity of Buyer and Seller

Problem with I.D.?   Yes

GENERAL TAXES DEPT
Approves transfer and stamps application if there are no outstanding taxes

BALADIYA
Validates transfer and verifies that transaction conforms to SOP

END   No

- For descriptions of departments, see next page.

Order of Procedure

Administrative Hierarchy

Source: U.S. Army.

Figure 3.4   Social Map

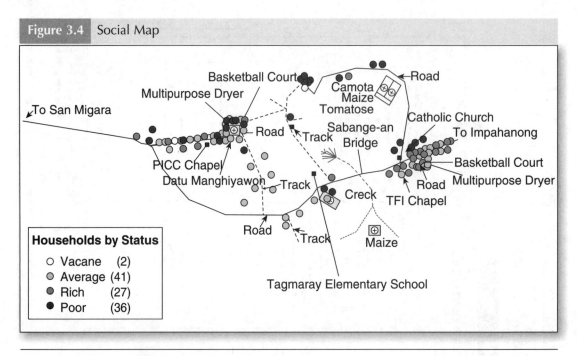

Households by Status

○ Vacane   (2)
◔ Average (41)
◕ Rich   (27)
● Poor   (36)

Source: Crumb and Purcell (2001).

Organizing Data

In many ways, organizing data from participant observation is similar to data organization for other types of qualitative research. The general principles and techniques are laid out in Chapter 7 of this book and will not be repeated here. There are, however, some special challenges to data organization that are inherent to participant observation. These are challenges presented by the field setting and the sheer volume of data that participant observation can produce.

In many participant observation settings, there will be limits on your ability to record your observations right at the moment they happen. This may be due to the physical setting (it is hard to take notes or operate a recording device while standing up outdoors during a rainstorm), the social setting (taking notes during a conversation slows it down and moves it from casual chat to formal interview), the need to maintain some secrecy about your role (if you suddenly start video-taping at your workplace, people may suspect you have an agenda other than earning a paycheck), or simply because the task you are participating in requires both hands (if you are helping to haul in a fishing net, you can't let go of it to jot down notes). The most standard approach to these challenges is to jot what notes you can, as soon as possible after the events, and then expand these notes at the earliest opportunity. For example, when a colleague of the authors conducted participant observation at a salmon fishing camp while working as a boat carpenter, he kept a small notepad in his overalls and would jot notes about camp activities and interactions whenever he was momentarily alone. Each night he would then expand these notes into as full a record as possible. The key is to minimize the loss of data due to the recall limits of human memory. Table 3.6 lists tips for field note taking, including the use of electronic note-taking aids.

Table 3.6   Note-Taking Tips for the Field
Field Note and Documentation Tips
Capture it quickly—the sooner you write down your observations, the more complete and accurate they will be.
Expand your notes as soon as possible—use the first possible opportunity to expand your notes into a full record; do not count on being able to remember "all the important stuff"—memory is fragile. In expanding your notes, fill in the complete story of *what* you observed first, before adding in interpretations or *what you think about what you observed*. The notes should provide a detailed record of "the facts," as well as your own commentary and developing understanding of those facts.
Use recording devices and assistants—in many cases, you do not have to do everything yourself. Modern digital photo/video/audio recorders, recording capabilities built into phones, and specialized note-taking devices, such as Livescribe (a combined pen–digital audio recorder that is excellent for field notes), can be used in many participant observation venues. If you are working in a team, having one person act as the note taker can help spread this burden and improve overall recall of observations.
Use time and labor saving tricks—develop shorthand for names/events/ideas that appear frequently in your observations. Develop and use forms and templates to streamline data capture for key topics.
Stay organized—Chapter 7 discusses data management. The sheer volume of data generated during participant observation makes this especially critical. The time you spend organizing your data as you collect them will be rewarded during data analysis. A little effort up front prevents a lot of frustration and wasted time at the next stage of the project.

How Long to Stay

As with any other field-based data collection method, the rule of thumb about participant observation is that you should stay long enough to get the data you need. In the case of large scale projects aimed at describing complex social scenes or entire cultures, this could be a matter of months or years. In these settings, it may take weeks or months to be fully accepted by your research participants, and in many cases, this is a gradual process. Typically, researchers conducting these long-term studies gradually become more of a participant and less of an observer as time goes by, moving through degrees of intimacy with others who are in the scene and at each stage, discovering new layers of insight and information.

Smaller, more focused projects, especially those where the topic of the participant observation is very specific and the general elements of the venue and behavior are already well-known, will not require such extended time frames. Workplace participant observation studies can often be completed in weeks or months rather than years, and commercial projects that hone in on narrow aspects of consumer behavior may have participant observation elements that last only a few days.

In the field of international development, it is common to use some form of participant observation as part of a rapid assessment study. In these settings, participant observation may be conducted on a very short time frame and will overlap with other forms of data collection. Most rapid assessment projects are completed in time frames ranging from a few weeks to a few months, with participant observation conducted for an even shorter period during this time.

Exiting the Venue

The longer time lines and personal interactions that are part of some participant observation studies mean that you may also need to give more consideration to how you leave your research venue(s) than might be necessary for other types of data collection. Friendships and collaborative relationships may develop that need to be respected as the research concludes. In some cases, the researcher may never fully

---

Before you leave . . .

Revisit your informed consent protocols—is there anyone whose consent is needed or is needed to a different degree than was true at the start of the research? As you begin to think about analysis and publication of your findings, be sure that all your consents and the records of them are in order.

Make sure your data are complete, organized, and backed up—the field site is the only place where raw data can be collected and the only place where you can effectively address gaps or recreate lost information.

Thank those who have helped you—recognizing those who assisted you is both polite and paves the way for researchers who might follow you.

Create a contact file—during data analysis you may need to recontact some of your research participants, or you may wish to share the research outcomes and outputs with them. Make sure the contact information you need is complete and up to date.

leave the venue, maintaining personal connections that last for years after formal data collection has concluded. The box below outlines some areas to consider as you depart your participant observation venue.

ETHICAL AND PRACTICAL CONSIDERATIONS

While Chapter 8 provides general guidelines on how to handle informed consent and research ethics in qualitative studies, the highly contextual nature of participant observation can present special ethical challenges to the researcher. The section that follows details the ethical and practical considerations that are unique to participant observation and provides solutions to the issues they present.

Informed Consent and Ethics in Participant Observation

For many smaller scale, short-term participant observation studies, especially those done for commercial or applied purposes, you may be able to follow the same informed consent procedures you would use for an in-depth interview or focus group. In these cases, you can provide all those who will be part of the scene to be observed with the needed information about their rights and responsibilities as a participant, answer their questions, and obtain a written or verbal record of their consent. This approach works well when the scope of the observation scene is limited in terms of the number of people involved, the size of the physical environment, and the duration of the study. For example, one of the authors conducted a participant observation study for the California Avocado Board in which consumers and chefs prepared their favorite avocado-based dishes in their own home or restaurant kitchens. In this case, only a small number of people were at each site—the participants and their family members or kitchen staffs—and everyone who was likely to be observed could be briefed and could give their informed consent.

But many participant observation venues are much more complex socially or physically. In a public or semi-public setting—an airport, a bar, a work site, a shopping mall, a video arcade, a village plaza, a store, a holiday celebration, a political rally, a playground, an online chat room—there could be anywhere from dozens to thousands of people on the scene, some there for extended periods and others only transiently. In these cases, it is often not practical, or would be simply impossible, to gain consent from all those with whom you might interact, let alone all those you might observe. Additionally, in some studies there might be multiple participant observation events spread out over a period of weeks or months, with different combinations of people at the location each time—turning traditional informed consent procedures into a logistical nightmare. When informed consent cannot practically be obtained, it is up to the researcher to conduct the participant observation in a way that still protects the rights of those being observed. Ask yourself the three key questions below to help make sure your participant observation is conducted ethically and respectfully toward all who are involved in it.

How public or private is the venue?

If the observed action is taking place in a truly public setting—a park, a political rally, or such—there is generally no expectation that what is said and done there, at least in terms of the primary action, will be private. As long as the observations you make are at the level of public behavior—public speech, the movements of people through the space and time of the event—you are generally free to collect data both via observation and interaction with the other participants, without gaining individual informed consent. Be aware, however, that some behavior that takes place in public settings may still carry an expectation of at least partial privacy. For example, participant observation of teenagers' activities in a shopping mall might include observation of how they utilize mall space, the amount of time they spend in each store, the food court, and just walking around—all very public behaviors with no expectation of privacy. But it might also include overhearing or even being part of their conversations about drug use, sexual behavior, bullying, or petty crimes—issues they might expect you to treat confidentially. It is your responsibility to recognize and respect the boundary between public and private behavior and speech—even in a public setting—and to adjust your informed consent procedures to get permission if your data collection and/or analysis shifts toward the privacy realm. Remember, it is not permissible to audio or video record any activity or conversation where there is a reasonable expectation of privacy without the consent of the participants. In many U.S. states, this is also subject to legal ramifications. If you are in doubt, get explicit permission before you record.

Online venues, such as chat rooms, also create challenges in terms of informed consent. Typically, conversations in the main areas of these online forums would be considered a public space with no expectation of privacy. But many online conversations include some private conversations that are not visible to the rest of the participants and where the expectation of at least some degree of privacy is clearly present. In these cases, the researcher may need to reveal her role in order to avoid an ethical violation.

What kind of data will you be collecting, and how will you analyze it?

Social interactions range from those that present very little potential for ethical concern to those that are inherently apt to raise ethical challenges. To return to our example of teenagers at a mall, few teen girls would be concerned about having a participant observer shadow and interview them about how they shop for, select, and purchase clothing. The same girls (and their parents) might have a far different view of participant observation in the same venue if the data collection focused on their conversations about boys and dating. Similarly, if the data collected are analyzed at a general level, that is, "Girl X spent 15 minutes discussing male-female relationship problems," most participants would have few privacy concerns and an ethical violation is unlikely. In contrast, a detailed personal narrative appearing in a published work—"Girl X described how her current boyfriend Y had pressured her for sex until she finally relented," requires a more formal approach to informed consent, even if the participants' names and towns are omitted.

How are you presenting yourself?

If you are making your role as a researcher clear to others in the participant observation venue, their observable behavior and interactions with you can often be considered to fall into the implied consent arena. This is the case with an anthropologist living in a native village—the anthropologist describes her role at the point of initial introductions, her actions as an interviewer-recorder-observer are openly visible, and it is assumed that from that moment forward everyone knows that she is collecting information about the local culture and way of life as she engages in the village's day-to-day activities and talks to its inhabitants.

At the other extreme are participant observation studies in which the researcher does not reveal her or his research agenda—for example, posing as a customer in a store, a co-worker in a factory, or a potential member of a political or social organization. (Not all writers on the subject consider these to be participant observation; Bernard, for example, classifies this role as "true participants.") These cases can pose genuine ethical dilemmas, since a certain degree of deception is built into the data collection protocol.

Some ethicists argue that research that requires deception simply shouldn't be done, whereas others point to the value of data that could not be collected without it. But most of us are somewhere in the middle, feeling that some studies warrant keeping at least some of the participants with whom we interact in the dark about our researcher role. In commercial research, the entire *mystery shopper* industry depends on participant observers playing the role of customers while collecting a wide range of data about retailers, restaurants, and service providers, and for the most part, no one questions the ethics of the firms engaged in mystery shopping, the researchers they hire, or the clients they serve. On a less commercial and more thought-provoking level, Barbara Erhenrich's (2001) famous participant observation study of low-wage workers, *Nickel and Dimed,* could not have been conducted if many of her co-workers, employers, and customers had known she intended to write a book about her experiences (some did know, but many did not). *Nickel and Dimed* is widely considered to be an important portrait of low-wage labor in contemporary America, and few have challenged Erhenrich's deception of those she encountered in the course of collecting her data. In contrast, controversy about the deception of other participants has surrounded Brooke Magnanti's (2005) description of prostitution, in which she worked as a London call girl and had paid sex with male customers—a venue in which it is safe to assume that many of the other participants would not have agreed to be part of a published work.

In answering the three questions above, you should be able to match the formality of your informed consent procedures to the needs of your study and respectful guardianship of the rights of your research participants. Remember that you, as the researcher, are the one specifically charged with making sure your study is conducted in an ethical manner. Participant observation studies raise unique opportunities for insight but also unique challenges to research ethics. Be sure that as you design your research protocols, you have fully considered the ethical ramifications of your work and that you have taken every step necessary to gather your data ethically.

Researcher Safety

Because it is often conducted at sites that are not fully under the control of the research team, participant observation can put the researcher in greater danger than would be encountered using other qualitative data collection techniques, such as in-depth interviews or focus groups. There are two main sources of risk to researcher safety in participant observation studies—risks posed by the venue and risks posed by those being observed.

Venue-Related Risks

Most researchers will be aware that some participant observation settings are inherently riskier than others. High-crime areas, corrupt bureaucracies, dangerous workplaces, ill-maintained vehicles, questionable roads, scenes of diseases and injuries, locations where illicit activity is conducted, and places where political oppression is occurring are just a few of the potentially risky venues that researchers have encountered during participant observation. And the participant observation does not have to be actually in a high-risk zone—high-risk adjacent is often enough to cause a problem. One of the authors, for example, once got teargassed while in the Indian *mercado* in Quito, Ecuador. The police were breaking up a student protest some distance from the *mercado* and, having extra tear gas on hand, apparently decided it would be amusing to teargas the marketplace—even though the Indians were not involved in the protest. Accordingly, the author's observations of the market swiftly turned into a participant observation of a crowd stampeding through the narrow cobblestone streets.

Participant-Related Risks

In some cases, the presence of the researcher or the researcher's data collection efforts may trigger a negative response from some of the people being observed. Sometimes this is caused by participants who assume the researcher is something else—a spy for a local or foreign government, a stoolie reporting to the boss or warden, a member of a rival gang, a policeman, a potential child snatcher, or someone from the political opposition. At other times, the negative response may be with full knowledge of the researcher's intention and role and simply be an expression of someone's dislike of being "a guinea pig" for your study, or, someone who fears that your findings will portray them in an unflattering light. In either event, people who take exception to your presence and your activities can a pose real dangers ranging from expulsion from the research environment to injury or even death.

Mitigating Safety Risks

Common sense and good planning are the best ways to protect yourself from the potential risks of participant observation. Assess the venues you will be in and learn what threats they might contain, human and otherwise. Do your best to make sure that your activities do not expose you, your research team, or your research participants to undue risks. If the environment is inherently dangerous, learn what local people do to lessen the threats and, if practical, do the same. Be aware that your presence may change the social dynamic and introduce new risks to a previously stable environment. Watch how others respond to you and around you. If you see that tensions are high, try to learn if you are the cause and what you can do to help things return to normal. Do a good job of your informed consent activities— make sure your explanation of your work is understandable and credible in local terms. Be especially cautious if you are working in a risky venue without explaining your role to other participants. Give long and full consideration to what might happen if you are "found out."

When selecting venues for participant observation, include risk assessment as part of your selection criteria. A risk assessment should include the following:

- Making a list of the reasonably foreseeable or likely sources of physical or social danger to the researcher(s) and any increased risks the research activity might create for the other participants
- Identifying ways of avoiding or mitigating any significant risks such as limiting the times of day of the participant observation to the least risky periods,

working in teams, hiring your own transport instead of relying on public or local sources, informing people of your whereabouts during data collection, making sure that communication with other team members, police, and other resources is available during the data collection, taking preventive measures to avoid injuries or exposure to disease, and having first aid on hand

- Assessing the overall risk to benefit ratio—making a realistic judgment of the value of the data you plan to collect in relation to the risks associated with collecting these—if the risks are disproportionate to the value, consider eliminating the venue in favor of a safer one, using a less risky approach or, in the worst case, abandoning the line of inquiry altogether

Legal Issues and Constraints

As you might expect, conducting participant observation can occasionally lead researchers into murky legal waters, especially in litigation-oriented societies, such as the United States. Researchers in the United States have been involved in a number of civil suits and criminal charges involving claims of invasion of privacy, libel and slander, theft of trade secrets or intellectual property, trespassing, and other claim types. Sometimes, these cases involve people who were only peripheral players in the research venue or who were not actually part of the research at all. When one of the authors was employed by Nissan North America in the early 1990s, a Southern California couple accused Nissan North America (NNA is the holding company for all of Nissan's operations in the United States and Canada) of invading their privacy. They had hosted a young Nissan researcher visiting from Japan who had arranged to live with them as a home-stay boarder during his internship at NNA's headquarters in Torrance, California. Shortly after he returned to Japan, the couple saw a published news story with Nissan researchers that mentioned doing participant observation of U.S. consumers at their homes and workplaces. They accused Nissan of having planted a spy in their home in order to conduct research without their knowledge and brought suit. Although the suit was soon dismissed by a judge, the publicity that surrounded the case was embarrassing to Nissan, hurtful to the young Japanese intern (who had believed he had a good relationship with his U.S. hosts), and made the company's research team extremely cautious about both home stays for interns and the communication of research findings.

Since, at least in the United States, anyone is entitled to sue anyone, at any time, for just about anything, there is no easy way to avoid all risk of legal complications when conducting participant observation. But a few rules of thumb can help researchers avoid legal pitfalls and stay within the boundaries of the law:

1. Know the law involving the types of activities you will be observing and/or participating in. If your research venue is a place where unlawful activity may occur, then do some research about the relevant law. For some types of crimes, an observer is not considered to be part of the criminal activity. For others, observing or even hearing about the crime after the fact and failing to report it makes you an accessory. Similarly, if you are working with a business, know what constitutes a trade secret. If you are working with individuals, households or social groups, know what makes an invasion of privacy, or a libelous, slanderous statement. Do not wait until you have already crossed the line into criminal or litigational territory to learn where the border lies.

2. Have a plan for dealing with sticky legal situations. Know what you are going to do if you observe or hear about criminal behavior during your participant observations. If possible (and safe!) inform others in the venue of your intentions. Whether you plan to keep your mouth shut, remove yourself from the scene during these moments, or run to the police, your safety and your freedom from criminal charges depend on having a good plan and being able to carry it out. And while the consequences in civil suits are usually less dire than in criminal law, the same principles apply. Know the risks, know the relevant law, treat confidential material appropriately, keep good records (often the best way to show you did nothing wrong), and don't wait until someone hands you a summons to decide what to do.

3. When in doubt, consult with an expert. Most researchers experience any legal consultation as an exercise in hearing all the ways every type of social research is a minefield of risks. Indeed, one of the authors once was asked by corporate lawyers to caveat data that showed that drivers of a certain make of car were less likely to wear seat belts than drivers of some other vehicles—an actual fact available in government statistics— to lessen the risk that someone seeing the data would interpret them as the car maker somehow encouraging its customers to drive without seatbelts. Nevertheless, if your research may take you into the fringes of criminal or civil law, there is no substitute for expert advice about the risks involved and ways to mitigate them. A consultation with an attorney in the relevant legal specialty can provide both ways to lessen legal risks and the comforting assurance that today's participant observation is not going lead to tomorrow's mug shot in the local newspaper. For researchers subject to institutional review board (IRB) approval, one of the things the IRB should do is to help identify and mitigate possible legal risks.

PARTICIPANT OBSERVATION IN INTERNATIONAL SETTINGS

Anyone who has even been a tourist in a foreign land has, in an informal way, been a participant observer. Many of us have delighted in the excitement of absorbing the human and nonhuman elements of a new environment and struggled with the mental exhaustion and occasional social disasters that come from trying to process an overwhelming stream of data. These joys and challenges are even more apparent when you attempt to conduct participant observation in an international setting.

The three most obvious international issues for participant observation are limits on how much of a participant the researcher can become, issues of language and translation, and the risk of a research failure due to poor interaction at the data collection stage or misinterpretation of the data during analysis.

Dealing With Social Limits

In many settings, there are significant restraints regarding how much of a participant you can become. Virtually all societies reserve certain roles for those who meet specific demographic and/or social criteria—sex and age; clan, tribe, and family membership; and particular skills or credentials—that may place constraints on the degree to which a particular researcher can embed in a particular setting. Being a foreigner can hugely increase and complicate these constraints. To do successful participant observation outside your own country, you must review every step in your preparations, choice of venue, and intended research approach with an eye to where and in what ways your lack of local origins may get in your way. In many cases, you can mediate the effects of your foreign origins—improving your language and cultural preparation before you enter the venue, spending more time building rapport and becoming acculturated, finding local guides and mentors to teach or sponsor you. But be realistic—there may be some areas or activities where you will never be welcome or able to participate. That doesn't mean you can't learn about these things—only that you may have to rely on data collection techniques other than participant observation.

That said, there are many international settings in which being from another country has little negative impact or even has a positive effect on participant observation. In many community and work settings, being a sympathetic listener or an extra set of hands can more than make up for being foreign. A colleague of the authors performed a very successful participant observation project on a construction crew in Afghanistan, despite being American and having only a basic command of the local language. His co-workers were happy to have an extra laborer and enjoyed telling him about their lives and answering his questions. The key to dealing with the issues surrounding being a foreigner is to use the strengths of being this type of outsider, mitigate the weaknesses of this role, and to be honest about the limits it may impose on your data.

Dealing With Linguistic and Cultural Translation Issues

Similar to the limits imposed by being foreign, a lack of fluency in the local language can constrain the effectiveness of participant observation data collection and analysis. Obviously, the greater your cultural and linguistic fluency, the more opportunities you will have for observation and participation. In many international settings, you need at least basic language fluency—or the ability to hire a good local interpreter—to move from being a pure observer to being more of a participant. Typically, there will be some activities and events that you can participate in and understand with only a limited linguistic capability and others that will be effectively off limits until your language skills are at a higher level. Similarly, you must have at least some cultural knowledge—social norms of dress, behavior, speech—to function socially among your chosen research participants.

While it is possible to use translators and interpreters, be careful about the effects of these activities on the data you are trying to collect. The conversational lag time created by waiting for the interpreter can interrupt the natural flow of the action you are trying to observe or cause speakers to be more thoughtful, brief, or cautious than normal. Additionally, the quality and accuracy of the translation or interpretation will have a direct effect on your data. If you use translators, interpreters, or local experts to help you analyze your data, their work will also become a feature of the data themselves. As with any other facet of your data collection environment, be aware of how the use of interpreters and translators may create biases and limits on the data you will analyze, and do what you can to make sure that you minimize any downside represented by your lack of cultural and linguistic fluency.

SUMMING UP

The deeply contextual insights and flexibility of participant observation make it a powerful source of qualitative insight. The density of data produced and the intensity of the data collection experiences it entails can produce meaning on both a professional and personal level that few other approaches can rival. While it can be time and labor intensive, participant observation is an important addition to any qualitative researcher's tool kit.

REFERENCES

Bernard, H. R. (2006). *Research methods in anthropology.* Lanham, MD: Altamira Press.

Dalby, L. (1983). *Geisha.* Berkeley: University of California Press.

Erhenrich, B. (2001). *Nickle and dimed: On not getting by in America.* New York, NY: Metropolitan Books.

Koester, S., & Hoffer, L. (1994). Indirect sharing: Additional risks associated with drug injection. *AIDS and Public Policy 1994, 9*(2), 100–105.

Leach. E. R. (1967). An anthropologist's reflection on a social survey. In D. C. Jongmans & P. C. Gutkind (Eds.), *Anthropologists in the field* (p. 14). Assen, Netherlands: Van Gorcum.

Mack, N., Woodsong, C., MacQueen, K., Guest, G., & Namey, E. (2005). *Qualitative research methods: A data collector's field guide.* Research Triangle Park, NC: Family Health International.

Magnanti, B. (2005). *The intimate adventures of a London call girl.* London, UK: Weidenfeld & Nicolson. (Re-edited and published in the United States as *Belle De Jour: Diary of an unlikely call girl*, 2006, New York, NY: Grand Central)

Malinowski, B. (1961). *Argonauts of the Western Pacific.* New York, NY: Dutton. (Original work published 1922)

Park, R. E., Burgess, E. W., & McKenzie, R. D. (1925). *The city.* Chicago, IL: University of Chicago Press.

Plimpton, G. (1966). *Paper lion: Confessions of a last string quarterback.* Guilford, CT: Lyons Press.

Spradley, J. P. (1980). *Participant observation.* New York, NY: Holt, Rinehart & Winston.

Webb, B. (1926). *My apprenticeship.* London, UK: Longmans, Green.

ADDITIONAL READING

Agar, M. (1996). *The professional stranger: An informal introduction to ethnography* (2nd ed.). San Diego, CA: Academic Press.

Anderson, G. L., Herr, K. G., & Nihlen, A. S. (2007). *Studying your own school: An educator's guide to practitioner action research* (2nd ed.). Thousand Oaks, CA: Corwin.

Bernard, H. R. (2006). *Research methods in anthropology* (chap. 13). Lanham, MD: Altamira Press.

DeWalt, K., & DeWalt, B. (2011). *Participant observation: A guide for fieldworkers* (2nd ed.). Lanham, MD: AltaMira.

Emerson, R. M., Fretz, R. I., & Shaw, L. L. (1995). *Writing ethnographic fieldnotes.* Chicago, IL: University of Chicago Press.

Jorgensen, D. L. (1989). *Participant observation: A methodology for human studies.* Thousand Oaks, CA: Sage.

Kvale, S. (2007). *Doing interviews.* Thousand Oaks, CA: Sage.

Seidman, I. (2006). *Interviewing as qualitative research: A guide for researchers in education and the social sciences.* New York, NY: Teachers College Press.

Spradley, J. P. (1980). *Participant observation.* New York, NY: Holt, Rinehart & Winston.

Van Manen, M. (1990). *Researching lived experience: Human science for an action sensitive pedagogy.* Ontario, Canada: Althouse Press.

EXERCISES

1. Choose an accessible social or cultural venue or event that is not familiar to you—a gathering place of a religious, ethnic, and/or cultural group outside your own, a social or community gathering that you would not normally attend, an event held by those of different heritage, interest, or values from yours. The more unfamiliar to you, the better. Go to the location and do a purely visual observation—note who is there (demographically); note signs of social differences (deference, use of space, identifying clothing, badges, etc.) and watch how people interact with one another. Note what parts of the scene are easy to understand and which parts are confusing to you as an outside observer. What sorts of additional data—interviews, secondary sources, or additional observation—would you need to conduct to get clarity on these issues?

2. List several potential participant research venues. In which of these would you make your research role known to all of the participants?

3. Choose a social scene that is familiar to you but that is not familiar to most others, such as an unusual hobby, job, or sport; an ethnic celebration that is not widely known among outsiders; or a localized event or tradition. What aspects of this scene would be hard for outsiders to understand? What behaviors distinguish insiders from outsiders? What would a participant observer have to know or learn in order for you to consider them to be a participant?

4. Choose a place, event, social gathering, or work setting that is highly familiar to you—one in which you have insider status and full membership. As one operating from the "complete participant" level (Spradley, 1980), try to observe with "fresh eyes" as a means for making the familiar "strange." What do you notice about how people interact with one another? Note signs of social differences and power differentials (e.g., How are people grouped together? Who is doing most of the talking? Who is listened to most?). Note patterns of discourse and conversational topics, behaviors, and norms.

5. Pick a section of a foreign film in a language you do not speak. Choose a part of the film that has a high degree of human interaction. Watch 5 to 10 minutes of the movie with the sound muted. Try taking notes about what you are seeing. What aspects of the action were clear to you? What aspects were confusing? Watch again with the sound on. What becomes clearer? What remains confusing?

If you were an actual participant observer in this scene, what sort of assistance might you need in terms of both linguistic and cultural interpretation?

6. If you speak a second language (even at a basic level), think what sorts of scenes and activities you could and couldn't act as a full participant observer in using that language. List at least five interesting social settings for which your current level of fluency would be adequate for good participant observation. List at least five for which your current level of fluency would place limits on what you could do and observe. What are some ways you could deal with these limits?

4

In-Depth Interviews

WHAT IS AN IN-DEPTH INTERVIEW?

The phrase *in-depth interview* conjures up the most iconic of qualitative data collection activities: a skilled interviewer engaged in a probing conversation with a suitably knowledgeable interviewee. Virtually all qualitative researchers use this technique to some extent, and for many projects and researchers, in-depth interviews are the primary or sole source of data. And there is good reason for the pervasiveness of this method: it is versatile across a range of study topics, adaptable to challenging field conditions, and excellent for not just providing information but for generating understanding as well.

On a basic level, an in-depth interview (or IDI) is just what its name implies, a conversation designed to elicit depth on a topic of interest. But it should be noted that not all interviews produce "in-depth" insights, and certainly there are other ways of discovering the answers to underlying *why* and *how* questions. There are several features that characterize IDIs and that are integral to the power and utility of the technique. In general, IDIs exhibit the following features:

Are Conducted One-on-One—The inductive probing at the heart of in-depth interviewing requires that the interviewer shape the probing questions in a dynamic fashion—keeping in mind both the objectives of an interview and the substance of the participant's previous answers. It is difficult to do this well if there are more than two participants in the conversation. The one-on-one format allows the researcher to focus precisely on the content of the interviewee's responses, paying close attention to tone, content, and body language. Additionally, for topics that are sensitive, confidential, or emotional, the one-on-one setting maximizes the ability of the researcher to gain rapport, ensure confidentiality, and extend empathy. Note that this unwritten one-to-one rule is sometimes broken for extenuating circumstances such as (a) when personal safety is an issue, (b) if using an interpreter, or (c) a separate note-taker is necessary.

Utilize Open-Ended Questioning—IDI questions are distinctively open-ended. Any planned questions in the discussion guide for an IDI are designed to lead the conversation into the topic of interest and are constructed so as to maximize the opportunities for discursive, detailed, and highly textured responses. Similarly, most of the inductive probing done during the interview will also feature open-ended questions that encourage the interviewee to share her understanding, beliefs, experiences, and point-of-view. Short-answer questions should be minimized, used only as a warm-up, as part of transitions from one topic to another, or to confirm factual details. If you want to ask a few structured questions—that is, to get basic demographics—this is fine. Be sure to do so before or after the IDI.

Use Inductive Probing to Get Depth—The single most defining characteristic of in-depth interviewing is inductive probing—asking questions that are based on the interviewee's responses and simultaneously linked to the research objectives. This is where a well-conducted IDI produces the meanings, insights and causal chains that provide the richness of qualitative data. Probing is the most difficult skill for beginning researchers to master, and missed or botched probing is one of the most common problems in conducting IDIs. This is why we've allocated an entire section to it within this chapter.

Look and Feel Like a Conversation—Skilled interviewers conduct IDIs that appear highly conversational, making the technique seem deceptively simple to outside observers. The trained interviewer is, in fact, using conversational norms to both build rapport with the interviewee and effectively steer the conversation toward areas relevant to the research objectives. The interviewee should experience the interview as talking with an ultrainterested and attentive conversational partner, not as being grilled by a reporter (or worse, a prosecutor!) or as providing answers to a "canned" set of questions.

An Interview Typology

In-depth interviewing is a specific type of interview that is part of a wider collection of general interview approaches. Bernard (2000) identifies "a continuum of interview situations based on the *amount of control* we try to exercise over people's responses" (p. 190). We refer to this level of control as the degree of structure within the interview process. The three most general terms used in this regard are unstructured, semi-structured, and structured, but as Figure 4.1 illustrates, these are markers

---

Figure 4.1   General Interview Typology

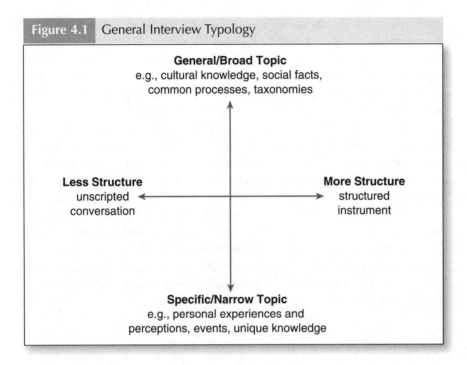

---

within a range (the x axis). On the one extreme are completely unscripted conversations, the type a researcher might have when doing participant observation or at the very beginning of an inquiry when almost nothing is known about a topic. At the other extreme fall highly structured interviews, in which the questions are asked verbatim and response categories are fixed. At this extreme, the interview has become a survey and is no longer qualitative in design. Most in-depth interviews are semi-structured and fall somewhere in the middle range of the x axis. We discuss interview structure in more detail later in the chapter.

In addition to structure, the breadth and depth of topical content is an important characteristic to consider (the y axis in Figure 4.1). Some topics are broad in nature and are experienced by a large portion of a study population. Examples of these are overt cultural norms (Is it OK to run through the streets naked?), social facts (What time does the market open?), commonly shared processes (How do people in the United States celebrate the 4th of July?), and indigenous typologies or taxonomies (How do people classify illnesses?). As described in Chapter 2, the more broadly shared something is—cultural knowledge, a socially shared experience—the easier it is to investigate and the smaller the sample size required. This is because responses to questions about broadly shared topics tend to exhibit minimal variation. Moreover, the purpose of such inquiries is typically to understand the norm, the usual, and the general process of something. While variation is not ignored in such cases, it is not the primary data point of interest. On the lower end of the y axis, the converse is true. If you're interested in personal experiences and unique events, perceptions, or knowledge, then your line of questioning and approach to data analysis will be more targeted, and variation will likely be of increased interest. The key point here is that the scope and structure of an interview depend on one's research objectives.

While the characteristics above provide a brief synopsis of what an IDI is, it is also important to note what it is not. Most importantly, an IDI is *not* a survey. IDIs are not a good or cost-effective way to do the things that surveys are most useful for—establishing the prevalence and frequency of behaviors, experiences, beliefs, or intentions and comparing these things across groups of people, points in time, locations, and so on. Before you embark on a project that includes IDIs, you should closely examine your study objectives and determine exactly what would count as an answer to the questions and issues the research is supposed to address. If you need simple facts and comparative data, a survey is most likely to be your method of choice. If, however, your research objectives require depth, nuance, and meaning, IDIs are more likely the way to go.

WHY USE IN-DEPTH INTERVIEWS?

The strengths of in-depth interviews are many. First, as the term implies, in-depth interviews allow researchers to get "deep" answers to their questions from "experts" on the issue. Generally, researchers seeking depth are trying to gain insight about some element of human experience beyond the basic facts of who, what, when, and where. Accordingly, IDIs are almost always, in part or in whole, about *how* and *why*, helping researchers to understand their interviewees' views of processes, norms, decision making, belief systems, mental models, interpretations, motivations, expectations, hopes, and fears. These are the things that make human experience more than mere facts—when you conduct an IDI, you are asking your interviewee to share not just the aspects of their experience that could be captured by a camera but also the aspects that can be captured only by a human being, someone who can tell you what that experience means.

Second, the conversational, open-ended style of a well-conducted in-depth interview is familiar to everyone. We all ask and respond to questions as a means of exchanging information in the course of a normal day. As Gorden (1992) defines the process, "Interviewing is a conversation between two people in which one person tries to direct the conversation to obtain information for some specific purpose" (p. 2). While the presence of an interview guide and the context of a research setting modify the conversational routine, people generally have an easy time answering questions in their own words. Also, respondents do not have to be literate to respond to an in-depth interview, and if they do not understand the phrasing or terminology in a question, the interviewer has both the opportunity to record that information *and* provide a rephrasing of the question so that the interviewee might provide a response. These are advantages over structured or closed-ended questionnaires or surveys.

Additionally, in contrast to other qualitative data collection methods, in-depth interviews are well suited to asking questions about polarizing, sensitive, confidential, or highly personal topics. Discussing these topics in a group or public setting could put the interviewee at risks that range from social embarrassment to financial loss to actual physical harm. To learn about these topics, the researcher must provide a space in which the interviewee can feel safe discussing matters that are usually kept private—exactly the environment that a skilled in-depth interviewer strives to create. In fact, it is often surprising what people will tell you—and to what level of detail— when you have built enough rapport and trust with them. For some sensitive or taboo topics, such as sexual activity, miscarriage, or death, an interview serves as a forum where people can reflect on their own attitudes, opinions, and behaviors in a way they might not in a regular conversation. Similarly, because the setting is one-on-one, interviewees may be less concerned about offending someone else or answering in the "right" or socially acceptable way than they might in a group setting (though potential for this kind of social desirability bias still exists).

IDIs can be used throughout the research process and at multiple points along the path of learning about a topic or issue, but they are especially useful for exploring and explaining phenomena.

Exploring

When enough is known about a topic or issue to formulate sensible research questions and identify potential interviewees, but not much more, IDIs are often the technique of choice. The open-ended nature of IDI questioning enables the researcher to get an initial sense of the subject, begin developing vocabulary, discover the steps in decision chains or sequential events, and start understanding systems and processes. Most importantly, doing IDIs at the exploratory stage helps researchers identify the boundaries of their own knowledge, to figure out the topics and questions that will become important as knowledge about the topic grows. There is nothing more frustrating than being far along a path of research— especially a time consuming and expensive one—and then learning that you have been asking the wrong questions, or using the wrong vocabulary, or questioning the wrong people. The time invested doing IDIs early on in the research process almost always pays benefits down the line.

Explaining

As mentioned above, IDIs are an excellent way to answer *how* and *why* questions. Often, quantitative studies reveal interesting patterns of behavior or opinion, but may offer little or no data to help explain why these patterns exist. For example, the U.S. census has shown a consistent trend of an increase in the percentage of Americans identifying themselves as having Native American ancestry, a trend far in excess of any rates of intermarriage or natural population growth. In fact, some of those who now identify themselves as having Native American heritage must have changed their ethnic identifications from one census to the next. Given that ethnic identification is both a deeply personal and socially meaningful choice, IDIs would be well suited to helping explain these patterns observed in the data.

Additionally, Weiss (1994) suggests that IDIs are useful for research that aims to develop detailed or holistic descriptions, integrate multiple perspectives or bridge intersubjectivities, describe processes, learn how events are interpreted, and/or identify variables and frame hypotheses for quantitative research. This multiplex utility of IDIs is one of the reasons why in-depth interviews are so often one element of mixed method approaches in commercial, government, academic, and nonprofit research. Almost any research topic that is addressed in a comprehensive manner will need exploration or explanation along these lines at one or more stages of an investigation. IDIs are a critical element of the researcher's tool kit to meet these needs.

One "commonly cited shortcoming of interviews is that they only provide access to what people *say*, not what they *do*. From a positivist perspective this is a problem, as interviews (people's accounts) are sometimes a poor substitute for empirical evidence" (Green & Thorogood, 2009, p. 102). This type of self-report bias, while a problem, is only slightly more so for interviews than it is for surveys, which also rely on self-report. Again, the purpose of the inquiry has to match the method. Structured direct observation would be a better methodological choice for studying the prevalence of teenage smoking, for example, but if you wanted to know *why* these teens had taken up smoking, an in-depth interview would be your method of choice. Bernard provides greater description of the types of response effects and suggestions for limiting their extent, concluding that "the problem of informant accuracy remains an important issue and a fruitful area for research in social science methodology" (2000, p. 219).

COMMON TYPES OF IN-DEPTH INTERVIEWS

While almost any topic can be approached using IDIs, there are several types of data for which IDIs are an especially appropriate, useful, and widely used tool.

Phenomenological Interviews

As described in Chapter 1, phenomenology focuses on "describing how people experience some phenomenon—how they perceive it, describe it, feel about it, judge it, remember it, make sense of it, and talk about it with others" (Patton, 2002, p. 104). The open-ended, discursive, and descriptive character of IDIs makes them ideal for capturing this level of lived human experience. Whether we are conducting market research to learn how consumers choose particular new cars from the hundreds of available makes and models, or trying to understand why young men use or fail to use condoms during potentially risky sexual encounters, or investigating what coping mechanisms enable people to survive wrenching disasters, the IDI format allows interviewees to share their experiences with researchers, who in turn obtain a deep view of how an issue or event affects a person's life.

Because they focus on individual lived experiences, phenomenological in-depth interviews are more difficult to systematically compare than others. An interviewer will likely start with one broad question and some affiliated follow-up topics, but must follow the participant's lead to a greater extent, focusing on the details of an experience that are most important to the individual. For this reason, phenomenological interviewing is most effective for exploratory or descriptive research aims, though some findings from phenomenological interviews are used in support of applied research aims. Phenomenological in-depth interviewing is popular in certain disciplines and traditions, including psychology and nursing. See Callister, Vehvilainen-Julkunen, and Lauri (2001) and Gibbins and Thomson (2001) for examples of studies where a phenomenological approach was employed.

Oral History

Similar to phenomenology in its approach, oral history interviewing emphasizes the experiences and perspectives of people who witnessed or lived through a specific event. The distinction is in the type of event: Oral history interviews are specifically geared toward collecting information on historical events or time periods from the people who were there. According to Sommer and Quinlan, "Oral history is primary-source material created in an interview setting with a witness to or a participant in an event or way of life for the purpose of preserving the information and making it available to others. The term refers both to the process and the interview itself" (2009, p. 1). Formal collection of oral histories has been a hallmark of a number of disciplines, with historical researchers and anthropologists making frequent use of this approach. Historians use oral histories to study the past of societies that have limited written records, where minority views of history and historical events may have been suppressed by oppressive ruling regimes, or where the points of view of particular individuals may illuminate key aspects of the historical record. Anthropologists collect oral histories as a way of learning how members of a culture live their lives, participate in their societies, and make sense of their worlds. Since the very essence of an oral history is the sequential tale of an individual's experience and their recollections and interpretations of past events, the intimate one-on-one format of an IDI is a natural and effective way of collecting these narratives. In this regard, in-depth interviews conducted as oral history have a very specific focus and scope, which helps to guide probing, often over the course of more than one interview with an individual. The output of oral history interviews is often a book or monograph rather than a journal article or report of recommendations (see Ward & Burns, 2007, for a recent example). Though its roots are in the fields of history and anthropology, "Oral history is now a multi-disciplinary method used in the humanities, social sciences, and interdisciplinary fields such as American studies, cultural studies, and gender studies" (Leavy 2011, p. 4).

Case Study

The idea of collecting case studies has its origins in medical research, where a particular case of a disease or syndrome is fully described in the medical literature. In this medical tradition, there are two types of case studies: those that define the *typical* symptoms and progress of a disease or condition—like the case of dementia in an elderly patient first described by Dr. Alois Alzheimer—and those that are *atypical,* such as case studies of the few patients infected in the early days of the HIV epidemic who never went on to develop compromised immune systems. In social research, case studies are often collected for similar reasons, either as exemplars of interesting social phenomena or processes or to examine unusual cases in which people behave in ways that are outside social norms or expectations. Depending on the research objectives, IDI-based case study research may focus on a single individual case or may collect a group of cases for analysis of common features, themes, or processes. Yin (2009, p. 46) details the basic types of designs for case study research. In applied sociobehavioral research, case studies are often used in association with other methods to add supplemental information to an evaluation or assessment and offer perspective on what happened and why (Neale, Thapa, & Boyce, 2006). Flyvbjerg (2006) provides a clear summary of what a case study approach to a research question can and cannot provide.

As Part of a Larger Study

As mentioned previously, the utility of IDIs for both exploratory and explanatory purposes often makes them a useful tool for large or long-term studies. Typically, such studies include a series of data collection phases using a mix of qualitative and quantitative data collection techniques to get at different aspects of the research topic. The larger study may be primarily qualitative or quantitative, sociobehavioral or clinical. Regardless of the situation, the flexibility and versatility of IDIs makes them one of the most widely used qualitative elements in such larger studies. In this context, where multiple methods are used to address multiple research aims and/or collect data from various sources, in-depth interviews often serve to (a) enumerate the range or breadth of a given phenomenon; (b) provide a rich description of the individual-level knowledge, attitudes, beliefs, or opinions of a population; and/or (c) to answer the *why* and *how* questions that more quantitatively-oriented inquiry often cannot. Guest and colleagues (2012) provide additional detail on the ways that qualitative, in-depth interview data can be incorporated into larger studies. The approach to in-depth interviewing in these cases should match not only the distinct goals of the interview study but also the broader aims of the larger study as well.

RECRUITING PARTICIPANTS

As reviewed in Chapter 2, recruitment of study participants refers to the process by which participants are first informed about and, if eligible, asked to join a study. As in any other data collection effort, recruiting participants for IDIs must balance the goals of the research with the practical limitations of time, money, physical logistics, and research team capabilities. Often with IDIs, the usefulness of your research findings will be dependent on a small number of interviews. The small sample sizes and intense use of research staff time underscore the need for recruitment to be done well. We therefore make efforts to minimize the chance of having interviewees who are unqualified or biasing the sample through recruitment efforts. For most studies, the recruitment process includes four key steps:

1. *Identify the types of people you need to talk to.* This may seem obvious from the research objectives, but formal definitions of targeted populations help to clarify who is being sought and why. For example, if the research includes conducting IDIs with "environmentally active residents of Smalltown, USA" you need to define what you mean by both "environmentally active" and "resident of Smalltown." What behaviors and/or attitudes will you use to identify "environmentally active" people? Which streets, neighborhoods, or zip codes will qualify someone as a resident? How long must residents have lived in the town in order to qualify to be interviewed? Your goal at this stage is to develop clear inclusion and exclusion rules—the screening criteria for your recruitment effort. You are ready to proceed to the next step only when

you—and any other relevant members of the research team and/or research sponsors—have screening criteria that would enable you to positively and invariably decide which people qualify to be interviewed and which do not.

2. *Develop the screening tool.* For some studies a formal screening questionnaire is not necessary. For example, if you are interviewing the inmates of a prison and all inmates are equally qualified to be interviewed, all you need is a current list of inmates—anyone on the list can be an interviewee. But in many cases, you will need to sift through potentially qualified people and screen them to identify those who actually meet your criteria. For the example mentioned above, you might intercept people attending a community event in Smalltown and then administer a short screening survey to determine who is a resident and which residents meet your formalized definition of environmentally active.

While no two screening questionnaires are alike, good rules of thumb in designing a screener are to:

a. put the screening criteria in a logical order, one that filters people in successive layers, generally from easiest to hardest. In the example above, you would ask the residency questions before the environmental activity questions because there is no point in asking about the behavior and attitudes of nonresidents.

b. keep it as short as possible. The idea is to screen, not to conduct a mini-interview. Don't waste your time, or that of potential interviewees, by asking questions that are not relevant to the recruiting decision.

3. *Select a recruiting method.* There are innumerable ways to recruit interviewees and all methods offer both advantages and drawbacks (see Table 2.2 in Chapter 2). The key in selecting a method is to pick one that meets your sampling needs and that is realistic in terms of the time, effort, and money your project can afford to invest in recruiting.

4. *Implement the recruitment plan.* With the exception of studies that intercept people and interview them on the spot, there is generally a lag time between recruitment and interviews. Allow sufficient time in your research plan to get the number of qualified interviewees you need. Use a conservative time frame when estimating how quickly you will attain your target study sample. It can take a lot of phone calls, intercepts, or waiting to find each qualified interviewee. Consider also whether or not it will be important to over-recruit in order to ensure that the desired sample size is reached. It is normal in commercial research to over-recruit or to recruit a few floater interviewees

who have flexible schedules and who will be interviewed only if another interviewee cancels at the last minute. Over-recruiting is often necessary in public sector work when the study population has transportation issues, a transient lifestyle, substance abuse issues, or any other qualities that make missed interviews more likely. Deciding how to lessen and deal with "no-shows" is part of the IDI recruitment effort.

The best recruitment approach for a given project will depend on the specific sampling strategy (see Chapter 2). For any technique, and particularly if using a passive recruitment approach, you will need to develop a thorough screening and eligibility log to keep track of the people who respond to a recruitment effort, their relevant characteristics, and if eligible, their contact information (see Chapter 7 for more details on these procedures). Also, note that self-selection bias can be something of a strength in recruitment for in-depth interviews, since people who take the time to respond to a flier or online ad are likely interested to some degree in the topic of the study and therefore probably have something to say. Random telephone selection of interviewees works somewhat less well in this regard, since those who are selected, if they agree to participate, may not be interested in the topic, may be suspicious of the legitimacy of the research, or may give brief answers to interview questions. When using referral techniques, you might add "talkative" or "opinionated" to the list of eligibility criteria you provide to those who are referring others.

PREPARING FOR AN INTERVIEW

Planning

Planning the logistics of an interview is as important as recruiting the right participant. Traditionally, in-depth interviews have occurred in person, face-to-face, and in this situation, selection of location is important. Popular sites for conducting IDIs include homes, workplaces, community centers, libraries, schools, medical facilities, restaurants, bars, hotel conference rooms and lobbies, markets and bazaars, research centers and focus group facilities, and even open-air locations, such as parks and streets. Choosing a location for your IDIs requires balancing several important elements of the human and physical environment. To select the location of your IDIs, you should ask yourself the following questions:

- *Where will the interviewee feel safe and comfortable?* Will your interviewees feel comfortable talking in your office or research facility, or will they speak more easily and frankly in a place that is familiar to them, such as their own home or work area? Is your interview topic so private or confidential that it needs to take place without the presence or knowledge of your interviewees' families or colleagues?

- *What location will be best in terms of building rapport and maintaining the tone and flow of the interview?* Is your interview topic one that will benefit from professional surroundings, or is it a more personal topic that naturally fits in a home setting? If interviews are conducted in the interviewee's home or workplace, will there be interruptions or distractions that could disrupt the interview? Will the interview benefit from being on neutral ground such as a school, community center, or other gathering place? Are there social or cultural norms that require you to play the role of host or guest when conducting your interviews?

- *What location will best serve the actual data collection?* Is your proposed location quiet enough to facilitate conversation, recording, and note-taking? Is there adequate and safe transportation for interviewees and/or the researchers to and from the site? If interviewees may have to wait their turn with an interviewer, is there a comfortable place for them to hang out? If they arrive with friends, spouses, children or colleagues, do you have a way to take care of these people? If you are offering refreshments to interviewees or observers, is there a place to store and a way to serve these items?

Green and Thorogood advise that "in most developed country settings it is preferable to interview in a private space that the interviewee feels is 'theirs.' This ensures confidentiality, and a relaxed atmosphere to develop rapport" (2009, p. 111). We agree, to an extent, but note that you do not have to pick one location to conduct all of your interviews; the selection will depend to a large degree on the interviewee. While home may be comfortable and convenient for one person, the next may prefer to meet you at your office. Offer options and follow the interviewee's lead. If you are conducting interviews some place unfamiliar to the interviewee, provide clear directions and parking information and meet the interviewee in the lobby or outside at a designated spot. When an in-person in-depth interview is not feasible given distance or schedules, telephone or internet interviews are another possibility. Special considerations for these types of in-depth interviews are provided later in this chapter.

As with location, the timing of your interviews should also be chosen with care. The general rule is to schedule the interviews at times that are convenient to both the data collectors and the interviewees, with greater emphasis being on the interviewees' schedules. If the people you wish to interview work during weekdays, you will probably choose to schedule your interviews over the lunch hour, in the evenings, or on weekends. In choosing interview times, you should also be aware of the natural rhythms of people of different ages and life stages. IDIs with teenagers are generally not a good bet at 7 a.m., and late evening interviews are not usually very successful with either senior citizens or the parents of small children. You may also have to adapt your schedule somewhat in order to have a suitable interviewing venue or to accommodate schedules. Shift workers may be delighted to be interviewed at 3 a.m., but finding a location—and interviewer—at that hour may be challenging.

With regard to the timing of an in-depth interview relative to recruitment, an ideal situation is to make an appointment with the interviewee a few days to a week in advance. Most interviews that are truly in-depth require from 45 to 90 minutes, depending on the scope of the topic. Others suggest than an hour and a half to 2 hours is more common (Weiss, 1994). When scheduling the interview, state your availability clearly and provide as much flexibility to accommodate the interviewee as you can. If the interview is estimated to take one hour, set aside an extra 15 minutes on either end to account for pre-interview preparations, informed consent, travel to and from the meeting point, and post-interview debriefing. In situations where an interview is scheduled more than a few days in advance, it is often helpful to provide a reminder call or e-mail the day before the interview, to remind the interviewee of your appointment, the location, any special instructions, and your contact information in case the interviewee has trouble finding the location or needs to reschedule. For interviews scheduled within a few days, you may still send an e-mail with this information as confirmation of the interview appointment. The Pre-Interview Checklist provided in the text box suggests steps you can take to be prepared for every interview you schedule.

Pre-Interview Checklist

One day before interview:

- Confirm that meeting location is still available/appropriate
- Call or e-mail participant with reminder about scheduled interview. Provide:
  - Date, time, and location of interview
  - Driving directions, parking instructions, or specific meeting location (outside, lobby)
  - Interviewer mobile phone number
- E-mail a copy of the interview guide (if applicable)
- Prepare interview packet, to include, as applicable:
  - Copy of the interview guide
  - Informed consent document(s)
  - Study incentive
  - Study incentive documentation (receipts or forms to be signed by participant)
  - Debriefing notes template (if applicable)

- Label interview packet with appropriate study ID
- Charge mobile phone
- Check batteries in recording equipment; charge or change if necessary

Day of interview:

- Pack interview packet, pen(s), recording equipment, extra batteries, notebook, mobile phone
  - Bring participant's contact information
- Arrive at designated location at least 5 to 10 minutes early; assess suitability for interview
- Adjust comfort features of location, as possible (temperature, light, sound)
- Test recording equipment in interview setting

In some situations, you may conduct a spontaneous or intercept interview that occurs at the same time and/or location as study recruitment (a common occurrence in traditional ethnography). These types of interviews are often used purposely in market research, to collect consumer opinions about a product or display at the point of purchase. Spontaneous, informal interviews may also occur as part of participant observation activities and may or may not be in-depth, depending on the context of the research. Or you might find yourself conducting an unscheduled, on-the-spot interview in the context of public health or educational research when you are trying to recruit a hard-to-reach or extremely busy person who says in response to your scheduling query, "I have time right now." In these situations, the interviewee may have limited time and focus to devote to the interview, which will affect how the interviewer establishes rapport and how deeply (or shallowly) responses are probed. Try to get an idea of how much time the person has before beginning the interview to make the most effective use of the time you do have. Gorden (1992) notes that "if an interview calls for in-depth exploration of the problems, symptoms, facts, values, and attitudes of the respondent, then the pace must be slowed down and time constraints must be removed" (p. 57). Though it is generally good advice, in an intercept situation, the removal of time constraints is unlikely. But there are ways to increase the likelihood of collecting all of the necessary information. If you are unable to complete the interview or if there are areas that could be explored more thoroughly, you may ask the interviewee for contact information so that you might follow up later via phone or e-mail. Or you may simply hand them a business card and ask them to contact you with any additional thoughts. While typically not ideal, interviews that are not scheduled in advance can still provide critical information to support research objectives, and they have the advantage of eliciting spontaneous thoughts about a topic, since the interviewee has not had time to prepare or think about the topic in advance.

Training

Planning for an in-depth interview takes more than having a place, a time, and an appropriate person to interview. The researcher or research team also needs to be physically and mentally prepared to conduct the IDI. Most central to the research effort is making sure that interviewers are properly selected and trained. While virtually any willing and socially competent person can learn to conduct an IDI, there is no question that some people get good at interviewing more quickly than others and that some show a positive talent for the technique. In general, successful interviewers have good people skills, are socially aware, have high levels of curiosity, and are quick thinking. It can be very challenging for those who are shy, quiet, and deliberate in their thoughts and speech to conduct IDIs. So if you are selecting potential interviewers and you have a choice, pick those who start with a natural propensity for the task.

For small studies where the principle investigator is also the primary or sole data collector, training may be confined to individual preparation and a few practice interviews using the interview guide. In team settings, it is important that all interviewers have consistent and thorough training (the next text box lists some of the essential elements for interviewer training); do not simply draft someone as an interviewer, hand them an interview guide, and put them in front of an interviewee. Prior to beginning interviewing, every interviewer associated with a project should be trained on the precise reason that each question was included on the guide so that he will know when to probe for further information and when the question's intended objective has been met. Practicing the interview several times with someone from the research team helps an interviewer better understand the objective of each question and begin to develop the range of probes he will use to ask people to provide information that more specifically addresses the goals of a given question. Flick suggests further that

> the application of the interview guide is taught in role-plays. These simulated interview situations are recorded (if possible on videotape). Afterwards they are evaluated by all the interviewers taking part in the study—for interview mistakes, for how the interview guide was used, for procedures and problems in introducing and changing topics, the interviewers' non-verbal behavior, and their reactions to the interviewees." (2009, p. 172)

Each of these elements can then be improved through recognition and practice.

Pretesting an interview guide serves the dual purpose of providing the interviewer with training on a specific interview guide and identifying questions or subquestions that are difficult to ask or understand. You might conduct a first pretest with a colleague unfamiliar with your research, to further familiarize yourself with the flow of questions, and to suggest any changes to order or language that would improve the interview. Try to avoid, if you can, using friends or family members as your practice interview respondents; the preexisting relationships and role expectations can disrupt the focus of the interview (Bernard, 2000). If you are supervising other interviewers, you may want to serve as the pretest interviewee to monitor interviewing technique and understanding, particularly for new interviewers; you may also think about providing opportunities for inexperienced interviewers to observe more experienced interviewers in action (Olson, 2011).

Next, we would advise conducting a pilot test interview with someone from the study population, particularly if your pretest volunteer was someone from your same discipline or background. In Namey's interviews on genetic research results, for instance, it became clear only after she pilot tested the interview guide with a member of the targeted study population that interviewers would need to provide a definition of the term *genetic research results* to ensure that people were interpreting questions the way the researchers had intended. The members of the research team that had prepared the guide all understood their own questions; it was essential to have someone unfamiliar with the topic complete the interview to help refine the phrasing.

The ultimate goal of practice with a specific guide is to develop an interviewer who is intimately familiar with all of the questions on the guide and their intended meaning, the general flow of the interview, and the larger research question behind the interviews. This level of familiarity will allow an interviewer to more closely follow what a respondent is saying rather than thinking, "What question do I ask next?" If the interview protocol allows, the interviewer may skip to a question directly related

Topics to Include in Training of Interviewers

Training for interviewers should include the following:

- Review of the research objectives
- Review of the recruitment plan and eligibility criteria
- Discussion of standards for appearance, dress, and greetings with interviewees
- Handling of informed consent and incentives (if applicable)
- Detailed review of the interview guide, including the rationale behind each question and possible areas for in-depth probing
- Interviewing practice and skill building, including both role play and critique by colleagues and, if possible, practice interviews with participants who in some way resemble the target interviewees.
- Review of interview documentation, note-taking, and data handling protocols, including practice using recording and data storage devices.

to what the respondent has just said, even if it is not next on the guide, to further the conversational style of the interview. Familiarity breeds confidence, and a confident interviewer is more likely to be at ease, which will in turn create a more comfortable environment for the respondent.

DEVELOPING AN EFFECTIVE INSTRUMENT

While an IDI should resemble a conversation when viewed from the outside and may feel very conversational from the interviewee's point of view, it is actually a very carefully planned and, to some degree, scripted event. The guidelines for how this research event will play out are embedded in your interview guide. A thoughtfully developed guide helps ensure that each interview provides a meaningful addition to your data, that key topics and questions are not overlooked in the give and take of discourse, and that there is ample opportunity for new themes, ideas, and information to emerge.

Process

The development of an effective in-depth interview instrument begins with a review of the project's research objectives, since the nature of the data you are trying to capture will influence the format and content of the instrument and the questions within it. Your research objectives will inform the scope of the interview and determine the specific questions and types of questions asked. In reviewing the research objectives, ask yourself:

1. What are the main research questions that the interviews are intended to answer?
2. What are the primary domains of content that should be covered in the interview?
3. What types of data are needed to provide these answers (opinions, experiences, knowledge, attitudes)?

In answering Question 1, you should be able to create a list of a few high-order research questions (not interview questions); answering these is the objective of the interview. Thinking about Question 2 will allow you to identify some domains, or subtopics, that are important features or characteristics of your research objective. The types of data necessary, in response to Question 3, will flow logically from these. From here, you can begin developing specific questions under each of the domains. Gorden (1992, p. 11) suggests a very similar process for formulating relevant questions. In Table 4.1, we provide examples of this process.

Table 4.1	Examples of a Stepwise Approach to Developing an Interview Guide Framework From Research Objectives		
(1) What are the main research questions the interview is designed to answer?	**(2) What are the primary domains of content that should be covered in the interview?**	**(3) What types of data are needed to provide these answers (opinions, experiences, knowledge, attitudes, lists)?**
Why do young women not seek care for condition Y?	❖ Knowledge of condition Y ❖ Personal experience of condition Y ❖ Barriers to care	→ Knowledge → Experience → Experience/Opinion
How do consumers choose among different brands of product Z?	❖ Known brands ❖ Preferred product qualities ❖ Experience with brands ❖ Decision-making factors	→ List → Opinion → Experience/Opinion → Experience/Attitude
How can the local library better serve the community?	❖ Current services provided ❖ Perception of current services ❖ Desired services/events	→ List/Knowledge/Experience → Attitude → List/Opinion

Once you have charted the broad outline of your research objectives this way, you have a good framework on which to construct your interview guide. We should point out here that not all in-depth interviews require that specific questions be defined a priori. When little is known about a topic and a highly exploratory approach is needed, just having domains of inquiry established may be enough, obviating the need for a guide. Most applied research contexts, though, are subject to time constraints and have a relatively narrow and defined topic focus, making a pre-established guide quite useful.

Below, we present the general process for developing a guide and then go on to discuss developing effective questions. The steps for creating an in-depth interview guide are adapted from Kreuger and Casey's approach to drafting an effective focus group guide (2009). The development process is essentially the same for both methods.

1. Brainstorming—Begin brainstorming possible questions to fit each of the domains and question types you identified. Try not to get hung up on specific language, order of questions, or flow during this process. Simply create three to five potential questions for each point. If you are working in a team, or have

colleagues who might be willing to volunteer some ideas, have each person generate a list of questions that map to these objectives. Two to three minds usually generate plenty of questions for consideration! When you (and the group) are finished, compare and collate the lists of questions, combining similar questions.

2. Phrasing questions—Have one person review the entire list of possible questions generated in Step 1 and choose about 20 that most directly address your research objectives. Revise each question to maximize clarity, while avoiding yes/no phrasing. Try to incorporate a variety of question types (more detail on this under *Types of Questions,* below).

3. Sequencing questions—Organize the rephrased questions into an order that flows logically. Often this entails starting with broad or background questions first and then narrowing the focus to address the research objectives more specifically, or, to get experiences or opinions in more detail. Also, the first questions of an interview should be easy, warm-up questions to help establish the interviewee's comfort and confidence. Difficult, sensitive, or complicated questions are likely the core of your guide and should appear in the middle, after rapport is securely established, but before there is any potential for interviewee fatigue. Some of the questions you have chosen may end up as follow-up or sub-questions related to a broader question, rather than as stand-alone prompts. You can add conversational transitions or explanations later to help orient the respondent to the interview flow but, for now, focus on the questions themselves. This will be your draft interview guide.

4. Estimating time—For each question on the draft interview guide, estimate the amount of time you anticipate allotting to it during the interview. Generally, listing questions will take less time than experience questions, for example, but it will depend on the topic. Remember that the desired range for an in-depth interview is generally 45 to 90 minutes and allocate time accordingly. If your estimate suggests that you have time to spare, you might revisit the questions generated in Step 1 to see if there are any that could justifiably (in terms of the research objective) be added; if your estimate suggests that the interview will take longer than 90 minutes, consider how much longer and whether you need to cut questions.

5. Team review—Once you have edited your draft interview guide to accommodate your time estimates, circulate it to the research team or colleagues who are familiar with the topic. To streamline the process, you might ask reviewers to focus on a few specific things: Do all of the questions relate to or inform the research objectives? Does the order of questions make sense? Is the phrasing of the questions clear? Are there any questions that could or should be omitted? Are there any questions missing that would be

important to ask? Once everyone has completed review, you might convene a meeting to discuss the comments or simply collect them and revise the guide accordingly.

6. Testing questions—At this point, with a peer-reviewed, revised interview guide in hand, you can begin testing the questions. Conduct a few mock interviews with peers to see how the guide works during an interview situation. You may need to repeat Step 5 after you receive some feedback and then repeat Step 6, pretesting the guide with a few people from the target population (or those very similar).

Types of Instruments

Once you have figured out what questions to ask, you must decide how you are going to ask them. Do you need all the interviewees to be presented with the topics and questions in the same order, or do you simply need to be sure that all the questions get addressed at some point during the interview? Comparability across interviews is greatly facilitated if the questioning follows a set pattern, and in some cases, the order of topics will affect the answers you get, making this a factor you need to control. For these reasons, the standard approach to a semi-structured in-depth interview is to list the interview questions, along with transition phrases, in the general order or sequence that they are to be asked. This type of interview instrument is called a sequential interview guide. That said, it is a universally experienced fact among researchers that interviewees do not always "stick to the script." They answer questions you haven't asked yet or wander off topic so that you have to revisit questions more than once. In some cases, especially with less experienced interviewers, this results in the disconcerting sight of a researcher flipping back and forth through a multipage interview guide, trying to figure out what they have covered and what they haven't, while an expectant, puzzled, or exasperated interviewee looks on.

Depending on the level of structure required for your objectives, interviewers may have more or less discretion in skipping around on the guide to follow the thoughts of the interviewee. If the interviewer has less of this discretion, numbering each question and sub-question can serve as an important visual reminder to interviewers that questions are to be asked in order to the greatest extent possible. In cases where the guide is less structured and the interviewer has more discretion, it is likely helpful to label the broad sections of the interview guide but not necessarily important to number each question within it, since they will not always be asked sequentially (see Figure 4.2 for an example of each style).

Figure 4.2   Sequential and Matrix Interview Guide Samples

Figure 4.2a   Domain-Organized Sequential Guide (partial) With Structural Features Identified

CONDOM USE

Let's now talk about condoms When you have sex with a woman, how is it decided to use or not use condoms? [if respondent does not mention, ask: Who usually makes the decision? What criteria are used to make this decision?]

Which circumstances would change your mind about using or not using condom? **sub-questions**

In thinking about the different kinds of sexual partners that you mentioned earlier, explain how your condom use may be different with different types of partners.

domain headers

COMMUNICATION   **rapport**

Thank you for your responses. Let's now move to the next section of the interview and discuss what you talk about before having sex with a woman.   **topic transition explanation**

What do you usually talk about with your sexual partners before having sex?

How is the conversation different with different types of partners?

question type transition explanation

RELATIONSHIP TERMS

Thank you for your responses. We are now at the last section of the interview. In this section, I'm going to give you three different words related to relationships between men and women. I will then ask you what each word means to you and ask you to give examples.

In the context of relationships between men and women, what does the word "faithful" mean to you? Please given me an example of being "faithful".

Figure 4.2b   Numbered Sequential Guide

DECISION ABOUT ENROLLMENT IN H1N1 VACCINE TRIAL

1. To begin, please tell me how you learned about the H1N1 vaccine trial here.
2. What were your initial impressions about participating in research about a vaccine for H1N1 flu virus during pregnancy?
3. Who did you talk to about enrolling in this trial?
4. What were the factors you considered before deciding to enroll/not enroll?

    a. What were the pros, or factors that encouraged you to participate?
    b. What were the cons, or factors that gave you reason to hesitate?

5. How do you feel about your decision now?

SEASONAL FLU VACCINATION
I'm also interested to know about your thoughts regarding the seasonal flu vaccine.

6. Have you also received the seasonal flu vaccine during this pregnancy? Why/not?
7. What differences were there in your decision-making about the seasonal flu vaccine, if any?

| Figure 4.2c | Matrix Guide |

	Set-up	Pre-Intimacy	Intimacy	Post Intimacy
Context	☐ *When & where meet?* ☐ *What else was going on at the time (e.g., social occasion, etc?)* ☐ *Who was around?*	☐ *Where were you?* ☐ *Where did you go?* ☐ *Was place familiar?*	☐ *Any discussion about condom use/previous sexual experiences?*	☐ *Any discussion about condom use/ previous sexual experiences and condom use this partner?*
Behavior	☐ *What did you do?* ☐ *Was meeting planned?*	☐ *What happened?* ☐ *Who made first move?*	☐ *What activities?* ☐ *Petting mastur-bation, oral*	☐ *What did YOU do/where go?* ☐ *What did HE do/ where go?*
Thoughts, Deci-sions, Condoms	☐ *What thinking?* ☐ *Did you think you would have sex with him?*	☐ *What thinking?* ☐ *Was sex planned?* ☐ *How decide on sex?*	☐ *What thinking?* ☐ *Condoms?*	☐ *What thinking?*
Feelings	☐ *What feeling (mood)?* ☐ *What do you think he was feeling (mood)?*	☐ *What feeling (mood)?* ☐ *What do you think he was feeling?*	☐ *What feeling (mood)?* ☐ *What do you think he was feeling (mood)?*	☐ *What feeling (mood)?* ☐ *What do you think he was feeling (mood)?*
Alcohol & Drug use	☐ *Who drank/did drugs?* ☐ *What? How much?* ☐ *Who started?* ☐ *What role did alcohol or drugs play in your decision to become more intimate?*	☐ *Who drank/did drugs?* ☐ *What? How much?* ☐ *Who started?* ☐ *What role did alcohol or drugs play in your de-cision to have sex?*	☐ *Who drank/did drugs?* ☐ *What? How much?* ☐ *Who started?* ☐ *What role did alcohol/drugs play in your decision to use/ not use condom?*	☐ *What drank/did drugs?* ☐ *What? How much?* ☐ *Who started?* ☐ *What role did al-cohol/drugs play in your decision to use/not use condom?*

Source: Ryan et al. (2009).

Another alternative in the less structured situation is to use a matrix guide approach. A matrix interview guide includes all of the questions for an interview in grid form, with column headings indicating the general topic of the questions within that column. The interviewer's job is to ask all of the questions (and mark that she has done so) during the interview, in whatever order makes the most sense to follow the content of the responses. This format frees the interviewer from flipping pages to skip ahead or return to previous sections. However, it also requires a skilled interviewer and produces data that are not conducive to comparison, since each interviewee will have heard and answered questions in a different order.

In the matrix interview guide example in Figure 4.2, the research was focused on condom use during sexual encounters by homeless women and the role of drugs and alcohol in whether or not condom usage occurred. In the one-page interview guide, the sequence of the sexual encounters organizes the grid columns, and the aspects of the experience the researchers wish to capture organize the rows. To do these interviews, the interviewer simply asks the interviewee to "Tell me about your most recent sexual hook-up." The interview might start at any point in the grid, and the interviewer asks whatever probe or follow-up questions are needed, checking the boxes as each piece of information is mentioned and moving about the grid and asking questions until all the information has been covered. The advantages of this type of interview guide are that it can produce very natural conversations, it is only a single page (useful in many in situ interview settings), and it is easy to see if and when you have gotten all your needed information. But it should be obvious that this type of interview guide works better for some topics than for others. Phenomenological studies of highly sequenced events are a natural for this type of guide, while studies that must cover somewhat disparate topics are less so. Additionally, this type of guide works best for very skilled interviewers who are good at steering interviewees through topics and who do not need a tightly scripted guide to get the job done.

Whichever style of guide you use, its content and structure must enable you to get the information you need, produce interviews that are reasonably comfortable for both interviewers and interviewees, and facilitate the data analysis that will follow.

How Much Structure Do I Need for My IDI Guide?

As discussed at the beginning of this chapter and as evident from the discussion of types of interview instruments, there are varying degrees of structure that can be incorporated into an interview guide. The degree of structure that you use will depend on three things. First, what are your research objectives? Are you more interested in describing the range of a phenomenon or comparing opinions within or between groups? Enhancing an instrument's structure facilitates comparability across participants, participant groups, and/or interviewers, yet there is a balance between structure and flexibility to follow up on participants' unique responses. Generally speaking, a study that seeks to explore or describe can be well served by a loosely structured guide, one where the interviewer covers all of the essential domains of inquiry but not necessarily in the same order. A study that seeks to compare things will require an interview guide with more structure, to increase the validity of the comparison (see Guest et al., 2012).

The second consideration is the scope of the research. The scope of an interview guide will depend on how much is already known about a topic, both in academic literature and by the general public. Generally speaking, the more that is known about a topic, the more structure can be incorporated into the guide (Johnson & Weller, 2001). Figure 4.3 illustrates the relationship between knowledge base and structure in relation to data collection. If little is known about a topic, your discussion guide may need to be very broad and minimally structured. If on the other hand, you are speaking to someone who experienced a well-known natural disaster, for example, then you may be able to dive more quickly into the specifics of their experience of the event. In general, figure out what is the broadest level on which you need to gain knowledge, start at that broad level then move to the specifics within the interview overall and within each topic area (domains of inquiry). Remember that the less that is known about a topic, the less structure is possible in questioning—you need to be very open-ended in order not to shut off possible domains of inquiry that you may not even know exist. But structure greatly facilitates comparative analysis—across time, space, and interviewers—so for even the most exploratory, early-stage-of-the-project IDIs, at the very least we suggest establishing interview topic areas. As illustrated in Figure 4.3, data comparability is greatly facilitated by structure.

Finally, consider the research environment that you will be working in. Are you conducting the interviews? If not, is there one designated interviewer for the project or several? As the team of interviewers grows, so does the need for a structured guide. We mentioned previously that training of interviewers on the style and intent of each question is essential. Building on that idea, providing a team of interviewers with the same training on the same questions that are intended to be asked in the same order helps to limit interviewer variation that could affect the quality or reliability of your data (Guest et al., 2012).

Types of Interview Questions

In Table 4.1, we provided some examples of general types of questions that you might ask to address a particular domain. It may seem like a simple concept, but you will elicit different information depending on the type of question you ask (and how you ask it). Spradley (1979) identified over 20 specific kinds of questions that were appropriate and useful for ethnographic interviewing. Other authors

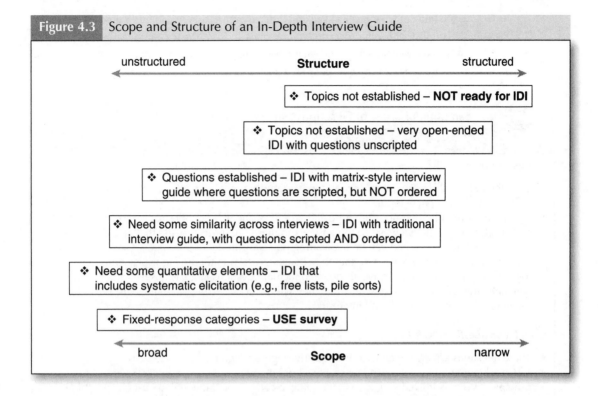

Figure 4.3 Scope and Structure of an In-Depth Interview Guide

and disciplines offer many other ways of categorizing questions. So while any list of question types will be far from exhaustive and somewhat open to dispute, the list below offers a simple typology of three major question categories—descriptive, structural, and comparative—and describes some of the question types within these categories that the authors have found most useful in doing IDIs across a wide range of projects and field settings. Table 4.2 (see page 138) provides a more detailed (yet still abridged) list of these kinds of questions as defined by Spradley (1979) and provides an example of each.

In general, descriptive questions simply ask the participant to describe something, often a recurrent or specific experience. These questions are easy to ask and answer, and as such, are commonly used at the beginning of an interview as a warm-up for both the participant and the interviewer. They might ask an interviewee to describe a typical day, a particular event or behavior, or an emotion. Perception questions fall within or are closely related to this category. We define them as questions intended to elicit attitudes, opinions, or knowledge about a topic. For example, How do you feel about the new school assignment system? Why do you think Americans have a relatively low house-hold savings rate? What do you know about the new health care law? If you are conduct-ing an evaluation or assessment of something, you will likely use perception questions to find out what people liked and disliked or how they would rate a product or service, coupled with other descriptive questions to have them describe what they thought worked well (and why) and what types of improvements they would suggest. Additional types of descriptive questions are detailed in Table 4.2.

Table 4.2 A Sampling of Types of Descriptive Interview Questions
DESCRIPTIVE QUESTIONS

"Reporter" questions

- Elicit the facts of the interviewee's experience, establishing the *who, what, when, where, how, and why* of the interview topic.
- Often the six reporter questions are especially useful at the exploratory stages of research and the early portion of an interview, since the answers to these questions provide the factual framework of the shared discussion and can be the starting points for in-depth probing.
- Care should be taken to make sure that they come across as naturally inquisitive and flow logically from one to the next. Detail-oriented factual questions can easily seem intrusive and can make interviewees self-conscious that they will get a fact wrong. Get the facts, but keep the tone friendly, conversational, and interested.

Grand tour questions (GTQs)

- These questions are also often used in the early stages of inquiry.
- GTQs ask about a topic at a very general level or get a description of a typical event, for example, "What is it like living here at the refugee camp?" or "How do you usually go about getting a meal on the table?"
- For these extremely open-ended grand tour questions the interviewees' responses tell you what they view as important and can reflect not only facts but also emotions, values, narrative styles, causative models, and vocabulary.
- GTQs can keep a researcher from straying into irrelevant or offensive lines of questioning.

*Remember the example cited in Chapter 1 about a project on employee benefits at a large copper mine? The moderator asked a grand tour question that was intended to simply be a warm-up to the specific topic of the benefits plan. But when the **grand tour** query, "What's it like working here at XYZ Copper?" produced a shouted "It sucks!", the researcher instantly understood that talking about the details of the 401(k) plan options was not important to the participants and that the research needed to go in an entirely different direction.*

Mini-tours

- Use the same question type but focus on a smaller element of a larger topic or sequence. For example, "You've given me an overview of a typical day out herding your flock, now could you tell me just about how you usually handle the mid-day meal?"

Guided tours

- The question includes the interviewee actually walking the interviewer (physically) through a task or event.

DESCRIPTIVE QUESTIONS

- The tour helps the interviewee remember details they might overlook in a purely narrative response and gives the interviewer new areas to probe.

Specific tours

- The interviewee is asked about a specific example rather than the general case, for example, asking, "What did you do yesterday from the time you got up until the time you went to bed?" instead of "What do you usually do each day from the time you get up until you go to bed?"
- For topics with low salience, such as routines, interviewees may recall details more clearly if they are answering about a specific case.

Example questions

- These can be extremely valuable in helping the researcher understand the boundaries, characteristics, and decision processes that organize interviewees' descriptions.
- Even if you believe you understand exactly what an interviewee means when she uses the phrase "hostile work environment," your interview should include a question asking "Can you give me an example of something that would make for a hostile work environment?"
- Examples improve not only your conceptual understanding of the topic, but they can also provide the quotes that help illustrate your analysis and drive home key points in the presentation of your data.

Experience questions

- Having people relate experiences and events that stand out to them can be another way of learning what is "normal" and what is exceptional from the perspective of your interviewees.
- Experience questions fall into the storytelling traditions of many cultures and can be an easy way of breaking the ice during an interview. Saying something along the lines of "You have probably had some interesting experiences while out fishing; can you recall any of them?" is bound to get an interview moving.
- The experiences people relate in response to these questions may be unusual or atypical, so use other types of questions to determine the norms.

Perception questions

- Some interviewees may assume they are supposed to stick with "just the facts," so if finding out about perceptions is one of your research objectives, you need to ask questions specifically aimed at learning your interviewees' feelings, interpretations, and opinions. As long as some rapport and trust have been established and the question flows logically, you should be able to ask such questions as "How do you feel about the new voting system here in Cairo?"

Source: Based on Spradley's (1979) typology.

Structural questions are designed to discover information about cultural or social domains, the basic units of shared knowledge in human groups, and can help elucidate how interviewees organize their world. Specifically, structural questions serve to elicit information on the range or parameters of a given domain: What are all of the ways that having a pet makes you happy? What are the kinds of cases you see here at the clinic? What brands of dishwasher detergent have you bought in the past year? You might notice that these examples essentially ask the participant to generate a list; the answers to these types of questions are therefore structured by the nature of the question. These types of question require a slightly different type of probing, since the aim is to generate an exhaustive list of elements of a specific domain. Each time the interviewee stops, the interviewer poses a question such as "Can you think of any more reasons, brands, or kinds?" until the interviewee cannot think of any new responses. Note that you may ask an interviewee to answer these questions on a personal, professional, or cultural level, depending on your research objective. "What are all of the types of drinks you serve to guests at home?" is a personal-level question, whereas the similar sounding, "What are all of the types of drinks served to guests in a home?" addresses the societal and cultural level.

Finally, comparison questions, as the name implies, use contrast and comparison to help identify relationships among items in a given domain. In some cases, this provides illumination to responses the participant has already given. In these cases, they are a little more difficult to write into an interview guide, but a well-trained interviewer can keep these in mind as potential clarification probes to get deeper, richer data. For example, if we heard from a participant that education, peers, and her job figured prominently in her attitude toward smoking, there are several comparison questions we could ask: Do education, your peers, and your job affect your attitude toward smoking in the same way, or are they different in some way? How would you rate those three factors you mentioned in terms of their influence on your attitude toward smoking? Are your education, peers, and job related in some way that they all affect your attitude? Some comparative questions can include asking interviewees to rank or rate items or to indicate a preference between two or more things.

Of course, there is no reason that these types of questions cannot be combined and juxtaposed on an interview guide—and they should be, both to address different research aims and to add variety to the guide to keep the interview (INT) interesting for the respondent (RSP). You might start with a structural question and follow up with a descriptive one:

INT: What are some of the places young men in the community hang out? (structural)

RSP: Well there is the square, the park, the bridge, and the local school yard.

INT: Can you describe what they do when they hang out at the bridge? (descriptive)

Or start with an experience question, "Tell me about your son's birth," and follow up with a perception question, "How did you feel about the interaction you had with your midwife?" Creating something like Table 4.1 will help you identify the types of data you need; you can then cross-reference those needs with the section above to get some ideas for specific question wording.

Finally, you will want to add some kind of closing question to your guide, one that allows the participant to provide additional comments on anything that has been discussed or to bring up something she feels is relevant that was not covered during the interview. A wrap-up question often takes the form, "Before we end the interview, is there anything else you would like to add?" or "Have we covered every-thing that you think is pertinent to this topic?" If the interviewee does offer additional information, be sure to ask the wrap-up question again, to determine whether there might be any other thoughts the participant would like to share.

Phrasing Questions

Once you have identified the types of questions that will best address your research objectives, you can begin thinking about how to phrase those questions. Berg relates the importance of well-phrased interview questions to the adage about garbage in/garbage out:

> Researchers must word questions so that they will provide the necessary data. . . . If the wrong questions are asked, or if questions are asked in a manner that inhibits or prevents a respondent from answering fully, the interview will not be fruitful—garbage will come out. (2009, pp. 115–116)

There are a few general guidelines that can help you in this effort. First, to maximize the inductive and conversational aspects of an interview, use simple open-ended questions. The corollary of this is to avoid or minimize use of yes/no or closed-response questions. In terms of language, this translates into beginning many questions with *what, how,* or *why,* or as a statement: "Please tell me about a time when you did *x.*" Questions beginning with *do you, who, how many,* or *when* are more likely to result in simple, one-word responses. That is not to say that you can't use these more survey-like questions, and in fact, they are the best way to elicit clear responses for some analysis purposes. For instance, if you are planning to conduct a comparative analysis, you may want to ask people, "Do you like the new gym?" to get a simple yes, no, or neutral answer before probing for the reasons why they answered as they did. This eliminates the need for analysts to later interpret answers to the similar question, "What do you think of the new gym?" and categorize them as like, dislike, or neutral, but it provides the same opportunity for a participant to describe in her own words what she does or does not like about it. In general, however, questions worded like this are the exception rather than the rule.

You should also aim to eliminate double-barrel questions, those that ask the respondent to reflect on two things at the same time (Berg, 2009). Double-barrel questions have the potential to leave you with partial, incomplete, or missing responses. For example, if we say, "Tell me how your clinic supports women with HIV and what the barriers are to improving that support," we are asking for two different kinds of information. A participant may focus on the answer to the first part, to the exclusion of the second, or vice versa. You can address the missing information using probes, but it is better practice to split the questions from the outset.

Finally, when phrasing interview questions, review the interview guide for any questions that are leading, or may be interpreted as leading. The intent, remember, is to treat the interviewee as the expert and collect his or her opinions, experiences, and/or knowledge as accurately as possible. What the interviewer knows or thinks about a topic is secondary. The obvious types of leading questions ask for or infer agreement with the interviewer's opinion and are often poorly phrased questions to begin with: "Don't you think the health care system here is great?" More subtly leading questions incorporate adjectives or judgments that the interviewee may hear as cues for the "right" answer, the one that the interviewer wants to hear. "What do you think about the great new development by the lake?" or "How do you think the rise of radical fringe groups, like the Occupy Wall Street movement, affects national politics?" are examples of less explicitly leading questions. The first pretty clearly inserts the opinion of the interviewer into the question, while the second, by labeling and coupling the Occupy movement with a radical fringe group, could be read as an indication of the researchers' own political views. Usually, leading questions are easy to identify in print and can be revised in the written interview guide; they often make their way into interviews via unscripted probes or follow-up questions, which reiterates the need to train interviewers carefully.

One other consideration in the phrasing of questions is the degree of consistency you want to maintain across interviewers, especially less experienced ones. Your research objectives, or in some cases the preferences of the research sponsors, will help you determine which, if any, of your questions need to be asked in precisely the same way for all interviews. If you go this route, make sure that all interviewers understand the need for the precise wording and that they train to get it right. There is no point in spending time carefully crafting exact words if interviewers cannot actually produce them when faced with a real live interviewee.

Sequencing Questions

The order in which you arrange questions on an interview guide deserves the same level of attention that you give to the phrasing of questions. As mentioned, a rule of thumb is to start out with "easy" questions—those that are both easy to understand and to answer—to continue the establishment of rapport and help both the participant and interviewer relax (Berg, 2009; Warren & Karner, 2010). Following this same reasoning, more sensitive questions are typically placed near the end of an interview. In terms of organizing the content of an interview in a way the interviewee can follow, researchers often use a funnel approach in which questions start out broad and move to the more specific as the interview progresses. "The danger in any interview is to rush into the central domain of the research question too quickly. Unless one understands the context surrounding the research question, the analysis will be very thin and general" (Olson, 2011, p. 56). We also advocate asking positive questions before negative ones, since people often have more to say (and with more emotion) about their negative opinions, and it is harder to bring them back to comment on the positive side of something once those emotions come into play.

Developing Transition Explanations

The final step in developing an interview guide is to create transition explanations to help the participant follow the logic or rationale for the sequencing of your questions. Scripted transitional text also serves as a touchstone for the interviewer as she leads the interview, though she will often paraphrase the written text. Transitional scripting (and scripting in general) is also extremely important in team-based research, to enhance consistency in procedures across interviewers. Transitional text is usually used at the start of the interview, as an introduction to the topics that will be covered; whenever the topic of discussion is shifting from, say, one domain to another; to provide the interviewee with a way to mark progress through the interview ("We just have two more sections to go."); or when the type of question is changing, from descriptive to structural, for example, and requires explanation. Olson provides an example of a transition statement she uses when approaching a topic in an interview that may be sensitive or difficult:

> I generally begin by saying, "Based on what you have told me so far, I have some additional questions that might be difficult to discuss. If you would rather not talk about them, please say so." . . . This approach accomplishes two important objectives. First, it emphasizes that the participant is in control of the topics discussed. Second, it gives the participant a few moments to "get ready" emotionally to discuss sensitive material if they wish to do so. (2011, p. 57)

Most guides will also include some text before and after the wrap-up question at the end of the interview, to thank the interviewee for his time and sharing his opinions and to provide any information about follow-up contact or logistics. The example in Figure 4.2a shows a sequential interview guide that includes various types of transitional statements, (annotated) in bold italics.

CONDUCTING AN IN-DEPTH INTERVIEW

After the often lengthy stages of planning and preparation for your IDIs, you will, at last, begin to actually conduct your interviews. If you have done a good job designing your project, have developed and tested an interview guide that effectively addresses your objectives, have trained your interviewers, selected suitable interviewees, and have all the interview logistics well in hand, then the actual data collection should proceed smoothly, even enjoyably. This is, after all, the beating heart of the research, the moment where questioning leads to data and, ultimately, to insight. This is also the place in which interviewer skill becomes critical. In particular, successful interviewers must develop strong skills in establishing rapport with interviewees, probing for depth, and handling interview problems.

Where/When to Conduct In-Depth Interviews

The section on planning an in-depth interview in this chapter identified the primary considerations with regard to where and when to conduct an interview. It bears repeating that in line with our respect for interview participants as experts whose time and contribution we value, the location and timing of the interview should be arranged as much as possible to suit the comfort and convenience of the interviewee. The environment of the interview, however, has implications beyond the comfort-level of the participant (Green & Hart, 1999). Conducting an interview at someone's home is obviously quite different from conducting an interview in an office building, academic institution, or health clinic. Each will have a different physical feel (sitting in arm chairs or across a table or in an exam room), will convey a different interviewer-interviewee relationship (whose "turf" you are on, who is the host with attendant responsibilities for welcoming the other, how much "authority" the interviewer carries), and come with various forms of potential interruptions (dogs barking, phones ringing, overhead music, background noise). Also, "the same person may stress different aspects of their identity in an out-patient clinic, a private room in their home, or in their workplace" (Green & Thorogood, 2009, p. 111). Think carefully in advance about what kind of interview environment a chosen location will present, and do your best to minimize any disruptive features you identify.

The timing of the interview, similarly, can have implications beyond convenience. Is the person leaving work to participate in the interview? Will she need child care at certain times? Is the interview scheduled to happen immediately before or after another appointment at the same location? Your efforts to identify these issues of timing and accommodate the interviewee will lay the foundation for good rapport during your interview.

Establishing Rapport

Imagine how off-putting it is to interact with someone who does not make eye contact, does not seem to be interested in what you are saying, or generally acts like an automaton going through the motions. Now imagine that this person has asked you to come to this interaction to help *him!* While politeness and social graces may get you through the encounter, you will likely hesitate to share information with this person and may want to end the interaction sooner than later. Thus, building rapport or a human, personal connection with the interviewee, is foundational to effective interviewing. King and Horrocks (2010) clarify, "Building rapport is not about ingratiating yourself with your participant. . . . Rapport is essentially about trust—enabling the participant to feel comfortable in opening up to you" (p. 48). As mentioned, there are things that you can do before the interview even begins to start developing rapport with an interview participant: You can return their calls or e-mails promptly, answer their questions with appropriate care, anticipate or accommodate their scheduling needs, and generally keep an open, friendly, responsive tone to all pre-interview interactions.

Once you are ready to conduct the interview, you continue to build on these previous interactions. Offer a friendly smile and a culturally appropriate greeting when you meet the interviewee at the designated location and have some small-talk topics in mind to fill the time it takes to get settled into the interview. Asking the person where they have come from or how their day is going, for example, can get conversation started. As you prepare for and start the interview, remember that nonverbal cues are important (and can constitute up to 65% of human communication!). Maintain appropriate eye contact and body positioning vis-à-vis the interviewee and use facial expression and verbal acknowledgements to show interest in the participant's story. "Rapport is built on the ability to convey empathy and understanding without judgment" (Patton, 2002, p. 366); sometimes this requires words, other times just body language. Try to avoid any distracting behaviors or gestures so the participant can focus on the questions you are asking, not the nervous thing you are doing with your hands. Related to that, think of a discreet way to keep track of time; an interviewee who sees you checking your watch or the clock may feel rushed or that he is boring you. However, keeping an appropriate pace is also important, both to keep the discussion moving and to ensure that you have enough time to complete the entire interview.

Another way to facilitate rapport is to be mindful of interviewer-interviewee characteristics. To the extent possible, try to match the gender and age of the interviewer to that of the sample population. In some cultures, this is essential, and you may need local cultural experts to help you determine the appropriate kinds of matching to consider. The social role, professional status, or perceived authority of the interviewer should also be considered. In some cases, having an interviewer and interviewee at the same professional level will be important so they can talk on a collegial, technical basis; in others, having a "novice" in a field interview an expert can be helpful in getting the interviewee to explain clearly and in simple terms information that she may otherwise have couched in discipline-specific jargon—or may not have expressed at all, having assumed it to be understood. It is important to avoid, to the extent possible, having someone in an authority relationship with the interviewee serve as interviewer (for example, a teacher interviewing students or a doctor interviewing patients). These preexisting role relationships have the potential to inhibit the interviewee's free expression of opinions and beliefs and, worse, may constitute undue inducement to participate in the first place.

Other social differences, including race, class, age, and gender can also affect the interviewer-interviewee relationship. Green and Thorogood provide an interesting example of the overlay of these characteristics and their effects on indepth interviews. They detail two female researchers, one White and one Caribbean, both of whom were conducting interviews with White and Caribbean women in Britain. The shared gender of the interviewers-interviewees in both cases was trumped by the ethnic and/or class differences perceived by the interviewees: The White researcher was more challenged to get rich information from the Caribbean women, and the researcher of Caribbean descent found the same with her White participants (2009, p.108). Matching is therefore less straightforward than it might appear, but this example illustrates the disadvantage that nonmatched interviewers face.

Presuming that you and the interviewee are well matched on at least some levels, you can also build "background" rapport into your interview guide by being mindful of the flow of questions, in terms of sequencing and transition statements. Descriptive questions are usually good conversation starters. And as mentioned previously, we advise starting with the easiest, least threatening questions, saving sensitive questions for last when the interviewee has had a chance to get comfortable with both the interview process and you personally as the interviewer.

General Interview Flow

Though every interview guide—and every interview—will be different, there is a general pattern to an interview that is maximally effective. This begins, naturally, with initial rapport building to set the interviewee at ease. When you transition from small talk to "official" interview mode, what we call "the spiel" is often a good segue. The *spiel* is simply a brief explanation of who you are, the research purpose, and what is expected from the participant. Both you and the interviewee are already aware of this information based on recruitment and scheduling interactions you have had, but restating this information signals that the interview session is about to begin, and provides another opportunity for you to reiterate the interviewee's role as expert. The informed consent process, whether written or verbal, follows next. Allow the participant enough time to actually read the consent form or study information sheet and ask any questions he may have. Before beginning the interview itself, ask whether the participant has any other questions—about the consent process, the study, or the interview itself.

Following the introductory pieces of the interview, the actual data collection on the research topic can begin. This does not mean, however, that we switch to a formal Question–Answer mode. Instead, the general flow is something like questions–probes–rapport, questions–probes–rapport, more questions–probes–rapport, and so on. As detailed earlier, questions are typically arranged so that the interview drills down to the core issues in a logical sequence that the interviewee can follow. And remember that your role as interviewer is to guide the conversation, but otherwise be a listener. As Bernard puts it, "The rule is: Get people on to a topic of interest and get out of the way. Let the informant provide information he or she thinks is important" (2000, p. 195).

At the conclusion of the interview, you will ask a closing question to ascertain that there is nothing more that the interviewee would like to add; then, you can take care of collecting demographic information or logistical details of incentive payments. Keep your digital recorder handy because often once the "official" interview has ended and you return to a more "normal" small-talk type of context, interview participants will add something that they had not previously thought of or had not thought relevant to your questions (Warren & Karner, 2010). It is perfectly acceptable—and advisable—to ask the participant if they would mind repeating their point on the record, and usually participants are happy to oblige. If you do not have the recorder with you or have left a suitable recording environment, write out detailed notes of the additional comments as soon as possible after the participant has left. You may also want to give interviewees the option of contacting you, via phone or e-mail, if they realize later that they have something to add to their comments from the interview. These postscripts provided after the participant has had some additional time to reflect on the topic of the interview can be very valuable, but if you are conducting a systematic thematic analysis, be sure to keep them in a separate "adden-dum" file related to the participant's interview file, since this information was not collected during the interview and is different from the "snapshot" of opinions collected in all of the other interviews (Guest et al., 2012).

To that point, in most cases we do not provide a copy of the interview guide in advance, just information on the general nature of the research and the types of opinions, attitudes, or experiences that will be covered during the interview. However, there are instances where sharing the guide in advance—or providing a copy of the guide at the interview—can facilitate the interview process and help the interviewee formulate richer responses to your questions. For example, in interviews one of the authors conducted on the return of genetic research results (Namey & Beskow, 2011), she e-mailed a copy of the interview guide to participants whom she could not interview in person for two, related, reasons. First, the interview covered a fairly complex topic that required clear communication about the definition of genetic results. Second, since some of these interviews had to be conducted via telephone, where facial expressions and other nonverbal communication cannot serve to express confusion or lack of understanding, provision of the guide allowed interviewees to follow along and reread passages if necessary before providing a response, without having to verbalize their confusion. This helped to ensure that responses were based on a clear understanding of the question and also served to lessen any disparity between phone and in-person interviews. Similarly, if you are asking participants to comment or provide their opinion on a hypothetical scenario or case that requires more than a few sentences to describe, it is helpful to provide a written copy of the scenario to the interviewee so that he or she might read along and refer back to the details as necessary.

Probing

In-depth probing of participant responses is the defining feature of in-depth interviews (and focus groups) and is critical to the success—in data collection terms—of an interview. So what is a *probe*? In qualitative research, we use the term to refer to an inductive, unscripted question asked by an interviewer based on a participant's previous response. Seidman (2006) proposes to call the process *exploring*, as "probe" conjures images of "a sharp instrument pressing on soft flesh [and] . . . also conveys a sense of the powerful interviewer treating the participant as an object" (p. 83). While we agree with both of these assessments, we use the terms *probe* and *probing* here for consistency with the literature and for the practical reason that there is both a noun and verb version of the term.

As questions asked in response to an interviewee's answer, probes are *not* sub-questions; they cannot be anticipated or written ahead of time. However, you can still train an interviewer on effective probing that is guide specific, since any probe used should be guided by the question objective, which *is* known from the outset. A probe that does not address the question objective wastes precious interview minutes; therefore, we do not probe out of curiosity or for the sake of probing only. Probes explicitly seek clarification or expansion of a respondent's answer and should be phrased in neutral language.

> The key to successful interviewing is learning how to probe effectively—that is, to stimulate a respondent to produce more information, without injecting yourself so much into the interaction that you get only a reflection of yourself in the data. Learning the art of probing takes practice. (Bernard, 2000, p. 196)

There are two main types of probes, indirect and direct. *Indirect* probes are those that keep the interviewee talking and encourage further explanation without asking another question. Examples include simple affirmations that the interviewer is listening and interested: a smile, nod of the head, "mm-hmm," or "I see." You might also rephrase and repeat what the participant has just said, "So you said you went to the clinic." Or, if appropriate, you might show that you have understood and can empathize with the person: "I can see why you say that would be hard for you." In all of these examples, the idea is to acknowledge the interviewee's response and encourage her to go further with it. Silence is also an excellent indirect probe; letting a response hang in the air while maintaining eye contact signals that you are anticipating or awaiting additional comment; it is also the most difficult type of probe to master (Bernard, 2000), because of our discomfort with "awkward" silence. But it is precisely this discomfort that you are relying on to encourage the interviewee to elaborate on her last statement.

Direct probes are less subtle. The interviewer asks clearly, "What do you mean when you say X?" or "Can you give an example of Y?" Probes may also be statements: "Tell me more about that," or "Explain that to me a little bit." Bernard (2000, pp. 196–201) provides several additional sub-types of probes that are variations on these types of questions.

The question or language of a probe is important only in terms of whether it elicits an expanded response. In refining their original answer in response to the probe, interviewees often sharpen their thoughts to provide what can be critical definitions or understandings of your research topic. This richness and depth of response is what distinguishes in-depth interviewing, in particular, from other data collection methods, and reemphasizes the importance of effective probing. In Table 4.3 (see page 150), we offer several tips for avoiding common probing mistakes; contrast the examples there with those presented in Table 4.4, Probing Exemplars (see page 151).

Table 4.3 Tips for Avoiding Common Probing Mistakes, With Examples From Transcripts

To Probe Effectively, DON'T . . .	Example
Finish participants' thoughts	RSP: Even [if] I don't have money to go [to] the doctor . . . INT: Yes . . . RSP: She ends up giving me money so that I see to it that— INT: You go see the doctor.
Push or pry too hard	INT: Can you explain for me the work your partner is doing? RSP: Yes, well I don't like explaining that to you. INT: You can explain to me. RSP: Mmm! INT: What kind of job? What kind of job is it that cannot be described? RSP: Well, I don't think it's the kind of work that can be explained, truly speaking. *[Might have tried, "Why don't you like explaining that?" instead.]*
Antagonize the participant, especially for information of limited use	INT: Well, how old was she? RSP: She was two years elder than me. While I was 14 she was 17. INT: You were 14? RSP: Mmm. INT: She is 2 years elder than you? Surely she must be . . . 16 . . . if she is 2 years older, she must be— RSP: Yes, she was 16.
Phrase your probe judgmentally	INT: If I may ask you . . . why do you have so many sexual partners?
Interrupt the participant	INT: Do you have any other word you can say to explain this sexual activity? RSP: Do you mean— INT: Your own explanation, what is your explanation of it? RSP: Well, my understanding if we . . . let me say "ke robetse" with this female person— INT: That is, when you sleep with a female person, what do you say when . . . ?
Accept simple answers at face value	INT: What qualities do you look for in a person to end up saying you love him? RSP: I look at how genuine his love is. INT: Mmm. *[Missed probes: "What do you mean by genuine? How can you tell his love is genuine?"]*

To Probe Effectively, DON'T . . .	Example
Read directly from the interview guide	INT: Did your views of the hospital change after your experience? If so, how? *[If so, how here is actually a sub-question, but an experienced interviewer will follow up the yes/no answer to the first question in a less abrupt/scripted way.]*
Focus on getting to the next question to the exclusion of probing	INT: How was your experience at the hospital? RSP: Pretty good. I felt well cared for. There was one jerk doctor who really made me mad, but otherwise, everyone was nice. INT: So they were nice. How was your room? *[Missed probes, if research objective is to learn about hospital experience: "Tell me more about the 'jerk' doctor. What made you mad?"]*
Lead the participant or insert your own opinions	INT: How do you feel about donating your frozen embryos for use in stem cell research? RSP: I'm still on the fence. It depends. INT: So you think stem cell research is good?

Table 4.4	Exemplary In-Depth Interview Probing
Research Question	**Interviewee Response and *Follow-up* Probe**
What makes a good birth experience for women?	RSP: But I didn't wanna scream, I didn't wanna yell, I wanted to be very ladylike about the whole birthing process, so I remember I did say "shit" once, and that was it. So I was proud of myself for that too. *INT: What about that was that important to you?*
	RSP: It's very important that you feel like you've got some control. Over the pain, over the . . . who's in the room, that kind of thing. *INT: Okay. So tell me a little bit more then about how you were able to feel that sense of control.*
	RSP: I finally let them give me an epidural, and that helped me a lot. *INT: How did the epidural help you?*

(Continued)

Table 4.4 (Continued)	
Research Question	**Interviewee Response and *Follow-up* Probe**
Why are there so many frozen embryos in storage?	INT: What has prevented you from deciding what to do with your frozen embryos? RSP: I haven't decided yet because I'm not crazy about the available options. *INT: What in particular about the options has prevented you from making a decision?*
	INT: How would you feel about donating an embryo to another couple if you had extra embryos? RES: I probably wouldn't do that. *INT: Okay, why would you be unlikely to do that?*

Most Common In-Depth Interview Mistakes (and solutions)

During our years as researchers, we have seen—and learned from—a lot of mistakes in the conduct of in-depth interviews. The text box below summarizes our tips for effective interviewing, to help you avoid common interviewing mistakes. One mistake is a simple lack of training on how to effectively conduct an in-depth interview. On paper, the only skills that seem necessary are the ability to read (the interview guide) and ask questions (of the interviewee). If this chapter has not convinced you that there is more to it than that, think about the last time you saw an amateur or guest interviewer on local television and compare that to a scene from Oprah or Larry King. In-depth interviewing for research purposes is different, but the same "art" applies. You have to be able to carry in your mind a general idea of the topics you want to cover, ask thoughtful questions, listen to the answer with one ear toward how the answer relates to the other topics on your list (to make smooth transitions) and the other ear toward the content of the response, so that you can pick up on and probe into interesting ideas or phrases (see also Seidman, 2006, pp. 78–79 for a description of the types of listening necessary for effective interviewing). With respect to listening, interviewing is analogous to interpreting, where you are listening/processing/speaking/listening simultaneously. And of course, an interviewer must perform this mental juggling act with a rapport-encouraging smile and body language as well (Green & Thorogood, 2009). Fortunately, the solution to lack of training is at least easily identifiable: training! "Interviewing is without a doubt a skill that improves with experience, perhaps above all in managing the potential tension between listening closely and maintaining a sense of where you are—and where you are going—in the interview as a whole" (King & Horrocks, 2010, p. 60). As detailed previously, we recommend role-playing exercises, mock interviews, pilot interviews, informal practice sessions—in short, whatever level of training and practice you need to master the basic skills of interviewing. Also, remember to practice your spiel and to be familiar with your recording equipment (if using) because confidence in these minor areas can bolster your overall sense of readiness.

The second mistake we often see in in-depth interviewing is relying on interviewing experience and skills in lieu of preparation for a specific set of interviews. Even the best interviewers will be challenged to enter an interview "cold"—with little background information or familiarity with the research topic—and then to elicit meaningful information that will address the given research objectives. We have said that probing is an essential feature of in-depth interviewing, and that the direction and intent of your probes should be based on gathering more research objective-specific information. Clearly an interviewer will not be able to effectively probe if she is not intimately familiar with the ultimate goals of the interview. Missed or misdirected probes are painful to read in an interview transcript, as some of the examples in Table 4.3 illustrate. The obvious solution to this problem is exposure to and understanding of an interview guide with sufficient time to review it and to practice the flow of questions. An interviewer should be able to mentally cross-reference research objectives and questions on the interview guide with ease and familiarity so that upon hearing an interviewee's response, he can evaluate whether it is sufficient or should be probed to elicit information more closely related to the research objectives.

Another common mistake relates to the personality of the interviewer. As we have mentioned, and as with any other professional skill, in-depth interviewing comes more naturally to some personalities than others. For instance, someone who typically sits back and listens to others will have an easier time than someone who likes to be the center of attention. Similarly, a person who is naturally sociable will find building rapport easier than someone who is shy or reserved. The worst interviews are those where the interviewer dominates the discussion or simply reads directly from the guide with no effort to engage the interviewee. In a great interview, the interviewer should be almost invisible, stepping in at appropriate intervals to ask a question, but otherwise letting the participant be the "expert" she is on the given topic. "You need to balance your personality with the interviewing situation. If you are too aggressive for the situation, back off a bit; if you are too passive, force yourself to follow up a bit more" (Rubin & Rubin, 2005, p. 81). Experience with different interview protocols in various settings with a range of respondents will best help you determine where your personality-related strengths and weaknesses lie, yet simply considering how aspects of your personality might affect your interviewing style can focus your attention.

Tips for Effective Interviewing

- Practice interviewing
  - Role-playing exercises, pilot interviews, informal practice sessions
- Practice using the equipment
  - Check batteries (have spares), microphone
  - Know how to use special features (do not use voice-activated recording)
- Know your research objectives
- Know your "spiel"
- Know your interview guide/topics
- Be respectful and be the novice
  - Humility is the single most important interviewer quality!
- Let the interviewee do 90% of the talking

Dealing With Emergent Issues

No matter how well prepared you or your interviewers are, there will always be conditions in an interview setting that are beyond your control: Someone gets paged and has to leave; the electricity goes out; a child or colleague repeatedly interrupts; you realize two questions into the interview that this person cannot answer your questions; your recorder breaks; the interviewee becomes extremely emotional. The list of potential issues that can disrupt an interview goes on and on. We try to minimize the effect of these issues on a case by case basis, but the general guidance in this type of situation is to manage the circumstances at hand with professionalism, respect for the interviewee, and a sense of humor. Consider how much time you (both) have put into the interview, how much data you have collected, how the issue or interruption is affecting the interview, whether rescheduling is an option, and how you feel about the possibility of "losing" this interview opportunity. In any case, where an interview is cut short, the interviewee should be provided whatever incentive was promised. Beyond that, assess the costs and benefits of continuing the interview under the current circumstances, communicate your assessment to the interviewee, and together, decide whether to address the issue and continue, continue without addressing the issue, or end the interview early (and potentially reschedule). For example, if the electricity goes out but there is plenty of light and the room is not uncomfortably hot or cold (and the outage is not caused by something dangerous), you can acknowledge the outage, be glad for your battery-powered recorder, and continue the interview. If that trusty recorder malfunctions at the beginning of an interview with a key stakeholder, consider whether your research would benefit more from canceling this appointment (in hopes of rescheduling) or keeping the appointment and relying on handwritten notes. In this scenario, as in most, each alternative has advantages and disadvantages to be weighed, and the right answer will depend on the interviewer, the participant's schedule, and the nature (and time line) of the research.

Below is a list of some of the most common problems we encounter when conducting in-depth interviews and suggestions for handling them.

Interruptions—Interviews conducted at homes, places of business, or in semipublic settings are subject to interruptions from family members, the press of business, or nosy bystanders. As much as possible, head these issues off before they start by selecting a location that is private or somewhat secluded, impressing on your interviewee that you will need their undivided attention during the interview and asking others for their cooperation in letting the interview proceed. That said, there is no way to stop small children from needing attention or to keep your interviewees from having minor personal emergencies. If these occur, relax, wait it out, and resume or reschedule the interview at a time that works better. If this is not possible, admit defeat, thank the interviewee, and move on to your next appointment. Not every interview will be as productive as you would like and many a colorful fieldwork story is built on "the one that got away."

Inappropriate participants—Despite all your planning, you may find yourself conducting an IDI with an interviewee with whom you cannot complete a usable interview. There are many ways this can occur—people sometimes misrepresent themselves during recruitment, they may have mental or other personal issues that make them unable to answer questions, the questioning may cause them to become emotionally distraught or belligerent, they may be unable to articulate their opinions clearly enough to give good answers, or they may simply be less knowledgeable about the topics than you expected. In each of these situations, you must ask yourself whether you can salvage any part of the interview. If you can, proceed with whatever parts of the interview seem viable. If you cannot, acknowledge this fact and quickly, politely, and safely end the session.

This can be difficult, especially with upset or belligerent interviewees. One of the authors (Mitchell) recently had to terminate an interview with a man who repeatedly became upset by the interview topic. Attempts to calm him worked momentarily, but his ire and agitation would return each time he touched on the topic. The interviewer was in the process of politely dismissing him when her efforts were preempted by two of her clients barging into the interview room. The client observers had become distressed watching the failed interview in the observation room because they feared the interviewer was in physical danger from the interviewee. While the interviewer did not share the clients' sense of imminent danger, she agreed the interview was not salvageable and helped remove the interviewee from the premises as gently as possible. Even in less extreme situations, there is no reason to waste your or the interviewee's time asking questions that the interviewee can't helpfully answer, so preparing an exit strategy and ending the interview is sometimes the best you can do.

Status issues—We mentioned that interviewers should be matched with their interviewees according to key demographic characteristics when it is likely to have an effect on the quality of the interview. This relates not only to modulating the personality of the interviewer, as discussed above, but also in limiting or managing status differences between interviewer and interviewee. In cases where the interviewer is perceived by the interviewee to be of higher professional, educational, or socioeconomic status, the interviewee may try to craft her answers so as to impress the interviewer—or to avoid embarrassment. This may occur when interviewing "elite" respondents as well, when someone in a position of authority offers "the party line" or PR-pitch rather than information based on personal experience or opinions (Green & Thorogood, 2009). In contrast, when an interviewee perceives herself to be of much higher status than the interviewer, this can sometimes lead to a struggle for control of the interview, with the interviewee asserting her expertise and knowledge not only over the domain of inquiry but also over the entire interview process, derailing the interviewer's attempts to guide the discussion. Status differences in both directions "can deleteriously affect the course of an interview in two ways: directly, by inhibiting interviewees from discussing particular topics (e.g., for fear of appearing ignorant or losing face), and indirectly, by preventing the building of rapport between interviewer and interviewee" (King & Horrocks, 2010, pp. 56–57). When these status issues arise unexpectedly during the course of an interview, you can adjust your tone, communication style (verbal and nonverbal), and approach to questions to minimize the differences.

DOCUMENTING THE INTERVIEW

When the interviewing is done, the analysis begins. But what, exactly, will you be analyzing? Your analytical capabilities and outputs will be shaped and limited by the methods you use to document your IDIs. As with any other data collection event, the more thorough your documentation, the more extensive and flexible your analysis can be. But doing research in the field often means making trade-offs, and documentation is an area where these trade-offs may occur.

Use of Audio-Recording

We have mentioned the recording of in-depth interviews several times in this chapter, so it will likely not come as a surprise that we recommend audio recording every interview, if possible. Digital recorders are so small, light, and dependable (and relatively inexpensive) that you can easily take one to any interview location, place it between you and the interviewee, and capture a more accurate and complete record of the interview than you could get with handwritten or typed notes. You may also choose to use video recording devices or a combined note-taking–recording device, such as Livescribe. These tools capture a complete verbal record of the interview sessions, with the capability of later synching specific handwritten notes with corresponding points in the audio recording. Such recording greatly improves the quality of the data collected and is a requirement for analytic approaches that require verbatim data, such as many forms of text analysis.

The reduced size and portability of digital recording equipment also means they are less obtrusive and that interview participants often forget about them quickly, reducing the potential impediment to openness that could come from being "on the record." However, be aware of the different associations that various people may ascribe to the recording process:

> For example, to a young offender it may be a reminder of procedures in the criminal justice system, and evoke suspicion or hostility. For others it may be seen as a sign of the "serious" nature of the project, and encourage them to make an effort to provide the interviewer with "what she wants." While you can never be certain in advance how any one person will react to being recorded, you can often anticipate likely responses and seek to take action to alleviate potential problems. (King & Horrocks, 2010, pp. 44–45)

Despite the convenience and rigor audio recording provides, compelling reasons not to record do exist. For example, the material you seek may be so sensitive that interviewees will not give permission for recording. Or the field setting may make recording problematic (too much background noise, dirt, wind, no reliable source of electricity or batteries), or having digital records may create a risk for you or your interviewees. In our experience, though, these are rare exceptions. As Bernard advises, "Use a tape recorder in all structured and semi-structured interviews, except where people specifically ask you not to" (2000, p. 204) or where extenuating circumstances prevent it.

Note Taking

If recording is not an option for some reason, try to plan to have a dedicated note-taker in addition to the interviewer. This again will allow the interviewer to focus on conducting the interview rather than documenting it. But where a dedicated note-taker is not available or where the presence of a note-taker might impede the flow of the interview, one person may have to act as both interviewer and note-taker. In some cases, even the presence of a note pad and pencil may not be allowed in the interview setting and documentation of the interview may not occur until the interview is completed.

In a situation where you do have a dedicated note-taker, establish roles up front for the interviewer and note-taker. Will the note-taker be allowed to ask questions or probe? Likely not. But he can ask "missed" questions at the end of the interview, if this is agreed upon ahead of time. In working with a note-taker, as with using a recorder, discretion is key to minimizing the interference that documentation of the interview can cause. Introduce the note-taker at the beginning of the interview so that the interviewee is aware of the note-taker's role. Then, the note-taker should fade into the background and avoid making eye contact with the interviewee or otherwise signaling that he should be included in the discussion.

The note-taker should have or develop a decipherable shorthand system and expand his notes immediately after the interview to capture as much detail as possible. The key to doing this well is to do it quickly. Human memory is fragile and field notes that made sense when they were written may be almost unintelligible (or unreadable) hours or days later. Unless your note-taker is a court stenographer, the initial notes from your interviews will not be a complete verbatim transcript of your interviews, so as soon as circumstances allow, the interviewer and any other members of the research team who were present during the interview should review and expand the notes.

If you are recording the interview, recognize that you still have the option of taking notes. Recording devices sometimes fail, storage media get lost, files get erased.[1] Duplicate documentation methods are cheap insurance against data loss or the expense of having to repeat interviews. One of the authors works frequently in market research, and her standard IDI documentation includes digital video, double digital audio—using two separate recorders—and a live note-taker. While this may seem like overkill to some field researchers, it is very reassuring to both the research team and the sponsors to know that every part of every interview will be available for analysis. And some interviews are "more unique" and less replaceable than others. Namey, for example, conducted 100 interviews on women's birth experiences, one of which was "lost" to equipment failure. This particular interview was with a mother who happened to experience a pregnancy complication that occurs in only 1 in 10,000 cases. The likelihood of someone else expressing the same perspectives on her birth experience was therefore

---

[1]In addition, in many contexts, the sight of someone taking notes during an interview gives the impression that what the interviewee is saying is important (and it is!) thus enhancing trust and rapport.

very small. In this case, the woman was gracious enough to repeat the interview so the data were not entirely lost, but the second interview was not exactly the same as the first. "A lot of very bad things can happen to tape [or digital recordings], and if you haven't got backup notes, you're out of luck" (Bernard, 2000, p. 206).

Not all researchers (including Guest) are convinced that note-taking is necessary for in-depth interviews that are audio recorded. Their rationale is twofold. They argue that the interviewer should concentrate entirely on the interview process and asking good follow-up questions rather than dividing attention between asking questions and taking notes (which is a skill in and of itself!). Having a dedicated note-taker working alongside the interviewer obviates this problem, but this is a luxury not often permitted in field research. Guest and others also contend that the risk of losing an interview is extremely low and not always worth the extra effort of taking notes. That said, if you have one chance to interview the president, a rock star, or some other type of unique, hard-to-recruit participant (such as the unique mother described above), then by all means employ multiple recording safeguards. The key is to balance the chance of possible loss with the cost (in money and time) of safeguarding.

Interviewing in Teams

While a one-on-one in-depth interview is ideal, there are times when a research project calls for team interviewing for purposes ranging from mentoring a novice interviewer to the need for a translator to the safety of interviewers. The addition of a third person to the interview dynamic can be awkward, so we suggest clarifying in advance who will be the primary interviewer. Explain this relationship and the reason for it clearly to the interviewee at the outset of the interview. As with the note-taker situation described above, the second interviewer should ideally fade into the background. It may be more appropriate in this instance for the second person to maintain eye contact and body language that suggests he is actively engaged in the interview, but unless there is a specific need for interviewers to take turns leading the interview, the secondary interviewer should save additional questions or probes for the end of the interview.

Post-Interview Debrief

Whether you are interviewing alone or with a partner, plan to set aside 15 to 20 minutes after the interview—or as soon as possible that day—to evaluate how the interview went. This type of debriefing can help you identify what information you collected in the interview that was new or novel, what themes you have heard before, which questions worked well or poorly, and any additional questions or sub-questions that you might want to add to the guide. You may also include information on the interview environment or your perceptions of the interviewee and how she received your questions. Warren and Karner suggest making notes on

> everything you can remember about the context of the interview: where it took place; how the respondent was dressed, looked and behaved before, during and after the interview; any body language that would not be captured in an audio recording; and your interpretation [set off in brackets like these] of the respondent's appearance, demeanor, and body language. (2010, p. 168)

Interview debriefing notes can be appended to the interview transcript (or inserted in a note at the beginning) so that others reading the transcript will have the benefit of your experience and observations in interpreting the data. Note, however, that these debriefing notes are not "source" data, from the interviewee, and should be coded and analyzed separately if included in an analysis (Guest et al., 2012). In Chapter 5, we share a sample focus group debriefing form (Figure 5.2). You might use this form as a template for structuring your in-depth interview debriefing notes as well.

IN-DEPTH INTERVIEW VARIATIONS

As mentioned briefly in the discussion of interview logistics, not every in-depth interview occurs face-to-face. Distance, timing, and convenience can all affect when and how an interview is conducted, and current technology has enabled variations on IDIs that allow researchers to use the technique in settings where they cannot be face-to-face with their interviewees. Logistics aside, you might also consider the sensitivity of the topic and whether remote interviewing might enhance a participant's feeling of anonymity in an important way—making her more likely to share information on socially "undesirable" behavior—(Warren & Karner, 2010), or, whether the topic is simply emotionally sensitive, in which case a face-to-face interview might be preferable (Olson, 2011). Figure 4.4 provides a comparison of characteristics of different modes of conducting IDIs (and focus groups), while Table 4.5 details the pros and cons of each.

Figure 4.4	Modifying the Medium for Conducting In-Depth Interviews				
Medium	Place	Time	Non-verbal Cues	Probing	Focus Group Appropriate
Face to face	Same	Same	Yes	Yes	Yes
Telephone	Different	Same	No	Yes	Yes
Email	Different	Different	No	No	No
Online/IM	Different	Same	Some	Yes	Some

Table 4.5	Advantages and Disadvantages of Different Remote IDI Media	
IDI Variation Type	**Interviewee Response and Follow-Up Probe**	**Cons**
Phone or voice-over-Internet	• Enables cost-effective IDIs with interviewees in geographically distant or highly dispersed locations • Can be useful when interviewees need to maintain a degree of anonymity	• Can be more difficult to build rapport without face-to-face contact • Interviewer loses the visual cues of body language to help in ascertaining interviewee's meaning or comprehension • Requires both interviewer and interviewee to have access to reliable phone connections
Internet—written	• Exchange of written questions and answers can be done "live" in a single session or as a threaded discussion over days or weeks • Generates a full written record of responses • For some interviewees, the process creates more thoughtful responses	• As with phone, rapport may be impaired, and body language cues are absent • Respondents who can't or do not like to type may give shorter, less complete answers • Requires literate interviewees with keyboard and Internet capabilities
Internet—video	• Often a good approximation of face-to-face interviewing • Cost-effective, and good for geographically distant or dispersed interviewees • Enables a full record of the session	• Requires broadband Internet, webcam/speakers and some degree of technical savvy on the part of both the interviewer and interviewee

King and Horrocks (2010) provide a detailed review of the reasons for conducting interviews remotely, highlighting the special considerations necessary for each mode. Here, we review a few of the major differences and challenges for conducting in-depth interviews via remote methods.

For telephone interviews, consider that establishing rapport when you cannot observe nonverbal communication can be more challenging, and it takes a little extra time at the beginning of the interview to try to establish a personal connection with the participant. You might also request that the interviewee be available on a landline if possible, in a private location, to lessen the potential for disruptions to the telephone connection or interview itself. Being visually disconnected from one another also provides more opportunities for the interviewer or interviewee's attention to stray, particularly if there are other things going on in the environment where they are taking the call (e-mail, colleagues, family members, television). That said, we have conducted telephone and in-person interviews within the scope of the same project and have not found substantial differences in the types of information elicited; Sturges and Hanrahan (2004) found the same. You may have to work a little harder or pay closer attention during a telephone interview, but it is possible to obtain important information from distant sources this way.

If you arrange an online interview, that might refer to either an instant message or chat session or a call via an online video-calling or -conferencing service, like Skype. The instant message route poses the same problems as telephone, with the added detraction of not having verbal cues (tone of voice, modulation, hesitations) to assist the communication. There is also the problem of asynchronicity of typing, where you may be typing a probe while the interviewee is adding a follow-up thought of her own, resulting in "cross talk" that disrupts the flow of the interview. For these reasons, if online interviewing is the ultimate choice, you may consider using voice or video services rather than instant messaging. Or, you may prefer to capitalize on the asynchronous nature of e-mail communication and "conduct" the interview by sending the interviewee the list of questions and having her send back her responses. Meho (2006) discusses the benefits and challenges of e-mail interviewing in detail.

IN-DEPTH INTERVIEW OUTPUTS

After completing a series of in-depth interviews, what do you have in terms of physical output? In the best case scenario, you have hours of clearly organized digitally recorded data ready to be systematically transcribed and analyzed, along with associated debriefing notes. You might also have free lists that were generated, pile sort data, drawings, photographs, time lines, and/or maps to augment your output (see Chapter 6). At worst you have a collection of interview guides with notes in the margins; audio files stored on your digital recorder, laptop, and a USB drive; and various other handwritten notes, lists, or sketches. No matter how well you conduct the interviews, the utility of the information you collect will depend on its being organized and accessible (see Chapter 7 for tips on data management). Table 4.6 details several of the common types of in-depth interview output and offers some of the advantages and disadvantages of each type for your consideration.

WORKING INTERNATIONALLY

Moving your research across borders or between cultures presents additional considerations for planning and conducting in-depth interviews. If you are planning to conduct your interviews in a setting where you do not speak the language and/or are

Type of Output	Advantages	Disadvantages
Summary notes	As a supplemental form of output (debriefing notes, for example), summary notes provide a quick overview of the important issues or themes discussed during the interview. These notes are helpful for small, time-sensitive studies with an immediate applied focus. (For example, an on-site program evaluation where you want to get a general feel for the range and types of challenges staff are encountering.)	As primary output, summary notes provide limited information and weak evidence for any findings you report; it is difficult to perform a systematic analysis on notes, and you will not have verbatim quotes to strengthen your argument. Also, you lose the richness and depth that are the strength of in-depth interview data.
Expanded interview notes (from a dedicated note-taker)	Expanded interview notes provide an acceptable record of the interview if recording is not possible. You may be able to do a structured analysis (providing all questions were asked of all participants), and you may have some verbatim quotes to augment your analysis findings. Expanded notes, done well, can capture the fundamental points of the interview for a descriptive, summary analysis.	The quality of expanded interview notes is very dependent on the skill of the note-taker; notes taken by an inexperienced note-taker may not provide much detail, nor adequately capture the participant's response. With expanded notes, it is still not possible in most cases to "reread" the interview to assess the participant's intended meanings.
Audio (or video) recordings	Interview recordings provide a verbatim account of the interview, which accommodates the widest range of analytic options, including thematic and linguistic analysis. They also capture the interviewee's tone and style of speech, which can be important in understanding a response.	It is difficult to work solely with audio or video files, so a transcript is often produced to provide a textual version for analysis. Also, if the interview is conducted in a language you do not speak, translation will be necessary.
Verbatim transcript	Typed transcripts of interviews are the most common form of output and, since they are based on the verbatim recording, present a similarly wide range of analysis options. Use of a transcription protocol (see Chapter 7) will help ensure consistency of transcript style for added rigor. The verbatim transcript is considered the gold standard of most in-depth interviewing.	Transcripts take time to produce (typically about 4 hours per hour of recorded text), and a one-hour interview may produce 20 to 30 pages of text, which can multiply quickly (consider 20 interviews is then 400–600 pages).

Table 4.6 Common Types of In-Depth Interview Output

not a native of or expert in the culture, your primary concern will be one of translation—not only in the sense of direct translation of the language but also more figuratively, in terms of translating the tips on interview logistics presented in this chapter to appropriately reflect the cultural and social norms of the participant population. Note that although this section was inspired by our work overseas, there are plenty of "international" research contexts, questions, and populations here in the United States where attention to linguistic and cultural detail will be as important (for example, working with Somali immigrants in Minnesota, Hispanic migrant workers in the Southwest, or Haitians in Miami). To acknowledge this breadth of context, we will use the term *field* to denote a setting outside of the researcher's native language or culture.

Wherever your field may be, if you are not fluent in the language or culture of a given population we recommend collaborating with a local researcher and research staff to conduct in-depth interviews. The benefits of "going local" in this regard are threefold:

1. You will have the advantage of having your research objectives and interview questions reviewed and critiqued by a cultural expert, who may be able to provide important contextual nuance to your data collection plans.
2. You will be able to conduct the interviews (via the local research staff) in the local language, which both widens the potential participant pool and facilitates participants' clear communication of ideas and experiences because they have access to local idioms, metaphors, and other parts of language-specific speech.
3. You will have access to an emic perspective or insider's interpretation of the data collected, which will complement and supplement the perspective you bring to the research.

Translation

Implementing research that is developed in one context and conducted in another (foreign) one immediately raises questions of translation—of the informed consent documents and interview guides and, ultimately, of the data. Translation here primarily refers to the process of converting written words and ideas from one language to another, which is never as literal or straightforward as it sounds. Even if you will end up working through an interpreter, it is helpful to present the interpreter with a professionally translated version of the interview guide from the outset, so that he can see the intended questions stated in the non-English language before any interviews begin. Once a translated version is drafted, it should be used alongside the

English version in training field staff so that they might provide additional insight and perspective on how effectively the translated language can be used to elicit the information required to meet the study objectives.

Interpretation

Sometimes budget constraints, time lines, or other logistical issues preclude collaboration with local research teams, in which case you might use an interpreter to help you conduct IDIs. This creates an interview situation similar to, but different from, the scenario of interviewing in teams described earlier in this chapter. Like interviewing in teams, interviewing through an interpreter requires clear delineation of roles, explanation of these roles to the interviewee, and strategic placement of the interpreter to minimize the distraction of a potential three-way conversation. However, an interpreter will be a crucial conduit through which questions are asked and answered; the interviewer cannot independently assess how well the information is being relayed. Screening and training of potential interpreters is therefore vital. Interpreters should be incorporated into the planning process of any in-depth interview research as soon as possible and given the same type of training that local interviewers would receive so that they are well versed in both the background and rationale for in-depth interviewing and probing, and, in the specific research objectives and interview guide. The interpreter will benefit from having a local-language version of the interview script, to become familiar with the types, nature, and wording of questions the interviewer will be asking.

Discuss with your interpreter what kind of interpretation you expect, whether more literal or verbatim (suggested) or a looser paraphrasing. You should also stress that the interpreter should not "screen" information or "make it nice" in an attempt to avoid interviewer–interviewee–interpreter discomfort or embarrassment, or, to in any way change the tenor of a response. However, there will always be judgment calls on the part of the interpreter. Green and Thorogood (2009, p. 99) provide a compelling example from Temple's work with British–Polish families of "the need for open and reflexive debate about how utterances are interpreted."

My translator had written the following:

"Women can organize everything, but they cannot lead."

Going back to the interview, I translated as

"Women are allowed to organize everything but to take the lead on nothing."
Discussing the differences with my translator we agreed that from a word
for word translation the statement could be translated either way. We

discussed our views on women's position in society and discovered that they were very different. (Temple, 1997, p. 616)

A professional interpreter will strive to convey the literal and contextual meaning of responses accurately, but on-the-fly interpretation (even more so than translation) inherently incorporates elements of the interpreter's own world view. But again, training and practice can help the interviewer and interpreter learn to maximize their shared relationship to and understanding of the interviewee.

As far as logistical considerations, United Nations interpreter protocol suggests that the interpreter sit behind the left shoulder of the speaker, in this case, the interviewer. This makes it easier for the interviewee to see both the interviewer and interpreter in one line of vision. The interviewer should ask the question of the interviewee, maintaining eye contact and body language as if they were speaking the same language, and maintain attention on the interviewee as the interpreter relays the question. Probes and follow-up questions should be asked in the same way. In terms of logistics, interviews that are conducted through an interpreter should be audio or video recorded so that there is a record of the conversation—including the interpretation—should it ever need to be verified. The later transcription may include only the English translation of the interview, but an independent bilingual person could assess the accuracy of the interpreted and/or translated data if there is a digital recording on file.

Matching Interviewers and Interviewees

As in domestic settings, appropriate pairings of interviewers and interviewees is an important consideration in field settings; the difference is in the "rules" about what constitutes a good (or bad) pairing. Characteristics such as gender, age, status, and professional role will have different relative importance in varied cultural contexts. Caste systems or tribal hierarchies, religious practices, gender norms, and age-group cohorts may all affect the interviewer-interviewee relationship. In a highly traditional Muslim culture, for example, a male-female pairing would not be acceptable in most cases. Or in a society with esteemed elders, it may be considered impertinent for a youthful interviewer to be asking personal and potentially sensitive questions of an elder. (Often the nature of the information being elicited factors in to these considerations.) A local cultural "expert" should be able to help you identify and strategize about potential problem pairings, and if you are working with a local research team, your team should be built to suit. If you are working with an interpreter, these same rules will apply.

Building Rapport

Interviewer-interviewee matching is a first step to building rapport. As discussed in detail in this chapter, good rapport with an interviewee encourages more open and honest responses to your interview questions. Here again, the rules for establishing rapport vary from field site to field site. If you are working with local research staff, your interviewers will likely know the acceptable—and effective—ways to build rapport with the sample population. Be sure to discuss ideas for enhancing rapport during interviewer training so that they will be explicitly aware of their body language and tone, as appropriate.

If you are conducting the interviews, alone or with an interpreter, make sure you have a good grasp of what is socially acceptable (and expected) within your field site's culture. For instance, in a strict Hasidic Jewish community, a man cannot shake a woman's hand; a fairly common American way of greeting someone is therefore off limits if gender matching of interviewee-interviewer is not possible. In Japan, you would be expected to bow upon meeting someone, and the depth of your bow indicates your level of respect for that person. In many Arab countries, it is insulting to show someone the bottom of your shoe, which may affect how you sit during the interview. Though small gestures, these types of culture-specific behaviors have the potential to deliver a big insult or offense. Take the time to become aware of the local customs—and your actions in relation to them.

SUMMING UP

The power and beauty of in-depth interviews lie in their ability to enable researchers to effectively and clearly comprehend the experience and understanding of their interviewees. In brief, an in-depth interview is a method of gathering information from a person in his or her own words by mirroring the back-and-forth, typically one-on-one structure of everyday conversation while keeping specific research questions and objectives in mind. When conducting an in-depth interview, you ask open-ended questions to elicit information on people's knowledge, attitudes, experiences, and behaviors in their own words, and follow their leads to uncover important issues you may not have thought to ask about. The one-on-one approach, along with well-established rapport, helps put research participants at ease, and often people are thrilled to have an "official" forum in which to express their views on a particular issue or experience.

In this chapter, we have provided tips and techniques for creating an effective interview guide, selecting appropriate times and places for interviewing, establishing rapport with interviewees, and conducting a successful interview. Kvale (2007) offers criteria for assessing the conduct and quality of an interview, which we have adapted for presentation in the next text box.

Criteria for Evaluating the Quality of an Interview

You can evaluate the success of an interview based on these factors:

1) The extent of spontaneous, rich, specific, and relevant answers from the interviewee; these should be plentiful.

2) The ratio of interviewer question length to participant response length; the shorter the interviewer's questions and the longer the participant's answers, the better.

3) The degree to which the interviewer follows up and clarifies the meanings of the relevant aspects of the answers; that is, consistent use of relevant, effective probing.

4) The degree to which participants' answers inform the research question or objective; the flow of the interview and specific probes should focus more and more narrowly on providing specific objective-related information.

5) The extent to which the interview is "self-communicating"; the interview is a story or narrative contained in itself that requires very little explanation.

Source: Adapted from Kvale (2007).

Ultimately, a successful interview is one in which the interviewer "lightly" but consciously directs the discussion to cover specified topics and collect information related to clear research objectives to produce a detailed report of an individual's views. The accumulation of these views through interviews with a number of respondents provides a rich qualitative dataset that can be analyzed to address the range, nuance, and complexity of important research questions. And whether the intent of these analyses is to advance commercial enterprises, guide public policy, or simply to help us better understand one another, there is no qualitative data collection technique as adaptable and effective as in-depth interviews.

REFERENCES

Berg, B. (2009). *Qualitative research methods for the social sciences* (7th ed.). Boston, MA: Allyn and Bacon.

Bernard, H. R. (2000). *Social research methods: Qualitative and quantitative approaches.* Thousand Oaks, CA: Sage.

Callister, L. C., Vehvilainen-Julkunen, K., & Lauri, S. (2001). Giving birth: Perceptions of Finnish childbearing women. *MCN, The American Journal of Maternal/Child Nursing, 26*(1), 28–32.

Flick, U. (2009). *An introduction to qualitative research* (4th ed.). Thousand Oaks, CA: Sage.

Flyvbjerg, B. (2006). Five misunderstandings about case-study research. *Qualitative Inquiry, 12*(2), 219–244.

Gibbins, J., & Thomson, A. M. (2001). Women's expectations and experiences of childbirth. *Midwifery, 17*, 302–313.

Gorden, R. L. (1992). *Basic interviewing skills.* Long Grove, IL: Waveland Press.

Green, J., & Hart, L. (1999). The impact of context on data. In R. Barbour & J. Kitzinger (Eds.), *Developing focus group research: Politics, theory, and practice* (chap. 2, pp. 21–35). London, UK: Sage.

Green, J., & Thorogood, N. (2009). *Qualitative methods for health research* (2nd ed.). Thousand Oaks, CA: Sage.

Guest, G., MacQueen, K., & Namey, E. (2012) *Applied thematic analysis.* Thousand Oaks, CA: Sage.

Johnson, J. C., & Weller, S. C. (2001). Elicitation techniques for interviewing. In J. Gubrium & J. Holstein (Eds.), *Handbook of interview research: Context and method* (pp. 491–514). Thousand Oaks, CA: Sage.

Kreuger, R. A., & Casey, M. A. (2009). *Focus groups: A practical guide for applied research.* Thousand Oaks, CA: Sage.

King, N., & Horrocks, C. (2010). *Interviews in qualitative research.* London, UK: Sage.

Kvale, S. (2007). *Doing interviews.* Thousand Oaks, CA: Sage.

Leavy, P. (2011). *Oral history: Understanding qualitative research.* New York, NY: Oxford University Press.

Meho, L. (2006). E-Mail interviewing in qualitative research: A methodological discussion. *Journal of the American Society for Information Science And Technology, 57*(10), 1284–1295.

Namey, E. E., & Beskow, L. M. (2011). Epilepsy patient-participants and genetic research results as "answers." *Journal of Empirical Research on Human Research Ethics, 6*(4), 21–29.

Neale, P., Thapa, S., & Boyce, C. (2006). *Preparing a case study: A guide for designing and conducting a case study for evaluation input.* Watertown, MA: Pathfinder International.

Olson, K. (2011). *Essentials of qualitative interviewing.* Walnut Creek, CA: Left Coast Press.

Patton, M. Q. (2002). *Qualitative research & evaluation methods* (3rd ed.). Thousand Oaks, CA: Sage.

Rubin, H. J., & Rubin, I. S. (2005). *Qualitative interviewing: The art of hearing data.* Thousand Oaks, CA: Sage.

Ryan, G. W., Stern, S. A., Hilton, L., Tucker, J. S., Kennedy, D. P., Golinelli, D., & Wenzel, S. L. (2009, October). When, where, why and with whom homeless women engage in risky sexual behaviors: A framework for understanding complex and varied decision-making processes. *Sex Roles, 61*(7–8), 536–553.

Seidman, I. (2006). *Interviewing as qualitative research.* New York, NY: Teachers College Press.

Sommer, B. W., & Quinlan, M. K. (2009). *The oral history manual.* Lanham, MD: Rowman Altamira.

Spradley, J. P. (1979). *The ethnographic interview.* New York, NY: Holt, Rinehart and Winston.

Sturges, J. E., & Hanrahan, K. J. (2004). Comparing telephone and face-to-face qualitative interviewing: A research note. *Qualitative Research, 4*(1), 107–118.

Temple, B. (1997). Watch your tongue: Issues in translation and cross-cultural research. *Sociology, 31*, 607–618.

Ward, G. C., & Burns, K. (2007). *The war: An intimate history, 1941–45.* New York, NY: Alfred A. Knopf.

Warren, C. A. B., & Karner, T. X. (2010). *Discovering qualitative methods* (2nd ed.). New York, NY: Oxford University Press.

Weiss, R. S. (1994). *Learning from strangers: The art and method of qualitative interview studies.* New York, NY: Free Press.

Yin, R. K. (2009). *Case study research: Design and methods* (4th ed.). Thousand Oaks, CA: Sage.

ADDITIONAL READING

Gordon, R. (1992). *Basic interviewing skills.* Long Grove, IL: Waveland Press.

King, N., & Horrocks, C. (2010). *Interviews in qualitative research.* London, UK: Sage.

Kvale, S. (2007). *Doing interviews.* Thousand Oaks, CA: Sage.

Rubin, H. J., & Rubin, I. S. (2005). *Qualitative interviewing: The art of hearing data.* Thousand Oaks, CA: Sage.

Seidman, I. (2006). *Interviewing as qualitative research.* New York, NY: Teachers College Press.

Spradley, J. (1979). *The ethnographic interview.* Belmont, CA: Wadsworth Group.

Weiss, R. S. (1994). *Learning from strangers: The art and method of qualitative interview studies.* New York, NY: Free Press.

EXERCISES

In-Depth Interview Exercise 1: Creating an Effective Interview Guide

1. Identify a peer or classmate with an interesting past job, hobby, or experience.
2. Once you have identified the person and topic, write out a clear research objective: What is it you want to find out about this person and why?
3. Develop five to seven questions you will ask in an in-depth interview with that person. Make sure that the guide has at least one of each of the following types of questions:
   a. Descriptive
   b. Structural
   c. Perception or Experience

4. Get feedback on your interview guide questions from a different peer or class-mate (NOT the person you plan to interview).
5. Prepare your introductory interview remarks and the spiel you will use to orient the interviewee.
6. Revise your interview guide as necessary, and practice it with a friend or family member. Remember to practice probing as well!

In-Depth Interview Exercise 2: Conducting an Effective Interview

1. Conduct an in-depth interview with the person you chose in Exercise 1, using your revised guide.

    *   Remember to establish rapport, provide an introduction, and review the spiel with your interviewee.
    *   Record the interview if possible.

2. Ask the interviewee for constructive feedback on your interviewing technique after the interview. What did you do well? What could you improve? Which questions worked well or need revision?
3. Listen to the recording and complete a self-critique.
4. Jot down the feedback as well as any insights from your own perspective and summarize as a form of debriefing notes.

5

Focus Groups

WHAT IS A FOCUS GROUP?

Focus groups have the distinction of being the only qualitative data collection technique with a name recognizable to the nonresearch public. Focus groups have been portrayed in panel cartoons, TV series (*King of the Hill*), and commercials (for Domino's Pizza—and one assumes that these commercials were themselves tested in front of focus groups, a stunning example of the self-referential nature of advertising). There is good reason for this high level of public visibility. Focus groups are ubiquitous in marketing and communications research, social-behavioral sciences, the health sciences, public policy, and political research. In commercial market research alone, there are an estimated 150,000 focus groups conducted each year in the United States, and there are hundreds of rooms in research facilities designed specifically for focus group data collection (Mitchell, 1998). The frequent use of the term, however, does not mean that everyone who says something about "focus groups" is really talking about the same thing. From a research standpoint it is important to define precisely what we mean when we say we are gathering data via focus groups.

As the name implies, a *focus group* is a carefully planned discussion with a small group of people on a focused topic. The group setting and group dynamics are integral to focus group data collection. Focus group discussion uses important elements of normal human conversation (sharing of experiences, opinions, perceptions, and reactions) and aspects of how we retrieve information stored in our memories (cognitive triggers) to enable the group to address the research objectives. Just as human groups have certain characteristics and capabilities that are not just the sum of their individual members (a person can run in panic, but only a group can "stampede"), so too do focus groups yield data and insights that are more than just the sum of the perceptions, beliefs, and experiences of those taking part in the discussion (Patton, 2002).

More explicitly, focus groups as a qualitative research technique generally have the following characteristics:

- A small group of people is brought together explicitly to participate in a research discussion regarding a defined topic. This is substantially different from a debate, a cocktail party conversation, or a town hall meeting.
- Similarity exists among group members in terms of some aspect of their characteristics, experiences, or situation that causes them to feel they all have something in common. This feeling of similarity is key to building the rapport that makes a focus group successful. Similarity is defined by the research objectives and could be anything from being a female Harley Davidson owner to American men who were circumcised as adults.
- Lack of preexisting social relationships between the group members is the norm, to limit issues of hierarchy and to facilitate trust and openness during the discussion.
- Discussion is moderated by a skilled researcher (usually called the moderator or facilitator) who controls the flow of questions and answers, and who explicitly uses group conversational norms and group dynamics to uncover information and gain insights.

The occasional misuse, of the term *focus group* means we should also draw distinctions between focus groups and other types of discussions that sometimes are labeled with the focus group name. A group of people simply talking about a topic of interest, even with someone leading the discussion, is not automatically a focus group. There are many common types of group conversations that are not focus groups. The interpersonal give-and-take that occurs at business meetings, community forums, and other public or organizational gatherings typically misses some of the elements that make focus groups work. There is either a lack of focus on specific informational objectives, there are prior relationships or power differentials between the participants that limit the quality of the data produced, or there is no meaningful use of group dynamics to illuminate the questions at hand. More insidiously, the term *focus group* is also sometimes used by unscrupulous researchers who bring together a group of people, not to learn something but rather to create bogus "research" to support predetermined points of view (this is similar to the fake quantitative "surveys" or "opinion polls" that are used to claim popular support for a candidate's position, generate lists of potential customers, or seed viral marketing schemes).

WHY USE FOCUS GROUPS?

Like IDIs, focus groups are a very versatile technique and can be used for a wide variety of topics and research interests. That said, there are some projects that can productively capitalize on the strengths of focus groups, while for others, focus groups may weaken the quality of data. As you might expect, groups are an especially good method for collecting data on things that are inherently shared or that have a public aspect. For example:

- Group norms and normative expectations—These can be at very broad levels, such as cultural norms; or they may be much more specific, such as workplace routines, expectations about what will occur during common events (e.g., a visit to the doctor's office, what people do following a minor car accident, etc.), what occurs during local festivals and celebrations, or how people would be expected to react when a particular situation, problem, or opportunity occurs.

- Opinions and perspectives—For topics on which a variety of viewpoints is known or expected to exist, groups can be a great way to explore the range of opinions. In these situations, the focus group moderator stimulates mild debate among the group members to discover how perspectives on the topic differ and how those holding different points of view support their positions.

- Reactions and responses—Focus groups are often used as a testing ground for reactions to such stimuli as ads or social marketing campaigns, product designs, public health interventions, service innovations, political positions, and so forth. The focus group setting can capture both the direction and strength of the response, while ensuing discussion can critique or improve specific elements of the stimulus material.

- Problem solving and brainstorming—The cognitive triggering in focus groups can often produce a team mentality in which the group members solve a problem, make suggestions, or brainstorm ideas for communications, products, or policies.

- Group processes and group dynamics—If your research topic is itself about a group process or about how people interact in groups, focus groups may enable you to observe these phenomena in action.

In addition to being especially useful for gaining the types of research information listed above, focus groups also overlap with in-depth interviews in types of data they can produce: Both offer the ability to drill down into the *how* and *why* of human experience, behavior, perceptions, and beliefs; with sufficient sample sizes, both can give some indication of norms and range of perspectives on a given a topic; and both are frequently used as a supplement to quantitative data. When the research objectives can be equally well served by either IDIs or focus groups, consider the following factors:

- Time limitations—An important advantage of focus groups is that they can be conducted quickly. Assuming you have a location, the ability to recruit suitable participants, a good discussion guide, and a trained moderator, the focus groups can be—and often are—literally conducted overnight. This makes them ideal for research in response to emerging events (e.g., natural disasters, national or international political or economic events, fast-moving crises) where the findings need to be made available right away. It is almost impossible to conduct enough IDIs fast enough to respond to these types of research and decision-making needs. Note, however, that the speed of focus groups does not mean they are a solution to all quick-turnaround situations—the research topic still has to be suitable for focus group investigation. There is no point to collecting data in a hurry if it isn't any good.

- Staff limitations—Closely related to the issue of timing are the limitations imposed by the size and composition of your research team. You may simply not have the people to get enough IDIs done to answer your research questions during the time you can allot to fieldwork, even when the project is not on a hurry-up schedule. Alternatively, if you have access to one superb focus group moderator, but would have to train IDI interviewers from scratch, it may make more sense to go with focus groups than IDIs.

- Sponsor preferences and expectations—Commercial research sponsors tend to like focus groups. Sitting in the back room observing the groups or reviewing the video recordings makes them feel engaged and excited about the study. Also, they can participate directly in the research by sending in questions that the moderator can introduce into the discussion (more on this later in this chapter). While clients or sponsors can be invited to observe or review IDIs, they are almost never as enthusiastic about this as they are about focus groups. One of the authors has, on multiple occasions, found her clients asleep in the observation room when they were supposed to be observing an IDI—something that rarely occurs among focus group observers. Additionally, sponsors who observe focus groups often find the eventual write-up of findings more credible than those who have not seen the actual data collection. So if your findings are going to need sponsor buy-in or if your sponsors simply want to be "hands-on" regarding the research, then focus groups may be your method of choice.

- Safety and comfort issues—In some field settings, it may be safer or more comfortable for your research participants to talk to you in a group. Cultural norms can play a big role in this. For example, in one of the author's studies, young mothers in a Middle Eastern country felt more comfortable talking about child health issues in a group of their age peers than one-on-one in their own homes or other settings. The group's composition freed them from restrictions about gender and age deference and, perhaps counter-intuitively, granted a sort of anonymity that helped them to freely express their views. Another, rarer field situation is when you are doing an IDI in a home or semipublic setting (e.g., man-on-the-street type intercept interviews) and bystanders keep joining the conversation. (This scenario is common in small villages where everyone knows each other and there is little else going on in terms of excitement.) If you cannot politely and effectively stop these interruptions and the research objectives allow it, it may be feasible to regroup and turn the lost IDI into a minifocus group by bringing the "interruptions" into the conversation and using group dynamics to get at your informational objectives (Baker, 1996). Flexibility is the key: be wedded to your research objectives, not to your preferred data collection methodology.

- Research topic—As mentioned in Chapters 1 and 4, focus groups are generally not well suited when soliciting information about personal, sensitive, or highly controversial topics. Resulting discussions can be contentious (or downright aggressive) or render information that is shallow in nature. Keep in mind that this guideline is not set in stone and in some cases focus groups can be used to collect, for example, personal data. One study conducted at Guest's organization was interested in understanding women's perspectives on using a vaginal microbicide as a potential form of HIV prevention. Women were recruited from the population of participants enrolled in a clinical trial testing the effectiveness of the microbicide. Despite being a highly personal topic (i.e., the insertion of a gel into one's vagina before having sex), women talked openly and freely about their experiences. The shared experience of participating in the clinical trial and using the product created a bond and mutual trust among these women, overriding concerns about privacy.

PRACTICAL DIMENSIONS OF CONDUCTING FOCUS GROUPS

Focus Group Size

There is no hard-and-fast rule about the size of focus groups, but there are limits to the number of people who can meaningfully participate in a group discussion. The size of a focus group, as with most things in research, will vary with the setting, topics, and research objectives of the project. The suggested focus group size throughout the methodological literature ranges from six to 12 individuals (with a few outliers on either end). Generally speaking, focus groups with fewer than six individuals may not be able to capitalize on the group dynamic so important to focus groups. And groups larger than 12 tend to lose momentum or become difficult to manage. Quieter participants often "hide" in large groups, and those who have to wait to speak may lose interest. Big groups can also be more difficult for the moderator to control and for the note-taker (or even electronic recording devices) to record.

The modal recommendation for focus group size in the methodological literature we've reviewed is eight people, and based on our personal experiences, this is indeed a good number for the majority of focus group contexts. It's small enough to allow (at least theoretically) everyone to speak and large enough to facilitate a group dynamic and capture a good range of responses.

Notwithstanding, certain research topics or circumstances may benefit from focus groups with more or fewer than eight individuals. The main factor to consider in this regard is the breadth-to-depth ratio most suitable for your topic and research population. Does the topic, for example, warrant a lot of detailed discussion among individuals, or is it more of a brainstorming type of endeavor? Table 5.1 provides some

Table 5.1 Guidelines for Adjusting Focus Group Size	
Use smaller groups when	**Use larger groups when**
• Participants are highly involved with the topic	• Participants have limited involvement with the topic
• The topic is emotional	• The goal is to hear numerous brief suggestions (e.g., brainstorming)
• Participants know a lot about the topic	• The topic is simple
• The topic is complex	• You're looking for generalities or social norms
• The topic is controversial	• The topic is not controversial
• You're looking for detailed narratives	

general guidelines to help you plan the size of your focus groups. We suggest starting with a default size of eight individuals and, if necessary, adjusting from there based on your research context and the recommendations below. Note that you can also adjust the size of your focus groups *during* the research process. If, for example, you observe side discussions regularly emerging, this is a pretty clear sign that not everyone is engaged and that you may want to decrease the size of your next focus group. Conversely, if your focus group isn't generating a broad enough range of responses, you may opt to increase the number of participants in the future.

Be aware that some authors refer to *mini* focus groups. The definitional size varies by author and field of use (e.g., social science, marketing, health sciences), but the term typically refers to focus groups with four to five individuals. Even smaller groups—dyads and triads—also sometimes make specific use of group dynamics. The advantages of groups this small are simpler logistics when space, recruiting specifications, or other constraints make full-size groups impractical, or when the psychological comfort of participants will be facilitated by being with a smaller number of people. The downside is that the range of combined experiences is relatively small, and you may not generate a very large array of responses in a given data collection event.

Incentives

You will need to decide whether to offer an incentive to your focus group participants, how much to pay, and in what form (cash, gift certificate, or something else). The same issues and cautions in using incentives for IDIs also apply to focus groups, but there are a few additional issues that can occur when using incentives with groups. (See Chapter 8 for a discussion on the ethical dimensions of incentives.)

Focus groups done for commercial purposes or at dedicated focus group facilities virtually always use an incentive, typically cash. If you are doing several groups, each with eight to 10 participants, the sum needed can be substantial, and this means you may need to hold, account for, and correctly dispense as much as several thousand dollars over the course of a single research session. Needless to say, someone other than the moderator should act as banker, and arrangements for secure storage and transfer of funds should be made.

The most common way to handle cash incentives at focus groups is to count the incentive amount for each participant into an envelope labeled with their name or other identification in keeping with your confidentiality protocol. The envelopes are generally handed out to the participants at the end of the group. It is a good idea to have each person count the sum in their envelope before they leave the premises, so as to be sure all have been paid correctly. Depending on the accounting requirements of your project, you may also need to have them sign a form acknowledging that payment has been made. Gift certificates can also be handled using the envelope method.

If you use a dedicated focus group facility, the reception staff there will handle the distribution of incentives and associated documentation. Otherwise, this role needs to be handled by someone on your research team. Make sure this is clear in advance. You do not want to complete a focus group and have 10 people eagerly awaiting their payment only to find that the incentives are in a locked safe, a team member's car, or are otherwise unreachable. Similarly, avoid waiting until the last minute to arrange to get the cash into the envelopes. You cannot get a sufficient sum in the right denominations from an ATM (although some of us have certainly tried), banking days, hours, and holidays vary widely from place to place, many focus group participants are leery of personal checks, and it is just plain embarrassing for researchers to have to scramble to gather the promised incentive.

Note that an unwritten, yet heeded, rule regarding incentives is that if (invited) people show up—for an IDI, focus group, or any data collection event—they receive whatever incentive is associated with the event, regardless of whether or not they actually participate. This situation may arise if too many people show up for a focus group, or some recruiting error was made and individuals who don't fulfill the eligibility criteria wish to participate. The same rule applies to participants who, for whatever reason, leave before the data collection event is finished.

If you are unable to provide monetary incentives, you may consider at least providing some kind of drinks, snacks, or meal to both encourage and thank your participants. Pizza is a staple of focus groups conducted with adolescents and college students. Boxed lunches or a sandwich station work well for focus groups conducted with professionals over the lunch hour or in early evening. Whatever you choose, consider the "crunch" factor of the foods and the "crinkle" effect of any wrappers. Provide enough time before the official start of the focus group for your participants to grab a bite to eat and unwrap anything that requires it so that your audio recording is not obscured by the rustling of people, plates, or plastic.

Recruiting Participants

The approaches for recruiting detailed in Chapter 2 generally apply to focus groups. There are, however, aspects of focus group recruitment that add a degree of complexity to the process, making some recruiting approaches more problematic than they would be for IDIs.

The most obvious constraint in recruiting for focus groups is that you are attempting to assemble a group of people at the same place at the same time. With IDIs, once you have located a suitable interviewee, you simply schedule him into a time slot of mutual convenience for him and the interviewer, and you are ready to proceed. With focus groups, in contrast, you are usually inviting people to come to a pre-set place and time. This means you are not just looking for qualified participants, you are looking for those that are both qualified and free at the right time. The implications of this are obvious—it is much more effort intensive to schedule an event involving 8 to 10 people (more if you count the entire research team, observers, facility personnel, etc.) than an event that may only involve two. The main requirement for successful recruitment of focus groups is to give yourself sufficient lead time.

In order to estimate how far in advance of the focus groups you need to begin the recruiting effort, approximate the prevalence of your desired participants within the recruiting environment and the expected effectiveness of your recruiting approach. Obviously, this can vary widely. A market research focus group with young men who consume McDonald's hamburgers can be assembled in a day and can use almost any contact approach (e.g., intercepting likely participants in a mall food court or college campus or random dial recruiting phone calls to households in the selected geographic area). But recruiting participants who are rarer or hard to locate or intercept will require more time (for instance, a colleague of the authors once assembled a focus group of male cross-dressers working as prostitutes in San Francisco).

If you are using a telephone recruiting method, estimate how many phone calls will be needed to locate each participant who is qualified, willing to come to the group, and available at the right time. Then, estimate the number of telephone hours that you must allow to get the needed number of participants. If you are using an intercept approach, estimate the prevalence of your participants in the population at the intercept site(s) and how many people each screening interviewer can successfully approach, screen, and recruit in an hour, day, or week at the intercept location. And for passive methods, such as posting fliers or online ads, allow time for communications back and forth with potential participants.

A general rule of thumb is that recruiting for high-prevalence participants (like the young men who eat at McDonald's) should start at least 1 week in advance of the groups. For moderately prevalent groups (e.g., Iraq war veterans who are also members of a fitness club, moms with kids in charter schools, etc.) allow 2 to 3 weeks for recruiting. And for hard-to-find participants, you may need to allow a month or more. The more focus groups you intend to conduct with each group or subgroup, the more participants you will need and the more time it will take. For research involving eight focus groups with four categories of participants (White and Black women with and without a particular health condition), it took Namey approximately 3 months to complete recruitment using fliers and once-a-week targeted intercepts in primary care clinics (about 90 participants recruited in total). Note that this time line was based on allocation of only 4 hours per week to the project, so the recruitment process may have been shortened with additional time and effort dedicated to the task. Generally speaking, if the research population exists in sufficient numbers, your approach is appropriate, and your effort diligent, you can assemble a focus group, even with highly restrictive screening criteria (one author brought together a group of Spanish-English bilingual general practice physicians who served Hispanic immigrant populations and who used a particular type of drug—not the most popular one—for treating cardiac ailments).

Dedicated focus group facilities often have staff available to conduct recruiting calls—a service normally done on a cost-per-recruit basis. Additionally, these facilities maintain databases of people who have expressed willingness to participate in market research. As noted in Table 2.2, these lists can be useful, but you should be cautious when employing them. People on research lists may be "professional respondents" who attempt to get into focus groups to get the incentive payment or simply because they like to share their opinions. If you are considering using any sort of panel or list for focus group recruiting, then give deep consideration to possible sources of bias that the list may introduce and what screening questions or other procedures you may need to put in place in order to screen out the professional respondent.

Of course, when you are recruiting from prequalified lists (e.g., employees of a company, local village leaders), many of your recruiting challenges disappear, and recruiting can be very fast and efficient. In these cases, your challenges may center more on who to put in which groups. As mentioned before, you should try to compose the groups to avoid the problems that can occur when hierarchy, social class distinctions, or prior social connections affect the group dynamics that your data collection depends upon.

Another issue in focus group recruiting is getting your chosen participants to stay recruited. Inevitably, some of your earliest recruits will develop time conflicts or otherwise lose their commitment to the research before the actual day and time of the group. Several techniques are available to ensure the desired number of participants shows up for your groups:

- Confirming and reminding—As soon as someone is recruited, they should receive a communication (e-mail, letter, follow-up call) confirming their participation, providing any directions or instructions, and repeating the day, place, and time of the group. A reminder communication should go out about 1 week in advance of the group (if the person was recruited more than 10 days prior to the group) and again about 24 to 48 hours prior to the group.
- Over-recruiting—Even with confirmations and reminders, some people will be no-shows on the day of the group. Common practice is to recruit 10 to 12 people to have eight to 10 in the group. If the extras all show up, the researcher can either run an extra-large group or "pay-and-dismiss" the additional people. If pay-and-dismiss is going to be used, it should be mentioned to recruits as a possibility during the initial recruiting conversation. You don't want people thinking they are being dismissed because you didn't like their looks or because they failed some sort of hidden test.

In your recruiting conversations and communications, you should instruct participants to arrive before the anticipated start time of the groups. This allows for the general tendency of people to straggle in late, have trouble parking and the like, and it also provides time for rescreening, documenting informed consent, and handling any other needed administrative details. Telling people to arrive 30 minutes ahead of the group start time is standard, and 15 minutes ahead is an absolute minimum. Even if you are doing groups in a culture where the norm is to arrive early or on time (e.g., the U.S. military), give yourself some leeway. If you are working in a culture that does not commonly use clocks or where it is considered odd or impolite to be exactly on time, then adjust accordingly—and if you are from an always-on-time culture, then be patient.

PREPARING FOR A FOCUS GROUP

Timing

The obvious and first rule of when to schedule your focus groups is to do them at times that make it easy for your desired participants to show up and when they will be reasonably alert and energetic. Groups done with employed people (other than groups done at their workplaces) are typically scheduled in the evenings or on weekends, when such people are most likely to be available. A typical timing of groups with this sort of average citizen or average consumer would be a midweek evening (most people like to do other things on Friday and Saturday nights) with a group starting at 5:30 p.m. and another at 8 p.m. (start any later and they'll be too tired/not talkative at the end). Alternatively, you might choose a weekend schedule—groups on Saturday at 10 a.m. and 12:30 p.m. are common. While there is no hard and fast "best" time for other categories of people, the list below shows some dos and don'ts for some commonly recruited types of focus group participants:

- Young people—Smaller children do best in daytime or early evening groups. Teenagers can do daytime or evening groups, but many are listless during the early morning.
- Parents—Unless you are providing babysitting during your groups, pick times when children are in school or when the other parent is likely to be available to watch the kids.
- Employees—Focus groups should be when employees are "on the clock"; no one wants to be at work extra hours, even if they are getting an incentive. If you are doing groups with shift workers, most people are more responsive at the beginning of the shift than at the end.
- Rural populations—In many communities, rural people keep early hours and can do groups in the morning right after the early chores are done. Harvest season can be problematic where crops are seasonal, while any "off" season when the local crops or animals require less care may be a good time for groups.
- Urban populations—If your participants must rely on public transport, know the hours when the trains, buses, and ferries run. Do not schedule groups at times that will strand people or make it hard for them to arrive or to get home.
- Senior citizens—Older participants, especially those at truly advanced ages or who have medical conditions, generally do best at late morning or mid-day groups.

Another consideration when scheduling your groups is holidays or local events that might occur at or around the time of the groups. These can make it difficult to recruit participants because people may tend to travel out of town or plan celebrations that would conflict with the groups. Additionally, public celebrations, such as parades, may block access to the focus group location or disrupt transportation networks. Recognize that potentially disruptive events are not confined to those that are permanently on the calendar—the authors have had groups disrupted by such events as spontaneous celebrations of local sports victories (watch the sports pages so you know if this is likely) and a presidential motorcade (watch the news for the potential arrival of dignitaries of this sort).

On some occasions, a scheduled event can work in your favor. Conventions, fairs, or other specialized gatherings can bring people with particular backgrounds together—often in great numbers. If you need to do groups with such populations, consider scheduling during such an event and holding the groups at or near the event location. The authors have conducted groups for high-volume sellers of goods on eBay (at the eBay Live convention), with rodeo stock companies (these provide "buck-ing stock"—bulls and broncos) at a large rodeo, and home canners at a county fair. (Groups are also sometimes conducted on cruise ships, but sadly, the authors haven't done any of these.) If your target participants have someplace they get together, take advantage of the event—you will probably also find that attending the event will fur-ther enrich the insights you get from the groups.

A final consideration in the timing of your groups is the number and spacing of groups on each day of data collection. Most focus group moderators are comfortable doing two or three groups (assuming the groups last 90 minutes to 2 hours each) in a day. It takes a lot of energy to do groups, and more than three will leave the moderator exhausted. Do not schedule your groups back-to-back unless there is no other option. You will need time between groups to let the earlier group depart, to check and down-load audio and video recordings, to clean up and prepare the room, and to welcome your next group and get them settled in the room. You also need time between groups, especially after the first one, for a quick debrief among the research team members so you can make any needed adjustments to the discussion guide or other elements of the research protocol. A final point in timing the groups is to remember that during a full day of groups, the moderator will need time to eat—back room observers can eat during the groups, but the moderator cannot.

Facilities

While focus groups can be conducted almost anywhere that there is enough space to gather a sufficient number of people, your choice of the space in which to conduct the groups can greatly facilitate or hamper your ability to gather and analyze your focus group data. At the minimum, your chosen focus group facility should feature the following:

- Sufficient space for the participants, moderator, and any equipment needed to run and record the group proceedings (white boards, flip charts, audio/video recording equipment, display space for stimulus materials, room for any supplemental activities that will occur during the groups, etc.)
- Culturally appropriate, comfortable seating (chairs, mats, pillows or rugs, lawn or flat ground space)
- Privacy or isolation to minimize interruptions (a closed room or if outdoors, a space at some distance from other activities)

The requirements listed above are a bare minimum and can generally be achieved in even the most challenging field environments—the authors of this book can personally attest that groups can be conducted successfully in locations as diverse as copper mines, film schools, isolated rural villages (under a tree), lawns, school rooms, church basements, and urban community centers. That said, however, having a space that offers more than the basics can offer huge advantages in terms of making the data collection simpler, more enjoyable, and more effective.

The gold standard in terms of focus group locations are purpose-built focus group rooms. Typically found in market research facilities, these rooms have a number of features that aid focus group management and data collection. Even if your research has budget, geographic, or other constraints that would make it impractical to use one of these rooms, you may be able to incorporate some of these features into whatever locations you do choose.

In North America, a dedicated focus group room will often be part of a market research facility or conference center—although a few large corporations also have purpose-built focus group rooms on their premises. The floor plan below shows a relatively large market research facility with several focus group rooms (with associated observation rooms and client lounges) supported by a central lobby or reception area.

The rooms in such facilities typically feature a conference table (or a specially built tapered table wider at one end than at the other so the faces of the participants are visible to the moderator and the video camera at all times); a set of chairs; a display ledge (for positioning photos/drawings or other stimuli); walls covered with cork or fabric to which paper items can be tacked; white boards and/or flip charts, video camera, audio–video microphones for dual audio recording, TV, and CD or DVD player for showing audio-video stimuli; side tables to hold questionnaires, stimuli and refreshments; and a supply cabinet for notepads, pens, pencils, crayons, and general office supplies. Dedicated focus group rooms also have an observation room attached that uses a two-way mirrored window to allow the observers to watch the focus

Figure 5.1   Floor Plan of a Market Research Facility

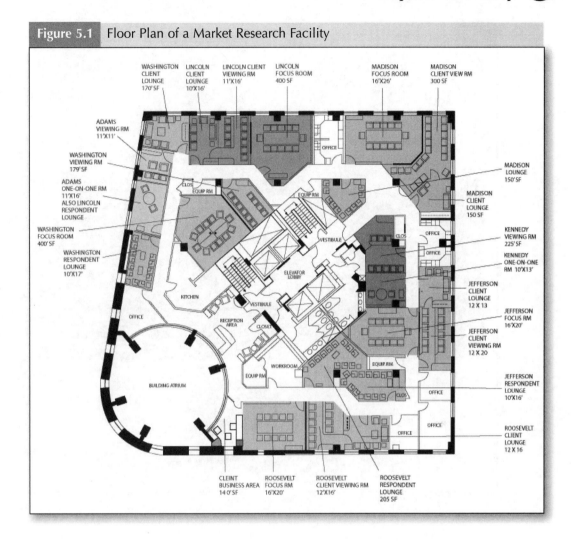

group proceedings (this window looks like a mirrored wall from inside the focus group room). The photos below show a typical focus group room and its attached observation room.

Since a steady volume of focus groups is needed to support a dedicated facility, these rooms are available in large cities throughout the developed world (the Market Research *GreenBook* provides a worldwide listing). Naturally, smaller towns and rural areas cannot support such specialized businesses. In these areas, hotel or office conference rooms, classrooms, community halls, factory break rooms or open spaces

---

Figure 5.2 Typical Focus Group Room and Observation Room

Lincoln Focus Room

Viewing Room

(lawns, parks, etc.) can be used. The table below lists challenges that occur in adapting these spaces, as well as some possible solutions.

As you can see from the list above, you must know the characteristics of your chosen space in advance in order to know what types of equipment you will need to make it workable as a focus group location. There is no substitute for on-the-ground reconnaissance of the space in advance (ideally, well in advance) of your groups. The people who run hotel conference rooms, conventional office meeting rooms, and other such spaces are well-meaning but do not really know what running a focus group entails. Every experienced moderator has had at least one experience in which

Table 5.2	Facility Challenges and Solutions
Challenge	**Solution**
Space too small for people/table/chairs	Remove table and conduct groups "therapy group" style; reduce number of participants per group
Space too large/echoing	Use temporary dividers to partition space and absorb sound
Space noisy/public	Use sound absorbing dividers; alter time of day to lessen noise from roads, factories, foot traffic; have assistants to direct possible sources of noise or interruptions away from the space during the groups
No place to display stimuli	Bring easels, chairs, folding tables; have assistant to hold and carry stimuli; redesign stimuli so it can be handed out on paper or projected onto walls
Space hot, cold, sunny, windy	Provide portable shade or umbrellas; create windbreaks; use portable heaters or fans; have jackets and blankets on hand for cold environments; serve hot or cold drinks
Poor lighting	Bring portable lights
No electricity/no electrical outlets	Minimize need for it; carry extension cords; use battery operated audio-video recorders (have extra batteries or a way to recharge); use a generator (if not too noisy)
No observation room	Connect video cam (in room) to closed circuit and place observers in a nearby room (have a monitor available); place observers in the focus group room (sitting quietly to one side)

the promise of a room that "is all set up for you" turned out to be a space hidden in a basement with no electrical outlets, next to a construction site where giant pile drivers were pounding 40-foot long construction anchors into the soil. Scout your site beforehand, bring everything with you that you could possibly need and be prepared for surprises. They do—and will—occur.

One of our field teams in Africa arranged to conduct a focus group in the one indoor space that could accommodate a group in the residential area where the women for the group lived (to limit no-shows based on transportation issues). This space happened to be a tavern that opened around noon. Despite plans to start the focus group at 9 a.m., the group ended up starting and running late, so the tavern opened and customers began to filter in and request that music be played. The resulting distraction of onlookers and loud music necessitated the early conclusion of the group. Even dedicated facilities can have problems—one of the authors was conducting a group in a dedicated facility when a lightning strike destroyed the electrical power. The focus group room had no outer walls or windows, so the group was plunged into total darkness. After a few minutes fumbling for a pocket flashlight, the audio recording was switched to battery power (the video recording was abandoned), a candle was located, and the focus group continued—albeit with somewhat more romantic illumination than is usual.

Training

As in any other research endeavor, all members of the research team should both be trained in the responsibilities of their role and in the specifics of the current project. It is easy for moderators who have done lots of focus groups to become cavalier about them and merely rely on experience to get them through the data collection. This is not ideal, and even those who have done hundreds of focus groups should allow sufficient time for training. Specific training issues for the key research team roles are outlined in the sections below.

The Moderator

The success of a focus group rests largely on the shoulders of the focus group moderator (also sometimes called the facilitator). No matter how well other parts of project have been designed or executed, it can all be for naught if the moderator loses sight of the research objectives, can't effectively direct the discussion, or lets unruly or talkative group members take control of the proceedings. A capable moderator:

- knows the research objectives and the discussion guide cold—In an IDI there may be time to refer to the interview guide, but there is very little "downtime" during a focus group. The sometimes free-wheeling nature of the discussion means the moderator must know, at all times, what material has been covered and what still needs to be pursued.
- has exceptional facilitation skills—The moderator must be able to draw out reticent participants, shut down blowhards, re-aim those who wander from the point, probe for the why and how beneath cursory responses and rationalizations, stimulate debate, and calm those who become overly emotional—all without upsetting anyone or losing track of time.
- is quick thinking—The moderator must quickly come up with good probing questions in the melee of a group conversation. Typically, good focus group moderators are fast thinkers who can formulate their thoughts and put them into words almost instantly.
- has mental and physical energy and stamina—Focus groups demand a lot of the moderator—the general rule is that you get as much energy and effort

from your groups as you put into them. To control a group discussion, the moderator will be constantly assessing, responding, querying, and suggesting and using words, tone, and gestures to drive toward the research objectives. People who tire easily or who are overwhelmed by the tumult of lively, talkative people will struggle in the moderator role.

From the description above, you can see that it is vital that the focus group moderator be well trained. In commercial research, the norm is to hire a professional moderator—typically, someone with years of experience, hundreds of focus groups under their belt, and often certificated from a research training institute (such as Burke Institute) or professional association (such as the Market Research Association of America). Professional moderators often specialize in doing groups for particular industries (medical and pharmaceutical, automotive, food, retailers, etc.), with certain types of research subjects (the elderly, various ethnic and linguistic groups, employees of large firms) or certain types of research problems (product design, customer satisfaction, advertising, political campaigns, public policy). If you are doing groups and your project's budget allows for it, you may wish to consider hiring a pro for this key role. The American Marketing Association *GreenBook* (see additional readings and resources at the end of this chapter) lists many moderators. To choose a good one, review their portfolio of videos of groups they have conducted, check out client recommendations, and be sure they have experience in areas relevant to your proposed groups. Expect to pay plenty for a top moderator—depending on the specialty, their fees can top $3K to $5K for a one-day set of 2 or 3 groups—and in many cases, this fee does not include the write-up of the findings (which is separately charged).

If you are not in the position to hire a professional moderator, most likely you or someone else on your team will perform the focus group moderator role. There are a number of ways you can prepare yourself to moderate your groups, including the following:

- Observe—Even if you have seen or participated in focus groups in the past, take every opportunity to watch more of them, either live or on video. Watch the methods and little tricks each moderator uses to control and direct the discussion. Note probes that were especially effective or that were missed. See how problem participants were handled. Professional moderators regularly watch each other and exchange tips and stories. No matter how many groups you have seen, there is always something new to learn.
- Read—There are a number of books specifically about focus groups (several are listed as additional readings to this chapter—Morgan and Krueger, 1998, is a keystone of this literature) and all contain tips and suggestions for focus group moderators. Additionally, read focus group transcripts and reports or

summaries of focus group findings. Watch these documents for things the moderator did that succeeded or failed or places where a potentially useful probe was missed.

- Consider taking a class—Classes and seminars that train focus group moderators are open to anyone with the entrance fee and provide excellent training in focus group moderator skills and, in many cases, a meaningful credential for future research work.
- Practice—The best training for moderating focus groups is moderating focus groups. If you haven't done actual groups before, find someone to practice on. Role play in groups among your research team, friends, or family. If there is a local charity, school, church, small business, or other worthy group that could use a little free research—volunteer to do a focus group for them.

The Note-Taker

Even when your focus groups will be audio-video recorded, it is useful to have a live note-taker. A live note-taker is not expected to catch an entire focus group verbatim (even court stenographers can't do this for a multivoice conversation) but is there to provide rapid capture of key quotes and the general flow of the discussion. Additionally, the note-taker may act as a second set of researcher eyes and ears during the data analysis phase of the research. And of course, the note-taker is the backup should the machine recordings fail or in situations where machine recording is not possible. Accordingly, these are the central characteristics of a good note-taker:

- Speed—The faster the typing or stenography, the more the note-taker can capture.
- Accuracy—The note-taker should have good hearing, understand the local vernacular or regional accent and any slang or industry jargon that is likely to be used in the groups. Agar and Macdonald (1995) discuss how focus groups are especially prone to use of "insider" language that can leave research teams baffled.
- Relevance—The notes should capture the research-relevant elements of the discussion, so the note-taker should know the research objectives well enough to distinguish the wheat from the chaff.

As with moderators, the best training for focus group note-taking is actual note-taking at real or practice groups. An easy way to do this is to have the note-taker watch videos of previous focus groups and try taking notes. Then, after the note-taker has expanded and cleaned-up the notes, other team members can review the notes and provide feedback to the note-taker. The performance standard is to imagine that the findings have to be written up using just the notes. If all the key insights and plenty of juicy, illustrative quotes have been captured, then the note-taker has mastered her job.

Depending on the focus group location, the note-taker may be either in the observation room or in the focus group room itself. An observation room setting allows the note-taker to really concentrate on listening and note taking—although clients and other observers may sometimes need to be reminded to be quiet so the note-taker can hear clearly. If the note-taker will be in the same room as the group, the note-taker should strive to be as unobtrusive as possible—typically by sitting off to the side and typing or writing quietly. The note-taker should also be ready to roll with the punches if the focus group gets lively. One of the authors once conducted a focus group at a factory that manufactures industrial gases. She was accompanied by a rookie note-taker. The focus group was all men, and the conversation was fast-paced, humorous, and, at times, raunchy. The note-taker was an excellent typist, and she was tapping furiously on her laptop, determined to capture every word of her first-ever focus group. Inevitably, one of the participants decided to emphasize one of his comments with a deliberate fart, causing his colleagues to erupt with laughter (fart jokes never grow old at an industrial gases factory). The note-taker froze, hands poised above the keyboard, clearly at a loss. The moderator stepped in by saying, "No need to transcribe that," giving the group a second chance to laugh and the note-taker a moment to compose herself, before the group moved on to the next question.

The Field Director

On a small research team, the role of field director may be an additional duty of the moderator or the note-taker, while on bigger teams or projects with large numbers of focus groups, someone may be dedicated to this role. But even if this is only part of someone's job, the field director's responsibilities should not be taken lightly. The field director makes sure that all the planning and logistics needed to conduct the group are taken care of. This includes all the arrangements that ensure that there is a place to do the groups, equipment and people to do them with, and that all paperwork and data associated with the groups are handled properly. Table 5.3 below lists the duties of the field director. As with other roles, it is useful for the field director to tag along with someone experienced in this role. For those who cannot shadow an experienced field director, Table 5.3 can be used as a guideline and checklist of the responsibilities of the role.

DEVELOPING AN EFFECTIVE INSTRUMENT

Focus groups are inherently a semi-structured form of interviewing, and accordingly, a good focus group discussion guide is developed in a similar way to in-depth interview guides outlined in Chapter 4. Many focus group questions are open-ended and

Table 5.3	Field Director Duties	
Place	**People**	**Things**
Selecting and, if needed, booking, the focus group room or site	Overseeing or conducting the participant recruiting effort	Maintaining screening questionnaires and recruiting records
Checking out the site to see what equipment is there and what will need to be brought	Overseeing or conducting all needed confirmatory communications with participants	Handling and maintaining incentive payments, informed consent agreements, confidentiality agreements, and incentive receipt forms and records
Arranging the room/space set for the focus group and observers	Arranging for participants, waiting room guests, and observers to be led to and from their proper locations at the right times	Transporting, setting up and testing any needed equipment—recording and display devices, closed circuit setups, cameras, and so on
Arranging for food and refreshments—for participants, waiting room guests, observers, moderators	Making sure all participants complete any needed paperwork—informed consent, receipt of incentives, confidentiality agreements, and so forth	Collecting, labeling, and organizing all focus group outputs—notes, video and audio recordings, photos, items produced during group activities
Restoration of focus group site to its original/agreed upon condition	Making sure participants leave with all their belongings, incentives, and where appropriate, contact information	Return/delivery of all equipment and data or outputs to their locations/recipients

virtually identical to an IDI question on the same topic, and a focus group moderator will often probe the responses in a similar way. But focus group discussion guides differ from IDI interview guides in that they typically contain at least a few built-in tricks and techniques that are specifically designed to use group dynamics. And, they are invariably shorter in length.

The examples below in Table 5.4 taken from several different focus group discussion guides) show how group dynamics can be "built in" to a focus group.

Focus group discussion guides are almost always laid out in a linear rather than a matrix format (see Chapter 4 for this distinction). The need to maintain control of the group makes the matrix-style too freewheeling for focus group use. As with IDI guides, focus group guides are divided into topic areas with sets of associated questions and may contain specific topic and question type transitions to help keep the

Table 5.4	Building-in Group Dynamics
Technique	**Example**
Using cognitive triggers to build a list—as one participant names something, it will cause other participants to think of their own examples. Also, lists of this type can start a discussion of rules—what belongs on the list and what does not.	Please list for me all the different places you might go for financial advice—not the specific organization or people's names—but the kinds of companies, people, organizations, or other resources that you might consider as sources of financial advice. RECORD LIST.
Using a rating to create debate—having people silently rate some idea or stimulus material ties them to their initial impression. Subsequent discussion of the rating elucidates the differing perceptions among the group.	How many of you gave this concept a high score (8, 9, or 10). What did you find appealing about this concept? Did anyone really dislike this concept and give it a low score (0, 1, 2, 3)? What did you dislike about it?
Having the group describe a process enables you to quickly learn the steps in the process, where different people experience the process differently, where problems occur, and what would count as possible solutions.	Walk me through what happens when you go through a checkpoint. Tell me what you see, do, and feel at each step.
Using a hypothetical scenario, "what next," can enable you to learn about norms, options, and alternatives and to probe about sensitive topics without embarrassing your participants.	Mr. Smith has both a wife and a mistress and has just learned that his mistress is HIV-positive. What should he do? What do you think he will do?
Brainstorming in a group can produce ideas for products, services, communications, and solutions to problems.	If you were in charge of cleaning up or improving this neighborhood, what would you do? What would you tackle first? What do you think is most important to do? What will be the easiest to do? The hardest to do?
Examples and ideals use cognitive triggering to produce colorful, detailed examples that can be analyzed for common themes or used to illustrate key findings.	What are some examples of bad customer service experiences? What would be the ideal process for getting financial advice?

group on track as the discussion proceeds from topic to topic. Focus group guides also generally include some sort of introduction to the focus group environment and some sort of warm-up questions—often, a self-introduction by each participant, as shown in the example below:

1. INTRODUCTION/WARM-UP (10 min)

   DISCUSS "GROUND RULES," PRESENCE OF OBSERVERS, AUDIO–VIDEO RECORDING, AND TOPIC FOR THE SESSION AND INTRODUCE MODERATOR AND RESPONDENTS

- Name
- Household makeup—who else is in the household with you, ages of kids, what financial services companies are used
- Purpose—to understand how parents like yourselves think about and talk about financial products, brands, and decision making with your kids and to show you some potential advertisements, promotions, or informational materials to get your reactions to them

As with an IDI interview guide, your focus group discussion guide should always conclude with a question asking the group if they have anything else they would like to add. Be sure to allow enough time for this at the end of the group.

Be very conservative when estimating how long it will take you to get through your discussion guide. Groups take longer—a whole lot longer—to answer questions than do individuals. You want the group dynamic to occur—so be sure that if you are asking a question that is apt to stimulate debate, you have allowed enough time for debate to occur.

CONDUCTING A FOCUS GROUP

Gauging the Group

The actual conduct of a focus group begins with the arrival of the participants at the focus group location. There should be someone to greet the participants, do any rescreening, handle any paperwork, and, if they will be waiting more than a few moments, direct them to seats and refreshments. The moderator should take this opportunity to look them over and get an initial sense of their mood and personalities. This is also a good time to watch their interactions with each other and with the research and facility staff. Note which ones are quiet and may need to be encouraged during the discussion. Watch for talkers and dominant personalities that may need to be held in check. And use this time to begin developing rapport. Thank them for attending the group, answer questions, reassure anyone who is nervous, and indicate that you are looking forward to hearing their opinions, perspectives, and reactions during the upcoming discussion.

When the group has been assembled in the focus group room, use the self-introductions to continue refining your sense of the group. Be prepared to adapt your style and your questions to raise the energy of a quiet group or tone down a bunch who may be overly exuberant. And make sure that one or more of your initial questions gets at mood more directly. If, for example, your topic is the performance of a company's promotion policies, ask a general question along the lines of, What comes to mind when I mention promotion policies here at Company XYZ? Then, adjust accordingly if the overall sense is that the topic is positive or problematic.

Setting the Tone and Expectations

The moderator's words, vocal tone, and body language set the example for the group and tell them how they are expected to behave and respond. A lively, smiling, joking, and energetic moderator gives them permission to smile and joke as well and sends the message that you expect quick answers. A more restrained, deliberate, and slightly distant moderator tells participants to be calm, thoughtful, and measured in their responses. You can use these aspects of the moderator role to adjust the group to the tone that will best help you achieve the research objectives.

Additionally, the moderator's introductory remarks can directly address your expectations. Usually, these remarks will include mention of the need to hear from everyone, being respectful of others' opinions, not holding back a minority opinion or perspective, limiting "me too" comments, keeping contributions relevant to the topic at hand, the need for the highly verbal to occasionally hold back, and the need for the quiet ones to speak out. If the group seems especially lively, you may wish to also mention that the moderator reserves the right to step in and redirect individuals or the group as a whole if someone is long-winded or the discussion simply needs to move on in order to cover the research objectives.

Probing in Focus Groups

Probing in focus groups is very similar to probing in IDIs. The moderator listens to a response or set of responses to an open-ended question and then asks a probe to learn more about a point relevant to the research objectives. A key difference is that often, in a focus group, the probe may be addressed to the group rather than just to the person who provided the initial response. Whenever possible, these probes should be explicitly designed to use group dynamics—eliciting norms, rules, and processes and highlighting range and contrasts, as in the sequence below from a focus group about small investors and financial advice.

Moderator: "James, how did you end up getting financial planning advice from Bank XYZ?"

James: "I had just gotten a big bonus and deposited it in my savings account. They started calling me about investing right after that. It was obvious from the timing that they were watching my account and that they wanted my money. Before that I don't think they knew who I was—when they started calling me like that, I felt hunted."

Moderator: "Has anyone else ever had a similar feeling of being hunted or targeted in their contacts with a financial advisor? What did they do that made you feel that way?"

The variations of focus group probes are limitless. Some useful examples follow:

- Does everyone feel the same way as Bob?
- Has anyone had a different experience than Mary?
- You have all mentioned X. Are there some people who might disagree with this?
- You have all mentioned X. I've heard that some people think Y. What do you think about Y?

Maximizing the Focus Group Dynamic

It is the combination of a good focus group instrument, a good environment, and a skilled moderator that enables the focus group dynamic to come fully into play. Table 5.5 below summarizes ways to capitalize on the full benefits of the group dynamic.

Managing Different Personalities

A critical moderator skill is managing the personalities of the group participants. Almost any focus group will have one or more people that require the moderator to exercise some form of control, guidance, or urging. Table 5.6 below summarizes some

Table 5.5	Maximizing the Focus Group Dynamic	
The Discussion Guide	**The Mental and Physical Environment**	**The Moderator**
• Most questions are open-ended—contain lots of opportunities to get contrasts, lists, and examples	• Room/location is physically comfortable (seating, lighting, temperature, etc.)	• Knows the discussion guide and research objectives fully
• Questions/activities designed to elicit differences, ranges, and points of debate	• Arrival environment is relaxed and welcoming, appropriate refreshments available	• Strong facilitation skills, trained/practiced/rehearsed on current project
• Focus on norms, processes, and group or public topics	• Warm-up/self-introductions used to set expectations about participant role	• Fast-thinking, able to probe in ways that use the power of the group

Table 5.6	Managing Different Personalities
Personality Type	**Solution**
Shy or reticent	Call on the person by name, ask for the person's specific response to a question or to the responses of other participants, reiterate your need to hear from all
Overbearing/interruptive	Direct questions to others in the group, use body language (such as a blocking hand) to ask them to hold their comments, directly ask them to hold back so others may speak
Long-winded	Ask a secondary element of the question to encourage them to conclude, directly ask them to come to the point, or answer the question
Wanders off topic	Remind them what question has been asked, point out that the group has limited time and much ground to cover, repeat the need for responses to be to-the-point
Self-appointed expert	Direct questions to others, directly ask them to hold back until others have spoken
Combative	Remind everyone to be respectful of others' opinions, directly address provocative remarks, consider removal from the group
Flirtatious	Remind everyone of the purpose of the group, directly address any inappropriate language

common personality traits and some ways of dealing with the challenges they present in focus groups.

Occasionally, one of your participants may be too disruptive, ignorant of the topic, or just plain socially maladapted to be in a focus group. In these cases, you may need to dismiss the person from the group. This is always a difficult decision because it may hurt the person's feelings, and it disrupts the flow of the group. But it does happen, and you should have a plan about how to do it smoothly. In settings with an observation room, set up a signal, in advance, to alert your note-taker or another team member to come to the room with a "message" for the disruptive individual. The colleague then comes to the room and has the disruptive person leave with them. In these situations, the disruptive one is then paid his incentive and dismissed. Make these conversations short, neutral, and to the point: "We appreciate your time and effort coming here, but feel we can better conduct the group without you." Don't get involved in a long drawn out discussion of why you feel that way. Pay them and get them out the door.

If you do not have an observation room set up or colleagues to assist in a participant removal, you will have to be more direct. Ask the person to come outside the focus group space with you. Explain that they are not contributing to the group in the way you had hoped and that you have decided to pay them and have them leave. Once again, do not get involved in a debate or discussion about your decision. Stay polite but firm, conclude the interaction as soon as possible, and get back to the group.

Closing out the Focus Group

At the end of your group, make sure that you have wrapped up all the data collection and administrative details of your focus group, including the following:

- Getting and asking any final or follow-up questions from observers
- Asking the group for any final thoughts on the topic
- Thanking the group and herding them out of the room (including any who have a tendency to stand around and chat)
- Paying incentives and filling out any final paperwork
- Restoring the room to its original condition
- Gathering and organizing all stimulus materials, notes, audio and video recordings, outputs of group activities
- Debriefing with research team and observers
- Packing, shipping, or transporting all equipment and materials that were brought to the site
- Getting everyone and everything to their next location

Most Common Focus Group Mistakes (and solutions)

As you might guess, there are a lot of things that can go wrong with focus groups. Table 5.7 below lists 10 of the most common ones, with tips for how to avoid or ameliorate them:

Table 5.7	Common Focus Group Challenges (and solutions)
Problem	**Solution**
Poor quality of participants (i.e., not knowledgeable, not verbal)	Good screening questionnaire, rigorous application of screening criteria, or rescreening when participants arrive; adding a verbal ability item ("tell me about the last movie you saw") to the screening questionnaire
Poor show-up rate, group too small	Allow adequate time for recruiting, actively confirm recruits, or over-recruit

Problem	Solution
Uncomfortable environment	Check out the room in advance, control potential sources of discomfort or disruption
Failing equipment	Test in advance, have back ups
Low energy in group	Moderator adds energy; do a group activity that requires movement, interaction, or debate; give them refreshments with sugar or caffeine
Rowdy group	Moderator asserts control: "One voice at a time please"; insert a quiet or individual activity ("write a paragraph about" or "draw me a picture of")
Observers butt in	Brief them on their role; assure them they will get their questions addressed
Participants struggling to answer	Revise the discussion guide; rephrase, shorten, or remove problem questions
Disruptive participants	Control or remove them
Groups running too long	Time the discussion guide, pare it down to the most important questions

DOCUMENTING THE FOCUS GROUP

As mentioned earlier, the quality of the notes and recordings from your groups is critical—these are the actual data you will be analyzing. Depending on the constraints of your focus group setting, you may be more or less dependent on one or another of these data capture approaches. Here are some tips about how to handle your various types of data:

- Video–audio recordings—Be sure all physical (CDs, DVDs, tapes, thumb drives) and digital (electronic) files are accounted for and properly labeled (group date, location, time, etc.). It is easy to get these mixed up, misplaced, or misfiled. Make sure that all supplementary documentation associated with the group—seating charts, participant rosters, outputs of group activities, screening questionnaires, informed consent and confidentiality forms—is also accounted for and appropriately labeled. If a full written transcript is to be made, arrange for transmission or transportation of the recordings to the transcriber.
- Notes—Follow the labeling and handling protocols for recordings. If notes will be the primary data source, they should be expanded and cleaned up as soon as possible following the group. Associated detail can be added, including notations of nonverbal elements of the group (body language, mood, gestures) or data from the screening questionnaire. When there is no video of the group, be sure to include a seating chart in the notes as shown in Figure 5.3 below.

Figure 5.3 Sample Note-Taker Form and Seating Chart

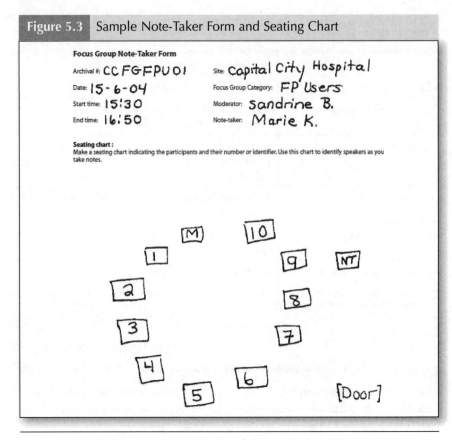

Source: Mack, Woodsong, MacQueen, Guest, and Namey (2005, p. 70).

Post-Event Debrief

After your focus group(s) and especially after the first one in a series, allow time for the research team (and possibly any observers) to meet and discuss the event. The checklist below shows elements that should be covered in this debrief. Figure 5.4 contains a sample debrief form.

- Research objectives—How well did the group address the research objectives? Are any changes needed in the discussion guide to better get at the desired information?
- Group length, or amount of time spent on each topic—Does the discussion guide need to be trimmed or rebalanced?
- Group tone and feel—Are any changes needed to make future groups go more smoothly or productively?

Figure 5.4   Sample Focus Group Debrief Form

Sample Focus Group Debriefing Form

Focus Group Debriefing Form
Archival #: **CCFGFPUOI**
Date: 15-6-04   Name of Study: FP-VCT Integration
Moderator: Sandrine B.
Note-taker: Marie K.

(1)   What are the main themes that emerged in this focus group?
- lack of FP supplies   ☒ Problems w/ FP will
- frustration w/ health services   affect integr
- still stigma re: FP (condoms)   of VCT

(2)   Did any information contradict what you learned in previous focus groups?
- Provider Int said follow up clients when
  not enuf supplies, give new appts but FG
  participants say don't even tell them to come back

(3)   What did participants say that was unclear or confusing to you?
"Go home and take care of yourself"
  -- What do providers intend w/this advice?

(4)   What did you observe that would not be evident from reading a transcript of the discussion (e.g. group dynamic, individual behaviours, etc.)?
- lot of frustration in gp
- R4 silent

(5)   What problems did you encounter (e.g. logistical, behaviors of individuals, questions that were confusing, etc.)?
Q7 & 12 overlap

(6)   What issues will you follow up?
- Ask about how clinic supplied - who? how often?
- Advice about changing methods when supplies
  run out   · Why do methods
- No follow up of clients?   prices change?

(7)   Does the note-taker have any suggestions for the moderator and vice versa?
- NT → try to get more quotes
- Mod → direct questions at participants
          who don't speak

Source: Mack et al. (2005, p. 74).

- Data capture—Are the notes, recordings, and so on accounted for and usable? Are any changes needed in the data capture protocol?
- Environment, equipment, and stimuli—Are any changes or improvements needed to the location and the things in it to make the groups better, more effective, or more enjoyable?
- Recruiting and participants—Are any adjustments needed in who is being invited to the groups or how they are being handled?
- Logistics—Are there any problems with transportation, parking, food, or anything else that needs to be addressed?

FOCUS GROUP VARIATIONS

In addition to the traditional face-to-face format, focus groups can also be done with groups of people who are not all physically present at the same location or, in some cases, even at the same time. Use of telephone and Internet technology presents both benefits and challenges in collecting focus group data. Below, we summarize some of the pros and cons of using one type of focus group medium versus another. Appendix 5.1 at the end of this chapter contains a detailed comparison of focus groups by media type by George Silverman. Readers should note, however, that the matrix in Appendix 5.1 is somewhat outdated (i.e., it doesn't include video-based, online technologies) and, given its basis in Silverman's market research experience, is rather biased towards telephone-based focus groups.

Telephone Focus Groups

Telephone focus groups utilize teleconferencing technology to enable what is essentially a conference call with a moderator. The key benefit of this variation is the ability to conduct a focus group with a sample that could not be assembled in a single location (at least not without sending costs through the roof). For example, you can conduct a telephone focus group with students who have applied to a specific university, but who are scattered across the country. This approach also works with rare individuals or those who are unable or unwilling to travel to a group (i.e., steel plant general managers, people with mobility disabilities). Additionally, telephone groups are usually less expensive than face-to-face groups—there are no charges for facilities, the research team does not have to travel, and, in some cases, incentives can be lower because of less inconvenience.

The drawbacks of telephone groups are those that are inherent to telephone conversations. Without the face-to-face contact, participants tend to talk over each other, the moderator (also the note-taker and participants) may have trouble figuring out who is speaking, there is no way to do activities or exercises that utilize visual stimuli, and the inability to see the body language of the participants makes the data somewhat less rich.

If you choose to do telephone groups, it is usually better to keep the number of participants relatively small—the larger the number of voices, the more difficult it is to manage the discussion and to correctly record the data. Be sure your teleconferencing service or software—and your recording devices—will work well with the number of participants you expect. Do a rehearsal to test how well everything will work, including how the note-taker or transcriptionist will perform their role. It can also be useful to have a moderator whose voice will stand out from the participants—that is, a female moderator running a mostly male group—otherwise, you may find that the participants are unsure who they should be responding to.

One of the authors conducted telephone focus groups to reach groups of medical residents at geographically dispersed medical schools. The residents were together in a conference room and could see each other as they were speaking, limiting the issue of respondents talking over one another. The moderator asked speakers to identify themselves before offering a response, and other members of the group helped to remind those who forgot. The conference calling service that was used offered audio-recording, which served as the primary mode of data documentation. It is certainly harder to establish rapport over the phone, but the resulting data were useful—and could not have been obtained as quickly or inexpensively otherwise.

Internet Focus Groups

There are a number of ways to use the Internet to conduct group discussions. Depending on what type of technology and software you use, these can range from chat room-style written group discussions to webcam setups that closely mimic the environment of a face-to-face focus group—even including a separate "observer room." All of these share the benefit of being able to conduct groups with people who are geographically dispersed. And all share the disadvantage of limiting the potential participants and researchers to those who have and can reliably use the requisite technologies. That said, as more and more people become web and webcam enabled and as focus group and chat room software improves, the opportunities to do Internet focus groups will steadily increase.

Chat Room–Style Groups

In chat room–style groups, the participants and moderator communicate only in writing—similar to any other chat room interaction. The moderator poses each question, and the participants type in their responses. There are two major chat room variations—the "live" group, which is confined to a short time frame similar to a regular focus group, and the "threaded discussion" or "bulletin board," which can be spread over several days. The live version has the problem of people generally being slower to type than to speak, so you get less data per focus group than you will in a face-to-face group done in a similar amount of time. Additionally, participants tend to type over each other, limiting the group dynamic. The threaded discussion solves these problems by spreading the discussion out over several days—the group finishes with a topic, and then the moderator moves them along to the next. Threaded discussions can produce very detailed and thoughtful responses and lots of give-and-take between the participants. An extra advantage of chat room groups is that they automatically produce a full transcript of the group proceedings.

Webcam Groups

There are several types of software available to facilitate webcam meetings, including some that are specifically designed for conducting focus groups. With the specialized software, the moderator and participants can see each other, observers and note-takers can see everything while not being visible to the group, observers can send questions to the moderator via instant messages that are visible only to the moderator, and exhibits, drawings, questionnaires, and other materials can be shown to the group. Less specialized Internet meeting software and services have some but not all of these capabilities. Depending on your needs and the sophistication of the software or web meeting service you use, webcam groups can be very effective and, of course, it is simple to do video capture of a webcam meeting.

The strength of these groups is also their weaknesses—they are completely technology dependent. You can do these only with tech-savvy participants and in places with reliable broadband connections. Even with every precaution, webcam groups are subject to technical difficulties—every now and then a participant will suddenly lose their connection and disappear—a disconcerting event that never occurs during a face-to-face group.

Large Group Discussions

From time-to-time, focus group type discussions are a part of hybrid quantitative-qualitative sessions with larger groups of people (20–50 participants is typical). In these sessions, the group responds quantitatively to some stimuli—answering a questionnaire about product concepts, prototypes, foods, or ads are common versions—usually by giving input via touch pads or Perception Analyzer dials. These data are instantly compiled, with the moderator-to-be watching the results as they come in. After the quantitative portion of the session is completed, the moderator enters the room and asks questions based on the quantitative findings as in these examples:

Moderator: "I see that quite a few of you said this vehicle prototype seemed youthful. Among those of you who answered that way, what about it gave you that feeling?"

Moderator: "It looks like almost all of you turned your dials way up at this point in the commercial. What about it made you do that?"

FOCUS GROUP OUTPUTS

Focus groups can create a number of types of data outputs. While the categories of outputs are limited only by the imagination of the research team, common forms of data generated through focus groups include the following:

- Notes—raw and expanded
- Transcriptions

- Audio files
- Video files
- Collages, drawings, written stories
- Ratings, rankings
- Ideas for products, services, communications
- Solutions to problems

Thinking about the type of output or data you'd like to generate will help you both in designing your focus group guide and in moderating and probing during the discussion itself.

WORKING INTERNATIONALLY

Conducting focus groups across national and cultural boundaries can be both extraordinarily challenging and deeply rewarding. Seeing how people respond, not just to your questions but to being in a group discussion in their own human and linguistic environment, can provide important insights into both your research topic and their national and ethnic cultures. It can provide both context for your findings and, if the data collection is done in more than one country or culture, the opportunity to discover commonalities and differences on a scale that would be invisible in monocultural or single-site studies.

Most of the issues, cautions and suggestions about recruiting or conducting IDIs in international and cross-cultural settings mentioned in Chapters 2 and 4 also apply to focus groups. But as with other aspects of conducting focus groups, there are some areas in which moving to a group setting in an international or cross-cultural environment demands extra consideration from the researcher.

Preparing for a Cross-Cultural or International Focus Group

In the United States and other developed countries, researchers typically have their choice of many possible meeting room type locations in which to conduct the focus groups—dedicated focus group rooms, hotel and office conference rooms, classrooms, community centers, and the like. These choices may be rare or nonexistent in less developed countries, especially in rural areas. As mentioned before, these locations require adaptations that may mean you are doing groups in someone's home, a restaurant, a bazaar, or under a tree in an open-air location. The key, as always, is to find a place that the participants can get to, where they will be comfortable talking, and where the group activities and data collection can go smoothly. Good reconnaissance of the site, thinking ahead as to human and equipment needs, and being flexible are vital to working in these locations.

Even in developed nations, local norms often mean that the researcher must adapt. In the United States, having participants sit around a large conference-type table is the norm, and Americans are very comfortable talking in groups in such a setting. In Great Britain, even dedicated focus group facilities often forgo the table and seat the participants in a circle of chairs in what looks to Americans like a group therapy session. This means that the group activities and the style of moderating need to shift to this somewhat more intimate layout. For example, if you're going to have them draw or write, you better have clipboards. And the large gestures that a moderator may use at a conference table will be muted. Learn in advance what a focus group in your target country looks and sounds like and how your participants will be seated, and make your changes accordingly.

If your research is in your home country but includes people from cultural or ethnic groups that differ from the dominant culture, then you may also need to alter some aspect of your focus group location. A focus group facility and protocol that is comfortable for Anglo-Americans may seem strange and intimidating to new immigrants from a small village in a less-developed country. Doing a few informational interviews may lead you to give up your well-equipped focus group room and plush observer lounge in order to make your participants more at ease. It's better to conduct lively engaged groups on a lawn than to try to get groups moving with participants who are cowed by the surroundings or, worse, suspicious that your activities are some sort of front for the CIA, the National Immigration Service, or repressive authority figures from their home country (and yes, the authors have been mistaken for all of these and more).

Your sampling and recruiting protocols may also need to adapt to an international or cross-cultural setting. Many types of recruiting that work in developed countries—phone calls, electronic databases, and so forth—are not practical in less-developed areas. Conversely, approaches such as snowball sampling may work quite well in such places. If possible, include someone who is a cultural or local expert on your research team who can advise you about how to approach people and who will keep you from wasting time and resources on inappropriate or locally offensive protocols.

You should also get local advice about the issue of incentives—what types, what amounts, and how to package them. Remember that cultures differ greatly in terms of how they deal with money and gifts. In Japan, for example, you never give someone money from your bare hand; an envelope (there are special ones for this purpose) is an absolute requirement, not just a courtesy as it is in the United States. Incentive amounts that would seem trivially small in the United States may be considered princely sums in other places, or, even be large enough to distort local economic relationships. If you cannot get a local expert to advise you, do some direct research about local prices and adjust your incentive accordingly. In the United States, typical focus group incentives are often in the range of a median day's pay for U.S. workers. Learn what workers in your target population are paid per day and use that as a guidepost.

Working With Groups in Cross-Cultural and International Settings

There are, of course, considerable cultural differences in terms of how people behave in group discussions, and these play a big role in how focus groups can be conducted. In Japan, for example, traditional etiquette dictates that people do not put their own opinions forward, especially if it might create a disagreement with some-one else. Consequently, focus groups in Japan require longer warm-up and introduc-tory phases and, in comparison with many other countries, Japanese discussion guides use more *what if* scenarios in which participants comment on what hypo-thetical others might say or do and fewer questions designed to stimulate debate. In contrast, groups in Latin America tend to be lively and full of social interaction—even among total strangers—almost from the instant the participants are in the room. One of the authors once witnessed a Latin American focus group moderator take off her shoes and walk the length of the conference table to refocus attention and assert control over her overly exuberant group.

The key to dealing with these cross-cultural differences is having some sense of them in advance so that the discussion guide and moderator style can be adjusted to local norms. There is no substitute for having someone with local knowledge on your research team. Even where you speak the language, there can be important differ-ences in the tone of group discussions—American researchers are sometimes baffled by the politeness of Canadian respondents (disagreements of opinion may seem so muted that the analysts aren't sure any differences were expressed), unable to pene-trate local jargon in Australia (a nightmare for an American transcriptionist), or shocked to find that British participants are allowed to have beer as a waiting room refreshment (moving the tone of the focus group toward the time-honored traditions of British pub discussion).

To conduct a focus group, the moderator must have native speaker level fluency in the local language—moderating a focus group just doesn't work well through an interpreter. The pauses caused by interpretation are death to group dynamics. If you don't have this level of linguistic skill on your team, this would be the time to hire a pro—ideally one who is also culture knowledgeable and can help review the discus-sion guide for cultural appropriateness. But for some places and languages, you may be forced to choose between a seasoned moderator who doesn't speak the language and a competent speaker who has never conducted a focus group (if you have neither of these, you're beat and probably shouldn't try to collect data via focus groups). While there may be exceptions in extraordinary circumstances, it is probably better to try to train the linguist to moderate a group than to try to moderate the group via an interpreter. If you think you will be in this situation, then bring along videos of focus groups that the linguist can watch for training purposes, involve them in the development of the discussion guide, give them a chance to practice or role play, and then hope for the best.

It is not just the group participants who may behave differently than in your home country. If your focus group observers are from a different culture or country than your own, you may need to make some adjustments for them, as well. Such adaptations may include food and drink in the back room—especially the issue of alcohol–no alcohol—what tone they adopt while watching the groups, and their expectations about debriefings after the group. It is generally a good idea to spend a little time with your observers before the groups start to discuss their needs, the observer role, and to set some boundaries. This can be especially important if you have observers who have never watched a focus group before. One of the authors was once moderating a group for a foreign subsidiary of a large America firm. The observers at the subsidiary were thrilled that their parent firm was finally spending some research dollars to learn about consumers in their country and a huge crowd showed up to observe the groups. But during the first group, the sounds of revelry began to bleed through the two-way mirror from the observation room. Concerned that this was becoming a distraction to the focus group participants, the moderator called a break and headed to the observation room to see what was going on. Apparently, sitting in a dark room watching the focus group had triggered the local equivalent of "group movie night" behavior in the observers—they were eating (a lot) and joking (loudly) with each other, and every flat surface in the room was covered with empty beverage containers, most of them alcoholic. The moderator delivered a short but pointed speech about focus group observer etiquette and the observers were not heard from for the rest of the group.

Interpretation and Translation in International and Cross-Cultural Groups

If your international or cross-cultural focus groups will have observers—and they expect to understand the proceedings as they occur—you will need to arrange for simultaneous interpretation. Interpreting a group is considerably more challenging than interpreting a one-on-one conversation, and you will need a very, very good interpreter. When you have an observation room, the interpretation setup is United Nations style—the interpreter has a headset with the audio feed from the focus group and speaks into a microphone leading to headsets worn by the observers. In less fancy surroundings, the interpreter may just sit with the observers in the observation area.

Note that it is almost impossible to do simultaneous interpretation for observers who are sitting in the same space as the focus group participants—hearing the interpreter distracts the participants from the discussion and constantly underlines that they are being observed.

The issue of language also has an impact on transcription of your focus groups. For major languages, you can find translator–transcribers, either in the Market Research *GreenBook* or by Internet search. For less widely spoken languages, you may have to do translation and transcription as separate steps. If this is the case, be sure to allow sufficient space in your project time line for this to occur—it will be a little while before you can jump into the analysis.

SUMMING UP

The power of group dynamics makes focus groups an enormously flexible and useful source of quantitative data. The old adage that none of us is as smart as all of us holds true for many research topics, and focus groups are definitely a way of harnessing the power of multiple minds, diverse points of view, and the variety of human experience. Additionally, they can be exciting and intense data collection experiences, giving the researcher (and often observers, as well) the chance to share in the insights and emotions that participants feel for the topics you question them about. By adding focus groups to your data collection tool kit, you will tap into rich sources of data and memorable field research events.

REFERENCES

Agar, M., & MacDonald, J. (1995). Focus groups and ethnography. *Human Organization, 54,* 78–86.

Baker, R., Parker-Brick, C., & Todd, A. (1996). Methods used in research with street children in Nepal. *Childhood, 3,* 171–193.

Mack, N., Woodsong, C., MacQueen, K., Guest, G., & Namey, E. (2005). *Qualitative research methods: A data collector's field guide.* Research Triangle Park, NC: Family Health International.

Mitchell, M. (1998). *Employing qualitative methods in the private sector.* Thousand Oaks, CA: Sage.

Patton, M. Q. (2002). *Qualitative research and evaluation methods* (3rd ed.). Thousand Oaks, CA: Sage.

Silverman, G. (n.d.). *A comparison between face-to-face focus groups, telephone focus groups and online focus groups.* Retrieved September 15, 2011, from http://www.nhtsa.gov/people/injury/newmediaforumweb/mediaforumplanner/images/face toface.pdf

ADDITIONAL READING

Krueger, R., & Casey, M. (2009). *Focus groups: A practical guide for applied research* (4th ed.). Thousand Oaks, CA: Sage.

Morgan, D., & Krueger, R. (1998). *The focus group kit* (Vols. 1–6). Thousand Oaks, CA: Sage.

www.greenbook.org. The online version of the American Marketing Association's *GreenBook*. It contains searchable listings of focus group moderators, facilities, and related market research companies worldwide.

EXERCISES

1. From your area of study, list five research topics suitable for qualitative inquiry. For each, write down the pros and cons of examining the topic via focus groups.

2. Think of two highly contrasting study populations—such as upscale Americans living in a suburb versus a rural population in a region in a less developed country where literacy rates are low and suspicion of outsiders is high. Write out your approach for handling informed consent, recruiting, and incentives for each group.

3. Locate an interview guide that you or another researcher has used for an IDI. Revise the guide for use in a focus group. What would you leave the same? What would you change? Can you add exercises, questions, or probes to maximize the group dynamic? Are there some topics or questions you would have to leave out? Are there things you could learn only from doing this in a group?

4. For the next 10 people you encounter in any setting, try to gauge what each would be like as a focus group participant. Who would need to be encouraged or drawn out, who might be overly talkative, who is opinionated, and who is shy about speaking their mind? Write down what techniques you would use to help each one be the most valuable participant they could be.

APPENDIX 5.1

A Comparison Between Face-to-Face Focus Groups, Telephone Focus Groups and Online [Chat-based] Focus Groups

Characteristic	Face to Face	Telephone	Online
Rationale	When the richness of group interaction is desired with people who can be brought into a central location.	When the richness of group interaction is desired with people who cannot easily be brought together face to face (geographically dispersed, hard to recruit, low incidence) or who you want in their own natural environment. Higher degree of openness makes this the preferred medium for remote groups.	Same as telephone focus groups, plus people you want to be online during the group.
First started	In the 1950's.	First viable telephone focus groups in 1969.	Unknown, but probably as a research methodology in the early 1980's. Didn't become widespread until the mid- to late- 90's.
Acceptance of methodology	Face to face almost totally accepted as a valid qualitative methodology.	The standard methodology in some industries, such as pharmaceutical and agriculture, increasingly in financial services and others. Telephone still not well accepted, or even heard of, in many industries.	Mostly used in high-tech applications. Rejected by most other industries, but acceptance growing.

Characteristic	Face to Face	Telephone	Online
Richest expression, greatest cues for interpretation. *(This is probably the most important issue.)*	Here, face-to-face groups have the clear advantage. You can see body language and facial expressions. More modes to express, more data to interpret.	Can't see body language or facial expressions, but most are translated into the richness of the human voice. When people are on the phone, their voices become more expressive because they know subconsciously that they can't be seen. Think about the voice, with its ironic sarcasm, slight hesitancies in answers (how do you spot a typing hesitancy?), chuckling that is unintentionally expressed on the phone but not expressed in text unless the person wants to call attention to it, strong vs. meek answers (in other words what would be in bold type if one could use it), tentative vs. energized ideas, speed, inflection, tone, strength, wavering, stress etc.	A distant third. All of this is lost in online text only groups. Emoticons, e.g., :-) or :-(, don't express the broad range of information, that can be heard in the voice.
Visual element	Has visual element.	Non visual, but telephone has the richness of the human voice. If this is the only way to get the participants, the lack of visual is not a high price to pay.	Non visual.
Stimulus materials	A virtually unlimited range of stimulus materials are possible.	Stimulus materials can be overnighted, faxed or presented on the Web.	May look different in different browsers.
Backroom interaction	Easiest to interact behind the one-way mirror. Sometimes it's too easy for the clients to interact and ignore the group.	Both telephone and online groups have virtual back rooms. There are no M&Ms available, but your favorite drinks are only as far away as your own refrigerator.	

Characteristic	Face to Face	Telephone	Online
Following the thread of the conversation	Not a problem.	Not a problem.	May be difficult to tell what respondents are responding to, since they are often typing in parallel.
Amount of information. Number of words per hour	About the same for Face to Face and Telephone.		About 1/3 less words per unit time for online.
Respondents can get their thoughts out without interruption in online	You want interaction, not thoughts running on without interruption. It's the very purpose of a focus group.		People in online groups are responding much more in isolation and in parallel than they are in telephone or face-to-face groups.

Characteristic	Face to Face	Telephone	Online
Technology bias	None.	None.	One person's bias is another one's sample. If you are selecting for technology sophistication, it is not a bias. If you are looking for a full range of technology attitudes represented, this method is extremely biased.
Rational, impersonal responses vs. full range of human interaction: emotional, cognitive, etc.	People tend to be somewhat inhibited, but get over it with expert moderation. Tremendous richness of expression is possible.	People get extremely emotional and personal on the telephone, since the anonymity, lack of visual element and naturalness of talking on the phone creates a great deal of psychological safety. .	While people feel safe online for the same reasons they do on the telephone, they cannot express themselves as well using text as they can using their voices. This essentially eliminates online groups for many sophisticated applications.
More honest, open, outspoken, less swayed by group, less reticent to speak	Participants somewhat inhibited.	The openness of people in telephone groups is legendary. People have compared the same groups of teenagers on the phone vs. face to face; the teenagers were much more comfortable talking on the phone. The production was much higher, gender groups could be mixed, and the phone groups were much superior in other ways. The argument that young people are more comfortable on the computer than they are face to face may be true.	No one has shown that online has any superiority to telephone on this cluster of attributes.

Characteristic	Face to Face Focus Groups	Telephone Focus Groups	Online Focus Groups
Whether people tend to tell the truth. Ability for moderator to detect lying	High degree of visual cues makes it easier to detect lying, but people more tempted to please each other or the moderator, play eye contact games, etc.	Telephone has been validated in individual interviews as being the medium in which people tend to tell the truth more, but this has not been validated for telephone *groups*.	Awaiting data.
Setting up the groups	Hardest. People have to travel to attend, so you usually have to identify people in the local area (exception: face to face at conferences.)	Easiest. People can be anywhere, everyone has a phone. Groups can be worldwide, or as narrow as a single building. High-level people want to participate to talk with old friends or just hear what people have to say across the country/world.	Not everyone can type, has access to a computer or wants to participate via computer with other people.
Show up rates	50–80%	90–100%	<50%
Ability to reach difficult-to-recruit participants.	Pretty poor. That's mostly why telephone and online groups were invented!	Best, for reasons already stated.	Better than face to face, but not as good as telephone, judging by acceptance and show-up rates.

Characteristic	Face to Face	Telephone	Online
Opportunity for dominators to sabotage group	Can be hard to control dominators. Hard to kick people out of group, without them getting a "message," which fools nobody and can destroy the dynamics of the group.	Much easier to control dominators in telephone groups than in face-to-face groups because people are more easily interruptible on the telephone. Can kick someone out of group privately and invisibly.	The fastest typist wins. Fifty words per minute is a pretty respectable typing speed. However, people who use voice dictation type at about 160 words per minute and can overwhelm an entire group easily. Easy to kick someone out.
Turnaround for recruiting, executing and reporting on groups	Usually much slower than telephone and online.	Both telephone and online are usually superior to face to face. Telephone probably has the edge because of its flexibility.	
Bias Issues	Lower potential for bias than than online, higher than telephone. Validated long ago as being roughly representative enough to generalize (if not, why are you running the groups?), although not *statistically* representative.	Highest recruitment rates mean telephone is the most representative. Like face to face, validated long ago as being roughly representative enough to generalize, although not statistically representative	Low recruitment rates mean that there is a much greater opportunity for bias. 10 people out of 2000, if that continues to be the rate, is unacceptable to many, unless it is proved that these ten people are not unusual. Online needs validation. Jury still out.
Greater participation from the client team	Difficult to get key people to participate in different cities.	Telephone has a slight edge here because it is easier to get access to a telephone than to a computer. If the client is stranded, he/she can dial in on a cell phone.	Computers aren't quite as ubiquitous as phones, but they are getting there.

Characteristic	Face to Face	Telephone	Online
Evaluation of websites	Face to face is a distant third because people have to be given computers in a usability lab. These are not their own computers, so they are not set up optimally for the person using it. On the other hand, if you need to observe them, face to face is the way to go.	Telephone is superior. People participate in a telephone group while using their computer. A variety of software and website services are able to direct them to websites, PowerPoint presentations, software screens or anything else that can be viewed on a computer screen. This can be under the control of the moderator or the participants.	When this is done as part of an online group, it is simply too unwieldy to expect people to click through and view websites while also typing their responses.
Fast turnaround with equal cost	About the same price as online, about 10% more than telephone. Can be more if a lot of clients are traveling.	Telephone groups are about 10% cheaper than face to face and online.	Online groups are reported to be approximately the same cost as face to face.
Cost-effectiveness	Least cost-effective.	Most cost-effective.	As of this writing, approximately the same cost as face to face.
Personal questions can be addressed, anonymity protected	Anonymity lowest face to face. This can make people clam up.	Anonymity can be protected just as well on the phone as it can be online	Unfortunately, authenticity can also be masked better online. Is the person who he/she says he/she is? Hardest to verify online, although there are abuses in all modes.

Characteristic	Face to Face	Telephone	Online
Sampling advantages, such as better mixture of people within the group, mixing heterogeneous and conflicting participants, and people who would be reluctant to participate together because they are competitors in a local geographical region	These are notorious problems with face to face groups.	Telephone groups have all of these advantages as well. Since the acceptance and show-up rates are higher for telephone, telephone probably has a more representative sample.	Online has all of these advantages over face to face, but equal to telephone. But telephone usually has more representative sample.
Availability of the technology to the participants	Traffic, bad weather, etc. can ruin show-up rate. Not everyone has a car available, ruling out non-drivers. This can be a problem with the elderly, infirm, some handicapped people, etc.	Everyone has a phone (many several). Worldwide: As long as they can get to a phone where they can be reached from the United States, they can be conferenced.	Not everyone has a computer. Not everyone is comfortable chatting on a computer.
Conversation flow	Usually natural, but can be stilted, easy to break into side conversations, or feel ignored.	Conversation is natural, with no side conversations possible. The illusion is created that the speaker is speaking to each person individually. It's extremely hard to talk while someone else is talking on the phone, but easy to interrupt.	If people are typing at the same time in parallel then trying to react to the burst of text, the flow is disjointed.

Characteristic	Face to Face	Telephone	Online
Catching cheaters, repeaters and impersonators	Easy to verify identities face to face in the same facility, difficult when there are many facilities in the same city.	Because of the high recruitment and show up rates, usually uses a closed list supplied by clients. This greatly reduces cheaters, repeaters and phonies.	This method is most vulnerable to abuses.
Difficulty of getting in-depth information	Face to face is widely acknowledged to be an extremely effective modality for getting in-depth information.	Telephone is even better.	Widely acknowledged, even by its practitioners, to be the least effective way of getting in-depth information.
Participation issues	Show up rates are unpredictable. Usually, after the warm up period, participants are extremely involved.	The modal show-up rate for telephone is 100%! It's extremely rare for someone to either hang up or get disconnected. Participants need virtually no warm up period. They get extremely involved.	Respondents can lose interest and drop out or get lost in the flow, especially in bulletin board forums. No-shows are high.
Group control issues	Groups can get out of hand, with side conversations, everyone talking at once, etc.	Extremely easy to control.	Amount of text streaming may overwhelm moderator and respondents.
Skills needed to participate	Usually need to drive (or have driver), speak clearly enough to participate, understand the language of the session.	Ability to use phone, speak and understand language of session.	Almost completely dependent on typing skills. Ability to follow simple log-in and participation instructions on a computer.

Characteristic	Face to Face	Telephone	Online
Travel time and expense	Another reason why telephone and online were invented.	Both telephone and online eliminate participant travel time and expense equally.	
Can be used to corroborate findings from in person groups that were done in only one or two markets	You have to go to many locations in order to get a cross-section of the nation.	Both telephone and online groups can be conducted in as many locations as there are participants. So a group of 9 participants can be from 9 different towns, or even countries. Or, they can be as narrow as from one office building in Los Angeles.	
'Sensitive' topics	Not as easy to get people to open up on sensitive topics as telephone and online.	Both telephone and online are ideal to create the psychological safety for sensitive topics. In some ways, they are better than individual interviews because of the group support effect.	

Characteristic	Face to Face	Telephone	Online
Participation on respondents' schedule	Impossible.	Impossible.	Bulletin board or list group style allows this. It is the only mode of running a focus group so far that not only repeals *geography,* but also repeals *time.* This is a very limited, but very important, application.
Ease of moderation	Face to face groups are slightly easier to moderate than telephone.	Telephone groups are probably the hardest to moderate.	Online groups are reported by some moderators to be a little easier to moderate because they do not require the moderator to think on his/her feet quite as quickly, especially in asynchronous groups, although an online moderator does have to process a lot of information. This whole issue is probably a non issue for *experienced moderators,* but could be a considerable advantage for inexperienced moderators. Asynchronous groups might even be a good training method, since the moderator could discuss possible probes with a teacher before actually committing to an intervention.

Characteristic	Face to Face	Telephone	Online
Psychological safety of participants (respondents)	Lowest of the three. People are easily intimidated by the other people's dress, manner, facial expressions, body language, etc. Even skilled moderators have to work hard to make people open up.	Almost as high as online. People can't see each other, and they may be from different parts of the country, so they tend to open up much more than in face to face.	Highest. People can't even hear each others' tone of voice.
Immediate transcripts	Transcripts can be ready the next day or two.	There are several services that can remotely record telephone groups and have the transcripts ready the next morning.	Transcripts are available even during the session.

Source: Excerpted from A Comparison Between Face-to-Face (F2F) Focus Groups, Telephone Focus Groups and Online Focus Groups (Silverman, n.d.).

6

Additional Qualitative Data Collection Methods

Traditional interviews and focus groups consist of a verbal exchange in which the interviewer/moderator asks questions, the participants verbally respond, and these responses are in turn inductively probed. This process is captured with notes and/or audio-recording, and a textual analysis ensues. These traditional approaches are time-tested techniques that work, which is why each has its own chapter in this book. Sometimes, however, a research objective can benefit from supplemental activities that can be completed *within* an in-depth interview or focus group. We cover the more common of these activities in the pages that follow.

Additionally, documents and other material artifacts sometimes serve as data in qualitative inquiry. Although not considered primary data—that is, they are not produced with the intent of informing a research objective—documents and other secondary forms of textual and visual representation can be highly informative. Since document analysis is considered a constituent component of qualitative research, we have included it in this chapter, despite the fact that it is not a form of data generation like the other techniques.

For ease of reference, we've divided the chapter into four main sections. The first three are based on which data collection context a particular supplemental activity is better suited to—one-on-one, group, or both. Note that these groupings are just general guidelines; exceptions exist. Additionally, while these activities are more commonly conducted within IDIs or focus groups, many of them can be adapted to use in participant observation in cases where the research objectives would benefit. The fourth section deals exclusively with document analysis.

PROJECTIVE TECHNIQUES

Many of the activities we describe below are considered *projective techniques*. Projective techniques originate from the psychoanalytic school of clinical psychology and are commonly used in a diagnostic capacity. The term itself comes from Frank's seminal article, "Projective Methods for the Study of Personality" (1939). The basic premise behind projective methods is that they allow "an individual to reveal his way of organizing experience, by giving him a field (objects, materials, experiences) with relatively little structure and cultural patterning so that the personality can project upon that plastic field his ways of seeing life, his meanings, significances, patterns and especially his feelings. Thus we elicit a projection of the individual personality's private world" (p. 403). Lindzey (1961) sorted these types of techniques into five general categories:

Association—Techniques in which participants respond quickly to a stimulus provided by the researcher. A commonly portrayed associative technique in popular culture is word association, where the researcher presents the participant with a term, and the participant says the first word that comes to mind.

Construction—These techniques require participants to construct stories, pictures, or other artifacts that are analyzed by the researcher.

Completion—Completion techniques are usually more structured than the previous two techniques. They present the participant with incomplete drawings or sentences and the participant is asked to complete or fill in the missing piece.

Ordering—Participants are asked to arrange pictures or other materials in an order that makes the most sense to them.

Expressive—These consist of activities such as role playing, drawing, taking photos, or any expressive activity that doesn't directly involve words.

Another way in which projective techniques can be categorized is along a continuum representing the degree of ambiguity in the stimuli used (Figure 6.1). Stimuli can range widely in the amount of information, structure, and clarity they contain. Some methods such as photo elicitation using pictures of familiar scenes within a community will fall on the less ambiguous side of the continuum, whereas others such as the Rorschach Ink Blot test (rarely used outside of the clinical setting) are extremely abstract and land on the more ambiguous end of the continuum. Conventional wisdom, backed by some research (Soley & Smith, 2008, p. 113), suggests that the more ambiguous the stimuli, the more likely responses will be projective of inner values, emotions, and beliefs. Less ambiguous stimuli will tend to

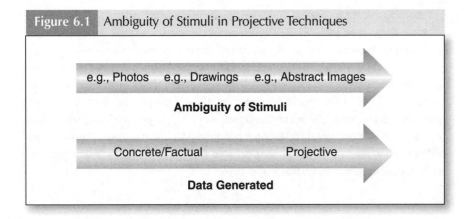

Figure 6.1   Ambiguity of Stimuli in Projective Techniques

elicit factual and more tangible responses. As an example of the latter, showing photos of actual events or places commonly encountered in an individual's daily routine, would most likely elicit factual information about those photos. Figure 6.1 depicts this relationship.

Note that for any of the activities described in this chapter, the researcher can control the degree of structure within a task. For expressive tasks, such as drawing or taking photos, the researcher can provide as little or as much instruction to participants as is appropriate. The outcome of a drawing activity, for example, would certainly be different if you asked participants to draw examples of (a) issues in their community, (b) health issues in their community, or (c) HIV-related issues in their community. Similarly, the degree of structure within construction or completion tasks can be controlled by the amount of information provided or omitted in the stimuli. The important thing to remember is that the type of activity and degree of structure you choose will depend on what it is you're trying to achieve with your data and research project.

Analysis Modes

Many activities we describe can be carried out either prior to or during an interview or focus group. Which route you choose depends on two primary factors—the time required to complete the activity and whether or not you wish it to be a collaborative endeavor (i.e., within a focus group). Most of the activities we discuss in this chapter are also analyzable in two general ways. A technique can serve as both a means and an end. In other words, you can directly analyze the output of an activity and/or utilize the activity to elicit knowledge, emotions, and beliefs that are represented in the discourse generated as part of that activity. If asking an individual to draw something, for example, you can analyze the resultant drawing and form interpretations based on its contents.

You can also ask the individual questions about the drawing and analyze their verbal response. Or you can analyze both. Which analytic approach you use depends on your research objectives and the specific activity in question. Some research objectives, for example, are more emotionally and/or core value oriented, in which case a more projective approach makes sense. Additionally, the output of certain techniques are more concrete than others and require less interpretation on the part of the researcher. We briefly describe analysis options for the activities covered, to give readers a better sense of why and how a particular technique might be used. Given the book's focus on data collection, however, we do not provide detailed analysis instructions, but rather refer readers to other resources for this purpose.

ACTIVITIES APPROPRIATE FOR BOTH IN-DEPTH INTERVIEWS AND FOCUS GROUPS

For each of the activities discussed in this section, the rationale for choosing a technique will differ between an in-depth interview and a focus group. We discussed criteria for choosing a focus group or in-depth interview in Chapters 1, 4, and 5. The same considerations apply here when choosing which data collection context—one-on-one or group—to use as a setting for the activities in this section. If you need response independence and/or the topic is highly personal or sensitive, a one-on-one situation is the way to go. If, on the other hand, you're interested in social processes or cultural-level knowledge and response independence isn't a concern, then a group setting is likely more appropriate.

Analytic options and the inferences that can be drawn from the findings will also differ between a focus group and individual interview context. As we've mentioned, focus groups lack response independence and so are limited in what can be inferred from some of the quantitatively oriented activities, such as ratings and rankings (an exception to this, of course, is the Delphi technique). Data collected in an individual context can be aggregated across participants and is more conducive to quantitative approaches to analysis, such as basic descriptive statistics or data reduction techniques.

Listing

If you have limited information about your research topic or a portion of it (on the less-knowledge/less-structured end of Figure 4.3), consider conducting a free listing activity in your in-depth interviews or focus groups. As Bernard (2000) observes, "[f]ree-listing is a deceptively simple but powerful technique" (p. 265). Free listing is an ideal technique for gathering information about the range and parameters of a specific topic or conceptual domain. The technique starts by asking participants to name or list all of the items they can think of in a conceptual domain, such as all of the health problems in their community, all of the fast-food restaurants they can think of, or all of the frustrating things about a given product or service. Free listing requires the interviewer to probe repeatedly, "Can you think of anything else?" to elicit an exhaustive list from each interviewee. Free list data can stand on their own or can additionally serve as starting points for further discussion. Free listing is a great way to begin an interview or focus group as it reveals the range of items or issues in a particular domain of inquiry. From here, the interview can build on items, by asking more descriptive and explanatory questions: "How does X prevent HIV infection" or "What is frustrating about Y?" to better understand the knowledge or reasoning that a participant used to generate items on the list.

Analyzing lists themselves is relatively straightforward. The lists are first "cleaned" by creating common terms for synonyms or different variations of the same word (e.g., *car* and *cars*). Calculating the frequency of items across the lists is the most common analytic method. An item's average rank across the lists can also be calculated, as well as its "saliency," which is a metric that incorporates both item frequency and rank. All of these measures—frequency, rank, salience—are presumed to be proxies for relevance and familiarity to participants. Free lists can also be analyzed comparatively, by noting the differences in item frequencies between two or more groups. Figure 6.2 depicts a comparison of data among five populations who were asked to list all of the causes of breast cancer (Chavez, Hubbell, McMullin, Martinez, & Mishra,

---

Figure 6.2   Five Different Explanatory Models of Breast Cancer

Salvadoran women (N = 28)	%	Maxican women (N = 39)	%	Chicanas (N = 27)	%	Anglo women N = 27	%	Physicians N = 30	%
Blows, bruises	29	Blows, bruises	64	Chemicals in food	30	Family history	67	Family history	100
Problems producing milk	29	Never breast-feeding	33	Environmental pollution	26	Radiation	26	Obesity	37
Breast implants	21	Chemicals in food	28	Blows, brulises	26	Unhealthy diet	19	Hormone supplements	33
Disorderly, wild life	16	Excessive fondling	23	Lack of medical atten.	26	Smoking	19	First child after 30	30
Excessive fondling	14	Problem producing milk	23	Family history	26	Birth control pills	19	High fat diet	30
Smoking	14	Birth control pills	18	Never breast-feeding	22	Environmental pollution	19	Prior history of cancer	30
Never breast-feeding	14	Breast-feeding	15	Smoking	19	It just happens	15	Age	27
Lack of hygiene	14	Lack of medical atten.	15	High fat diet	11	Blows, bruises	15	No children	20
Family history	11	Smoking	13	Large breasts	11	Never breast-feeding	11	Smoking	17
Abortions	11	Too much alcohol	13	Too much caffeine	11	Fibrocystic breasts	11	Fibrocystic breasts	13
Illegal drugs	11	No children	13	Birth control pills	11	High fat diet	11	Ethnicity	13
Dirty work environment	11	Lack of hygiene	8					Early menses	13
		Illegal drugs	8					Birth control pills	13
		Family history	8						

[a]Respondents often listed more than one risk factor. Consequently, percentages do not add up to 100.

Source: Chavez et al. (1995).

1995). These data show distinct differences among groups in terms of their explanatory models. Data such as these are quite useful for educational and social marketing efforts. If, for example, one were trying to get more Mexican and Salvadoran women to conduct breast self-examinations, the data below reveal a (culturally driven) cognitive obstacle that would have to be overcome—the perception that excessive fondling and blows and bruises *cause* breast cancer.

List generation is often followed up by open-ended explanatory questions—for example, the whys, whats, and hows—to further understand the domain. See Bernard (2000) and Weller and Romney (1988) for more detailed explanations of how to do free listing activities. Borgatti (1999) and Bernard and Ryan (2010) provide additional information on the uses and analysis of free list data.

Categorizing

If you have a list of things, you can ask participants to sort items on that list. Lists may be generated by the researcher (based on theory or a real-world problem) or by participants within the study population as part of a free-listing task. A common categorizing technique is called "pile sorting" or "card sorting." A good number of items for a pile sort task is between 20 and 40, so lists will often have to be strategically truncated to accommodate this activity (see Borgatti, 1999).

In a sorting activity, the interviewer instructs the participant to put predefined items (words, pictures, objects, drawings, etc.) into piles that make the most sense to them. In an "unconstrained" pile sort, the only additional guidance participants receive is that they cannot put each item into its own pile, nor all of the items into one pile. Often participants are asked why they grouped certain items together. A researcher can also decide to "constrain" the sorting task by asking participants to sort the items into X number of piles. Which method you choose depends on your research objectives, but in either case, the composition of piles are recorded (see Weller & Romney, 1988).

Though the process is a structured qualitative activity, the analysis of pile sorting results is primarily quantitative. The first step is to aggregate data across individuals, creating an N by N similarity matrix. Similarity matrices capture the perceived *similarity* between items, as indicated by the total number of times items were put in the same groups. Figure 6.3a shows a hypothetical, individual similarity matrix for five items. Figure 6.3b shows a similar matrix but aggregated (i.e., summed) across a group of individuals.

Similarity matrices are commonly analyzed with graph-theoretic techniques, such as multi-dimensional scaling (MDS) and cluster analysis. Figure 6.4 (see page 230) shows the MDS plot generated from the analysis of pile sort data of occupations.

Figure 6.3a	Five-Item, *N* by *N* Similarity Matrix—Individual				
	Item A	Item B	Item C	Item D	Item E
Item A	–	0	1	1	0
Item B	0	–	0	0	0
Item C	1	0	–	1	0
Item D	1	0	1	–	0
Item E	0	0	0	0	–

Figure 6.3b	Five-Item, *N* by *N* Similarity Matrix—Aggregated				
	Item A	Item B	Item C	Item D	Item E
Item A	–	2	15	12	1
Item B	2	–	4	6	4
Item C	15	4	–	8	11
Item D	12	6	8	–	2
Item E	1	4	11	2	–

Spatial proximity between occupations in Figure 6.4 is associated with the degree to which items (occupations in this case) were grouped together, on average, by participants. Note that although the analysis is quantitative, interpretation of the output is qualitative. In other words, the two dimensions depicted in Figure 6.4—indoor/outdoor and mental/manual occupations—are subjectively interpreted by the analyst. For another good example of applying MDS to pile sort data, from the field of ethno-medicine, see Weller (1983).

Cluster analysis is another graph-theoretic technique, but it uses a different algorithm than MDS. Cluster analysis generates a dendrogram as its primary output

Figure 6.4	Multi-Dimensional Scaling Plot of Occupations

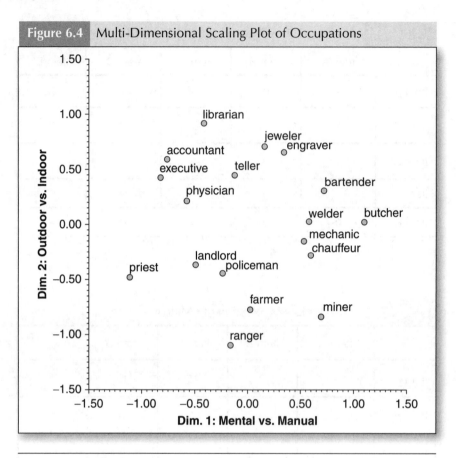

Source: Sadler and Shoben (1993).

instead of an MDS plot. Figure 6.5 shows a hierarchical cluster analysis based on pile sorting of transportation modes, among nine participants. The analyst's interpretation of the clusters are annotated on the dendrogram. While various software programs can be used for pile sorts (e.g., statistical programs, Anthropac), the web-based Optimal Sort is a good resource: http://www.optimalworkshop.com/optimalsort.htm.

As with MDS, interpretation of the output of cluster analysis is subjective, particularly in terms of where the demarcation between groups is established. This is why the qualitative data and supplemental information about the piles collected during the interview activity are important. They are extremely helpful in developing an interpretation that reflects the participants' view of the conceptual domain being studied.

Note that cluster analysis is especially useful for depicting taxonomies as it produces a tree structure commonly used in taxonomic construction. In anthropology,

---

Figure 6.5   Cluster Analysis of Transportation Modes With Analyst Interpretations

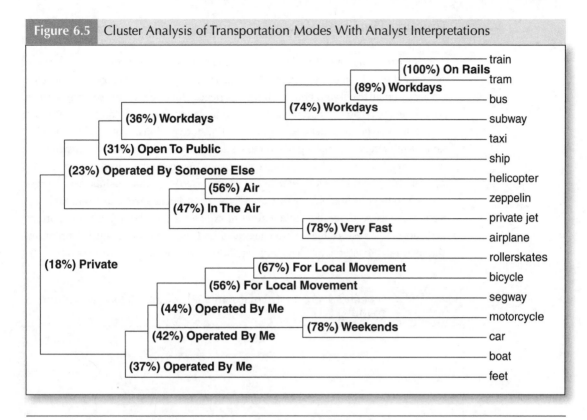

Source: http://www.userpoint.fi/tools/card_sort_cluster_analysis_tool/index.php?sample.

---

pile sorting is often used to reconstruct cultural taxonomies for a given domain such as poisonous plants or types of diseases (Bernard, 2000). For a more applied example, consider the project that CARE Nicaragua undertook to help staff know what food is available and being consumed by pregnant and lactating women, infants, and young children and to help answer why specific foods are being consumed (CARE, 2009). Women were shown cards and asked to sort them into piles of food they would and would not eat after having a baby. The interviewer then asked about the placement of each card, discovering all the taboos and traditional beliefs that restrict women to a diet of corn drink, tortillas, and soft cheese for 40 days after delivery (CARE, 2009).

Pile sorting can also elicit judgments of similarity among items in a group or identify attributes people use to distinguish items. As mentioned earlier, researchers often ask participants to explain why they put items in one pile and not another or what features distinguish one pile from another. The resulting data are analyzed qualitatively to reveal patterns of logic among participants. For more details on the mechanics and math behind MDS and cluster analysis as they're applied in socio-behavioral research see Borgatti (1994, 1997).

Creating Timelines

You cannot be sure what kind of information you might get if you ask an interview participant to tell you everything that happened as part of a certain experience. Imagine asking a woman to tell you about her birth experiences, for example. Answers might range from 2-minute versions, which require extensive probing, to half-hour-long narratives that leave little time for more detailed follow-up. A timeline creation activity in the context of an in-depth interview can help to structure participants' responses and the ensuing discussion by allowing a participant to succinctly detail the points she considers most important and allowing the interviewer to follow up on a selection of those points that are most relevant to the research objectives. Generally, when a timeline technique is used, interviewees are asked to recall a certain event or experience and sketch out the important activities or tasks associated in chronological order. Figure 6.6 shows a timeline produced through in-depth interviews identifying significant environmental events in Guam.

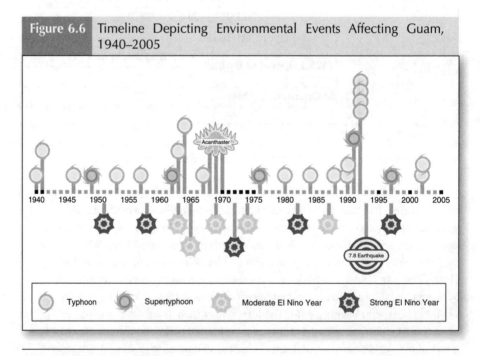

Figure 6.6 Timeline Depicting Environmental Events Affecting Guam, 1940–2005

Source: Amesbury (2005–2006).

Timelines can also be used to facilitate recall of specific actions or behaviors. Consider a question in HIV research that asks an interviewee to identify how many sexual partners he has had in the past 3 months. For those with few partners, this may be an easy question. For those with more than a few, giving an accurate answer may be difficult. Asking the participant to develop a timeline or calendar of the past 3 months—marking important holidays, travel, or significant dates—may help to jog the interviewee's memory and contribute to recall (see, for example, Sobell and Sobell's [1996] *Timeline FollowBack User's Guide* technique). In another study, Barry (1997) employed a seven-step process to examine academics' information-seeking activities. Barry's study combined diaries, activity logs, semi-structured interviews, and bibliographic information to construct "research timelines." The timelines were then compared to observe common patterns of research behavior as well as to identify individual differences.

Berends (2011) reports on an alternative version of the timeline process. The authors used timelines to explore pathways to treatment among 112 substance abusers. After generating individual timelines during in-depth interviews, Berends plotted recurring themes of individual timelines onto a "typical timeline." The purpose of this analytic approach was to identify and highlight *common* elements of substance abuse. Figure 6.7 depicts one of the resulting timelines.

| Figure 6.7 | Typical Timeline of Substance Use and Treatment Seeking for Someone Whose Recent Main Drug Is Alcohol |

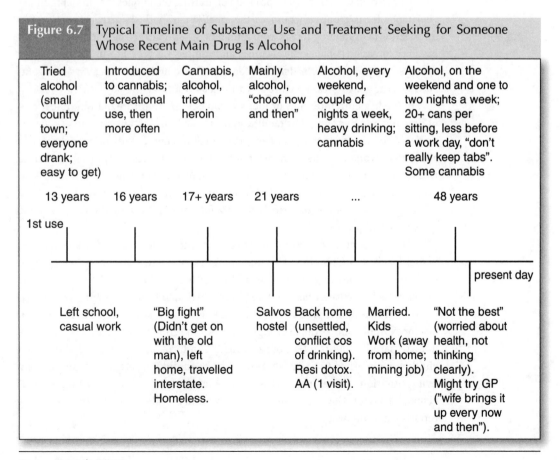

Source: Berends (2011).

Timelines may also be used in participatory action research where the goal is to re-create events within a community's history. Participants in a focus group mark important dates, names, and events on the timeline. The advantage of creating timelines in a group context is that you have a larger and more diverse knowledge base from which to draw. The interviewer can also probe about these key events: "Was this generally perceived as a good thing?" "A bad thing?" Creating and commenting on timelines facilitates discussion about changes that have occurred over time in a community.

Drawing and Mapping

Bagnoli (2009) argues that applying "drawing methods in the context of an interview can open up participants' interpretations of questions, and allow a creative way of interviewing that is responsive to participants' own meanings and associations" (p. 547). We concur that the incorporation of drawing techniques into in-depth interviewing or focus groups encourages the creativity of both the participant and the interviewer in examining topics from mundane to complex. Visual methods of information expression enhance the accuracy and completeness of the information that is conveyed by providing a bridge between experience and recall (Denzin & Lincoln, 2003). As the adage goes, a picture is worth 1,000 words.

In the in-depth interview or focus group context there are many applications of drawing and mapping that facilitate discussion. For instance, if you ask someone to draw the daily market scene, they may include details (stray cats in the alley) that would not have made it into their verbal description of the same. Drawings or maps also give interviewees a chance to think about and process a given topic before trying to put their thoughts or description into words, and they serve as supplemental (or primary) data for interviewers in their subsequent questions and probes.

For topics with an emotional aspect or for interviewees who are not highly verbal (such as young children), making a drawing can sometimes help people explain themselves in ways that would be difficult otherwise. Additionally, the drawing task itself can help put research participants into a highly expressive conversational mode, producing richer answers to subsequent questions. Figure 6.8, for example, shows the drawings made by nine children living in the neighborhood of Canudos in Novo Hamburgo, Brazil (Cauduro, Birk, & Wachs, 2009). These children were asked to draw what they liked and did not like in relation to their living situation. These images relate to the latter topic and served as a powerful visual basis for the discussions of community violence—and the resulting report—that followed.

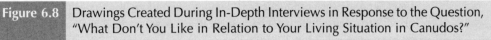

Figure 6.8   Drawings Created During In-Depth Interviews in Response to the Question, "What Don't You Like in Relation to Your Living Situation in Canudos?"

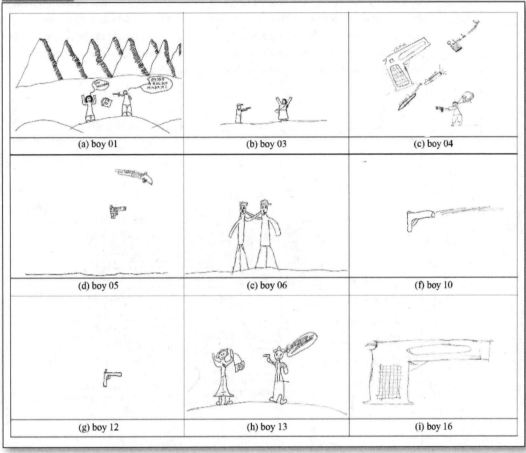

Source: Cauduro et al. (2009).

Hand-drawn maps can also provide interesting data. You might ask participants to draw a map depicting their daily routine, including the places they go and the general distance they travel. This single map might relate to a research objective on multiple topics such as city planning, fuel conservation, or time management. Conversely, there is a wide range of items that you might ask an interviewee to map for the same purpose: resources (health clinics, local farms, grocery stores), community areas (residential, leisure, commercial), social ties (family, friends, neighbors), or socioeconomic and demographic information (wealthy areas, poor areas, particular ethnic neighborhoods). Below is an example of a community map created by members of a small village in India, as part of a situation assessment (Mascarenhas & Kumar, 1991). Researchers asked the villagers to make a map of the existing situation in their village. Starting with a physical layout of the village and key structures, villagers then added socioeconomic and health dimensions such as demographics, locations of ill persons, and so on. (Figure 6.9)

| Figure 6.9 | Social Map Drawn by Villagers of Ramenhally, India |

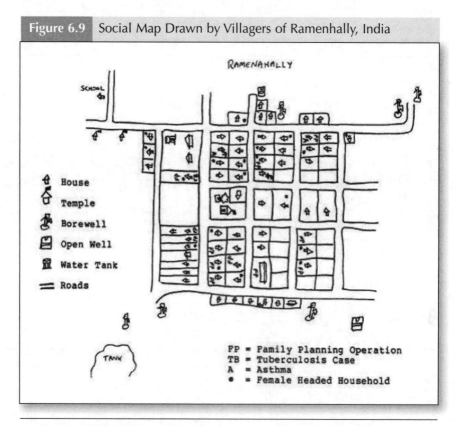

Source: Mascarenhas and Kumar (1991).

Concept maps are another type of useful mapping exercise. You can ask interview participants to draw out relationships between concepts, that is, to sketch out the main ideas related to a topic in visual form that represents the relationships and connections among them. Figure 6.10 displays traditional and free-form versions of concept maps used by Wheeldon and Faubert (2009) to clarify the definitions and uses of concept mapping in qualitative research.

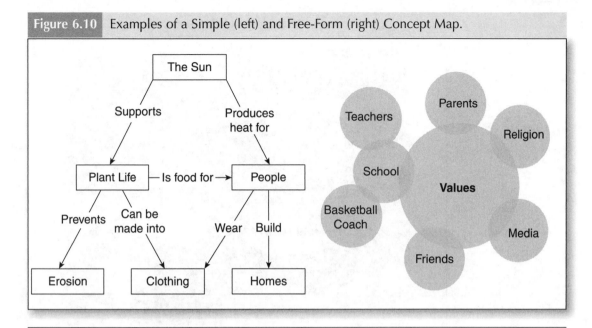

Figure 6.10 Examples of a Simple (left) and Free-Form (right) Concept Map.

Source: Wheeldon and Faubert (2009).

Building a Collage

A creative expressive technique, and nice alternative to drawing and mapping, is building a collage. The researcher typically provides magazines or other sources of images, and the participants are asked to build a collage that represents their reaction to an idea, object, or event. Collages can be created and discussed in both group and one-on-one contexts. The techniques work particularly well in cultures where making collages is a common activity for children; adults revert, often enthusiastically, to their childhoods when performing this activity. Collage-building produces a lot of energy in groups, and the collages can then be used as a stimulant for group discussion and/or analyzed separately. Collages can also be generated individually before-hand and discussed in a subsequent focus group or in-depth interview. Below is an example of a collage created by an eighth grade girl on the topic of math that she brought to a focus group (see Figure 6.11 on page 238).

During the focus group, students were asked to talk about their collages. Here is what the creator of the collage had to say:

> I put in a lot of nature and things that would calm a person, and that's just because in my math environment, I feel really calm. But at the same time, I

Figure 6.11   Eighth Grade Student's Collage of "Math"

feel focused and ready to work. This is specific with my math teacher because she's a very encouraging person, so I put, "Find the strength you never knew you had," and "Inside you've got it." She really encourages us and pushes us to try to take the next step because math is always with levels. I think it's really cool with math that you can keep on going and going, and keep on excelling. My math teacher is so supportive of us. I really like math because we do a lot of hands-on. (Retrieved from http://www.mathmirror .org/research/collages/emilys-collage/)

Visual Elicitation Techniques

The power of visual methods to convey information is not limited to drawings or maps that are created by the interview participant during the interview. Interviewers can also use visual aids prepared ahead of time—by the interviewer or interviewee—to their advantage. There is an extensive literature on visual anthropology and ethnography that details the uses of photography, film, and other visual media in understanding social and cultural phenomena (Banks, 2001, 2007; Pink, 2007; Stanczak, 2007). Another branch of relevant literature is found in clinical psychology under the rubric of "projective techniques," which have been adapted to social science and marketing research (Soley & Smith, 2008) and which we briefly described at the beginning of the chapter. We encourage interested readers to seek out additional information in these bodies of literature for more in-depth information about, and theory behind, these techniques.

Photos

Like drawings, photographs can quickly convey depth and detail that words cannot match. As an interviewer trying to elicit information on knowledge or attitudes, for example, providing the interviewee with a photograph and asking her to describe what she sees or how she interprets it can open interesting channels of discussion. The picture might show a scene, a specific location, a person, event, action, or product. The questions you ask will be as varied as the photographs themselves and the research objectives behind them: What do you see here? How does it make you feel? What kinds of people might go here? What is this person doing? Can you describe how the items in this photograph fit together?

Nazarea, Rhoades, Bontoyan and Flora (1998) used photo elicitation, in a variation of the thematic apperception test, to document ecological conceptions among inhabitants of the Manupali watershed in the Philippines. Nazarea took 20 photographs of the watershed, depicting various types of production activities (which varied in terms of the Western concept of sustainability) and conducted individual interviews among 51 participants across three sites in the watershed. The researchers showed each participant the photos, one by one, and asked them to "tell a story" about each photograph. Researchers scored the responses based on dominant themes to identify locally relevant indicators of sustainability and quality of life. The authors found that local indicators differ significantly from externally defined (i.e., Western) indicators and that local indicators varied in relation to sociodemographic variables.

Alternatively, you might provide a camera to participants prior to the interview or focus group and ask them to document a certain aspect of their life, community, or behavior over a given time period and then have them bring the resulting photographs to the interview. They can then describe the content, imagery, and/or rationale for each photo's inclusion in the collection. You might ask participants to sort them or arrange them chronologically as well. In this type of in-depth interview, you obtain two sets of data: the images that the participants took as well as their verbal description of them and their responses to your questions about them. An increasingly common version of this technique, derived from a participatory action perspective, is Photovoice (Blackman, 2007; Wang, 1999; Wang, Yi, Tao, & Carovano, 1998). The method is community-based and explicitly designed to influence policy and community-level outcomes. Key community members are first assembled to discuss community issues, to become familiarized with the Photovoice concept, and to identify a theme to guide the subject of the photographs they will take. The SHOWed method, a set of six questions, is often used to guide photographic efforts:

What do you *see* happening here?

What is really *happening* here?

How does this relate to *our* lives?

Why does this situation, concern, or strength exist?

How could this image *educate* the community/policymakers, and so on?

What can we *do* about it?

After participants take photographs over a prescribed period of time, they meet again to discuss their pictures. At this point, they also decide on a format in which to share their photos and stories with policymakers or community leaders.

Photovoice is often used in public health research and advocacy. A project in Dar es Salaam, Tanzania, for example, used Photovoice to understand household behavioral risk factors for diarrheal disease (Badowski et al., 2011). Participants took a total of 127 photographs from 13 households, and 13 interviews were conducted with household mothers. The photographs and interviews revealed insufficient hand washing procedures, unsafe disposal of wastewater, uncovered household drinking water containers, a lack of water treatment prior to consumption, and inappropriate toilets for use by small children. A quick review of PubMed (database)—using *Photovoice* as your search term in the title—will generate numerous other examples, for those interested.

Objects

In some cases, you might use an object other than a photograph to facilitate discussion. In market research, you might provide a sample product. In public health, you might have an incidence map. The range of possibilities is virtually infinite. In a study conducted by Mitchell for an automotive trade school, for example, interviewees were asked to bring an object to the interview that represented how they felt when working on a car. These young men brought in favorite tools, Hot Wheels toy cars, and pictures of their fathers and sons, all great starting points for "tell me about this" probing.

In another example, Kerner, McCarthy, Bishwa, and Lundgren (n.d.) used plastic animals to elicit perceptions of gender norms among young adolescents in Nepal. The authors presented participants with the following instructions:

- Choose an animal that represents a typical man and woman in your community.
- Why did you choose that animal? Tell me more.
- What does it mean to be a typical man? Typical woman?
- Now choose animals that describe a "Real man" or "Real woman."

- Can you describe someone you know who you consider to be a real man?
- Can you describe someone who you do not consider a real man?
- How does the typical man differ from the real man? Woman?
- How do boys learn to act like men? How do girls learn to act like women?
- What isn't a boy/girl allowed to do?
- Who tells him what he is not allowed to do?
- What if a boy/girl acts differently? What happens?
- Now choose an animal that you think represents your father or a man in your family? And your mother or a woman in your family?
- What type of animal represents how you want others to view you when you are older?

As the authors point out, it is not so much the animal that a participant chooses that is important, but rather the words that follow and the emotions they convey. And it is the latter which were ultimately analyzed for thematic content and which provided the foundation for a behavior change curriculum.

Rating and Ranking

Sometimes in qualitative research, especially in an applied setting where policy guidance is your goal, the most effective way to address your research objective is to include a few rating or ranking questions interspersed with the open-ended questions on your topic. These provide a standard "language" used by all participants that can easily be compared between participants or among groups (although response dependence issues still remain in a group setting). An open-ended follow-up question, asking participants to explain why they chose the rating they did, provides information that can be thematically analyzed in association with the summarized and quantified rating responses. Namey and colleagues (Beskow et al., 2011), for example, conducted in-depth interviews with participants in genetic research to gather their opinions on returning individual research findings to participants when researchers wanted them to take part in additional research. Because this study's objective was to contribute to policy development on return of these results, the researchers incorporated several rating questions into the interview guide. For example, they asked an open-ended question first, "How important would it be to you to receive aggregate results from the study, even if you didn't receive individual results?" To be sure that they could compare the answers to this question among sub-study populations, the researchers subsequently asked, "On a scale from 1–5, where 1 is not at all important and 5 is very important, how important would it be to you to receive aggregate study results?" The responses to the second question were summarized quantitatively, as illustrated in Table 6.1 (see page 243).

Given the varied and small sampling sizes in the study, the authors decided not to include this type of table in the final manuscript. Rather, they used the table to help them identify trends in the data (for example, in this case, that a majority of participants in each sub-study thought that aggregate results were important), and to guide subsequent qualitative inquiry. The authors reported the trend in the body of the results section and included a table summarizing the relevant themes with substantiating quotes (see Table 6.2).

Rating scales like the one used in the example above can be created for any number of concepts or attributes, and may be presented to interviewees numerically, descriptively, and/or graphically. In the example above, the researchers provided both a numerical scale (1–5) and verbal descriptions of the ends of the scale (*not at all important—very important*). You might also provide a written scale as a visual aid to help the interviewee pinpoint his response. An advantage of rating is that most people in the United States are familiar with this type of question, and, enjoy being afforded the opportunity to provide additional explanation.

Ranking questions or activities are similar. You ask an interviewee to rank items (e.g., from most to least desirable or most important to least important) in terms of a specific characteristic. The items that are to be ranked may be predetermined by your research objectives and included on your interview guide, or they may be the items generated by the interviewee in an earlier question or listing exercise. In either case, with complete rank ordering, the interviewer instructs the participant to order all of the items in a list or set according to some attribute. This can be accomplished verbally, with pen and paper, or by presenting a stack of cards on which item names are written and asking them to arrange the cards in order as they relate to the given characteristic or attribute. Another possibility is pairwise comparison, where each item is paired with every other item and you ask the interviewee to choose which is better, preferred, worse, or whatever comparison is relevant. Rank ordering of all the items is then established by counting the number of times each item was chosen, within and across interviews (see Bernard, 2000, p. 275 for more information on paired comparison). This again is a structured qualitative exercise that produces quantitative data to be interpreted using the qualitative comments also collected. This method, like rating scales, enables more effective comparison of differences among individuals.

Ranking in a group setting is similar in principle, but the execution and analytic aim are different. If you ask individuals within the group to rank or rate things, the interdependent nature of the data in a group setting restricts what you can infer from them. The quantitative output in this case should only serve as a general guideline or be used to inform subsequent processes in the focus group event. Calculating and reporting percentages, as in the in-depth interview example above, would not be

Table 6.1 Quantitative Summary of Responses to a Rating Question Used in an In-Depth Interview, "On a scale from 1–5, where 1 is not at all important and 5 is very important, how important would it be to you to receive aggregate study results?" (Beskow et al., 2011)

	Site 1 N = 9 Study A		N = 15 Study B		Site 2 N = 29 Study C		Site 3 N = 13 Study D		N = 5 Study E		N = 7 Study F		TOTAL N = 78 All studies		
Rating 1 or 2	0	0%	2	13%	2	7%	1	8%	0	0%	0	0%	5	6%	not important
Rating 3	4	44%	3	20%	5	17%	0	0%	0	0%	1	14%	13	17%	neutral
Rating 4 or 5	5	56%	8	53%	21	72%	12	92%	5	100%	6	86%	52	67%	important
Total:	9		13		28		13		5		7		70	90%	

243

Table 6.2	Presentation of Thematic Analysis of Same Information From Table 6.1 (Beskow et al., 2011)	
Response	**Theme**	**Example Quotes**
Important	Outcome of contribution	• "I would like that. That would be very interesting. It would be nice, if I participate in a study and a paper is written, to get the paper even though I wouldn't understand probably the abstract, but I could look through it and see that I feel that I've made a contribution. Whether mine actually helped or not I can at least think it did." (Biobank-C10) • "It's important to know what they're doing, why they're doing it. They're not just coming around and giving you a test and saying, 'Okay, filled out, see you later.' No, you'd like to know that your time and effort is getting some kind of results." (Epilepsy-D06) • "I mean I'm curious, Has this helped anybody? Have they found any great answers? Are they coming up with new methods?" (Diabetes-S08)
	Stay updated	• "It's important to me. I find the research interesting and obviously we have a personal interest in it, but even if the information wasn't something that was going to be directly applicable to my family or something, I think it's helpful to know. I want to know as much as I can." (Autism, SAGE-S24)
	Provide information to family	• "Even if I don't know for a fact it's for me, it would allow me to know that a possibility is there that it could be hereditary. And that it could still be something I could look for in my kids." (Epilepsy-D29)
	Answers	• "It would be very important, I mean I think it would make me understand exactly how my daughter got it." (Diabetes-S03)

appropriate. An alternative would be to ask focus group members to *collectively* rank or rate things. Observing and analyzing the discussion involved in the process can be highly informative, as it will elicit participants' rationale for their choices. Moreover, if you have these data from enough focus groups, you can compare data between different subpopulations (e.g., focus groups with men versus women).

Another difference is the manner in which rankings or ratings are recorded. A focus group typically consists of six to 10 people, so the method for ranking needs to be quick and efficient. The number of ways in which this can be done is limited only by a researcher's imagination. Some that we've used and like are the following:

- The moderator moves a real or imaginary dial, and the group indicates where the arrow should stop.
- Members of the group can use hand gestures as a 5-point Likert scale in response to a question (e.g., 1= thumb down and waving, 2 = thumb down and stationary, 3 = thumb at mid-level, 4 = thumb up and stationary, and 5 = thumb up and waving)
- Participants are given a certain number of stickers (3–5 is a good range), and they then are asked to attach one sticker to each of their top choices (ranking) on a flip chart or white board. A variation of this is to allow participants to put more than one sticker on any one choice (rating). Or participants can simply be asked to stand next to their first choice. An added benefit of these types of activities is that they get participants up and moving.

Post-Event Reflection

Post-event reflection activities can be used for any in-depth interviews or focus groups that are transcribed. Participants are provided a copy of the transcript after the event and are asked to comment on it. The basic idea behind this method is that it allows participants more time to think about what was said, which is ideal for topics that are exceptionally complicated. During this reflection period, participants can amend or elaborate on what they (or others) said, or be asked to clarify specific parts of the interview or discussion. An advantage of this technique is that it can be done remotely, assuming that the study population is computer literate and has Internet access.

ACTIVITIES BEST SUITED FOR FOCUS GROUPS

As we've mentioned earlier in this chapter, and in previous chapters, some data collection and generation techniques work better in certain contexts than others. In general, group activities are better suited to research contexts in which:

- Response independence between individuals is not needed;
- The research objectives are concerned with group dynamics or social processes;

- The topic of inquiry is not overly personal;
- A broad range of perspectives is sought; and/or
- The activity itself is conducive to a group situation.

The techniques we describe in this section satisfy one or more of these criteria.

Delphi Method

The Delphi method is a group forecasting technique, in which a panel of experts independently answer survey questions in two or more rounds of data collection (Brown, 1968; Linstone & Turoff, 1975; Rowe & Wright, 1999). The purpose of forecasting techniques is to generate a reasonably accurate quantitative estimate of a future outcome. Survey questions center on quantitatively estimating (i.e., forecasting) parameters associated with the topic of study. After each survey round, the facilitator provides an anonymous summary of participants' forecasts as well as the self-disclosed rationale behind each participant's forecast. Participants are then encouraged to rethink, and potentially revise, their estimation after hearing what other members of the group have said. The goal of the successive process is for the range of answers to progressively converge toward a "correct" estimate. The process is typically stopped after a predetermined criterion (e.g., number of rounds, degree of consensus, or stability of results), and the mean or median estimates from the last round are the final outcome. The method has been shown to be an effective forecasting tool (Rowe & Wright, 2001). For a thorough, yet readable, set of instructions for planning and implementing the Delphi method, see Cuhls (n.d.).

Although the Delphi method is really a mixed method approach with a quantitative outcome, it does include qualitative components, which is why we've included it in this chapter. And it can be used to address virtually any type of research question that has a quantitative estimation as an outcome. Colton and Hatcher (2004), for example, used a web-based variation of the Delphi method to validate content on a human resource development (HRD)–related research instrument. In the authors' words,

This study demonstrated the power of technology in enhancing a classic and ethical Delphi research process, in facilitating in-depth discussion among diverse participants separated by time and place, and in providing a venue for voting, all while preserving the anonymity of the participants. It yielded rich qualitative and rigorous quantitative data resulting in a content validated instrument. . . .[This resulted] in a more in-depth content validation, applicable to educational, business, industrial, and government research as well as using the tenets of adult learning principles in 21st-century technology. (Colton & Hatcher, 2004, p. 188)

Another example of the Delphi technique is the work of Fletcher-Johnson, Marshall, and Straatman (2011), who used it to identify, and reach a consensus on, research priorities for academics and clinicians in the field of child care health and development. The researchers recruited 114 clinicians and academics throughout Canada. Three phases were conducted until consensus was achieved for the five most pressing research priorities. A total of 38 respondents completed at least one of the three phases of the process. All responses were analyzed, and five questions in phase 3 achieving a level of consensus ranging from 64% to 80% were identified as the top five research priorities. The results of the study can be used to inform and prioritize a framework for an ongoing program of research in Canada.

Creating a Campaign

The energy and cognitive triggering that occurs in groups makes them great for building a possible communications campaign or outlining an action plan to address a problem. This works very well in public policy or community-based research projects where local buy-in is important. Krueger and Casey (2009, p. 49) recommend warming participants up to the task by asking introductory questions such as "What is a campaign?" "Tell us what happens in a campaign," and "Describe a campaign you recently experienced." The moderator then instructs participants to plan and develop a campaign and provides them with creative materials such as markers, colored paper, and so on. The active nature of this technique is well suited to youth and other active groups. The output is a campaign concept that can be used or adapted in a real marketing or educational campaign.

Campaign activities are particularly useful in research designed to inform behavior change strategies. In the late 1980s, an organization tasked with procuring and organizing organ donations in the western United States discovered a large disparity between the need for donor organs among Hispanic residents and the number of people of Hispanic heritage who were registered as potential organ donors (a tragically important disparity, because tissue similarity is an important factor in the success of organ transplants, and many Hispanic potential organ recipients were dying while waiting for a donor organ). Focus groups with Hispanic participants revealed a number of beliefs that presented barriers to organ donation. Chief among these was a belief that the Catholic Church did not endorse the practice of organ donation and that good Catholics needed to be buried with their bodies intact. In fact, the Catholic Church did not hold this position, and a statement by the Pope endorsing organ donation was shared with participants in the focus groups.

The groups were then asked to outline the key points of a communications campaign to increase Hispanic organ donation. The participants developed a public service message that could be aired on English and Spanish-language television and that was also the basis for print ads, posters, and community outreach efforts. Messages contained the following key elements:

- The statement of need: Mentioning the mismatch of donors to potential recipients in the Hispanic community, illustrated by showing a young Hispanic boy and his worried parents, as he suffers the ravages of liver disease while awaiting an organ donation that might not happen in time.
- The statement of permission/blessing: A video insert of the Pope reading his statement about the desirability of becoming an organ donor.
- The payoff: The same boy shown after his organ transplant, smiling, playing, and surrounded by his happy family.
- The how-to: Information about how to become a registered organ donor or make an in-hospital donation.

The campaign was launched with considerable success: large numbers of Hispanics in the region registered as potential organ donors in the months following the campaign.

ACTIVITIES BEST SUITED FOR INDIVIDUAL INTERVIEWS

Some data collection activities are better suited for a one-on-one context. Typically, research utilizing individual level activities share one or more of the following characteristics:

- Response independence between individual responses is required.
- Personal narratives are sought.
- Depth of information is more important than breadth.
- The topic of inquiry is highly personal or sensitive in nature.
- The activity itself is conducive to a one-on-one situation.

The two techniques outlined below have one or more of these features in common.

Laddering

Laddering is an interviewing technique commonly used in marketing research (see Reynolds & Gutman, 1988). The theoretical perspective behind the technique is the means-ends theory of consumer decision making (Gutman, 1982), which holds that there are different levels of product knowledge and emotional significance that influence consumer decision making. A key premise is that deeper levels of knowledge and emotion—that is, one's core values—are more influential over behavior than shallower levels such as rational evaluation of product attributes. The data collection method itself is simple. The researcher begins with questions about what attributes of a product (or program, or anything to which the participant has been exposed) appeal to the participant and then continue with a series of "why" questions until deeper core values associated with the product are reached. The output of these interviews resembles a ladder of motivations, with product attributes at the top and core values at the bottom. The laddering example below (only part of the interview) centers on understanding why consumers buy certain brands of shoes over others (from Peter and Olson, 1990).[1] Observe how the researcher progressively moves the conversation from a product attribute (shoe's lacing pattern) to a core value (self-esteem).

Researcher: You said that a shoe's lacing pattern is important to you in deciding what brand to buy. Why is that?

Participant: A staggered lacing makes the shoe fit more snugly on my foot.

Researcher: Why is it important that the shoe fit more snugly on your foot?

Participant: Because it gives me better support.

Researcher: Why is better support important to you?

Participant: So I can run without worrying about injuring my feet.

Researcher: Why is it important to you to not worry while running?

Participant: So I can relax and enjoy the run.

Researcher: Why is it important to you to relax and enjoy the run?

Participant: Because it gets rid of the tension I have built up from work.

Researcher: Why is it important for you to get rid of tension from work?

Participant: So when I go back in the afternoon, I can perform better.

Researcher: Why is it important for you to perform better?

Participant: I feel better about myself.

Researcher: Why is it important to feel better about yourself?

Participant: Because it just is! [End of interview]

Laddering is intended to access an individual's core values, since they are thought to be primary drivers of behavior and therefore potent change agents. Core values can be data driven, identified by the researcher as themes within the data themselves. Alternatively, you can use, or modify, existing models of intrinsic motivation such as Reiss' taxonomy of 16 motives (Reiss, 2004, p. 187) or Maslow's hierarchy of needs (Maslow, 1970).

---

[1]The technique described is an example of "soft" laddering, which is the most commonly used form of the technique. For a comparative description of this and two other types of laddering, see Russell et al. (2004).

It should be mentioned that because laddering moves toward deeply held values, it can be both very demanding of interviewer skill and, at times, highly emotional for interviewees. Most people have strong psychological defenses that keep them from revealing their core values and subconscious motivations during normal conversation, and these will often make it difficult to move the interview to the deepest level. Skilled interviewers learn how to help interviewees break through these barriers, and in actual use, laddering interviews are somewhat more complicated than simply asking *why?* (which often produces a rationalization or avoidance, rather than a move to the next level).

Some core values, such as the desire to experience a sense of family and belonging or the desire to be a good parent, are so important to people and so highly emotional that interviewees may become distraught or start crying during an interview that approaches these values. One of the authors regularly conducts laddering interviews and always warns interviewees about the possibility of strong emotions, assures them that it is all right if those feelings occur, and keeps a box of tissues on the interview table. She has also been hugged by interviewees who found these more emotional interviews "therapeutic." So if you plan to include laddering in your interviews, try to watch a skilled laddering interviewer before you try it yourself and be prepared if some of your interviews become intense.

Ethnographic Decision Modeling

Ethnographic decision modeling (EDM) is a data collection and analysis technique that results in a decision tree that can fairly accurately predict decisions with dichotomous outcomes. EDM, as outlined by Gladwin (1989), is a multistep process that begins with establishing what the two alternatives are for the decision of interest. To build the decision model, about 20 individuals from the study population are independently asked about decisions they made in the past pertaining to the behavior of interest. The in-depth interview consists of eliciting "if/then" statements (e.g., if it rains heavily in spring, then I plant corn). These statements are then combined to construct a draft decision tree for the first participant. As more participants are interviewed, the decision tree is amended, resulting in an aggregate EDM in the form of a decision tree, or dendrogram. Creating a perfectly accurate model that predicts every single decision among everyone in a population is an impossible task. The commonly accepted rationale is that it is more informative to have a model that accounts for the decisions of, say, 90% of the participants interviewed with just a few decision rules than a model with 20 different sets of ordered reasons that can, on the surface, account for all 20 participants' decisions. So, for the sake of clarity and simplicity, not every rule is added but rather only those that inform the research objectives.

The final step in ethnographic decision modeling is to test the model with a different sample from the same population, with the typical goal of having a model that accounts for at least 80% of the decisions with the fewest number of rules (Bernard & Ryan, 1998). Participants are asked all of the questions in the model (i.e., they are probed for all of the reasons and constraints given by the first group). A model that works should be able to predict the outcome decision based on the second group's answers, with 80% accuracy.

Ethnographic decision modeling has been used in multiple applied settings and has been shown to predict behavior with 80% to 90% accuracy (Bernard, 2000). The method has recently been shown to have good external validity as well. In a recent study of recycling behavior, Ryan and Bernard (2006) found that ethnographic decision models from a sample of 21 interviews could account for 85% of reported behavior in a national sample (n = 386).

One of the most compelling reasons to choose EDM methodology is that resulting dendrograms are highly informative from a programmatic perspective, as each decision point can also be considered a potential intervention point. Figure 6.12

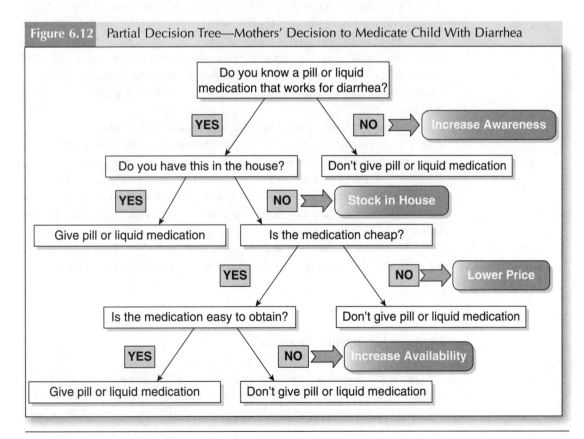

Figure 6.12 Partial Decision Tree—Mothers' Decision to Medicate Child With Diarrhea

Source: Ryan and Martinez (1996, as cited in Hill, 1998, p. 149).

shows an abridged decision tree, from Ryan and Martinez's (1996) work among rural Mexican mothers (cited in Hill, 1998, p. 149). We've added hypothetical intervention points to illustrate the practical utility of the method.

DOCUMENT ANALYSIS

Document analysis consists of selecting (as opposed to generating) documents, both textual and visual, and analyzing their contents. The term *document* in this context is broadly defined and can refer to a number of different forms of text: public records (e.g., court transcripts, institutional literature, congressional documents, websites), historical archives, periodicals (e.g., newspapers, magazines), personal narratives (e.g., diaries, letters, blogs), corporate documents (e.g., annual reports), or artifacts of popular culture (e.g., print advertisements, graffiti). The variety of visual "documents" is equally as diverse and might include things such as TV or movie images, photographs, and drawings. Theoretically, the universe of documents and images (and artifacts) that can be analyzed is infinite in scope. Document analysis has been carried out on a wide range of topics and media ranging from sexual content of graffiti in restrooms (Bates & Martin, 1980), to iPhone apps and smoking cessation (Abroms, Padmanabhan, Thaweethai, & Phillips, 2011), to people's trash and consumptive behavior (Rathje, 1992).

As with other forms of secondary data analysis, the main disadvantages of document analysis are that (a) it is usually not possible to follow up with the person or persons who generated the document, image, or artifact, (b) the data are not generated specifically to inform your research objectives and may not be as directly relevant to your study as you might like, and (c) in many cases, the quality of data is unknown. On the other hand, secondary data already exist and so circumvent the need to generate primary data, which in turn can save time, money, and eliminate the need for regulatory oversight. Another advantage of analyzing documents, as Padgett (2008, p. 123) points out, is "their lack of reactivity," since the researcher is not present at the time the data are created.

Steps in Document Analysis

The key to document analysis is finding data sources that are most relevant to your research objectives. Start by asking yourself Questions 1 and 2 below. When considering these questions, remember to be open minded and consider all of the various types of media, both hard copy and electronic, as well as physical artifacts that may relate to your topic:

1. What documents, images, or artifacts, if any, have been produced by my study population that are conceptually related to my research question(s)?
2. What public documents, images or artifacts, if any, contain information that can inform my research question(s)?

Once you have a sense of what your data sources might be, ask yourself,

3. How accessible are these sources of data?

Based on your responses to Question 3, narrow your list to those sources that are most readily available and proceed to Step 4.

4. Choose sampling units, coding units, and code attributes for your analysis. This entails moving to a finer level of granularity, a process Krippendorf (2004) calls "unitizing."

Sampling units in document analysis refer to the discrete units that are selected for inclusion or exclusion in an analysis—from a larger population—and which serve as the unit of analysis in a given study. Some examples of sampling units are newspaper issues, websites, or movie titles. In the case of restroom graffiti, the sampling units could be individual restrooms or stalls within restrooms.

Coding units are those units of data (image, text, artifact) that are selected for coding. Coding units are often contained within sampling units, though in some cases they can coincide with (but can never exceed) a sampling unit. Whereas sampling units often have natural boundaries (i.e., a specific movie or newspaper issue), coding units are often less concrete and more subjective than sampling units. For example, one may be looking for particular predetermined themes in newspaper editorials, political speeches, or advertisement content in magazines. In these examples, themes will invariably weave in and out of a given sampling unit. Coding units can, however, be relatively discrete and have clearly defined boundaries, for example, characters in a movie or individual personal ads within a newspaper issue. Generally speaking, the more defined coding units are, the easier the analysis.[2]

Coding attributes are the specific features or attributes you look for in your coding unit. For confirmatory analyses (which we describe below), in which themes and codes are predetermined, these are derived from your hypotheses or existing sources

---

[2]This process is similar to what is called "segmenting" in text analysis. See Guest et al. (2012).

and are defined up front. Code attributes in document analysis vary as much as the topical content and sample media observed in the field of document analysis. You can, for example, record types or frequency of behaviors in images, expressions of particular themes in text, or virtually any attribute associated with your research objectives that might be observed in the materials you're analyzing. This includes physical objects. If studying cigar smoking, for example, you might examine cigar butts, in which case your coding attributes could be pretty much anything about the cigar: for example, brand, length and circumference of the butt, tar concentration in the tobacco, where the butt was found, and so on. To cite a text-based example, Hirshman (1987), in a study on personal ad content, created ten code categories (derived from her hypotheses related to resource theory): love, physical attractiveness or beauty, money, occupational status, educational status, intellectual status, entertainment services, information-personality, information-ethnic, information-demographic. Two coders then independently looked for the presence of these themes in the content of personal ads (see the text box that follows for more on Hirschman's study). Note that data can be recorded in a dichotomous form (i.e., presence/absence), as in Hirschman's study, or interval form (i.e., number of occurrences). Themes and codes can also be scaled in terms of intensity or some other dimension of interest.

Analytic Approach to Documents

Two general approaches to analysis of documents exist.[3] One approach is hypothesis driven, which has a deductive orientation and is confirmatory in purpose. The other is a content-driven, exploratory, approach that is inductive in its orientation. Table 6.3 provides a brief summary of the differences between these two approaches.

Hypothesis-Driven (Confirmatory) Document Analyses

As indicated in the table above, confirmatory content analysis is a hypothesis-driven enterprise that entails defining categories (often themes) *prior* to reviewing the data and then systematically searching the data for instances or expressions of these categories. Often, the goal in such an approach is to assess one or more hypotheses generated by the researcher. Given the confirmatory nature of these types of analyses, much attention is given to reliability in coding procedures, and probability sampling measures are typically employed. Often a checklist, matrix, or some other form of worksheet is used in this process. Checklists and templates are often dichotomous in design—that is, was this theme, item, or criterion present in this sampling

---

[3]Note that not all researchers agree with this categorization. Hsieh and Shannon (2005), for example, demarcate content analysis into three general approaches—directed, conventional, and summative.

Table 6.3	Summary of Differences Between Exploratory and Confirmatory Approaches to Document Analysis	
Exploratory ("content-driven")	**Confirmatory** ("hypothesis-driven")	
• For example, asks: "What attributes are observed/identified in sample X?" • Inductive orientation • Specific codes/analytic categories NOT predetermined • Coding is open-ended • Codes derived from the data • Can use either non-probability or probability sampling	• For example, hypothesizes: "X attributes will be found more often in data from source Y than from source Z" • Deductive orientation • Specific codes/analytic categories predetermined prior to analysis • Coding has some predetermined structure • Codes generated from hypotheses or borrowed from existing sources • Generally uses probability sampling	

unit (e.g., document, piece of text, etc.)? But they can also record interval level data, such as how often a particular attribute occurs in a sampling unit. Appendix 1 at the end of this chapter provides examples of structured content analysis templates.

The text box below, "Three Examples of Hypothesis-Driven (Deductive) Document Analysis", contains examples of hypothesis-driven content analysis, each using a different media source (newspapers, movies, and websites). For more detailed information on this type of content analysis, we refer readers to two comprehensive books on the subject in the Additional Readings section (Neuendorf, 2002; Krippendorf, 2004).

Three Examples of Hypothesis-Driven (Deductive) Document Analysis

People as Products

Hirschman (1987) wanted to test how certain resource theories applied to personal ads. She developed several hypotheses about offering and seeking 10 different types of resources and conducted a content analysis of 400 personal ads in the *Washingtonian* and the *New York Magazine*. To start, she verified that her 10 resource types were identifiable in the ads. To do this, she gave 10 men and 11 women lists of 100 resource examples from ads and had them put the examples into her 10 resource categories, to ensure items were exhaustive and mutually exclusive. Once confident that her categories were valid,

Hirschman then randomly sampled 200 ads per periodical—100 male placed ads and 100 female placed ads from each. One male and one female coder—both blinded to the hypotheses—then independently coded the ads. A third coder resolved any discrepancies, of which there were less than 17% from of a total of 3,782 items. Hirschman statistically compared code frequencies within male and female placed ads and found that men were more likely to offer financially related resources and women were more likely to seek such resources. She also found that women were more likely to offer physical attractiveness.

Who Survives in Slasher Films?

Cowan and O'Brian (1990) generated hypotheses about what types of characters survive in slasher films. They sampled 56 slasher movies containing a combined total of 474 victims. They coded for gender, survival, and character attributes including physical attributes and personality traits. Their analysis found, among other things, that (a) slashers are men, (b) men and women are equally likely to be victims, (c) female survivors are less sexual and less attractive than female victims, and (d) male survivors tended to be more cynical, egotistical, and dictatorial than their deceased counterparts.

Websites and Smoking Culture

This study by Ribisl, Lee, Henriksen, and Haladjian (2003) examined smoking culture and lifestyle websites listed on Yahoo! The study objective was to determine whether the sites were easily accessible to youth, featured age or health warnings, and mentioned specific tobacco brands. The researchers conducted a content analysis of photographs on 30 websites to assess the demographics of individuals depicted and the amount of smoking and nudity in the photographs. The authors found that cigarette brand names were mentioned in writing on 35% of the sites and brand images were present on 24% of the sites. Nearly all of the photographs (95%) depicted smoking, 92% featured women, and 7% contained partial or full nudity. From these data, the researchers conclude that there is a need for more research and monitoring of smoking-related Internet content by health educators and tobacco control advocates.

Content-Driven (Exploratory) Document Analyses

Document analysis can also be inductive, where themes, codes, and items to be recorded are emergent within the data. No predetermined categories—that is, coding attributes—are created. Rather, researchers derive attributes from the data themselves as the analysis progresses, and analyses are typically descriptive in nature, outlining key themes identified in the data (although a descriptive comparison between two or more datasets can be carried out).

It's important to point out that inductive analysis does not mean that coding of the content is arbitrary. Open coding has to be framed by at least your research objectives and questions. Otherwise, the utility of the analysis will be diffuse at best, and nonexistent at worst. Appendix 2 contains two examples of worksheets for inductive, content-driven analyses. For more in-depth coverage of open, inductive coding and analysis, we refer readers to the works of Guest, MacQueen, and Namey (2012) and Charmaz (2006), cited in the Additional Reading section. In the text box below we provide examples of content-driven, exploratory, document analyses.

Two Examples of Content-Driven (Inductive)

Using Wall Graffiti to Reconstruct Inmate Culture

With the intent of gaining insight into the structure of inmate societies and the process of socialization in correctional communities, Klofas and Cutshall (1985) conducted a document analysis of wall graffiti in an abandoned correctional facility. The researchers analyzed text from the walls of 95 general population rooms in the facility. They transcribed the text from the walls and documented the room from which each piece of text was extracted. Discrete units of graffiti were determined by handwriting, subject matter, and writing tool. Chained responses by multiple authors were treated as discrete graffiti units. The units were initially grouped into 38 content-driven categories. This number was later reduced to the following 13 categories. The authors further recorded the frequency of instances, in the form of percentages (in parentheses):

- Personal identifier (35.7)
- Group identifier (4.6)
- Slurs and insults (1.9)
- Teen romance (21.8)
- Criminal justice related (7.8)
- Activism (6.6)
- Race (1.3)

- Outlaws (1.5)
- Drugs (1.1)
- Sex (1.0)
- Religion (2.5)
- Obscenity (2.0)
- Miscellaneous (12.3)

From these and other data, the authors were able to reconstruct the processes individuals go through as part of adjusting to incarceration and how this process changes throughout inmates' period of incarceration.

Using Listserv Content to Understand Communication Among Physical Educators

Pennington, Wilkinson, and Vance (2004) examined physical education teachers' conversations posted on the National Association for Sport and Physical Education listserv (NASPE-L), a listserv on which teachers share information about their needs and concerns while working in their school environments. Data were collected from 333 messages in the listserv archives for one randomly selected month. The researchers analyzed the content inductively and identified six common themes: professional issues, teaching activities, instructional strategies, technology in physical education, professional conferences, and advocacy. Findings from their study indicate a professional nature of the conversations on the listserv. From these data, the authors also conclude that individuals participating in the listserv forum appear to care deeply about the profession as a whole along with their own teaching and programs. Data suggest that teachers are willing to share and support others within the profession thus potentially alleviating feelings of isolation.

WORKING INTERNATIONALLY

All of the cross-cultural issues discussed in earlier chapters also apply to the activities outlined in this chapter. Images, however, present an additional translational challenge. Verbatim, text-based data collection instruments are difficult enough to translate from one language and/or culture to another. The situation is amplified substantially with visual stimuli. Consider the following example from an international public health organization with offices in more than 25 countries, including the United States. One of the U.S.-based colleagues wanted to use the image of a string tied around a finger in an intervention to denote the concept of a "reminder." In order to see if this was in fact a universally accepted meaning of the symbol, the researcher sent an e-mail to individuals in all of the organization's international locations. Below is the initial query and a select sample of responses:

> **Query:** *I am currently working with a partner on an international campaign and need to know if the symbol of a finger with a string around it is understood universally as a sign of a reminder. This is the case for the US, but would this resonate around the world?*

Responses:

- *In my culture in Northern Nigeria, it will surely tell everyone who notices that the person is mentally sick.*

- *In some parts of Malawi, it signifies a suicide case (needs to be handled carefully and all the rites followed). In the northern part of the country, a string tied on the small toe stops diarrhea.*

- *Mischief, that's all I read! But a promise is sealed with the little finger wrapped round the other young person's little finger from the opposite hand. Especially if it is of the opposite sex, and you know what for! The deal is sealed.*

- *In my community, a boy ties his finger with a string during a special visit to his uncles and aunties to announce he's ready for traditional circumcision!*

- *In Southern Africa, it might be misunderstood to mean a bandaged/wounded finger or hanging a person—suicide.*

- *I have no idea what it means and am a Zimbabwean.*

- *In Tanzania we think it's another white man's trick.*

- *In East Timor we'd assume snakebite.*

The responses above are a clear example of how much the meaning behind visual stimuli and symbols can vary cross-culturally. If using any of the more visually based methods described above in other cultures, it's important to make sure that the stimuli used are appropriate for the data collection objective. Moreover, directly analyzing the output of expressive tasks, such as drawings or photos, becomes even more difficult when working outside of your own culture. The flip side to this is that less structured forms of data elicitation allow more room for cultural interpretation, and image-based techniques can be used in nonliterate populations (Gates, 1976). Notwithstanding, we recommend sticking to analyzing the discourse generated from expressive activities carried out in cross-cultural research, unless you are either an expert in that culture or have local collaborators who can aid in interpretation of the data.

SUMMING UP

As illustrated in this chapter, nontraditional data collection activities can be incredibly useful and informative, particularly for certain types of inquiry that require deeper probing of thought processes and emotive valences. The majority of the activities we've discussed can be implemented in a number of different forms, contexts, and temporal arrangements. The same can be said for analysis of the data these activities can generate. You need to think about all of these parameters in order to better plan activities involving the techniques covered. Table 6.4 includes a summary

Table 6.4	Data Collection Techniques and Characteristics	
Method/ Activity	Key Characteristics	More Appropriate Context
Listing	• Great activity for identifying range of items/concepts in a domain of inquiry • Good starting point for data collection activities • Lists can be analyzed quantitatively and qualitatively	Group AND One-on-One
Categorizing	• Useful for understanding how individuals or groups perceive the relationship between items/concepts in a domain of inquiry • Pile sorting is a commonly used method • Typically represented visually, using graph-theoretic techniques (e.g., MDS, cluster analysis) • Often used to identify and visually represent cultural/sub-cultural taxonomies	Group AND One-on-One
Timeline Development	• Extremely useful for any research question that has a temporal dimension • Time period depicted can vary immensely, (one day to one century) • Timelines are often augmented with other data sets—both quantitative and qualitative	Group AND One-on-One
Drawing	• Drawing is often used as a projective technique, to reveal underlying values or cognitive and emotive processes that verbal questioning may not reach • A great method for children	Group AND One-on-One
Building a Collage	• A type of projective technique that works well in both individual and group contexts • Good technique for children	Group AND One-on-One
Mapping	• Very useful for any research question that contains a spatial dimension • Map scale can range in size considerably (from an individual's room/office to a region of a country) • Maps can include both quantitative and qualitative dimensions and can be annotated with social, behavioral, and other non-geographical data	Group AND One-on-One

Method/ Activity	Key Characteristics	Appropriate Context
Visual Elicitation Techniques	• Range of visual stimuli a researcher can use is infinite • Can be researcher- or participant-led • In general, visual elicitation techniques are projective in purpose, designed to reveal underlying values or cognitive and emotive processes that verbal questioning may not reach • As a general rule of thumb, less ambiguous stimuli will tend to elicit more factual and tangible responses. More ambiguous stimuli are presumed to better reveal inner values, emotions, and beliefs • Good methods for children	Group AND One-on-One
Rating and Ranking	• Excellent techniques for situations where items/ideas/etc. need to be prioritized • Data can easily be compared between participants or among groups	Group AND One-on-One
Post-Event Reflection	• Can be used for any data collection technique • Most useful when you want participants to think in-depth about or reflect upon a particular topic, finding, or dataset/data point	Group AND One-on-One
Delphi Method	• Used to generate "expert" forecasts or estimations for a given topic • Can also be used to generate consensus among a group of experts • Output is primarily quantitative, but qualitative data should also be captured during the process to reveal the rationale(s) behind the estimations	Group
Creating a Campaign	• Very useful in marketing and social marketing research • Works well in a group context, since multiple perspectives are brought together to build the campaign	Group
Laddering	• If done properly, laddering can reveal an individual's core values regarding a particular belief or behavior • Requires well-developed interviewing skills	One-on-One

Table 6.4	Data Collection Techniques and Characteristics	
Method/ Activity	Key Characteristics	Appropriate Context
Ethnographic Decision Modeling	• Excellent technique if your research objectives require documenting decision processes • Has been shown to be highly predictive • Great for applied research, as it can reveal potential intervention points • Requires specific, well-developed interviewing skills	One-on-One
Document Analysis	• Not truly a form of data generation, but commonly used in qualitative inquiry • An advantage of document analysis is that the data do not need to be generated (which circumvents regulatory issues governing human subjects research) • The range of "documents" that can be analyzed is extremely broad, so the technique can be used for almost any topic and in any context	NA

Note: NA = Not applicable.

of the techniques covered and some of their key characteristics, to help you with the planning process.

With the above table and your research objective(s) in mind, ask yourself the following questions. How you answer them should guide which activity (if any) you choose, how you implement that activity, and how you analyze the data generated from the activity.

Question: *Does my research objective warrant a nontraditional data collection activity and/or output?*

Suggestions:

• Using nontraditional activities often requires additional effort and expertise. Be parsimonious; not all research topics will benefit from these activities. Weigh the costs, in terms of time and effort, with the potential benefits of using a particular activity.

Question: *Should I use a group activity or would an individual context be better?*

Suggestions:

- Individual data collection methods are better for research topics that are highly personal or sensitive.
- Use individually based techniques when your data analysis requires response independence. The majority of peer-reviewed journals look more favorably on individual techniques rather than group techniques.
- If consensus or group outcome is desired, then employing a group-based activity is the appropriate route to take (as long as it does not contradict the point above).

Question: *Am I interested in deeper, more emotional and value-based information?*

Suggestions:

- If the answer to this question is "yes," consider using a projective technique.
- The less factual, and more emotional, the data you desire, the more ambiguous you should make the stimuli.
- If you need to direct your query to a specific product or topic, laddering provides better control over the data generation process. Note that laddering can be used in conjunction with other, visually-based, projective techniques.

Question: *If I'm selecting a projective technique, which of Lindzey's five activity types should I use (association, construction, completion, ordering, or expressive)?*

Suggestions:

- The answer to this really depends on your research topic, objectives, and study population. You need to think carefully about which type of activity best suits your research context.

Question: *If using an expressive activity, do I want to directly analyze the outcome (i.e., drawing, photo, etc.), the discourse generated during the activity, or both?*

Suggestions:

- More commonly, researchers analyze the discourse generated during the discussion about the stimuli. This is because direct analysis of visual representations requires much more researcher interpretation than analyzing what participant's say. Notwithstanding, some pictures (e.g., Figure 6.8) speak for themselves.

Question: *Should I assign the activity before the interview or focus group takes place? Or is it something better left for the event itself?*

Suggestions:

- Generally, complex topics that require a lot of thought are good candidates for preassigned tasks.
- Preassignment of activities allows more time during the interview or focus group process to *discuss* the activities and their outputs.
- More interviewer-directed activities (e.g., decision modeling, laddering), or group process activities (e.g., building a campaign), however, are better suited to a real-time context.

Question: *Would I get additional, insightful data from asking participants to review and reflect on the data generated from the initial data collection activity? And, is it logistically feasible to do so, in terms of time and participant ability/willingness?*

Suggestions:

- If you answer "yes" to both of these questions, post-event reflection is a good option that can deepen your understanding of your research topic.

Question: *If using a visual technique, should I use a more researcher-driven approach (e.g., the researcher provides the stimuli) or a more participatory approach (participants play a larger role in determining the study parameters, such as choosing stimuli)?*

Suggestions:

- The answer to this depends on how much control you want over the process and outcome. If you want to guide participants in a specific direction, then providing some structure to the task is helpful. If, conversely, your research topic is highly exploratory and you want participants to more fully drive the process, use a more participatory approach.

Question: *Is there a temporal dimension to my research objective(s)?*

Suggestions:

- If the answer is "yes," think about using a timeline approach in your data collection process.

Question: *Do I need some form of quantitative output as part of the activity?*

Suggestions:

- If you or your audience require quantitative outcomes, choose a method that is more conductive to a quantitative analysis, such as free listing, rating/ranking, or the Delphi technique.

Question: *What types of documents (including images and artifacts), if any, can inform my research objectives?*

Suggestions:

- Observe or visualize your study context. Talk to people from your study population. Identify text/objects/images that are accessible and that can yield information about your research topic that other data collection techniques cannot. The possibilities are limitless, so choose your items carefully.

Question: *If I choose to carry out a document analysis, what is the most appropriate analytic approach to take?*

Suggestions:

- If you have hypotheses you want to test, choose a confirmatory approach. This type of approach requires rigorous sampling and data analysis procedures, as well as predefined themes or categories.
- For most qualitative field research, content analysis of documents, images, and objects has an exploratory objective. A content-driven analysis identifies themes inductively, as they emerge from the data.

We have just skimmed the surface of document analysis and nontraditional elicitation activities in this chapter; a myriad of other techniques and derivatives of those techniques exist. Page limits restrict the amount of detail we can provide, so we refer those interested in these techniques—and others not covered—to the Additional Reading section at the end of this chapter.

While the repository of published works on elicitation techniques is large, it is dwarfed by the infinite number of possible techniques and their permutations that have yet to be tried. These are limited only by the imagination of researchers. Integrate and mix and match techniques if it makes sense for your study. Consider the possible variations of any one activity. Be creative; there are no hard and fast rules. The most important thing is to be explicit and transparent about your procedures.

REFERENCES

Abroms, L., Padmanabhan, N., Thaweethai, L., & Phillips, T. (2011). iPhone apps for smoking cessation: A content analysis. *American Journal of Preventive Medicine, 40*(3), 279–285.

Allen, S., & Bartram, P. (2008). *Guam as a fishing community* (Administrative Report H-08-01). Honolulu, HI: Pacific Islands Fisheries Science Center, National Marine Fisheries Service, NOAA.

Amesbury, J. (2005–2006). *Monitoring and forecasting ecological changes in the Mariana Archipelago.* Presentation to the Ecosystem Social Science Workshop, Honolulu, January 2006, to the 129th Council meeting, Guam, November 2005, and to the meetings of the Joint Plan Teams and the Scientific and Statistical Committee, Honolulu, October 2005.

Badowski N., Castro, C. M., Montgomery, M., Pickering, A. J., Mamuya, S., & Davis, J. (2011, September 28). Understanding household behavioral risk factors for diarrheal disease in Dar es Salaam: A photovoice community assessment. *Journal of Environmental and Public Health* [E-journal]. doi: 10.1155/2011/130467

Bagnoli, A. (2009). Beyond the standard interview: the use of graphic elicitation and arts-based methods. *Qualitative Research, 9*(5), 547–570.

Banks, M. (2001). *Visual methods in social research.* Thousand Oaks, CA: Sage.

Banks, M. (2007). *Using visual data in qualitative research.* Thousand Oaks, CA: Sage.

Barry, C. A. (1997). The research activity timeline: A qualitative tool for information research. *Library & Information Science Research, 19*(2), 153–179.

Bates, J., & Martin, M. (1980). The thematic content of graffiti as a nonreactive indicator of male and female attitudes. *Journal of Sex Research, 16,* 300–315.

Berends, L. 2011. Embracing the visual: Using timelines with in-depth interviews on substance use and treatment. *Qualitative Report, 16*(1), 1–9. Retrieved from http://www.nova.edu/ssss/QR/QR16-1/berends.pdf

Bernard, H. R. (2000). *Social research methods: Qualitative and quantitative approaches.* Thousand Oaks, CA: Sage.

Bernard, H. R., & Ryan, G. (1998). Text analysis: Qualitative and quantitative methods. In H. Bernard (Ed.), *Handbook of methods in cultural anthropology* (pp. 595–646). Walnut Creek, CA: AltaMira Press.

Bernard, H. R., & Ryan, G. 2010. *Qualitative data analysis: Systematic approaches.* Thousand Oaks, CA: Sage.

Beskow, L. M., Namey, E. E., Cadigan, R. J., Brazg, T., Crouch, J., Henderson, G. E., Michie, M.,. . . Wilfond, B. S.]. (2011, December). Research participants' perspectives on genotype-driven research recruitment. *Journal Empir Res Hum Res Ethics, 6*(4), 3-20.

Blackman, A. (2007). *The PhotoVoice manual: A guide to designing and running participatory photography projects.* London, UK: PhotoVoice.

Borgatti, S. (1994). How to explain hierarchical clustering. *Connections, 17*(2), 78–80.

Borgatti, S. (1997). Multidimensional scaling. Retrieved from http://www.analytictech.com/borgatti/mds.htm

Borgatti, S. (1999). Elicitation techniques for cultural domain analysis. In J. Schensul & M. LeCompte (Vol. Eds.), *The ethnographer's toolkit: Vol. 3* (pp. 115–151). Walnut Creek, CA: Altamira Press.

Brown, B. (1968). *Delphi process: A methodology used for the elicitation of opinions of experts.* Santa Monica, CA: RAND.

CARE. (2009). *Window of opportunity annual report 2009.* Atlanta, GA: Author. Retrieved August 2, 2011, from http://windowofopp.files.wordpress.com/2010/11/annual-report-20091.pdf

Cauduro, M. T., Birk, M., & Wachs, P. (2009). Arts-based investigation: A Brazilian story. *Forum Qualitative Sozialforschung / Forum: Qualitative Social Research, 10*(2), Art. 33. Retrieved from http://nbn-resolving.de/urn:nbn:de:0114-fqs0902335

Chavez, L., Hubbell, F., McMullin, J., Martinez, R., & Mishra, S. (1995). Structure and meaning in models of breast and cervical cancer risk factors: A comparison of perceptions among Latinas, Anglo women, and physicians. *Medical Anthropology Quarterly, 9,* 40–74.

Colton, S., & Hatcher, T. (2004, March 3–7). *The web-based Delphi research technique as a method for content validation in HRD and adult education research* (pp. 183–189). Paper presented at the Academy of Human Resource Development International Conference (AHRD; Symposium 9-1), Austin, Texas.

Cowan, G., & O'Brian, M. (1990). Gender and survival vs. death in slasher films: A content analysis. *Sex Roles, 23*(3–4), 187–196.

Cuhls, K. (n.d.). *Delphi method.* Retrieved November 2011, from http://www.unido.org/fileadmin/import/16959_DelphiMethod.pdf

Denzin, N. K., & Lincoln, Y. S. (2003). Collecting and interpreting qualitative materials. (2nd ed.). Thousand Oaks, CA: Sage.

Fletcher-Johnston, M., Marshall, S., Straatman, L. (2011). Healthcare transitions for adolescents with chronic life-threatening conditions using a Delphi method to identify research priorities for clinicians and academics in Canada. *Child Care Health and Development, 37*(6), 875–882.

Frank, L. (1939). Projective methods for the study of personality. *Journal of Psychology, 8,* 389–413.

Gates, M. (1976). Measuring peasant methods to modernization: a projective method. *Current Anthropology, 17,* 641–665.

Gladwin, C. (1989). *Ethnographic decision tree modeling.* Newbury Park, CA: Sage.

Guest, G., MacQueen, K., & Namey, E. (2012). *Applied thematic analysis.* Thousand Oaks, CA: Sage.

Gutman, J. (1982). A means-end chain model based on consumer categorization processes. *Journal of Marketing, 46,* 60–72.

Hill, C. (1998). Decision modeling: Its use in medical anthropology. In V. de Munck & E. Sobo (Eds.), *Using methods in the field: A practical introduction and casebook* (pp. 139–164). Walnut Creek, CA: AltaMira Press.

Hirschman, E. C. (1987). People as products: Analysis of a complex marketing exchange. *Journal of Marketing, 51,* 98–108.

Holcomb, J., Okumus, F., & Bilgihan, A. (2010). Corporate social responsibility: What are the top three Orlando theme parks reporting? *Worldwide Hospitality and Tourism Themes, 2*(3), 316–337.

Hsieh, H., & Shannon, S. (2005). Three approaches to qualitative content analysis. *Qualitative Health Research, 15,* 1277–1288.

Kerner, B., McCarthy, P., Bishwa, R., & Lundgren, R. (n.d.). *Using projective techniques to explore gender norms with young adolescents in Nepal.* Westport, CT: Save the Children.

Klofas, J., & Cutshall, C. (1985). Unobtrusive research methods in criminal justice: Using graffiti in the reconstruction of institutional cultures. *Journal of Research in Crime and Delinquency, 22,* 355–373.

Kreuger, R. A., & Casey, M. A. (2009). *Focus groups: A practical guide for applied research.* Thousand Oaks, CA: Sage.

Krippendorf, K. (2004). *Content analysis: An introduction to its methodology* (2nd ed.). Thousand Oaks, CA: Sage.

Linstone, H., & Turoff, M. (Eds.). (1975). *The Delphi method: Techniques and applications.* Reading, MA: Addison-Wesley.

Lindzey, G. (1961). *Projective techniques and cross cultural research.* New York, NY: Appleton-Century-Crofts.

Lopez Levers, L. (2001). Representations of psychiatric disability in fifty years of Hollywood film: An ethnographic content analysis. *Theory & Science* [E-journal]. http://theoryandscience.icaap.org/content/vo1002.002/lopezlevers.html.

Mascarenhas, J., & Kumar, P. (1991). Participatory mapping and modelling users' notes. *RRA Notes, 12,* 9–20.

Maslow, A. (1970). *Motivation and personality* (2nd ed). New York, NY: Joanna Cotler Books.

Nazarea, V., Rhoades, R., Bontoyan, E., & Flora, G. (1998). Defining local indicators which make sense to local people: Intra-cultural variation in perceptions of natural resources. *Human Organization, 57,* 159–170.

Padgett, D. (2008). *Qualitative methods in social work research* (2nd ed.). Thousand Oaks, CA: Sage.

Pennington, T., Wilkinson, C., & Vance, J. (2004, Jan). What is on the minds of teachers in the trenches? *Physical Educator, 61*(1). Available from www.highbeam.com

Peter, P., & Olson, J. (1990). *Consumer behavior and marketing strategy* (2nd ed.). Homestead, IL: Irwin.

Pink, S. (2007). *Doing visual ethnography* (2nd ed.). Thousand Oaks, CA: Sage.

Rathje, W. (1992). *Rubbish!: The archaeology of garbage.* New York, NY: HarperCollins.

Reiss, S. (2004). Multifaceted nature of intrinsic motivation: The theory of 16 basic desires. *Review of General Psychology, 8,* 179–193.

Reynolds, T., & Gutman, J. (1988). Laddering theory, method, analysis, and interpretation. *Journal of Advertising Research, 28,* 11–31.

Ribisl, K., Lee, R., Henriksen, L., & Haladjian, H. (2003). A content analysis of web sites promoting smoking culture and lifestyle. *Health Education and Behavior, 30,* 64–78.

Rowe, G., & Wright, G. (1999). The Delphi technique as a forecasting tool: Issues and analysis. *International Journal of Forecasting, 15,* 353–375.

Rowe, G., & Wright, G. (2001). Expert opinions in forecasting: The role of the Delphi technique. In J. Armstrong (Ed.), *Principles of forecasting: A handbook for researchers and practitioners* (pp. 125–144). New York, NY: Springer.

Russell, C., Busson, A., Flight, I., Bryan, J., van Lawick van Pabst, J., & Cox, D. (2004). A comparison of three laddering techniques applied to an example of a complex food choice. *Food Quality and Preference, 15,* 569–583.

Ryan, G., & Bernard, H. (2006). Testing an ethnographic decision tree model on a national sample: Recycling beverage cans. *Human Organization, 65,* 103–114.

Ryan, G., & Martinez, H. (1996). Can we predict what mothers do? Modeling childhood diarrhea in rural Mexico. *Human Organization, 55*(1), 47–57.

Sadler, D., & Shoben, E. (1993). Context effects on semantic domains as seen in analogy solution. *Journal of Experimental Psychology: Learning, Memory, and Cognition, 19*(1), 128–147.

Sobell, L., & Sobell, M. (1996). *Timeline followback: A user's guide.* Toronto, Ontario, Canada: Addiction Research Foundation.

Soley, L., & Smith, A. (2008). *Projective techniques for social science and business research.* Milwaukee, WI: Southshore Press.

Stanczak, G. C. (2007). *Visual research methods: Image, society, and representation.* Thousand Oaks, CA: Sage.

Wang, C. (1999). Photovoice: A participatory action research strategy applied to women's health. *Journal of Women's Health, 8,* 185–192.

Wang, C., Yi, W., Tao, Z., & Carovano, K. (1998). Photovoices as a participatory health promotion strategy. *Health Promotion International, 13,* 75–86.

Weller, S. (1983). New data on intracultural variability. *Human Organization, 42,* 249–257.

Weller, S., & Romney, A. (1988). *Systematic data collection.* Thousand Oaks, CA: Sage.

Wheeldon, J., & Faubert, J. (2009). Framing experience: Concept maps, mind maps, and data collection in qualitative research. *International Journal of Qualitative Methods, 8*(3), 68–83.

ADDITIONAL READING

Borgatti, S. (1999). Elicitation techniques for cultural domain analysis. In J. Schensul & M. LeCompte (Vol. Eds.), *The ethnographer's toolkit: Vol. 3* (pp. 115–151). Walnut Creek, CA: Altamira Press.

Charmaz, K. (2006). *Constructing grounded theory: A practical guide through qualitative analysis.* Thousand Oaks, CA: Sage.

Guest, G., MacQueen, K., & Namey, E. (2012). *Applied thematic analysis.* Thousand Oaks, CA: Sage.

Krippendorf, K. (2004). *Content analysis: An introduction to its methodology* (2nd ed.). Thousand Oaks, CA: Sage.

Krueger, R. (1998). *Developing questions for focus groups.* Thousand Oaks, CA: Sage.

Linstone, H., & Turoff, M. (1975). *The Delphi method: Techniques and applications.* Reading, MA: Addison-Wesley.

Neuendorf, K. (2002). *The content analysis guidebook.* Thousand Oaks, CA: Sage.

Perkins, C. (2007). Community mapping. *Cartographic Journal, 44,* 127–137.

Soley, L., & Lee Smith, A. (2008). *Projective techniques for social science and business research.* Milwaukee, WI: Southshore Press.

EXERCISES

1. Choose two or three qualitative articles in your field of research that employ standard in-depth interview or focus group techniques. For each study, think about how some of the activities discussed in this chapter could have enhanced understanding of the subject matter.

2. Search the research literature—preferably in your field of interest—for two or three studies that employed nontraditional qualitative data elicitation techniques not covered in this chapter. In a few paragraphs per technique, describe the context in which the technique would be most useful, how the activity is conducted, and the type of output the activity generates.

3. Choose one or two techniques described in this chapter. Create one or more innovative variations of these techniques. In a paragraph, describe what particular context would be best suited for each variation created.

4. Choose two qualitative articles in your field of research that employ standard qualitative data collection techniques. List all the types of documents, including images and artifacts, that might have been able to inform each of the research studies. Think about what sampling and recording units, and overall sampling strategy, would be most appropriate for these analyses.

OR Think about a research project that you are planning or would like to do. List all the types of documents, including images and artifacts, that could inform your research objectives. What type of analysis approach would you use (exploratory or confirmatory), and why? Think about what your sampling and recording units would be and how you would sample them.

APPENDIX 6.1

Examples of Confirmatory, Structured, Document Analysis Worksheets

Example 1: Corporate Reporting of "Corporate Social Responsibility" (CSR): Matrix of Content by Top Three Theme Parks (content from websites, annual reports, and CSR reports)

CSR areas	Walt Disney World	Sea World Parks	Universal Orlando
Environment			
Conservation	X	X	X
Architectural integration (cultural heritage)	X		X
Community			
Community support and charities	X	X	X
Employee volunteerism	X	X	X
Jobs for disadvantaged	X		

CSR areas	Walt Disney World	Sea World Parks	Universal Orlando
Market place			
Business Partners and suppliers(diversity)	X	X	X
Safety and well being of customers	X	X	X
Vision and values			
Mission/vission statement	X	X	X
Code os conduct(ethics)	X	X	X
Board conducted CSR review	X		
Workforce			
Employee diversity	X	X	X
Employee welfare programs	X	X	X
Child care	X		

Source: Holcomb, Okumus, and Bilgihan (2010).

Example 2: Rank Ordering of Iconography of Psychiatric Disability by Total Frequencies in Hollywood Films (icons created a priori)

ICON	TOTAL	FILMS	RANK
lighted window w/door	277	**19**	1
seated	226	18	2
cage	175	14	3
held/guided by warders	172	17	4
staff (long stick)	101	10	5
eyes cast down	95	18	6
music icons	68	12	7
restrained	65	12	8

ICON	TOTAL	FILMS	RANK
hiding hands	51	12	9
ship of fools/confinement	49	9	10
scampering fools	46	6	11
clotes in disarray	45	10	12
any body invasive techinque	42	12	13
dark asylum	39	15	14.5
dance icons	39	9	14.5
hands grasped to face	31	10	16
clenched fists	30	11	17
facial expression of fear	28	8	18
naked	27	8	19
flailing limbs	26	8	20
shaft of light	23	6	21
criminal insanity/deviance	22	6	22
wringing hands	20	7	23
Feather cap	19	4	24.5
straightjacket	19	4	24.5
chained	18	3	26
facial expression of horror/terror	15	3	27
lunatic's ball	14	2	28
bedlam	7	3	29
individual illuminated by light	7	2	29
sexual deviant	7	2	29
tearing hair	6	5	32
tearing clothes	5	2	33
ecstatic swoon	4	3	34

ICON	TOTAL	FILMS	RANK
sluggish dog	1	1	35.5
demons/exorcism	1	1	35.5
rats (appeared in still art, but not film)	0	0	37

Source: Lopez Levers (2001).

APPENDIX 6.2

Examples of Exploratory, Open-Coding, Document Analysis Worksheets

Example 1: Generic Worksheet

Document Analysis Worksheet

Name _____

Document Title _____

Type of Document(check one):

_____ Newspaper   _____ Map   _____ Advertisment

_____ Letter   _____ Congressional Record _____ Telegram

_____ Speech   _____ Press Relaese   _____ Census Report

_____ Book   _____ Report   _____ Other

Date of the Document _____

Author/Creator of the Document _____

Background of the Author: (position, nationality, gender. occupation, social class, religion, etc.)

For what audience was the document written? _____

Document Information: In your own words, list in three main ideas from the document. Cite a quote from the document that illustrates each main idea.

1. _____

    _____

    _____

2. _____

    _____

    _____

3. _____

    _____

    _____

Example 2: Written Document Analysis Worksheet, "Was Lincoln an Abolitionist?"

Name: _____

Date: _____ per.:_____

1. IDENTIFYING "NAME" OF THE DOCUMENT:

2. TYPE OF DOCUMENT(*Check one*):

——— **Newspaper**	——— **Memorandum**	——— **Press release**
——— **Letter**	——— **Map**	——— **Report**
——— **Patent**	——— **Telegram**	——— **Other...**

3. UNIQUE PHYSICAL QUALITIES OF THE DOCUMENT *(check one or more, describe details)*:

——— **Interesting letterhead**	——— **Notations**
——— **Handwritten**	——— **"RECEIVED" stamp**
——— **Typed**	——— **other**
——— **Seals**	

4. DATES(S) OF DOCUMANT

5. AUTHOR (OR CREATOR) OF THE DOCUMENT:

    POSITON (TITLE):

6. DOCUMENT INFORMATION *(Quote the document as part of your answer. Continued on the back.)*

    A. List up to THREE sentences from the document that may offer insight into Lincoln's position on slavery or abolition **(how do these statements help you understand Lincoln's view on slavery?):**

7

Qualitative Data Management

WHAT IS DATA MANAGEMENT?

Compared to the skills and complexities of qualitative data collection (and analysis), data management seems rather straightforward. And if it's planned in advance and executed well, it can be. Defined as "a designed structure for systematizing, categorizing, and filing materials to make them efficiently retrievable and duplicable" (Schwandt, 1997, p. 61), *data management* is simply an organizational process.

Despite its apparent simplicity (or maybe because of it), data management is often overlooked in the planning and data collection phases of research. And literature on the topic is limited (Lin, 2009; MacQueen & Milstein, 1999; McLellan-Lemal, 2008a). This may be because qualitative data management is so tightly bound up in both data collection and analysis that it is not perceived as a distinct step in what is already a nonlinear process (Huberman & Miles, 1994). As such, some authors conflate data management with coding and/or data analysis. Take, for instance, the chapter in the *Handbook of Qualitative Research*, second edition, titled "Data Management and Analysis Methods" (Ryan & Bernard, 2000). Despite the title of the chapter, the text does not contain a definition of qualitative data management, nor does it mention any logistical considerations for "managing" data. In their chapter, Ryan and Bernard (2000) treat data management almost as a synonym for data analysis, a phenomenon observed in other published works as well (e.g., Ray, 1997; Ritchie, Spencer, & O'Connor, 2003). In other cases, scholars view qualitative data management as merely a software related issue and focus on the various features and functions of particular software packages for managing and analyzing qualitative data (e.g., Ross, 1994; Russell & Gregory, 1993).

Although qualitative data management is related to both data analysis software and analytic procedures, the process is much larger in scope than both of these combined. The traditional, and limited, focus embodied in the approaches above represents what MacQueen and Milstein (1999) refer to as the "black box of data management," where data management is mentioned in reports as a necessary part of qualitative data collection and analysis, but without reference to the nitty-gritty details of how one kept track of the data collected or the methods and processes used to analyze it. When it comes to research, and aspirations for transparency of process, the devil is indeed in the details. In this chapter, we examine data management within a larger framework and describe relevant details that—if considered in advance—can enhance the efficiency, organization, and security of your data.

WHY IS DATA MANAGEMENT IMPORTANT?

Imagine that you were asked to join a qualitative rapid assessment project in the middle of its 12 week lifespan. Upon arrival at the field site, you are handed a cardboard box and told, "Here's the data." The box contains over 80 audio cassette tapes representing as many in-depth interviews, conducted with people from three stakeholder groups at each of three field locations by different interviewers. Each tape is labeled with different information—date of in-depth interview (IDI), location, maybe stakeholder type, or interviewer ID. All are mixed and jumbled in the box. You have 8 weeks to transcribe and analyze these data (a very truncated timeline, reflecting the rapid assessment nature of the project) and produce a mid-term report. Where would you start?

Now imagine that instead of one box, you are handed three separate boxes, one for each field site. Inside the boxes, tapes are systematically arranged according to their labels, which consistently and clearly identify the site, type, date, interviewer, and unique ID number associated with the interview on the tape. Additionally, you receive a log detailing how many IDIs were conducted with each category of stakeholder at each site and by whom. Does this sound like a little less daunting way to get started?

The first situation is what one of the authors stepped into during graduate school; the latter describes what she did first with the big "box of data." Data "messes" like this happen. Researchers and field teams can be so excited about and busy with data collection (which is admittedly more fun than data management) that they overlook the importance of keeping clear, consistent, legible, and accessible information on what they're doing and collecting. This type of information is essential for preparing even the most basic of "analysis" reports—a project summary. How many IDIs have been conducted? Where? On which topics? Have the data been "processed" yet (transcribed or translated)? Are they secure? How do data collected match up with the sampling design for the study? Who is left to be interviewed, or which remaining interviews should be prioritized? A data management plan, incorporated from the beginning of a research project, allows you to quickly and easily answer these questions to guide both data collection and analysis. Put succinctly, the benefits of good data management practices in a qualitative study include the ability to:

- Organize your data;
- Quickly distinguish distinct items, types, and versions of data;
- Sort or filter your data;
- Monitor data quality;
- Coordinate and systematize team-based research;
- Standardize transcription and translation to enhance quality and facilitate analysis;
- Secure your data against accidental loss or theft;
- Protect the confidentiality of your research participants;
- Keep track of the sources of your data;
- Mark recruitment progress against sampling goals;
- Measure project completion against timelines, deadlines, and budget considerations; and
- Maintain an ongoing record of analysis decisions to enable replication (internal or external).

Systematic Data Management—Basic Considerations

A good data management plan should allow you to address the following questions and issues:

- How many files do you have?
  - You should know at any given point (and without counting individual files) how many participant observation IDI/focus group events have been conducted for a particular project.
  - This information is important for comparing data collected to the sampling parameters defined in your research design, to guide subsequent recruitment and data collection efforts.

- Where are your files, physically?
  - On the digital recorder? Uploaded to a laptop? In a shared network folder? In cloud or other offsite/dispersed/secure storage?

(Continued)

(Continued)

> o You should be able to produce any data, consent forms, payment receipts, or other data-related documents upon request.
>
> - Where are your data, figuratively, in the data management process?
>   o Which files have been transcribed? Translated? Coded?
>   o This information is essential for assigning data processing tasks and keeping track of data-related study timelines.
>
> - How secure are your data?
>   o Are data stripped of identifiers? Password protected? Are there files on personal or shared network drives? Hard copies lying on your desk?
>   o Data security is an essential element of ethical research and the protection of participant confidentiality.
>
> - Which file is which?
>   o Do you have different versions of the same file? (If so, which is most recent?) Does file name IDI02S1 represent the second of the IDIs or the second of all of the files? Is the S1 for Site 1 or Stage 1?
>   o Clear and consistent file-naming conventions become increasingly important as the number and inter-relatedness of data files increases.
>
> - Which files go together?
>   o Can you easily link source data (audio/video or notes) to transcribed or expanded versions? To the related consent form? To associated demographic information?
>   o File naming, data logs, and file organization structure all facilitate coherent and comprehensive use of data.

IDENTIFYING SOURCES AND LABELING DATA

Consider all of the pieces and permutations of data and documentation you could collect from a single interview: an audio recording, the associated transcript, notes from the IDI, demographic information about the interviewee, a consent form, data from additional activities, and so on. The first consideration in data labeling then, as alluded to earlier, is to ensure that all of the information and documentation related to a particular source of data (an interviewee, focus group discussion, or participant observation event) is clearly, accurately, and consistently marked in a way that permits someone to identify the salient characteristics of the data file quickly. You will want to then extend your labeling protocol beyond this single case so that all of your files follow the same labeling system.

There are at least three different elements of identification to distinguish here, Source ID, data labels, and file names:

Source ID

A source is a person or event that provides primary data for your study. A source is typically a person, in the case of interviews and focus groups, or a particular event in the case of participant observation. The Source ID, then, is a unique reference number assigned to each contributor of primary data, usually in sequential order. For example, if you interview Mary, Bob, and Stan in that order, they would be Source01, Source02, and Source03, and you might assign Source IDs S01, S02, and S03.

Data Labels

Any physical data that you collect—consent forms, audio cassettes, demographic information sheets, drawings, or interview notes—will need to be labeled to reflect the source with which it is associated. Oftentimes, the data label will be the same as the Source ID. Continuing the example from above, all of the physical data associated with Mary would be labeled S01, Bob's data would be labeled S02, and Stan's would be labeled S03.

File Names

If your data collection efforts produce any electronic information—digital audio or video recordings, scanned consent documents, transcripts—these will also need to be labeled so that they can be linked with the original source. Because electronic files all look generally the same in a folder (there is no physically distinguishable difference), electronic file names often include more description than just the Source ID. For example, the audio recording from Mary's interview might be given the file name "S01 IDI audio," while the transcript of this audio recording would be named "S01 IDI transcript."

The relationship among Source ID, data labels, and file names, then, looks something like Figure 7.1.

We will focus our discussion on data labeling and file naming in this section, but note that both are predicated on Source IDs, and many of the same considerations apply to all three.

| Figure 7.1 | The Three Elements of Data Identification |

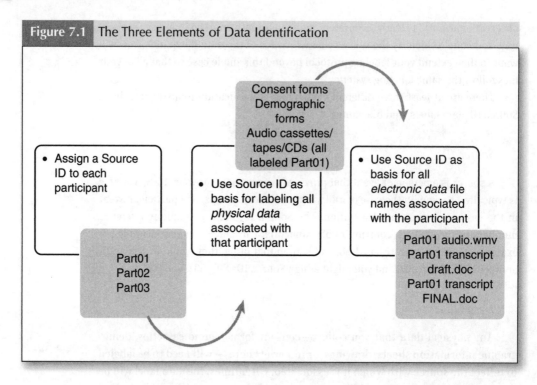

Data Label and File Name Confusion

How much information is enough when it comes to a data label or file name? Consider the following example of a list of file names:

Sarah1

Sarah2

Sarah3

How would you interpret these? They might indicate a series of three interviews with a person named Sarah. Or maybe they are three versions of a transcript produced from the same interview, each a revision of the previous. Maybe Sarah1 is the original audio file, Sarah2 is the text transcript, and Sarah3 is a coded document or translation. Or perhaps there were three Sarahs in this study, and each file corresponds to a separate person's interview transcript. The point is that we don't know based on these file names. While this example is a bit extreme, it illustrates the importance not only of agreeing upon a data labeling protocol but also in spelling it out in a reference document or key, which might say, using this example, "All files will be labeled with the first name of the interviewee followed by the number representing the stage of the study during which the interview took place (Stage 1, 2, or 3). File extensions will serve to indicate whether the file is audio or text." [Note: We don't recommend using participants' names, particularly full names, in data or file labeling as a confidentiality precaution. Leading with names in a data label or file name also makes it harder to arrange the data sequentially or chronologically, which may be important to your analysis. If you do decide to use first names in your data labels, specify the procedure for dealing with duplicate names.]

Here's an example from the other end of the file name continuum and its key:

> *File Name:* **SNA_Site1_IDI_01_DC_20110101**
> **SNA_Site1_IDI_02_DC_20110116**
> **SNA_Site3_IDI_03_AB_20110303**

Key: study name abbreviation_code for site_type of data collection_archival (sequence) number_data collector's initials_date of interview (year month day)

This file name contains a lot of information but is also very long. You can imagine that it would be difficult to pick out a particular interview if you were viewing a list of 20 of these file names. The simpler the better, as long as it is clear what is being represented in the file name.

The specific details of what is included in the Source ID, data label, or file name will vary by project, depending on the nature of the research and the scope and characteristics of the dataset. However, thinking about the types of information that would be helpful in quickly identifying or describing the file contents offers suggestions for items you might consider including. We provide a list of some common data and file label characteristics below.

- Source ID—A unique reference number assigned to each data collection event, usually in sequential order
  - 001, 002, 003, and so on. Note that the number 12 will appear before the number 2 in an electronic-sequential list, so consider the number of leading zeros you will need to keep files organized sequentially.

- o Different sites may each have sequential archival numbers distinguished by the leading number (e.g., Site 1 begins with 100, Site 2 begins with 200, etc.).

- Source information—Descriptive information about the person/people or event from which the data originated:
  - o Interviewee category or stakeholder group
    - Nurse, teacher, politician, mother, fisherman, engineer
  - o Relevant demographic details
    - Gender, race, region, religion, age, employment status
  - o Location information
    - Study site, PO setting

- Data type—A reference to the type of data collection method used to obtain the data
  - o In-depth interview (IDI), focus group (FG), participant observation (PO)

- Date—An indication of the date that the data collection event occurred, which can be used to organize data chronologically if archival numbers are not used.

It is not necessary—and is likely confusing—to try to include all of this information in a data label or file name. Select the features that are most important to identifying unique sources, organizing and linking your data, and understanding where files are in the research process at a glance. Table 7.1 provides some examples of file naming protocols.

Once you have established a procedure for naming files as they are created, think about how you will indicate changes to or versions of these files. For example, if "D07ResIDI audio.mp3" is the name of the audio file for the seventh data collection event at site D, which was an IDI with a resident, and "D07ResIDI transcript.doc" is the associated transcript, what will you call the proofed version? Or the version translated into English? In these cases, extending the file name to include descriptive text, version numbers, or dates is often worth the extra file name length. You should be able to tell, without doubt, which file is the most recent or final version for use in analysis. Also, despite the longer file name, you can always use the shorter Source ID version (D07ResIDI) in qualitative data analysis software (QDAS), since you will either have only one version of the file (e.g., transcript), or will be able to distinguish the two versions within the program anyway (e.g., audio and transcript). Finally, it's a good idea to create a footer that includes the file name on any printed versions of electronic material so that the hard copy is clearly labeled.

Table 7.1	Sample Source ID, Data Labeling, and File Naming Protocols		
	Example 1	**Example 2**	**Example 3**
Description of study	30 IDIs at one site with doctor/patient pairs	20 IDIs and 10 FGs at each of two sites (A and B)	40 IDIs conducted at two points in time with the same participants by two interviewers
Source ID key	Sequential study ID, by participant type (D=doctor, P=patient)	Site prefix-Data collection type-Sequential study ID (by data collection type)	Sequential respondent ID, Month and Year of interview, interviewer initials
Source ID/ Data label	D01 P01 D02 P02 D03 P03 D04 P04	A-FG-01 B-FG-01 A-FG-02 B-FG-02 A-IDI-01 B-IDI-01 A-IDI-02 B-IDI-02	R01May10AB R02May10CD R03May10AB R01Aug10AB R02Aug10CD R03Aug10AB
File names	D01 audio.mp3 D01 transcript.doc D01 notes.doc	A-FG-01 video.wmv A-FG-01 notes.doc A-FG-01 debriefing.doc A-FG-01 responses.xls	R01May10AB audio. wma R01May10AB final transcript.doc
Rationale	Since the two types of interviewees are related, we want to be able to easily match the specific doctor and patient in analysis and therefore gave them the same ID number with a different prefix. Since all data collection involves IDIs, we did not feel it necessary to include this information in the source or data label.	We will code and analyze the data from the two sites together, beginning with focus group data. Though the data will be combined, we want to be able to easily separate data from the two sites for comparison, thus, the parallel (rather than combined) sequential numbering.	We want not only to keep all of the interviews from the first data collection period (May 2010) together but also want to be able to match the individual files to a person's second (August) interview. Additionally, we want to make sure that the same person conducted both interviews, so we have included the interviewers' initials as both documentation and verification tool.

DATA CONVERSION

Analysis of qualitative data often requires several rounds of data conversion, beginning with the "coding" of participants' names into Source IDs, and continuing (potentially) through transcription, translation, coding, quantification, and data reduction activities. Of these processes, transcription and translation often form a bottleneck within the research process. Raw audio or video recordings of interviews or focus groups are often not coded or analyzed until they are converted into a text document through transcription, and certainly not until they are translated into the language of the analysis team. These conversion processes are time consuming and, if not done well, can create problems for subsequent analyses. In this section, we highlight issues that can hinder or facilitate transcription and translation of qualitative data.

Transcribing

For small samples with relatively short responses to questions, or for data collected on a specific topic with a very short turnaround time, you might skip the step of data transcription and simply make a running list of the types of answers to each question. If you are audio or video recording your in-depth interviews or focus groups for more extensive analysis, you will likely want to produce a transcript of the media file to facilitate analysis. While qualitative data analysis software offers increasing capabilities for importing, coding, and analyzing audio and video data sources, the size of these files often slows down the processing of the software. More importantly, it is impossible to "eyeball" 10 audio files coded at a particular theme the way you can scan text, and it's this simultaneous juxtaposition that often enhances efforts to compare and contrast cases reporting a similar theme. Videos offer the visual dimension but are again difficult to watch and interpret side-by-side. And so we very often end up with the task of transcribing interview and focus group responses.

Though sometimes tedious, the task of transcribing audio or video files seems relatively simple: Type whatever you hear. Yet, based on our experience, if you give that instruction to five people, you will get five very different transcripts in return. Some might identify the interviewer and respondent as INT and RES, while others ascribe sections of the data by ID number or initials. Some may produce a verbatim transcript suitable for linguistic analysis, including pauses, hesitations, and notes on tone of speech, laughter, or body language; others may paraphrase to capture the gist of what the speaker was saying. The specific style you choose for your project will depend on the nature and objectives of your research, the level of experience of your transcriptionist, and your study timeline. McLellan-Lemal (2008b) offers an extensive review of the different types, purposes, and styles of transcripts. The bottom line is that every project should incorporate a transcription style that is consistent across files and supports the goals of the analysis. Key elements to consider include formatting (headings, font, margins, spacing), header information, speaker attribution, level of linguistic detail, and any notes marking corresponding time from the media file. Table 7.2 (see pages 286 and 287) describes the importance of each of these considerations, and Appendix 7.1 includes a sample transcription protocol, which you can use as a starting point for developing your own.

Whether you opt for verbatim or paraphrased transcription will depend upon your research objectives and should be decided on in advance. If your goal is to analyze the mode and manner of communication along with the content of responses, you will need some form of verbatim transcript. If, on the other hand, you are most interested in simply gathering the range of responses to listing or "feedback" type questions (e.g., "What did you like about your stay there?"), a paraphrased or targeted summary approach to the transcript may suffice, particularly if your interview or focus group guide is fairly structured among respondents or groups. Most studies fall in the middle and are well served by a "clean" verbatim transcript, in which the responses of the participants are transcribed verbatim, but filler words and interviewer confirmations (mhmms) are omitted.

The specificity and detail of your transcription protocol will depend in part on the level of experience of your transcriptionist as well. A professional transcriptionist can transcribe, proofread, and format an hour's worth of recorded speech in about 4 to 8 hours, depending on recording quality, subject matter and terminology, the number of speakers, their dialects or accents, the placement of the microphone with respect to all of the speakers, extent of background noise, and so on. Usually an hour of good quality recorded interview would take about 4 hours to complete, while that same hour of recording of a focus group with several speakers could take from 6 to 8 hours, depending on the conditions mentioned above. A novice transcriber will require more time to accomplish the same tasks.

Increasing transcription speed is mainly a function of practice; it takes training and repetition to work a playback foot pedal, listen to the audio, and process the sounds in your ears to your fingers on the keyboard. Another way to enhance speed is to find ways to maximize typing efficiency. One trick experienced transcriptionists use to enhance efficiency is to select a standard repeated letter to indicate interviewer speech (*iii*) and another to refer to participants' speech

(Text continued on page 288)

Table 7.2   Essential Elements of a Transcription Protocol

Topic	Examples	Importance
Formatting	Heading styles Font size and style Margins Spacing	The formatting styles you select will depend on how your files will be analyzed. If you are using qualitative analysis software and a structured or semi-structured data collection guide, use of specific and consistent heading styles for each distinct question on the guide can enable auto-coding features. Font size and style, as well as margins and spacing, should make for easy reading, particularly if you have a large volume of text. Keeping these characteristics standard across the dataset makes for a uniform reading appearance and avoids unintentionally giving more or less weight to the text of a particular transcript. Finally, consider how you want to demarcate each piece of the conversation, either with a hard return after the speaker attribution or a colon and a tab, for example. Use whatever maximizes readability and spacing for the reader (and check to determine whether software that you may use has requirements about this level of formatting for importation or auto-coding functions).
Header information	Interview date/type Interview ID Interviewer Transcriptionist Translator	By header here, we are referring to the first few lines of each transcript (rather than a header in the margin at the top of each page). A header with study management, data labeling, and demographic information provides the reader of a transcript with a quick overview of the details surrounding the collection of data contained in the transcript. [Note: You may also wish to consider adding a footer to each page of a transcript, indicating the data label or file name associated with that transcript. Be aware that this footer information will be lost when files are imported into most qualitative data analysis software and is also redundant if you include the data label as the speaker attribution for each response in the transcript.]
Speaker attribution	Interviewer or focus group moderator Respondent(s)	As with other elements of the transcription protocol, simplicity and clarity are paramount when indicating who is speaking in a transcript. For that reason, we typically prefer to use the interviewer's initials and the participant's Source ID to denote the speaker for each question and response. Both are short and highly specific. If you use something like INT/RES, consider how you will quickly identify which study participant provided the response when you are reading through a list of responses

Table 7.2 (Continued)		
Topic	**Examples**	**Importance**
		to a particular question (since all of the different interviewers and respondents will look the same). Also, it may be more difficult to run quality control checks by interviewer if a specific interviewer is not identified for each transcript/ question. Identifying individual speakers is even more important for focus groups so that a reader can identify whether one particular person is driving the conversation or keeps making the same point.
Level of linguistic detail	Verbatim Clean verbatim Paraphrase Select summary	The gold standard for a transcript produced from an interview or focus group is a verbatim record of the conversation, including background noises, every filler word, nonverbal communications (yawns, stretches, hesitations), and so on. This level of detail is important for linguistic analyses, where *how* people say things is as important as what they say. From there, you may specify lesser levels of detail that would still be appropriate. For instance, you may not need to know that a truck honked its horn outside, or that a group of schoolchildren ran past. In a clean verbatim transcription protocol, you may ask the transcriptionist to omit any extraneous filler words, such as "um," "uh," "ah," or the "mhmms" that the interviewer says to keep the respondent going, but which do not add to the content of the data (and can often detract from one's reading of it). An even "looser" transcription protocol using paraphrasing or selected summaries of key points may be acceptable if your research is intended to quickly summarize opinions, generate ideas for a survey, or is otherwise not going to be analyzed in-depth on its own. The idea with these types of transcripts is to focus limited time capturing essential ideas or themes in the exact words of the participants, while allowing a paraphrased summary of the rest.
Tagging media file references	Time stamping	There are several reasons why it can be helpful to include time stamps in an interview transcript. If the transcriptionist is unable to understand or hear a section of audio or video, she can mark the exact time segment that is inaudible so that the interviewer or another team member can review the source data file to try to fill in the missing section. Similarly, if a particular speaker within a focus group audio file is unidentified, another research team member can review relevant portions of the source file later to try to attribute the voice. Or if you identify an excellent quote and want to cut a snippet of the audio or video file to include in a multimedia report, you can use time stamp markers at the top of each page to give you a rough idea where to begin searching for the quote in the source data.

(*ppp*), since these speaker attributions will appear over and over in the transcript and often involve data labels with case-sensitive alphanumeric combinations that can be cumbersome to type. These series of three "placeholder" letters are unlikely to appear in the content of the transcript, so you can then do a "search and replace" at the end of transcription to turn the *iiis* into the interviewer's initials, the *ppps* into the participant's ID number, and add any punctuation offsets required by the transcription protocol. In general, the more detailed your transcription protocol (and the more special characters, indications of tone, or other specifics about the communication style), the longer the transcription process will take. And the more technical the subject matter, the longer the transcription process. If you are a "one man show" and will be transcribing all of the data yourself, you might want to transcribe a few interviews or focus groups before you decide upon your preferred format and style.

Translating

If your source data will be collected in a language other than the one you will conduct your analysis in, then translation of the source files is in order. As with transcription, the process of translation is less straightforward than it sounds and requires careful consideration of how translation will affect the quality and validity of the data and subsequent findings (Birbili, 2000). As we mentioned with regard to in-depth interviews in Chapter 4, one of the more procedural issues to consider is the process by which the translation will be produced. There are two main approaches to translation when an audio or video record of the data collection event is the source material (Figure 7.2).

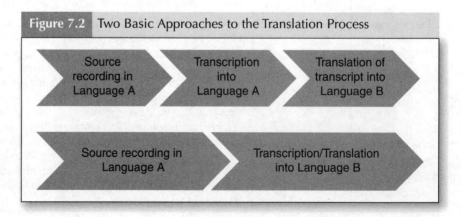

Figure 7.2 Two Basic Approaches to the Translation Process

Source recording in Language A → Transcription into Language A → Translation of transcript into Language B

Source recording in Language A → Transcription/Translation into Language B

The three-step process is generally favored in social and behavioral research, despite the additional step, for a few reasons. First, it is extremely difficult to listen to speech in one language and transcribe it in another; this process requires skills in interpretation (as opposed to translation from text to text) as well as transcription. Second, the three-step process provides a written (usually verbatim) account of the source material in the original language, which can be used as an easy reference to check the subsequent translation. It is much more difficult to have someone verify or check a transcript in Language B when the comparison is an audio file in Language A. For translations of consent forms and interview guides, we typically employ a two-step process of translation that involves bilingual, bicultural translators. Many institutional review boards outline two versions of this process, which you might use for translation of informed consent materials and interview guides:

- *Option A—One forward and one back translation by different bilingual and bicultural translators*

  (a) forward translation from English to non-English by the first translator; and
  (b) back translation by a second translator, who has not seen the original English document; and
  (c) review and approval of both the forward and back translations by the lead researcher and/or IRB.

- *Option B—Two forward translations by different bilingual and bicultural* translators

  (a) forward translation from English to non-English by the first translator; and
  (b) forward translation from English to non-English by the second translator. However, instead of doing the second forward translation from scratch, the second translator will review the forward translation already done by the first translator, compare it with the original English version, and revise it as necessary; and
  (c) discussion between the two translators to reconcile any differences and produce one consensus forward translation. (This discussion must be documented by e-mail or other notes.)

Though not explicitly listed in Option A, the discussion between translators presented in Option B is a helpful, and often necessary, step in the translation process and may include discussion with the researcher as well, to clarify the meaning and intention of specific wording. If you are working in a fairly common language (Spanish, Chinese, Arabic), many professional translation firms offer web-based services so that you do not necessarily have to find two bilingual, bicultural people in your area; instead, you can upload or e-mail your source documents, specify any special instructions (back-translation), and receive the translated version, along with certification (notarized if necessary) of the translators' qualifications and the process followed. If you are working in a less common language or dialect, you might ask your field team to perform and cross-check the translation.

While these processes work well for standard study documents (guides and consent forms), translation of interviews conducted in a local language is a bit of a different story. Assuming the interviews are recorded, you will have a non-English, nonwritten account of the interview as your primary data source. In the studies we have worked on in Africa, we typically have local team members (not necessarily those who conducted the interviews) transcribe the audio files into a text version in the local language and then pass them back to the original interviewer to work on the translation into English. Having the person who conducted the interview perform—or at least review—the transcription enhances the validity of the process, since the interviewer was present for the asking and answering of the question and may more clearly articulate the thoughts or ideas into their English equivalents. As mentioned, in some cases, transcription and translation can occur simultaneously, with the transcriber-translator listening to the non-English audio and mentally translating before typing it into English. Though this is more efficient, you lose the ability to refer quickly to a source document if you have questions about translation or meaning.

One work-around is to have translators include the original language for idioms or other hard-to-translate speech in the English transcript, allowing others who are bilingual to assess the accuracy of the translation. Also, some portion of translated data should be spot checked by another member of the team, as part of the quality assurance process. Given the length, complexity, and volume of in-depth interviews collected, it is not feasible to perform back-translation or double translation of all interview transcripts, but you should have some level of review built in to enhance confidence in the translated data. Whichever method you use, a data tracking system is essential to keep tabs on who is working with the data, how files are labeled, and where the various versions can be found.

If you are not fluent in both languages yourself, you will need to collaborate with an experienced translator and train her on your specific project. As Singal and Jeffery (2008) point out,

> Whoever is doing the translation needs a thorough understanding of both languages and the cultures or sub-cultures within which they are being

used. There is sometimes a trade-off between knowing the local "language" (dialectic, slang, jargon, etc.), on one hand, and understanding the purposes of the research and the academic language (of sociology, or whatever) on the other. Depending on the research context, one person rarely has both sets of skills.

For this reason, we recommend bringing the translator into the research team from the beginning so that she receives all of the same training on the research objectives and data collection tools as her peers who will be collecting the data. If you choose to have data collectors translate their own interview material, be sure to train them on a translation protocol as you would someone new to the project. For instance, you may be interested in a more nuanced than literal translation, to capture the essence of the respondent's thoughts rather than the specific words. Or you may wish to ask the translator to keep key phrases or sentences in the original language, with a translation and explanation of any important concepts in brackets alongside.

For example, in interviews with community (volunteer) health workers in Uganda, a translated transcript read, "People now know me as a *musawo* [the term for doctor, which implies respect] who provides family planning methods." Here, the use of the Luganda term *musawo* and the affiliated denotation and connotation provide the necessary context to interpret the speaker's remark; that local community members refer to the volunteer health worker as *musawo* indicates they respect her knowledge as well as services. Local idioms or metaphors, in particular, are often kept in the original language and roughly translated and explained so that a non-native speaker of the language can understand the intended use of the term. Table 7.3 shows excerpts of metaphors from the Oluluyia language of western Kenya describing HIV/AIDS as something that happens by accident (Kobia, 2008).

In the examples in Table 7.3, the direct translations of the metaphors often require some explanation. "He has hit the wall," for instance, is explained to be in reference to a bird that hit the wall of a house while flying and died; in other words, like an accident, nobody can predict when HIV/AIDS will hit him or her (Kobia, 2008, pp. 52–53). Requesting these types of explanations alongside the original language will provide needed guidance to the translator and context to the reader. You may also specify that responses not be cleaned in any way, to make the respondent sound better, or to use official terminology where the respondent used slang (like metaphors, slang can be difficult to translate).

The line between translation and interpretation is often a blurry one, so the more guidance you can provide, the better. Having field teams think about translation issues as they are practicing with the data collection guide and conducting

Table 7.3	Metaphors About HIV/AIDS in the Oluluyia Language	
Dialect	**Metaphor (Oluluyia)**	**English**
Olunyala	Kauna muonjoka	Pierced by a thorn
Olunyala	Omuya kwa futukhile	Slow puncture
Olunyala	Kanywa amachi amatumbufu	Has drank dirty water
Luwanga	Yasena khubembe indoro	He stepped on a piercing grass
Luwanga	Yanyola epanja ya kalaha	Slow puncture
Luwanga	Yasena ewa kalulire	He stepped where the brew was strongest
Luwanga	Yasena khwiva	Stepped on a thorn
Lwisukha	Yali nachenda butukhu ni yituya khushisishi	As he was traveling at night he was hit by a stump
Lwisukha	Waituya mwisisi	He has hit the wall

mock interviews can help to raise some of the specific types of translation challenges that you might face in the actual data, and discussing them as a group can serve both to generate possible solutions and reach consensus on the best approach.

KEEPING A RECORD OF EVENTS

Maintaining a dynamic document of what has (and hasn't) happened so far in your project also facilitates data management. Two tools that are helpful in this regard are the participant screening log and the data tracking log. The screening log is a recruitment tool that serves as a centralized place for documenting each recruitment encounter—whether phone, mail, e-mail, or in person—and its outcome. It is a spreadsheet created to include all of the necessary screening information for your study (eligibility criteria that are checked in advance), potential participant contact information, record of whether contact was successfully made, and the final outcome (eligible/ineligible, scheduled/not scheduled). This document can help identify problems in recruitment such as poor follow-up, a troublesome eligibility criterion, or sample homogeneity. You can also use it to calculate your "hit rate," or the ratio of potential participants contacted to those who eventually screen eligible and enroll, which can help you plan your timeline, budget, and resource allocation related to recruiting your intended sample of participants. Screening logs are particularly important for organizing focus groups, since you need not only eligible participants but also need them to be grouped according to specific characteristics and available at the same time. Appendix 7.2 provides a few sample recruitment screening logs.

Where the screening log contains details about potential participants, the data tracking log documents the movement of enrolled participants' data through the research process. Once a person agrees to participate in an interview or focus group, his relevant information can be moved to the data tracking log and associated with a unique study identifier or Source ID (see Chapter 8 about linking participant names and study IDs). Starting with the scheduled interview or focus group date, the data tracking log includes things such as the Source ID and interviewer assigned, whether the interview has been completed, whether the interview audio or video file has been sent for transcription or translation, the date and author of transcription and translations, whether the transcript has been coded and by whom, and the location of all related study documents and materials. We have provided a sample data tracking log in Appendix 7.3.

If you are working alone or in a small team, the data tracking log is tremendously useful for helping you maintain a record of where your data are in the collection, conversion, and analysis processes. If you are working in a larger team or multisite group, a data log is essential for keeping track of the various data, people, and tasks associated with a project. You can consider this data log as a map or flow chart for the processing of each new piece of data; drawing a flow chart might serve both as a visual depiction of the expected movement of data through the project and as the basis for identifying what columns to create in your data log. The flow chart in Figure 7.3 corresponds with the data tracking log in Appendix 7.3.

MONITORING DATA QUALITY AND STUDY PROGRESS

Implicit in the transcription protocol and data tracking discussions above is the need to perform quality control and assurance checks as part of systematic data management activities. These quality checks can take many forms. Early in the data collection phase, you may want to review incoming transcripts for several things:

Figure 7.3 Flow Diagram of Data "Processing" Plan for Sample Project

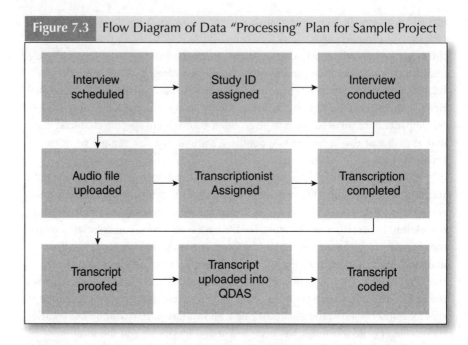

Are the transcripts prepared according to the transcription protocol? Does the transcribed text match the audio or video recording of the data collection event to the extent required? If translated, is the appropriate level of meaning captured? How are interviewers or moderators doing in their job of asking nonleading questions and probing to elicit information that will address the research objectives? Are all questions being asked of all participants, as intended? Are there any "dud" questions that just don't seem to be working? This kind of data management, again, is a repetitive, nonlinear process, in that these kinds of data reviews will need to be conducted intensively at the beginning of the project and at specified intervals once an acceptable level of quality has been reached on each of the issues indicated. Similarly, you may want to review the participant screening log and data tracking log at the beginning or end of each week, to help identify progress made, areas for follow up, or anticipated delays.

A large portion of data review will involve the assessment and verification of transcribed versions of original source material. Depending on the number of data collection events you have planned, who is doing the transcription-translation, and the size of your research team (if you have one), you may want to check every transcript against the audio, review only a certain number each week, or randomly sample portions of transcripts at given intervals. Transcript review also includes proofreading the typed material for spelling mistakes or sensitive or identifying information that should be omitted or replaced prior to working with a final transcript. While it is possible to do some limited editing in qualitative data analysis software (QDAS), the capabilities are not as robust as those in standard word or media processing software. Furthermore, you should aim to import the "final" version of transcripts or other files into QDAS to avoid version discrepancies between QDAS and archival files or among research team members.

ORGANIZING AND STORING DATA

A cardboard box, like the one used to collect interview audio recordings in the example at the beginning of this chapter, is clearly a suboptimal way to store and organize data. But what is optimal? Consider that the level and type of organization of your data can directly affect the thoroughness, accuracy, and efficiency of your analysis (Mason, 2002). And the security of your data is essential both for you as a researcher (no one wants to "lose" data or the time and effort that went into collecting it) and for the confidentiality of your participants. At a minimum, then, you should have a secure and dedicated space—both physical and electronic—to store the materials for each project you work on. Below, we list some additional tips and considerations for data organization and storage.

- *Use folders to your advantage*—Electronic data storage in a folder-based system can greatly enhance the organization of your data. Think about diagramming a file folder system before you have any data files so that you can identify the advantages and disadvantages of grouping particular data or documentation together. See Figure 7.4 for some examples of different emphases in file organization.

  If you are working with paper-based files alongside or in place of electronic files, sturdy, easy-close envelopes are a handy way to group all of the documents and files related to a particular source together in one place. In this case, it often makes the most sense to label the envelope according to the Source ID related to the documents within and to file the envelopes sequentially in a locked filing cabinet or office. When using envelopes or other physical file folders, you have the added option of color coding the materials (by site, data collection method, or stakeholder group, for example) to assist in file retrieval.

- *Maintain consistent Source IDs to link files together*—The assignation of consistent Source IDs, in addition to consistent file names, facilitates the linkage of two or more pieces of data or documentation from the same source. For example, if you have a spreadsheet with demographic information or survey responses from the same people who participated in interviews or focus groups, the Source IDs for each person will be identical across all files in order to accurately link multiple data points from the same source.

- *Determine the most secure location for files and back-ups*—Do you have access to a secure server? Will you need "offline" access to your source materials? How many people will need to access the source or back-up files? If you are working in hard copies, where will you store copies of the data? The answers to all of these questions will point you toward potential file storage options. At the minimum, your data should exist somewhere other than on a single laptop or desktop computer. Laptops are insecure in terms of their portability (easily stolen, and the material on them easily retrieved if the hard drive is not encrypted), and both have the potential to crash and wipe out any data saved on them. Additionally, "It is not uncommon for servers to crash, electronic files to become corrupted, or documents ruined; hence, it is recommended that multiple archival mediums be used to store records" (McLellan-Lemal, 2008a, p. 179). Redundancy is key. The standard for hard copies of data and study files is that they are stored in a locked cabinet in a locked office and that the keys to both are accessible to only one or two people. Back-up copies should be stored in a different physical location, in case of fire, theft, water damage, and so on.
- *Define procedures for data back-ups*—From the outset of data collection, you should have a clear idea of how and how often you will back up your data. As each interview recording or video comes in, will you immediately make a copy and place it somewhere other than the main study file location? Will you do the same for the transcription? How often will you do a study-level back up, copying everything in your study folder to the secondary or back-up location? Planning for data back up from the outset is a simple way to avoid losing data.

Note that the three sets of files in Figure 7.4 are all are based on the same project, which includes 30 in-depth interviews (with two groups of participants) and 10 focus groups at each of three sites. The number of combinations and permutations of folders is virtually endless; what we look for in a data organization system is a structure that is clear and which facilitates data management and analysis. The first example is structured by type of file and provides a specific location for different versions of data files as they move from source audio or video to text transcript, to final, proofed transcript ready for upload into qualitative analysis software. The second example focuses more explicitly on the fact that there are three data collection sites and two data collection methods; it provides specific folders for FG and IDI files (type and version unspecified) from each site. This organization suggests central management of the study, since all project management folders are shared rather than site-specific. The third example stresses the centrality of the data; all FG and IDI data files are collected at a central level, regardless of study site, while study management and ethics

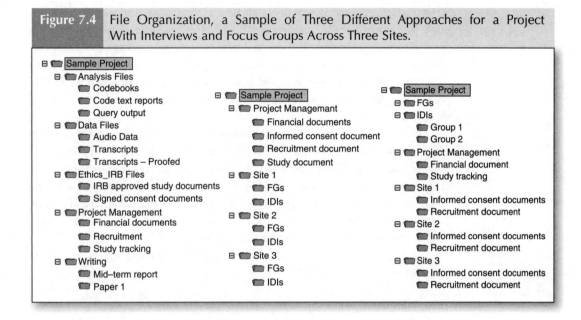

Figure 7.4   File Organization, a Sample of Three Different Approaches for a Project With Interviews and Focus Groups Across Three Sites.

documentation are designated as site-specific. There is no right or wrong configuration, but note that stratified or split hierarchies will require more clicks to access all of a particular type of document (for example, to upload all of the transcripts from the site-specific folders in Example 2 into QDAS would require opening and selecting from six different folders), while centralized or lumped hierarchies will require more careful searching for particular files or sets of files. QDAS programs allow (and to an extent require) similar decisions about data organization, though they have the added flexibility of allowing for sort, filter, and grouping options beyond the particular folder where a file is stored.

ARCHIVING

As you work through your project, you can begin to archive or even dispose of some data, particularly if the study is multiyear or multiphased. By archiving, we are referring to the process of creating a final version of the data, files, folders, QDAS projects, and/or associated study materials that can be stored securely for a predetermined amount of time after the conclusion of the study. The first step in the process is to decide which materials need to be archived. It's possible that you do not need to keep any of the original audio or video files from IDIs or focus groups once the associated transcript has been checked against the original for accuracy. These audio and video files might be destroyed at the completion of the transcript verification process or at the point of archiving. Similarly, you may not need the original demographics form that each participant filled out if you have completed and verified an aggregate participant demographics spreadsheet that includes the information for all participants. The aggregated file would be archived; the original hard copy forms could be shredded.

Once you have determined which materials will be archived, assess whether there are any institutional requirements for the location, organization, or duration of archived materials. All of these are likely to vary according to the study situation and/ or institution, but if materials are going to be stored for several years (many IRBs require at least 5 years after completion of the study), consider a location and organization that will be both secure and accessible if any or all of the study team members leave their current position during the time the data are in the archive.

The following considerations for developing data archiving plans are adapted from McLellan-Lemel (2008b):

1. How many people will require access to the data once archived?
2. How much storage space will be required (physical or electronic)? What modifications will need to be made to the storage area to ensure that it can accommodate the data and that the data are secured (e.g., locked cabinets, computer firewalls)?
3. When will the data be disposed? Can some parts be disposed sooner than others? What is essential to retain? Are there institutional requirements that define what must be archived?
4. In storing electronic data long term, what software considerations must be made to ensure that changes in technology do not negatively impact data access and usability?

CREATING AN "AUDIT TRAIL"

Participant screening and data tracking logs provide records of who has done what with which data during recruitment, data collection, data conversion, and the initial stages of analysis. To provide a parallel record of activities undertaken during data analysis, we suggest developing an *audit trail*—that is, a running record of tasks assigned and performed related to codebook development, coding, summary text reports, queries run, and so on. Maintaining audit trails is an oft cited example of good qualitative research practice (e.g., Cesario, Morin, & Santa-Donato, 2002; Guest & MacQueen, 2008; Hills, 2000; Miles & Huberman, 1994; Sharts-Hopko, 2002).

Qualitative data analysis software programs provide some functions to assist with this type of analysis trail, recording all project events carried out during a given session with date stamps and user logs. However, no automatic log can document what you or another analyst was thinking when particular changes were made, organizational tasks were performed, or codes added, revised, or deleted. We therefore recommend that you create a coding and analysis log, in either a text document or within QDAS, where you can keep a running annotated log of codebook development and revision activities, thoughts about organizing or reorganizing data and other materials, a list of code summary reports and coded text queries that have been run (and the location of the output), and the dates and results of any intercoder agreement exercises performed during coding and analysis. Appendix 7.4 provides an example codebook development log, and Appendix 7.5 provides a sample data analysis log. These logs serve not only as an important reminder about decisions made during the analysis process, but also they serve as documentation that can be used to corroborate or replicate an analysis if your findings or interpretations are ever questioned.

WORKING INTERNATIONALLY

Throughout this chapter, we have referred to the importance of well-planned, -implemented, and -communicated data analysis processes whether research is conducted by a "lone" researcher, in teams, or across multiple sites. If some or all of the data collection sites happen to be distributed around the globe, the challenges of coordinating data management—and the benefits of following a coordinated plan—are multiplied. Below, we review many of the data management issues discussed in this chapter and provide additional information and tips for addressing these issues in an international context. We recognize that translation is often required in international research, but since the process is discussed earlier, it is not addressed below.

- *Identifying sources and labeling data*—The greater the diversity of your data collection events (in terms of location, data collectors, language[s] spoken, and so on), the greater the need for a systematic and coordinated source and data labeling convention. If you are working with different data collectors in different countries, all of whom are "in the field" simultaneously, you'll want to assign each team a set of Source IDs during training for the study and explain the rationale and process behind assigning new Source IDs and relating those to data labels and file names. Consider whether file names should be typed in the source language or in English. For instance, if interviews in West Africa are conducted in French, can the field team maintain their electronic files using French names for files and folders? When these items are shared with you, do you want them in English? Consider how linguistic differences might affect your Source ID or file naming conventions: If you have a site in Cote d'Ivoire, should that site be abbreviated as CI—or IC for Ivory Coast? While these issues seem minor, inconsistencies among source and file names can cause big headaches and confusion when it comes time to link data points or merge datasets.

- *Transcription*—If you are working in resource-poor settings, the lack of a typewriter or computer can greatly impede the efficiency of transcription efforts. Even where computers are available, access to transcription machines (foot pedals or software)—not to mention trained typists—can be a limiting factor. Transcription in the field can therefore take roughly 8 to 12 hours per hour of recorded data, particularly if one person handwrites the transcript while listening to the audio (and stopping and starting the recording manually) and another then types the handwritten transcript. Building adequate time—and staff and equipment if possible—into your study budget will help you avoid compromising the quality of the transcripts with rushed work or the stress of impossible deadlines. Where equipment is available, level of experience and training in transcription is likely variable (as it is in the United States), so training on the specific transcription protocol for your project can help to get everyone started on the same page. If electronic data files are to be passed along to a central location for transcription, be sure to investigate the security of electronic data transmission options.

- *Keeping a record of events*—If your work includes international sites, it is unlikely that you will keep a day-to-day or file-by-file log of what is happening at those sites. However, you can share your participant screening and data tracking logs with the site and assign a data manager who will be responsible for making sure that all recruitment and data activities are logged and that the log is shared with you on a routine basis (weekly, biweekly, monthly). Include training for the data manager on these aspects of study documentation.

- *Monitoring data quality and study progress*—As with domestic research, data quality monitoring should be one of your top priorities during the first month of data collection. Are participant observation field notes in the correct format and at an appropriate level of detail? Are transcription and translation protocols being followed? Are the interview or focus group questions eliciting the types of responses that will address the research objectives? Examining and addressing these questions from the outset allows for corrections and revisions early in the process to streamline the subsequent data collection and conversion tasks.

- *Data organization and storage*—The primary concern with data storage when working internationally is the security of study related files—as they are stored physically and electronically in the local setting and as they are transmitted or sent to a central or coordinating site. In some cases, we have budgeted for study-specific file cabinets for our field sites (along with the envelopes to go in them), to ensure that study files would have a dedicated and secure space in the field office. In others, we may arrange for access to a shared secure server via cloud computing or other online services so that data can be uploaded to the central site and backed up at the same time. If you are using a shared electronic storage space, agree upon a file folder system and location in advance.

SUMMING UP

Data management includes, "all the processes necessary for systematically and consistently collecting, tracking, preparing, processing, organizing, storing, securing, retrieving, verifying, and sharing qualitative data so that it can be used to (a) inform subsequent data collection and (b) perform data analysis" (McLellan-Lemal, 2008a, p. 168). As such, there is no single data management "step" to be performed on qualitative data; it is an ongoing, dynamic series of activities that is interwoven with recruitment, data collection, coding, and analysis. The appendices to this chapter provide a range of data management tools and templates that will help you plan your data management strategies and procedures so that you can quickly and easily locate, identify, link, and/or verify the various elements of your qualitative research project. Below is a summary list of qualitative data management activities and practices that can be used as a checklist of sorts, to ensure you have at least considered many of the data organizational elements associated with qualitative research.

- Establish a system for assigning source and data labels—Determine what information you will include in Source IDs, data labels, and electronic file names.
- Develop a transcription protocol—Determine what should be included in each transcript and how it should be formatted.
- Create guidelines for data translation—Decide on a translation style (literal or figurative) and how idioms and other hard-to-translate phrases will be handled.
- Draft a recruitment screening log—Create a spreadsheet structured according to your eligibility criteria as well as your sampling targets where you can assign Source IDs for eligible, enrolled participants.
- Develop a data tracking log—Create a spreadsheet to keep track of primary data—as they relate to your sources, and as they are processed, or converted.
- Create a system for monitoring the quality of your data—Develop a data monitoring plan, including which data items you will monitor, how you will check quality or verify accuracy, and how often these quality checks will occur.

- Establish a data storage and organization plan—Determine which data will be stored where and how they will be organized.
- Determine your data archiving policies—Decide when and where you will archive your data.
- Create a data analysis log—Prepare a spreadsheet or other system for tracking analysis progress, decisions, and changes.

REFERENCES

Birbili, M. (2000). Translating from one language to another. *Social Research Update, 31.* University of Surrey, UK. Retrieved from http://sru.soc.surrey.ac.uk/SRU31.htm

Cesario, S., Morin, K., & Santa-Donato, A. (2002). Evaluating the level of evidence of qualitative research. *Journal of Obstetric, Gynecologic and Neonatal Nursing, 31*(6), 531–537.

Guest, G., & MacQueen, K. M. (Eds.). (2008). *Handbook for team-based qualitative research.* Lanham, MD: Altamira.

Hills, M. (2000). Human science research in public health: The contribution and assessment of a qualitative approach. *Canadian Journal of Public Health, 91*(6), 4–7.

Huberman, A. M., & Miles, M. B. (1994). Data management and analysis methods. In N. K. Denzin & Y. S. Lincoln (Eds.), *Handbook of qualitative research* (2nd ed., pp. 428–444). Thousand Oaks, CA: Sage.

Kobia, J. M. (2008). Metaphors on HIV/AIDS discourse among Oluluyia speakers of western Kenya. *Critical Approaches to Discourse Analysis Across Disciplines, 2*(2), 48–66.

Lin, L. (2009). Data management and security in qualitative research. *Dimensions of Critical Care Nursing, 28,* 132–137.

MacQueen, K. M., & Milstein, B. (1999a). Systems approach to qualitative data management. *Field Methods, 11*(1), 27–39.

Mason, J. (2002). *Qualitative researching.* Thousand Oaks, CA: Sage.

McLellan-Lemal, E. (2008a). Qualitative data management. In G. Guest & K. M. MacQueen (Eds.). *Handbook for team-based qualitative research* (pp. 165–188). Lanham, MD: Altamira.

McLellan-Lemal, E. (2008b). Transcribing data for team-based research. In G. Guest & K. M. MacQueen (Eds.), *Handbook for team-based qualitative research* (pp. 101–118). Lanham, MD: Altamira.

Miles, M. B., & Huberman, A. M. (1994). *Qualitative data analysis: An expanded sourcebook* (2nd ed.). Thousand Oaks, CA: Sage.

Ray, L. (1997). Qualitative data management using Folio VIEWS. *Qualitative Health Research, 7,* 301–308.

Ritchie, J., Spencer, L., & W. O'Connor, W. (2003). In J. Ritchie & J. Lewis (Eds.), *Qualitative research practice: A guide for social science students and researchers* (pp. 219–262). Thousand Oaks, CA: Sage.

Ross, B. (1994). Use of a database for managing qualitative research data. *Computers in Nursing, 12*, 154–159.

Russell, C., & Gregory, D. (1993). Issues for consideration when choosing a qualitative data management system. *Journal of Advanced Nursing, 18*, 1806–1816.

Ryan, G., & Bernard, H. R. (2000). Data management and analysis methods. In N. Denzin & Y. Lincoln (Eds.), *Handbook for qualitative research* (2nd ed., pp. 769–802). Thousand Oaks, CA: Sage.

Schwandt, T. A. (1997). *Dictionary of qualitative inquiry* (2nd ed.). Thousand Oaks, CA: Sage.

Sharts-Hopko, N. C. (2002). Assessing rigor in qualitative research. *Journal of the Association of Nurses in AIDS Care, 13*, 84–86.

Singal, N., & Jeffery, R. (2008). *Qualitative research skills workshop: A facilitator's reference manual.* Cambridge, UK: Research Consortium on Educational Outcomes and Poverty (RECOUP). Retrieved from http://manual.recoup.educ.cam.ac.uk/

ADDITIONAL READING

Guest, G., MacQueen, K., & Namey, E. (2012). Choosing qualitative data analysis software. In *Applied thematic analysis* (chap. 9, pp. 217–240). Thousand Oaks, CA: Sage.

MacQueen, K. M., & Milstein, B. (1999a). Systems approach to qualitative data management. *Field Methods, 11*(1), 27–39.

McLellan-Lemal, E. (2008a). Qualitative data management. In G. Guest & K. M. MacQueen (Eds.). *Handbook for team-based qualitative research* (pp. 165–188). Lanham, MD: Altamira Press.

McLellan-Lemal, E. (2008b). Transcribing data for team-based research. In G. Guest & K. M. MacQueen (Eds.), *Handbook for team-based qualitative research* (pp. 101–118). Lanham, MD: Altamira.

McLellan, E., MacQueen, K., & Neidig, J. (2003). Beyond the qualitative interview: Data preparation and transcription. *Field Methods, 15*, 63–84.

Powers, W. (2005). *Transcription techniques for the spoken word.* Lanham, MD: AltaMira Press.

QSR International Pty Ltd. (2011). NVivo qualitative data analysis software, Version 9. Cambridge, MA: Author.

EXERCISES

1. Read the following study descriptions and come up with at least two different Source ID and file naming conventions for each to represent the data that will be generated.

    (a) In this study, we will interview shoppers at two different grocery stores on three consecutive days (Thursday, Friday, Saturday for both). We will aim to interview 10 people each day. We plan to compare the data based on the day of the interview as well as the time of day (morning, afternoon, evening).

(b) In this study, we will conduct participant observation during after-school hours at three high schools. We will then conduct 10 interviews and four focus groups at each of the high schools with students and others who use the school grounds after hours.

2. Create a flow diagram and file organization plan for each of the studies described in Exercise 1.

3. Review the three transcript excerpts in the table below. List the advantages and disadvantages you recognize in each, in terms of the information they contain, format, and style.

Exercise 3 Sample Data

Study A
1.19.11

Interviewer:	Today is January 19th. I am speaking with A01. Is it okay if I record you?
Participant:	Yes, ma'am.
Interviewer:	And do you agree to participate in this study?
Participant:	Yes, ma'am.
Interviewer:	Thank you. So as you know, we're looking to learn about . . .

Study B
Participant ID: Vax00
Interviewee Summary: 25, white, grad degree, upper SES
Vaccine trial: Yes
Date of Interview: 2/10/10
Interviewer ID: WX
Transcriptionist: YZ

–WX–
Okay so today is February 10th. Is it okay if I record you?

–VAX00–
Yes.

-1WX-

And do you agree to participate in this study?

-VAX00-

Yes.

-WX-

Okay so today is February 10th. Is it okay if I record you?

-VAX00-

Yes.

-WX-

And do you agree to participate in this study?

-VAX00-

Yes.

-WX-

All right, thank you. So we're interviewing you today because . . .

Study C
Educational Assessment Focus Groups
Focus Group 1
3.9.11
Moderator: MM

MM: So today is March 9th. Could you let me know verbally whether you all
are willing to participate in this group?

All: [Sure/Yeah/Yes.]

MM: Great, thank you. Okay, so to start, I'd like to know generally what you
think of the educational sessions you've received so far? Particularly,
what are the things you like or you think are done well?

RES4:   Are you talking specifically about the Friday morning sessions?

MM: Yes, sorry.

RES3:   So far, I have really liked the way that . . .

APPENDIX 7.1 **Sample Transcription Protocol**

Data Preparation and Transcription Protocol

Adapted from McLellan et al. (2003), *Field Methods, 15*, 74–81.

Source Labeling

Participant IDs begin with the alpha character that designates the data collection site, followed by the individual's two-digit identification number (e.g., D07 = Site D interviewee number seven). Interviewer IDs will consist of the interviewer's first and last initials. (Emily Namey = EN)

Site designators for individual interviews:

D = Site D

C = Site C

S = Site S

Text Formatting

General Instructions

Please use the following formatting:

1. Arial 10-point font

2. One-inch top, bottom, right, and left margins

3. All text at the left-hand margin (no indents)

4. Entire document left justified

5. Page numbers inserted, bottom right of page

Labeling for Individual Interview Transcripts

Individual interview transcripts include the following labeling information left justified at the top of the document:

Participant ID:

Participant demographics: (age, gender, race, education level)

Interview Category/Subgroup:

Site/Location:

Date of Interview:

Interviewer ID:

Transcriber ID:

Insert a single blank line between the file labeling information and the actual interview transcription. Use a double hyphen (--) before and after each speaker identification label. Use a single hard return immediately after the ID. The participant's/interviewer's response/question should begin on the next line. Leave one blank line between each speaker's comments.

Example:

Participant ID: D00

Participant demographics: 37, M, white/NH, college degree

Interview Category/Subgroup: Epilepsy study/Not Recontacted – opted-in

Site/Location: Site D/participant's home

Date of Interview: 2.25.10

Interviewer ID: Emily Namey

Transcriber ID: Emily Namey

—EN—
OK, before we begin the interview itself, I'd like to confirm that you agree to participate in this interview.

—D00—
Yes, I do.

—EN—
Do you have questions before we proceed?

—D00—
No.

End of Interview

Indicate when the interview session has reached completion by typing END OF INTERVIEW in uppercase letters on the last line of the transcript along with information regarding the total length of the audio recording. A double space should precede this information.

Example:

—EN—
Is there anything else that you would like to add?

—D00—
Nope, I think that about covers it.

—EN—
Well, thanks for taking the time to talk with me today. I really appreciate it.

END OF INTERVIEW (53:13 minutes)

Content

Audio recordings should be transcribed verbatim (i.e., recorded word for word, exactly as said) to the extent that narrative flow is not lost or interrupted, including any wordless sounds (e.g., laughter, sighs, snaps fingers, pauses).

- Nonverbal sounds shall be typed in parentheses. Example: (short sharp laugh), (small sigh), (raps table for emphasis).
- If interviewers or interviewees mispronounce words, these words will be transcribed as the individual said them. The transcript shouldn't be "cleaned up" by removing foul language, slang, grammatical errors, or misuse of words or concepts. If an incorrect or unexpected pronunciation results in difficulties with comprehension of the text, the correct word shall be typed in square brackets. Example: I thought that was pretty pacific [specific], but they disagreed.
- The spelling of key words, blended or compound words, common phrases, and identifiers shall be standardized across all individual transcripts. Enunciated reductions (e.g., betcha, 'cause, 'em, gimme, gotta, hafta, kinda, lotta, oughta, sorta, wanna, coulda, could've, couldn't, couldn've, couldna, woulda, would've, wouldn't, wouldn've, wouldna, shoulda, should've, shouldn't, shouldn've, shouldna) plus standard contractions of is, am, are, had, have, and not will be used.
- Filler words such as hm, huh, mm, mhmm, uh huh, um, mkay, yeah, yuhuh, nah, huh, ugh, whoa, uh oh, ah, and ahah will be transcribed whenever said *by the participant*. If said as acknowledgement

by the interviewer, these words can be included in the narrative text of the participant within brackets, or omitted if overlapping with speech. Example: "I thought that I would receive my research results [mhmm], but no one ever told me anything about it."

- Word or phrase repetitions should be transcribed. If a word is cut off or truncated, a hyphen should be inserted at the end of the last letter or audible sound. Example: "I wen- I went to the clinic even though I didn't wanna."
- The transcriber should identify portions of the audiotape that are inaudible or difficult to decipher. If a relatively small segment of the audio (a word or short sentence) is partially unintelligible, the transcriber shall type the phrase "inaudible segment." This information should appear in square brackets. Example: "I received a letter in the mail saying there was a new study, but I didn't [inaudible segment]."
- If a lengthy segment of the tape is inaudible, unintelligible, or is "dead air" where no one is speaking, the transcriber should record this information in square brackets. In addition, the transcriber should provide a time estimate for information that could not be transcribed. Example: [Inaudible: 2 minutes of interview missing].

- *Overlapping Speech*

If individuals are speaking at the same time (i.e., overlapping speech) and it is not possible to distinguish what each person is saying, the transcriber should place three dots (...) after the last clear word and place the phrase "cross talk" in square brackets after the last identifiable speaker's text, picking up with the next audible speaker (again using three dots if this thought is midstream). If individuals are speaking at the same time but both can be distinguished, follow the sequence of conversation as closely as possible in the transcript and use three dots (...) to indicate that there is overlap.

Example 1:	Example 2:
—EN—	—EN—
So you were saying that . . .	So you were saying that the researcher called you back . . .
[cross talk]	
—D00—	—D00—
. . . after I had already agreed.	. . . Right, and I didn't understand because it was after I had already agreed.

- *Pauses*

If an individual pauses briefly between statements or trails off at the end of a statement, use three dots (...) to indicate the pause. A brief pause is defined as a two to five second break in speech. If a substantial speech delay occurs (more than five seconds), use "long pause" in parentheses.

Examples:

—D00—

Well . . . I think that it's okay. But . . .

—D00—

 (Long pause) That's a tough one. I really don't know.

- *Questionable Text*

If the transcriber is unsure of what a speaker has said, this statement should be placed inside brackets with a question mark on either side of the word.

Example:

—D00—

I went over to the [?neuro clinic?] to meet with the study team to talk about joining the study.

- *Sensitive Information*

If an individual uses his or her own name during the discussion, the transcriber should replace this information with the brief interviewee identification label.

Example:

—D00—

My family always reminds me, 'D00, think about things before you open your mouth.'

If an individual provides others' names, locations, organizations, and so on, the transcriber should enter an equal sign immediately before and after the named information. The study team will use this labeling information to easily identify sensitive information that may require substitution.

Example:

—D00—

I went to the clinic on =Main Street= and saw =Dr. Doolittle=.

Reviewing For Accuracy

The transcriber/proofreader shall check (proofread) all transcriptions against the audio recording and revise the transcript file accordingly. All transcripts shall be audited for accuracy by the interviewer who conducted the interview or by the study data manager.

Saving Transcripts

The transcriber should save each transcript as an individual Word document with a .doc or .docx extension. Individual interview transcript files should be assigned the study name followed by the brief participant ID (e.g., StudyA D00 = Study A, Site D participant number one).

Example 1. Recruiting interview participants from a clinical trial; must not be pregnant and have experienced side effects to be eligible

Last name	First initial	Contact date	Contact info	Preferred contact	MRN	Gender	Race	Ethnicity Age group	Age group	Pregnant?	Side effect?	Eligible?	Interview scheduled	Notes
Jones	J	7.17.11	e-mail home# cell#	e-mail	123456	F	Black	non-Hispanic	26-30	N	Y	Y	7.22.11	
Martin	M	7.17.11	e-mail# cell#	cell	654321	F	White	non-Hispanic	56-60	N	N	N	N/A	

Example 2. Recruiting interviewees who experienced poor customer service; must have had specific incident in the last 30 days and live in Area A, B, or C to be eligible

Last name	First initial	Contact date	Contact info	Preferred contact	Gender	Race	Age group	Date of poor customer service?	Area of residence?	Eligible?	Interview scheduled	Notes
Kent	Clark	2.21.11	home# cell#	home#	M	Asian	21-25	2.14.11	B	Y	2.24.11	Sounds very upset about what happened. Notify interviewer so can prepare
Lane	Lois	2.24.11	e-mail home# cell3	cell	F	White	41-45	1.27.11	D	N	N/A	

(Continued)

APPENDIX 7.2 (Continued)

Example 3. Recruiting focus group participants who attended specific program; must be available on one of the FG dates to be eligible

Last name	First name	Contact date	Contact info	Preferred contact	Gender	Age group	Attended program?	Available 10.10.11?	Available 10.17.11?	Eligible?	Notes
Well	S	6.5.11	e-mail home# cell#	e-mail	F	31-35	Y	Y	Y	Y	
Rex	T	6.8.11	e-mail cell#	e-mail	m	26-30	y	N	Y	Y	Might be available for 10.10 group; call to confirm if needed

Interviews

Scheduled interview date	Study ID - assigned	Interviewer assigned	Date interview completed	Date Audio uploaded	Transcriber assigned	Date audio file sent for transcription	Date transcript received	Proofer assigned	Date transcript proofed	Date transcript uploaded into date	Coder assigned	Date coding completed	Associated documents	Date processed
4/2/2011	SSIDI01	AB	4/2/2011	4/2/2011	CD	4/2/2011	4/2/2011	EF	4/11/2011	4/11/2011	GH	4/13/2011	signed consent IDI notes Demog form	4/2/11 4/11/11 4/2/11
4/5/2011	SSIDI02	AB	4/6/2011	4/6/2011	CD	4/6/2011	4/13/2011	EF	4/13/2011	4/13/2011	GH	4/14/2011	signed consent Demog form	4/6/11 4/6/11
4/11/2011	SSIDI03	ST	4/11/2011	4/11/2011	X	X	X	X	X	X	X	X	signed consent IDI notes demog form	4/11/11 X 4/11/2011

Focus group

Focus group date	FG ID assigned	Moderator	Note taker	Date Audio uploaded	Transcriber assigned	Date audio file sent for transcription	Date transcript received	Proofer assigned	Date transcript proofed	Date transcript uploaded into QDAS	Coder assigned	Date coding completed	Associated documents	Date processed
3/9/2011	SSFG01	MD	NT	3/9/2011	TR	3/9/2011	3/9/2011	NT	4/1/2011	4/1/2011	MD	4/4/2011	signed consents FG notes Describing forms Demog forms	3/9/11 4/1/11 4/1/11 3/22/11
3/31/2011	SSFG02	NT	MD	3/31/2011	TR	3/31/2011	4/8/2011	MD	4/9/2011	4/9/2011	NT	X	signed consents FG notes Debriefing form Demog forms	3/31/11 4/9/11 4/9/11 3/31/11

APPENDIX 7.4 Codebook development log

Code name	Original definition	Revision1	Revision2
Trust necessary	*Full definition:* Discussion of the necessity of trust before participant will discuss sexual matters with another woman; if there is no trust, will not talk about it *When to use:* Have to know somebody's "character" before talking personally; can't trust just anybody and often don't know most of the women well (R1) (07.12.07)	*Full definition:* Discussion of the necessity of trust before participant will discuss sexual matters with another woman; if there is no trust, will not talk about it *When to use:* Have to know somebody's "character" before talking personally; can't trust just anybody and often don't know most of the women well; includes statements on confidences coming back to haunt you (R2) (07.25.7)	*Full definition:* Discussion of the necessity of trust before discussing sexual matters with another woman; if there is no trust, will not talk about it *When to use:* Have to know somebody's "character" before talking personally; can't trust just anybody and often don't know most of the women well. Includes statements on confidences coming back to haunt you; includes setting the right atmosphere (sharing own personal information, creating a safe space etc.) before asking personal questions (R6) (08.04.07)
Talk with sex worker (SW) friends	*Full definition:* Talk between the participant and a close friend who is a SW *When to use:* Often occurs as: can only share very personal matters with one to two close friends (concept of space, can go to their rooms but nobody else's) (R1) (07.12.07)	*Full definition:* Talk between the participant and a close friend who is a SW *When to use:* If using the word *friends* in this discussion, use this code; often occurs as: can only share very personal matters with one to two close friends (concept of space, can go to their rooms but nobody else's) (R1) (07.13.07)	*Full Definition:* Talk between the participant and a close friend who is a SW *When to Use:* If using the word *friends* in this discussion, use this code; often occurs as: can only share very personal matters with one to two close friends (concept of space, can go to their rooms but nobody else's); use if obvious/implied that the friend is a SW, even if not specifically stated (R2) (07.09.07)

Source: Excerpted from Guest, G., Bunce, A., & Johnson, L. (2006, February). How many interviews are enough?: An experiment with data saturation and variability. *Field Methods*, 18, 59–82.

APPENDIX 7.5a   Sample Data Analysis Log, Document Version From NVivo 9 (Powers, 2005; QSR)

These memos will constitute a chronological history of progress in the project. Prior to closing out for any given day, please briefly summarize your daily progress here. Always start with a date–time stamp and your name.

6/2/2010 8:13 AM Effie:

Added some additional source material (government documents that Henry found). Changed Betty and Paul from a one-entry transcript to a verbatim one because accents can be hard to understand. Continued to code.

6/3/2010 7:25 AM Wanda:

Considered whether we might want to have our images in an "audiovisual" source category, and have attribution there instead of in the description?

6/3/2010 2:45 PM Henry:

Created a new node today—"Environmental change"—and coded interviews to it through Robert. Need to resume with Susan.

6/3/2010 3:16 PM Henry:

Coded the recordings of Helen and Ken.

Here are the definitions of the numerical categories that we used to define how long respondents have lived Down East.

- 0 = people who own property Down East, but neither they nor their forebear have ever lived there (i.e., people who have purchased property with intent to build but haven't built yet)
- 1 = people who are in the first generation of their family to reside (either full-time or part-time) Down East
- 2 = people whose families have resided Down East (full-time or part-time) for two generations
- 3+ = people whose families have resided Down East (full-time or part-time) for three or more generations

These definitions don't differentiate based on how much of the year a person spends Down East.

6/3/2010 5:36 PM Wanda:

Added Endnote library. Wanted to do some word frequency queries, but didn't want to count the interviewer's words. I created sets of the nodes for interviewees, because this would exclude the interviewer text. I also created sets that added survey respondents and all sources, each of which used person nodes rather than interview sources to exclude interviewer voice for word frequency queries.

6/24/2010 12:59 PM Wanda:

Auto-coded codable columns in survey data and created tag clouds comparing what respondents considered development that they would or would not want to see Down East. Some interesting things here: (a) some positive words for business and commercial, highest use of family, high use of affordable and small; (b) negative use of condos, developments, high, and large. These results will be interesting to investigate further.

APPENDIX 7.5b   Sample Data Analysis Log, Tabular in Excel

Date	Analyst	Analysis task(s) completed	Notes
05.04.11	AB	Created new project "Sample study" Imported IDI files D01-D15 Imported FG files: DFG01-DFG08 Created folders for each set of data Imported demographics spreadsheet Linked data sources and demographic info Posted copy of QDAS project to shared drive	Will need to create site-specific folders, sets, or attributes at some point
05.05.11	CD	Created folders for structural and content codes Added all structural and content codes as currently defined to project "Test" coded files D01and DFG01 Posted version of the QDAS project dated 5.5.11 to shared drive	These will need to be coded again by someone else. I didn't have any problems with the codes as I used them.

8

Ethical Dimensions of Qualitative Research

BASIC ETHICAL PRINCIPLES IN RESEARCH

Before embarking on data collection involving participant observation, in-depth interviews, or focus groups, it is important to understand some of the basic ethical dimensions of qualitative research. Like biomedical or quantitative research, good qualitative research is designed and conducted within the parameters of internationally recognized ethical guidelines that emphasize the principles of *respect for persons, beneficence,* and *justice.* As defined by the *Council for International Organizations of Medical Sciences and the World Health Organization* (World Health Organization, 2002, pp. 17–18):

Respect for persons incorporates at least two fundamental ethical considerations, namely,

(a) respect for autonomy, which requires that those who are capable of deliberation about their personal choices should be treated with respect for their capacity for self-determination; and

(b) protection of persons with impaired or diminished autonomy, which requires that those who are dependent or vulnerable be afforded security against harm or abuse.

Beneficence refers to the ethical obligation to maximize benefit and to minimize harm. This principle gives rise to norms requiring that the risks of research be reasonable in the light of the expected benefits, that the research design be sound, and that the investigators be competent both to conduct the research and to safeguard the welfare of the research subjects. Beneficence further proscribes the deliberate infliction of harm on persons; this aspect of beneficence is sometimes expressed as a separate principle, non-maleficence (do no harm).

Justice refers to the ethical obligation to treat each person in accordance with what is morally right and proper, to give each person what is due to him or her. In the ethics of research involving human subjects, the principle refers primarily to distributive justice, which requires the equitable distribution of both the burdens and the benefits of participation in research. Differences in distribution of burdens and benefits are justifiable only if they are based on morally relevant distinctions between persons; one such distinction is vulnerability. *Vulnerability* refers to a substantial incapacity to protect one's own interests owing to such impediments as lack of capability to give informed consent, lack of alternative means of obtaining medical care or other expensive necessities, or being a junior or subordinate member of a hierarchical group. Accordingly, special provision must be made for the protection of the rights and welfare of vulnerable persons. (2002, pp. 17–18)

Together, these three principles (and their attendant considerations) form the foundation of ethical research. It is beyond the scope of this chapter to detail the history or elaborate upon each of these principles; instead, we will discuss the principles in the context of the dominant ethical issues and considerations that accompany the qualitative research methods described in the preceding chapters. To supplement the information on issues specific to qualitative research ethics presented here, we highly recommend that you complete some form of research ethics training prior to undertaking any qualitative data collection. There are several excellent online research ethics training resources available free of charge, and we have listed a few of those under the Additional Reading section at the end of this chapter.

WHAT IS DIFFERENT (OR NOT) ABOUT THE ETHICS OF QUALITATIVE OR SOCIOBEHAVIORAL RESEARCH?

The majority of guidelines, regulations, and laws relating to research with human subjects were developed as a direct result of ethical misconduct, exploitation, and/or abuses that occurred in the context of biomedical research.

Despite the fact that these regulations apply to all types of research with human subjects, their origin in the primarily controlled or clinical setting of biomedical research affects their scope and structure. Often, this presents challenges for researchers conducting less structured, less (physically) invasive, and/or less predictable types of studies—the types of studies where qualitative methods are often employed. How do we apply these ethical guidelines or approaches to qualitative research then?

One line of thinking, posited by Ramcharan and Cutcliffe (2001), is that "social research is largely—unlike, for instance, drug trials—*not a treatment* that will or will not have an intended *specifiable* outcome. Consequently, the question should be raised: Do the same rules apply to such research as apply to treatments that have the potential to change the life of a human physically, and perhaps, irremediably?" (p. 363). They argue for a different "ethics as process" approach for qualitative research, one that consistently monitors the benefit-to-risk ratio for participants to ensure that it is always on the side of benefit.

Others take a slightly different tack in comparing biomedical and (qualitative) social science research:

> Social scientists, perhaps to a greater extent than the average citizen, have an ethical obligation to their colleagues, their study population, and the larger society. The reason for this is that social scientists delve into the social lives of other human beings. From such excursions into private social lives, various policies, practices, and even laws may result. Thus, researchers must ensure the rights, privacy, and welfare of the people and communities that form the focus of their studies. (Berg, 2009, p. 60)

There is a parallel in Berg's view between the physically invasive nature of biomedical research and the socially invasive nature of sociobehavioral (often qualitative) research: Both place research participants at some level of risk and require minimization of potential harm. The difference in the ethical considerations for qualitative research is in the *types* of potential harms that are most likely to occur. Though there is relatively low risk of physical harm for qualitative research participants, there are varying, and potentially high, risks of social or emotional harm that can result. Fundamentally, however, the goals of designing ethical qualitative research are the same as those for biomedical or any other research initiative: "At a minimum, ethical researchers strive to leave people no worse off than they were before the research. Ideally, people should experience some improvement or benefit" (MacQueen, 2008, p. 22).

WHAT IS AN "ETHICAL" QUALITATIVE RESEARCH DESIGN?

The conventional answer to this question is that an ethical qualitative research design is one which respects the three primary principles of research ethics. In practice, however, there are as many "ethical" qualitative research designs as there are studies. In the United States, the federal government has a set of standard regulations called the Common Rule that serves as guidance for researchers and institutions alike in their evaluations of the ethics of proposed research (U.S. Department of Health and Human Services [HHS], 2009; see Additional Readings section for link to the full text of the Common Rule). Any research center, academic institution, or other organization that receives federal funding to conduct research of any kind with human subjects must have an institutional review board (IRB) composed of a variety of experts and lay persons to review and approve all research activities that take place under the direction of or that involve members of that institution. Variously called an ethics committee, human subjects research committee, or protection of human subjects committee, an IRB is responsible for ensuring that all research conducted meets the minimum ethical requirements spelled out in the Common Rule, and that ultimately participants are protected from research-related harms.

Do You Need to Have Your Qualitative Study Reviewed by an IRB?

As we alluded to earlier, the ethics of qualitative research get a little tricky when you try to apply the Common Rule—written to cover all research, but with a biomedical orientation—to qualitative research. The first step is to determine whether your research project is actually "research." As defined by the Common Rule,

> *Research* means a systematic investigation, including research development, testing and evaluation, designed to develop or contribute to generalizable knowledge. Activities which meet this definition constitute research for purposes of this policy, whether or not they are conducted or supported under a program which is considered research for other purposes. For example, some demonstration and service programs may include research activities. (HHS, 2009, *Protection of Human Subjects, Title 45* CFR 46.102 Definitions)

The key phrases here, cited by most IRBs as the distinguishing features of research, are "systematic investigation" and intended "to develop or contribute to generalizable knowledge." However, both of those key phrases are subject to interpretation. Let's imagine that we wanted to conduct a series of in-depth interviews to evaluate a new public health program. We will interview a randomly selected sample of the people who participated in the program to assess their attitudes and opinions about the effectiveness and clarity of the program's messages. This sounds like a systematic investigation, but will it produce or contribute to generalizable knowledge? Probably not; the information collected may apply only to the public health program in question. Does that mean that this activity is therefore *not* research, and will not require IRB review and approval? Maybe.

There is a whole class of activities that are considered research and yet are exempt from the Common Rule, including research in educational settings that involves normal educational practices; research involving educational tests; surveys; interviews; or observations of public behavior (HHS, 2009, *Protection of Human Subjects, Title 45* CFR 46.101b1,2). Note that when we say exempt, we don't mean that an IRB is uninformed about a study. An exemption means that someone from an IRB has looked over the proposed research plan and has decided that it does not need to be reviewed any further by the IRB. Interviews and participant observation—two of the qualitative methods covered in this book—are specifically identified as types of research that do *not* need to be approved by an IRB or meet the federal guidelines. (Some interpret focus groups to fall under this exclusion as well.) Based on this information, even if our example project is determined to be research, it would be considered exempt research (meaning exempt from the Common Rule) because it employs interviews as the primary method of data collection.

But there's another piece to consider. Will we be collecting and retaining identifying information about interviewees? Might that information, if disclosed outside the research setting, put interviewees at risk of criminal or civil liability or be damaging to their financial standing, employability, or reputation? If the answer to *both* questions is *yes*, the project is no longer considered exempt and would require IRB review and approval, pursuant to the federal regulations (HHS, 2009, *Protection of Human Subjects, Title 45* CFR 46.101b1,2). If the answer to only *one* of the questions is *yes*—we are keeping identifiable information, but its disclosure would not result in harm to our interviewees, for example—our evaluation project is indeed exempted from compliance with the Common Rule.

As mentioned, if we are working within an organization or institution that has an IRB, we will still have to submit our proposed project to the IRB for review (not approval). The IRB will then make the final determination of whether the study is, in fact, exempt. As MacQueen notes, "The exemption criteria are often poorly understood [by IRB professionals] and may not be used as fully as they could be . . . [Additionally] some IRBs may be uncomfortable with the notion of exempting any research from review, and they are within their rights to refuse to allow exemptions" (2008, p. 24). In these cases, most qualitative research is still deemed "minimal risk," meaning that the potential harms or discomforts are no greater than those that you might encounter in daily life (HHS, 2009, *Protection of Human Subjects, Title 45* CFR

46.102 Definitions). IRBs often provide "expedited" review of minimal risk studies, in which the proposed research is reviewed by one or two members of the IRB rather than by the whole panel. Compared to exempt research, expedited review gives the IRB a chance to review more carefully the potential harms of participating in the study, along with the researcher's plans to minimize risk of those harms. Full IRB review of qualitative research—where the proposed study is reviewed and discussed by all of the members of the IRB at one of their regular meetings—is usually reserved for studies that are integrated into a biomedical or mixed methods research design or for studies where the potential consequences of loss of data confidentiality are severe. For instance, full IRB review may occur if interviews will collect identifiable information about illegal activities (drug use or dealing) or may put a person at risk of physical harm (domestic violence). Research with particularly vulnerable populations, such as children or the homeless, may also warrant a full review.

So the short answer to the question, "Does my study need IRB review," is "It probably requires review, but not necessarily approval/oversight." In addition to the levels of distinction spelled out in the Common Rule, all IRBs are different in their interpretations of it. Some may not offer tiered levels of review; some are specifically designated as sociobehavioral IRBs while others (many) operate on a more biomedical model; and each likely has slightly different requirements for the types of documentation necessary for review of research and during the course of the study. Expedited review of qualitative research is probably the most common scenario. The following text box lists the types of information typically requested by IRBs, if review is required.

Common Requirements of an Institutional Review Board Proposal for a Qualitative Study

- Purpose of the Study—objectives and aims
- Background and Significance—should support the scientific aims of the research
- Design and Procedures—describe the research design and methods of data collection
- Selection of Subjects—list inclusion/exclusion criteria and how subjects will be identified
- Subject Recruitment and Compensation—describe recruitment procedures, including who will introduce the study to potential subjects. Describe how you will ensure that subject selection is equitable and all relevant demographic groups have access to study participation (per 45 CFR 46.111(a)(3)). Include information about approximately how many subjects will be recruited. If subjects are to be compensated, provide specific amounts to be provided for expenses such as travel and/or lost wages and/or for incentive to participate.

- Consent Process (if applicable)—address the following:

  o What type of consent will be sought—oral or written?

  o Who will conduct the consent process with prospective participants? Give the person's role in this study (principal investigator, study coordinator, etc.).

  o What arrangements will be in place for answering participant questions before and after the consent is signed? Describe the steps taken to minimize the possibility of coercion or undue influence.

  o What provisions will be in place to obtain consent from participants who do not read, are blind, or who do not read/understand English?

- Subject's Capacity to Give Legally Effective Consent—if subjects who do not have the capacity to give legally effective consent are included, describe how diminished capacity will be assessed. Will a periodic reassessment occur? If so, when? Will the participant be consented if the decisional capacity improves?

- Risk/Benefit Assessment—include a thorough description of how risks and discomforts will be minimized (per 45 CFR 46.111(a) (1 and 2)). Consider physical, psychological, legal, economic, and social risks as applicable. If vulnerable populations are to be included (such as children, pregnant women, prisoners, or cognitively impaired adults), what special precautions will be used to minimize risks to these subjects? What is the importance of the knowledge that is expected to result from the research?

- Data Analysis Considerations—provide a detailed description of how study data will be analyzed, how ineligible subjects will be handled, and which subjects will be included for analysis. Include planned sample size and rationale.

- Privacy, Data Storage, and Confidentiality—explain how you will ensure that the participants' privacy will be protected. Consider privacy interests regarding time and place where participants provide information, the nature of the information they provide, and the type of experience they will be asked to participate in during the research. Describe how research data will be stored and secured to ensure confidentiality. How will the research records and data be protected against inappropriate use or disclosure or malicious or accidental loss or destruction?

Source: Example adapted from Duke University Health System IRB research summary instructions.

Note that almost no qualitative research carried out on behalf of corporations is reviewed by an IRB. The main reason is that corporate research—typically marketing related—is carried out and funded within the private sector and is therefore not bound by the Common Rule. And, unlike academic, government, or nonprofit research organizations, corporations are not associated with any IRBs. This does not mean the corporate research is exempt from ethical guidelines and practices, but rather, it is not subject to the same formal oversight as research in other sectors.

Are There Other Forms of Review or Consultation You Will Need?

For some studies, particularly those situated within distinct geographical communities and/or following a participatory approach, you may need the input, review, advice, and perhaps approval of a Community Advisory Board (CAB). CABs comprise volunteers from the local communities who

- assist in the planning, development, and implementation of the research,
- assess community impact and ensure community concerns are considered, and
- serve as a voice for the community and study participants.

CAB members may also help members of the general community to understand the science and methods underpinning the research. CABs have often been used in public health research (see Newman et al., 2011 for a synthesis of best practices).

In terms of the ethical conduct of qualitative research, CABs can often help to address issues related to the principles of beneficence and justice: How can research objectives and community concerns be balanced to maximize benefit to the research participants? What is fair treatment of research participants, in terms of the compensation, services, or other goods they receive as part of the research? CABs also help to address what some have proposed as a fourth principle of ethical research, *respect for communities.* Respect for communities "confers on the researcher an obligation to respect the values and interests of the community in research and, wherever possible, to protect the community from harm" (Weijer, Goldsand, & Emanuel 1999, p. 275).

The participation of CABs in qualitative research raises some questions about research ethics themselves:

- Would the act of obtaining [IRB] approval undermine the very meaning of [community] collaboration and partnership building?
- Should community advisory board members be allowed access to original data so they can participate in its analysis and interpretation, or would that constitute a breach of confidentiality if they are not paid members of the research staff?
- If community partners and IRBs differ with regard to how they believe informed consent should be obtained, how should those differences be reconciled? (MacQueen 2008, pp. 35–36)

It is likely that different IRBs and researchers will provide different answers, but the questions suggest important areas for consideration, in terms of both the design and ethical conduct of qualitative research. Minkler (2004) provides additional detail on the ethical challenges of community-based participatory research.

ETHICAL CONSIDERATIONS FOR PARTICIPANT OBSERVATION, IN-DEPTH INTERVIEWS, AND FOCUS GROUPS

Across the qualitative research methods detailed in this book, the most common ethical concerns relate to elements of the principle of respect for persons. These range from ensuring that sampling and recruitment procedures do not exploit dependent or otherwise vulnerable populations, to making sure that research questions are relevant to participants, to the sensitive elicitation of highly emotional or personal experiences (Green & Thorogood, 2009). Whiteford and Trotter provide a dissection of the principle of respect for persons that is helpful in identifying key elements for consideration:

> The concept of respect for persons includes three guiding conditions—respect for individual autonomy, free will, and self-determination—that establish four basic actions that researchers must accomplish when they conduct ethical research: (1) assuring that participation is voluntary (voluntary participation), (2) determining that individuals recruited into the project are competent to participate (competence), (3) preserving confidentiality for participants (confidentiality), and (4) providing a thorough and accurate informed consent process (informed consent). (2008, p. 57)

While actions 1 and 2 seem to flow naturally from the necessity to respect individual autonomy, actions 3 and 4—ensuring informed consent of potential participants and maintaining the confidentiality of the data participants provide—are perhaps less intuitively related to the principle of respect for persons. Yet these are precisely the issues that are the most common sources of potential ethical conflict in qualitative research. We discuss each in turn. There are slight variations among the three methods in how informed consent and confidentiality are conceptualized and practiced, which we point out as we discuss each.

Informed Consent

Informed consent, as a concept, consists of three elements: information, comprehension, and voluntariness (National Institutes of Health [NIH], 1979). "The goal . . . is to insure that people understand what it means to participate in a particular research study so they can decide in a conscious, deliberate way whether they want to participate" (MacQueen, 2008, p. 29). In order to attain this goal, informed consent must be conceived of as a process, not just a way to get the interview started, or a form that you get research participants to sign. Informed consent starts with the design phase of your research and continues throughout your interaction with your interviewees.

Most sponsored research, whether commercial, governmental, or nonprofit, requires formal (often written) informed consent, and good informed consent procedures should be adhered to even where they are not explicitly required. While the ethics codes of various research institutions and professional organizations vary in how they define informed consent, most converge on a description of "consent given by a competent individual who: has received the necessary information; has adequately understood the information and; after considering the information, has arrived at a decision without having been subjected to coercion, undue influence or inducement, or intimidation" (World Health Organization, 2002, p. 32). The operationalization of this definition includes three key steps: figuring out what information you need to provide, finding a way of communicating the information clearly to your potential participants, and determining and recording their decision.

Step 1: Informed Consent Information

Whether delivered in a written or oral format, *informed consent* means disclosing and explaining key aspects of the research and the data collection to your potential participants. The text box, Essential Elements of Informed Consent Information, describes seven types of information to be included in informed consent for qualitative research.

Essential Elements of Informed Consent Information

Include these elements in your informed consent communications:

- Study description—explaining that the study is for research, outlining the objectives of the study, describing the responsibilities expected of the participant and researcher, describing what procedures are involved in the interview and the duration of both the data collection event and the overall study (including when the results might be available or would be put into use).
- Risks—outlining any anticipated or foreseeable potential physical, social, or psychological risks that the participant might incur as a result of agreeing to be part of the research. Risks should be described in understandable, culturally appropriate terms.
- Benefits—describing, without exaggeration or hyperbole, any benefits to the participants, their community or other groups of interest that might occur as a result of the research, along with the anticipated timing of those benefits.
- Confidentiality—indicating the degree of confidentiality the researchers are promising, the measures used to protect confidentiality (if appropriate), and what persons or organizations may have access to the information.

- Compensation—outlining what incentive or compensation, if any, is being offered (see Table 8.3 for more on this issue) and what the participant has to do in order to receive the incentive.
- Contacts—listing contact names, telephone numbers, and e-mail addresses for research-related questions or for concerns about the participant's rights as a research participant. Any contacts provided must be realistic and viable so that those who wish to ask a question have a reasonable expectation of reaching someone who can and will respond.
- Voluntary participation—clearly and explicitly stating that participation is absolutely voluntary, the participant has the right to discontinue at any time, and that there is no penalty for refusing to be interviewed or refusing to answer particular questions during the interview.

Source: Rivera, Borasky, Rice, and Carayon (2009, *Research Ethics Training Curriculum*, 2nd ed., Research Triangle Park, NC: FHI 360)

Step 2: Communicating the Information

Depending on the nature of your research, your interviewees, and your field setting, you may choose to convey your informed consent information orally, in writing, or using a combination of both. In developed countries with literate populations, written informed consent is the norm, and written consent is often a requirement of institutional review boards, study sponsors, and funders or is needed for legal reasons. While the Common Rule (45 CFR 46.116 [HHS, 2009]) states only that "the information that is given to the subject or the representative shall be in language understandable to the subject or the representative," most IRBs recommend that informed consent language be written at a sixth-to eighth-grade reading level and free from jargon or technical terms. These recommendations are based on the National Adult Literacy Study (Kirsch, Jungeblut, Jenkins, & Kolstad, 2002), which estimated that the "average" American reads at or below the eighth-grade level. Using active voice, keeping sentences short, and using simple words (*person* rather than *individual*, for example) can help to increase the readability of the language. MS Word can generate a reading level metric (Fleish-Kincaid) as part of its Spelling and Grammar function. The following text box contains a checklist produced by the National Cancer Institute (NCI, 2011, Simplification of Informed Consent Documents section, Appendix 3) to assist in the creation of easy-to-read consent forms. Some IRB websites also offer lists of simple words or lay language for medical terms (Stanford, 2011; University of Michigan, 1999).

NCI "Checklist for Easy-to-Read Informed Consent Documents"

- Words are familiar to the reader. Any scientific, medical, or legal words are defined clearly.
- Words and terminology are consistent throughout the document.
- Sentences are short, simple, and direct.
- Line length is limited to 30–50 characters and spaces.
- Paragraphs are short. Convey one idea per paragraph.
- Verbs are in active voice (i.e., the subject is the doer of the act).
- Personal pronouns are used to increase personal identification.
- Each idea is clear and logically sequenced (according to audience logic).
- Important points are highlighted.
- Study purpose is presented early in the text.
- Titles, subtitles, and other headers help to clarify organization of text.
- Headers are simple and close to text.
- Underline, bold, or boxes (rather than all caps or italics) give emphasis.
- Layout balances white space with words and graphics.
- Left margins are justified. Right margins are ragged.
- Upper and lower case letters are used.
- Style of print is easy to read.
- Type size is at least 12 point.
- Readability analysis is done to determine reading level (should be eighth grade or lower).
- Avoid:

  o Abbreviations and acronyms.
  o Large blocks of print.
  o Words containing more than three syllables (where possible).

Written consent procedures are generally not appropriate for studies with illiterate populations, for groups or places where written documents are culturally suspect, or where the physical circumstances of the interview setting make handling and control of paper documents problematic. In these cases, you can convey the informed consent information orally, by reading or reciting it to the potential interviewee. Note that this does not mean that the information itself should be skipped or attenuated—just that the information delivery needs to be adapted to the circumstances. You will often need to file for a waiver of written informed consent from the relevant IRB(s) if you plan to use verbal consent for a nonexempt study.

Step 3: Determining and Recording Consent

In most cases, determining whether or not someone has consented to participate in your study is obvious: The interviewee takes pen in hand and signs your consent document or they nod, say "sure," and gaze expectantly at you, waiting for the first interview question. But in some cases, their decision may not be so clear cut. In many cultures, saying yes or no directly may be considered impolite or may be impolite for some social groups. In some contexts in Japan, for example, people may avoid giving a direct negative answer to a request and say something like, "Chotto muzukashi desu," which translates literally to "It's a little bit difficult." You would need to fully understand the cultural and contextual environment where the consent process was taking place to know whether this meant something like "I'm not comfortable, but I'll do it," or "No freakin' way!" Closer to home, people in highly authoritarian environments may have trouble freely saying no to a person in a position of authority or respect (which may include a researcher). Understand the local rules for saying yes and no before you start asking for consent.

If you are getting consent in writing, the signed consent document is your record of having provided and discussed the informed consent information and received permission to do the interview or focus group. If consent procedures are oral, it is common to record the verbal consent on digital audio or video (if you are capturing the data using such a device) or to note the time, date, and place that oral consent was given, if you are only taking notes. Data collectors are also often required to sign a statement that the informed consent process has taken place, the participant has had a chance to ask any questions, and that the participant has provided consent to enroll or begin. Please note that if you are using cameras or audio recorders, permission to use these must be part of your informed consent information.

This informed consent process is essentially the same for in-depth interviews and focus groups. In a focus group setting, we recommend obtaining individual informed consent *before* a participant enters the room or location where the focus group will be held, to avoid any undue group influence or feeling of social pressure to stay in the room with other focus group members. People may also be more comfortable asking questions about the study, their participation, or any other part of the informed consent materials if they are in a one-on-one situation. Obtaining individual consent in this way usually requires the help of a note-taker or other member of the research team so that the moderator can remain in the focus group setting and greet the participants once they have provided informed consent. At the beginning of the focus group, then, the moderator can get the group to provide verbal consent or assent, both to their participation in the study and to the recording of the focus group, if applicable.

Specific procedures for obtaining and documenting informed consent will reflect the context of risks in the research. With in-depth interviews, the main risk is often to the confidentiality of the information that the interviewee provides. In some cases, where names and addresses of respondents are not collected or maintained as part of the research, a signed consent form may serve as the only source of identification linking a person with a particular study. In these cases, documentation of informed consent may *increase* the risk of loss of confidentiality (and therefore study participation), so verbal consent may be more appropriate. As Whiteford and Trotter relate,

> Researchers in countries undergoing political strife, or where recent political action has occurred, may find people willing and able to participate because they have important stories to tell and information to share from their experiences; however, they may be reluctant to put their name on any form that might eventually surface and endanger them . . . [or] for example, when ethnographers are working on HIV/AIDS prevention projects with individuals who are engaged in illegal activities (drug use, prostitution), having those individuals sign a consent form creates a confidentiality risk if those forms can be accessed by a law enforcement agent, while a verbal informed consent process provides better protection for the participants. (2008, pp. 66–67)

The flexibility in how the process of informed consent is implemented helps to assuage the "concern that relying only on codes of research ethics risks compartmentalizing ethical aspects of research, and shutting them off into a preamble to research" (Shaw, 2008, p. 400). If we remember that the point of informed consent is to give the potential participant sufficient information to make a decision about participating—at the outset of research and as it progresses—the emphasis on the process rather than the documentation relieves some of the tensions between informed consent requirements and confidentiality. To this end, the Common Rule provides provisions for waiving written consent in cases where

1. the only record linking the subject and the research would be the consent document, and the principal risk would be potential harm resulting from a breach of confidentiality. Each subject will be asked whether the subject wants documentation linking the subject with the research, and the subject's wishes will govern; or
2. the research presents no more than minimal risk of harm to subjects and involves no procedures for which written consent is normally required outside of the research context. (45 CFR 46.116c [HHS, 2009])

Similarly, verbal consent following a simplified or short-form study information sheet may be more appropriate for minimal risk research if a long and/or complicated consent form and associated documentation requirements might create distrust with interviewees. Alternately, if distrust already exists in a given research community, a more detailed, written consent process may be needed, even for minimal risk research. Context, along with institutional policies, will dictate the appropriate approach to informed consent for a given research situation. Figure 8.1 provides an example of a simple, straightforward informed consent document.

Figure 8.1   Informed Consent Form

INFORMED CONSENT

RELATIONS BETWEEN TRADITIONAL AND SCIENTIFIC KNOWLEDGE OF THE KOTZEBUE SOUND ECOSYSTEM

You have been asked to participate in a study of Traditional Ecological/ Environmental Knowledge of the Northern Kotzebue Sound Ecosystem. We will be interviewing around 100 individuals from Kotzebue on the natural resources of the region. The purpose of the research is to see how traditional knowledge compares to scientific ecological knowledge about environmental changes and to investigate the importance of subsistence activities within the Kotzebue Sound.

All information you tell the interviewer will remain confidential. This means that you will not be individually identified as a participant in this study to anyone. All names you provide will be replaced by ID numbers to insure all information remains confidential.

What do I need to do if I consent?

The interviewer will ask you the same questions all participants will be asked. These are questions about your hunting and fishing, your knowledge of the Kotzebue Sound and its animals and fish, and your thoughts on how the environment has changed over time. You will be asked to answer these questions as completely and honestly as possible.

What are my rights?

You have the right to refuse any question you do not want to answer without giving any reason. You have a right to end the interview at any time after it begins if you wish. You have a right to know the results from the study after it has been completed. You have a right to call the people responsible for this study at the numbers below and ask any questions you wish.

What are my benefits from participating?

By answering the questions honestly and completely, you will be contributing to the knowledge base about the Kotzebue Sound from the Inupiaq point of view. There is a good possibility that the data you provide will go into school programs to teach young children about the value of Inupiaq environmental knowledge, and help design museum exhibits about Inupiaq knowledge. This study will also produce a profile of the Kotzebue Sound ecosystem and other valuable information for the Kotzebue IRA.

Who can I call if I have questions?

If you have *any* questions about this study or its results, you may contact

I certify that I have read all of the above, asked questions and received answers concerning areas I did not understand, and have received satisfactory answers to these questions. I willingly give my consent for participation in this research study. (A copy of this consent form will be given to the person signing as the subject or as the subject's authorized representative.)

Participant's Name (print) Date	Signature of Participant
Signature of Interviewer Date	

Finally, there is the sometimes tricky issue of informed consent for participant observation activities. In most contexts, participant observation activities fall under the exempt research category of the Common Rule, and informed consent is not required. Provided that you are conducting participant observation in a public place and have notified any gatekeepers of your presence and intentions, you do not have to get the express consent of every person there before you observe. Of course, it's a good idea to have a succinct and truthful answer ready if someone asks you what you are doing. And if your observations and informal chatting with people morph into a more formal interview mode, we recommend you notify your conversation partners about the research you are conducting and go through an informed consent process (verbal or written) before proceeding to collect interview-type data. As discussed in

Chapter 3, the goal in participant observation is to "be discreet enough about who you are and what you are doing that you do not disrupt normal activity, yet open enough that the people you observe and interact with do not feel that your presence compromises their privacy. In many situations, there is no reason to announce your arrival at the scene; in many others, however, it is essential that you openly state your identity and purpose" (Mack, Woodsong, MacQueen, Guest, & Namey, 2005, pp. 16–17). The latter pertains particularly to educational research, where studies frequently involve both observation of classrooms and supplemental data collection of student assignments or test scores (see Howe & Moses, 1999, starting on p. 45, for more on the ethics of educational research specifically). In these cases, parental or guardian informed consent is required, as is consent from the teachers being observed. And prior to fielding your study, you'll likely need permission from various levels of administrative officials (county, district, school). Part of the rationale for obtaining consent here is that your observations include a vulnerable population (children) and a subordinate population (teachers, to principals, administrators). We seek informed consent in these types of situations to avoid potential for coerced or mandated participation. The text box titled Informed Consent and Participant Observation provides some tips on when and how informed consent should be implemented in participant observation activities.

Informed Consent and Participant Observation

Is it feasible to receive formal informed consent from every participant in a group with which one interacts? At what point is informed consent required, given the numerous roles and statuses the researcher adopts? Can one receive "collective" consent by approaching group leaders or spokespersons?

There are no easy answers to these questions. They vary by setting and by the nature of the research. However, the researcher should seek the highest standards in applying the principle of informed consent when using participant observation. In so doing, the researcher should:

- Ensure that participants are aware of the researcher's identity and purpose among the group;
- Disclose and disseminate as broadly as possible through general announcements or other more informal means the researcher's purpose, research topic, and data gathering method. Participants should be aware that any of their interactions with the researcher may constitute some form of data gathering;

- Seek permission from group leaders or spokespersons, where appropriate, but especially if they can help to broadcast to a community the researcher's identity, purpose, and method. However, researchers should also be careful to avoid situations where such public endorsements and announcements to the community can create pressure to participate. Participants should remain free to avoid all interaction with the researcher;
- As much as possible, the researcher should obtain informed consent from each individual participant with whom the researcher will be interacting. It is especially important to remain aware that some participants might not be fully informed despite general announcements in public. As the researcher gains awareness of the level of information individual participants have about the researcher's identity, purpose, and method, he or she should make every possible effort to disclose such information individually.

Source: University of Toronto Social Sciences and Humanities Research Ethics Board (SSH REB; 2005, pp. 3–4).

Confidentiality

In qualitative research, the most serious risk and potential for harm is typically related to the issue of data confidentiality. This applies to all three data collection methods detailed in this book. As mentioned previously, the more sensitive the nature of the research and questions you'll be asking, the greater the potential for confidentiality-related harms. While many qualitative studies ask participants about seemingly harmless topics (preferred brand of toothpaste, experience with a particular program, views on genetic research), many also collect information on very sensitive subjects (prostitution, drug use, infidelity). Depending on the field, most qualitative research probably falls somewhere in between these two points, exploring experiences and opinions on personal, though perhaps not sensitive or illegal, topics. It is your job (aided by the IRB perhaps) to identify the potential risks associated with loss of confidentiality for participants in your research and to come up with ways to minimize risks or prevent breaches of confidentiality from occurring, and to manage potential harms if they do. Table 8.1 provides examples of some common confidentiality-related risks and ways to address them.

Even if you are conducting research on the "less risky" end of the continuum, the nature of qualitative research—exploring human values, attitudes and behaviors in

Table 8.1	Common Confidentiality-Related Research Risks and Suggestions for Minimizing Harm
Confidentiality Risk	**Risk Minimization Strategy**
Data may be identifiable, even without names attached	• Strip other identifying details from study documents; include instructions for replacing sensitive data in your transcription protocol. • Maintain strict control over access to the data. • Consider whether there is another way to get the information you need with less potential for identification of participants.
People in positions of power or authority will want to see what someone said	• Same as above. Also: • Communicate clearly with people in positions of power or authority to let them know that only aggregate results will be presented; no individual responses will be shared.
Data could be stolen or inadvertently shared	• Prepare a data security plan for both physical and electronic data. • Use encryption tools to further secure electronic data. • Develop a protocol for file-sharing that requires sign-off by a key member of the research team (principal investigator or study manager). • Have all external personnel (transcriptionists, off-site collaborators) sign confidentiality agreements.
Data collection seen by or interrupted by outside party	• Hold interviews or focus groups in a private place. • Provide transportation to a private location if needed. • Meet with those who do not wish to participate if there are potential consequences to those who do not participate. • Enroll "controls" or "extras" if participation in the research will otherwise identify someone as belonging to a particular group (HIV+, for example).
Written consent or payment forms will identify participants	• Apply for waiver of consent or written consent. • Look into mechanisms for providing incentives that do not require a written receipt (this can be an issue at institutions that require documentation on each research subject that receives study incentives to comply with IRS reporting regulations).
An external transcriptionist or translator might discuss the data	• Have all external staff sign a confidentiality agreement. • Remind participants at the beginning of a data collection event to avoid using names or other identifying descriptors. • Strip identifiers from the original data to the extent possible.

the participant's own words—presents unanticipated challenges to confidentiality. Imagine, for example, that you are conducting interviews about how people use the Internet to enhance their efficiency at work. One of your findings is that work-time use of the Internet includes a lot of *personal* browsing, shopping, e-mailing, and so on.

The manager of a local company from which you recruited participants reads the findings and wants to know which of his employees participated in the study—and more importantly—what amount of personal web-surfing they admitted. Even if you do not divulge participation information or data, the manager might conduct a review of Internet log-ons and web-use for all of his employees, which may result in harm to the professional standing of some of your research participants. Unexpected findings can lead to unintended consequences. And though there is sometimes a lower threshold for informed consent and confidentiality applied to participant observation activities, Warren and Karner (2010, pp. 34–35) present four cases where researchers' field notes were subpoenaed as court evidence, presenting a clear challenge to the confidentiality of information collected during qualitative participant observation activities. This underlines the point that, whichever data collection method is used, there is the potential that information collected through qualitative research—even when seemingly innocuous—can have negative consequences if disclosed outside of the research setting in an identifiable manner.

In the case of some applied studies, such as in commercial market research, or studies involving social deviance, illegal behavior, or the military, IDIs may also include information that is potentially subject to patent or intellectual property law, criminal prosecution, or even relevant to state security. The more potentially sensitive the topic, the more important it is that the informed consent process clearly explains the potential risks and that the study procedures provide participants with proper protection of their rights and interests (see the text box Certificates of Confidentiality for one means of addressing these heightened concerns).

Certificates of Confidentiality

If you know from the design phase that your research will address a topic that is highly sensitive, involves illegal behavior, or could be the source of future legal proceedings AND you will be collecting and keeping identifiable information, you might consider (and your IRB may recommend) a Certificate of Confidentiality.

Certificates of Confidentiality are issued by the National Institutes of Health (NIH) to protect identifiable research information from forced disclosure. They allow the investigator and others who have access to research records to refuse to disclose identifying information on research participants in any civil, criminal, administrative, legislative, or other proceeding, whether at the federal, state, or local level. By protecting researchers and institutions from being compelled to disclose information that would identify research subjects, Certificates of Confidentiality help achieve the research objectives and promote participation in studies by helping assure confidentiality and privacy to participants.

Certificates are recommended for many types of research, including the following:

- Research on HIV, AIDS, and other STDs
- Studies that collect information on sexual attitudes, preferences, or practices
- Studies on the use of alcohol, drugs, or other addictive products
- Studies that collect information on illegal conduct
- Studies that gather information that if released could be damaging to a participant's financial standing, employability, or reputation within the community
- Research involving information that might lead to social stigmatization or discrimination if it were disclosed
- Research on participants' psychological well-being or mental health
- Genetic studies, including those that collect and store biological samples for future use
- Research on behavioral interventions and epidemiologic studies

Source: HHS (2011, "Certificates of Confidentiality Kiosk").

Focus groups pose issues of confidentiality and consent that go beyond those that arise in one-on-one data collection efforts. By their very nature, focus groups require that individuals reveal their experiences, perceptions, beliefs, and reactions in the presence not just of the researcher, but of their fellow focus group participants. This means that on a very fundamental level, the researcher cannot prevent information that is shared in the group from later being passed on from group participants to their friends, families, bosses, co-workers, or even the general public. Table 8.2 below outlines some of the risks and possible approaches to mitigate them when using focus groups.

No matter what steps the researcher takes, focus groups are simply not as confidential a forum for data collection as IDIs. The more interesting the topic—and the livelier the discussion—the more likely your participants are to chatter about the group proceedings to others. The researcher's job is to mitigate the potential negative consequences of this aspect of human nature and to make an honest judgment as to whether these risks are low enough to conduct focus groups.

Table 8.2	Potential Ethical Issues in Focus Group Research and Tips for Mitigating Risk or Harm
Potential Risk	**Risk Minimization Strategy**
Embarrassment of participants due to revelation of personal information	• Mention this risk during informed consent process. • Avoid recruiting people who know each other or share personal/professional connections. • Emphasize the need to respect the privacy of others during the moderator's introductory remarks ("What happens in the focus group, stays in the focus group"). • Design the discussion guide and lead the discussion in ways that minimize the chance of overly revealing comments.
Professional or personal reprisal aimed at participants	• Similar to above. • For groups that involve community members, employees, or others where anonymity is not possible, avoid having those in power (leaders, doctors, teachers, bosses, parents, etc.) in the same group with those they oversee or control.
Release of confidential stimulus materials (photos, documents, prototypes, drafts)	• Maintain tight control of all copies of stimulus materials used in the group. • Forbid/limit the use of recording devices (e.g., smart phones) by participants. • Mask potentially confidential elements (names of people/companies, product details/features, release dates). • Have participants sign a confidentiality agreement (these are generally unenforceable in law but help to emphasize to participants that they are handling/evaluating confidential ideas and materials).
Release of information or rumors about the research itself	• Give participants an accurate sense of what the research is. • Keep lines of communication open with those who might consider themselves stakeholders in the research (local community groups, the press, etc.). • Consider during research design phase what impact premature or inaccurate release of information might have on your research. o If such release would be fatal to conducting the study or using the findings, focus groups may not be the correct method for data collection.

Focus group observers are another potential source of breaches of confidentiality. The presence of observers (the norm in commercial research and common in other fields, as well) is an important feature of the research environment, and if observers will be present—whether visible in the focus group space or watching from an observation room—you must mention them as part of your informed consent process. Prior to your group, brief any observers on their role and responsibilities. Emphasize that they are part of the research team and are expected to conduct themselves accordingly, respecting the rights and privacy of the focus group participants. It is easy for observers, especially those watching groups from a concealed observation room (the norm in dedicated focus group facilities), to fall into a TV-viewer mode, fixating on the personal characteristics of the participants rather than the research objectives. Make sure that observers know not to discuss the group proceedings in any way or in any forum that might compromise the assurances of confidentiality you provided during the informed consent process. No matter how entertaining, salacious, or outrageous the focus group participants or their comments, observers (and other research staff) will have to resist the temptation to turn them into fodder for post-group storytelling. Such conversations can easily contain details that could identify and embarrass the focus group participants.

As detailed earlier, there are several questions related to confidentiality to consider prior to data collection: How will you ensure that participants' privacy will be protected? How will the research records and data be protected against inappropriate use or disclosure, or malicious or accidental loss or destruction? How will research participants' identities be kept confidential? The last question raises a point related to the data management procedures outlined in the previous chapter. If each person who participates in the research is given a Source ID and all data (physical and electronic) are labeled with this Source ID or some variation of it, where will you keep track of which person is associated with each Source ID? Usually, this is in a master key that is accessible to only one person and that has an extra layer of security (in a locked drawer in a locked office in a locked building or in a file protected by a password that only one person knows). This master source key contains only two columns: participant name and Source ID. The idea is to keep all of the data separate from this key so that someone with the data could not identify the participant and someone with the key would not have access to the data (unless authorized). In highly sensitive research, this key may exist for only a short time, during recruitment perhaps, and would then be destroyed upon completion of each data collection event (i.e., once an interview is complete and the participant's contact information is no longer necessary) or at the end of all data collection. These sorts of details are typically considered prior to data collection, presented to an IRB for approval, and explained to potential research participants during informed consent. Since breaches of confidentiality damage the trust between research participants and researchers (and may jeopardize subsequent research), the additional time and effort put into protecting participant confidentiality benefit both parties.

Incentives

The topic of how to compensate qualitative research participants for taking part in the research relates to the principle of justice: What is an appropriate recognition of and reciprocation for the time and information that research participants share? For in-depth interviews or focus groups, this could be a gift card or cash, a small gift, or reimbursement for travel and parking. Incentives are typically not provided in the context of participant observation activities. If there is an incentive provided for participation, it's a good idea to make it commensurate with the participant's status and social context, so as to avoid both inducement and offense. Inducement exists when the incentive or compensation for research participation is "too good to pass up" and creates the potential for people to agree to participate simply for the payout (and perhaps despite some of the study requirements). On the other hand, you may offend or insult participants with an "incentive" that is not at all an incentive for them to participate because it undervalues their time, expertise, or experience. For this and other reasons, IRBs and researchers struggle to find an appropriate term for incentives, with some favoring "reimbursement" or "compensation" or "token of appreciation," or avoiding a single term all together and phrasing it as "What you will get for participating."

If you are not familiar with the research population, colleagues who have conducted similar research, CAB members, or members of the research population directly can provide a ballpark estimate. Consider also that giving equal incentives to all interviewees may insult high-ranking individuals, while giving unequal incentives (even where culturally appropriate) may result in charges of unfairness. In our experience in the United States, incentives for participating in an in-depth interview or focus group average about $50 for a "regular" participant. This rate increases as a function of both the rarity of a participant's attributes and how much their time is worth in the general workplace. You might provide incentives of over $1,000, for example, for an in-depth interview with an African American female neurosurgeon. Outside of the United States, incentives are determined based on consultation with local researchers who provide guidance on what constitutes a tremendous inducement or an egregious insult.

Using incentives can make it easier to find willing interviewees, offer thanks in tangible form for the time and insights participants have contributed to your study, and can help build rapport. But incentives are not without their drawbacks, and no type of incentive is perfect for every study. Table 8.3 details several common types of incentives and the pros and cons of each. Keep in mind that research institutions often require study participants to sign or provide identifying information upon receipt of an incentive, which can again pose a confidentiality risk as documentation of someone's participation in a study, particularly if no other identifiers are being recorded.

Table 8.3	Common Types of Incentives Offered for Participation in In-Depth Interviews and Focus Groups	
Incentive Type	**Pros**	**Cons**
Cash	Cash is easy to handle, available everywhere, and valued by most interviewees.	Cash incentives can have unintended consequences: They may create a "market" for being interviewed, causing those who get the incentive to be the target of jealousy, and/or they may also attract unqualified people to try to become interviewees. Very wealthy interviewees may disdain cash incentives. Many U.S. academic institutions will not allow cash incentives due to accounting regulations.
Checks	Transferrable to cash. Satisfy the requirements of institutions concerned with fiscal audits of research funding.	Checks require a bank account or check-cashing option and are therefore less convenient than cash. Checks also often have to be "processed" by an institution, creating a 2 to 6 week time lag between interview and receipt of incentive.
Gift Certificates	Useful in developed countries and sometimes safer to carry (for both interviewers and interviewees) than cash. Useful for wealthy interviewees who may view more favorably a certificate to a store or restaurant than the same amount in cash.	Certificates must be meaningful/ usable for interviewees. Not useful in some countries or areas where the gift certificate concept is not familiar.
Gifts and donations	Can create a sense of personal warmth and build rapport. Gifts to children are often welcomed by parent interviewees, donations to communities or charities allow the interviewee to provide something for a group or organization they value. Donations can be especially good for motivating/thanking wealthy interviewees	Requires a good sense of what gifts and donations would be welcomed by the target interviewees. Runs the risk of the incentive being viewed as insulting, inappropriate, or simply not motivating. Some research funding sources prohibit the donation of grant funds on behalf of research participants (as incentives).
Raffle or lottery	Useful for situations where you have limited funds or limited ability to distribute incentives (online interviewing, ethnographic field research). The "prize" is discussed, every research participant is entered into the drawing, and winners are selected at predetermined intervals (once a month, at completion of project).	Requires extra documentation and oversight to track eligibility and manage a fair drawing. Some IRBs may not approve a "selective" incentive; that is, they may prefer that everyone who participates receive the same item or amount rather than the same chance to win a larger item or amount.

Also, we recognize that for many students conducting project-related or dissertation research, there may not be any funding to provide monetary incentives. Personal, face-to-face recruitment is helpful in these situations: People may not respond to a flier or letter inviting participation in a study without an incentive, but if you have a chance to explain your research and the significance of their contributions in person, they may be willing to help. In these situations, it is often helpful to stress the minimal amount of time or effort required to participate in the research and extend your sincere thanks to each participant for their altruism. People in your own social or professional networks may be a good place to start your recruitment, but recognize the limits that snowball or chain-referral recruitment may have for your data (see Chapter 2).

MONITORING YOUR RESEARCH

Whatever your study or data collection methods, you will need to monitor the research as it progresses to be sure it remains compliant with ethical principles and regulations. This is especially true if your research team involves more than one person. Many of the data management tools described in Chapter 7 can help to provide checks on the processes and implementation of your research. For instance, you may have a column on your screening log to document whether informed consent was obtained at the time of screening, or on your data tracking log to note whether a written informed consent form was signed and filed for a particular source. In addition to process- and document-related monitoring, you will want to assess whether there have been any social harms or confidentiality breaches during the study.

Guest and colleagues (2008) provide a helpful monitoring checklist that identifies specific items that may be reviewed or audited at predetermined intervals during the course of a team-based sociobehavioral study. The list below is an abridged version of that checklist, specifying ethics-related documentation that a research study should have on hand at all times:

- Copy of ethics committee approval
- Interim or annual reports to the ethics committee
- Protocol amendments
- Deviations from the protocol
- Signed staff confidentiality agreements
- Staff ethics training documentation
- Informed consent documentation for each enrolled participant (written with participant signatures, verbal with interviewee signatures, or verbal recorded on audio or video)

- Social or physical harms related to study participation
- Breaches of confidentiality

As Whiteford and Trotter note, sometimes ethical issues in qualitative research are less clear cut: They are

> unplanned, unanticipated, and revolve around conflicts between ethical principles rather than violation of them. These ethical challenges cannot always be resolved if [researchers] follow simple, formulaic, rules-based, mechanistic approaches to resolving ethical dilemmas in research—especially if they try to do so without taking the context and cultural conditions into account. (2008, p. 97).

These are often more challenging issues to identify and describe during study monitoring. For these situations where ethical principles are in conflict, Whiteford and Trotter provide a practical six-step ethical problem-solving guide "to allow the researcher (or an ethics review panel) to explore the issues involved in a particular case and devise a solution that does the least amount of harm to everyone concerned" (2008, p. 98). The process includes (1) determining the facts of the research case, neutrally and nonjudgmentally; (2) identifying the values of researchers and research participants that are at risk; (3) describing the primary ethical dilemma and the primary area of conflict(s); (4) determining a range of possible solutions or courses of action; (5) choosing one solution or course of action from among those generated in Step 4; and (6) defending your solution or course of action to the key stakeholders in terms of the primary ethical principles that are being upheld (Reprinted by permission of Waveland Press, Inc. from Whiteford & Trotter, Ethics for Anthropological Research and Practice. [Long Grove, IL: Waveland Press, Inc., 2008]. All rights reserved.). Whether you adapt and use the monitoring checklist and/or the ethical problem-solving guide will depend on the size, nature, and scope of your research, but at the very least, be prepared to identify ethical issues as they arise during the conduct of a study. As Olson summarizes, "The task of the researcher is to design his or her study in ways that minimize harm as much as possible, but it is also incumbent on the researcher to know how to recognize harm if it occurs during a study and not to simply assume that harm is unlikely" (2011, p. 80).

REPORTING PROBLEMS

So what happens if and when you do identify an ethical issue in your research? The answer depends on the severity of the problem. In nearly all cases—whether it involves a deviation from the study protocol, an unsigned consent form, or a serious breach of confidentiality—you are typically expected to prepare a report of the lapse or violation, along with your plans to correct it or prevent recurrences, and submit it to the relevant parties overseeing your research (ethics committee, CAB, sponsor, funder). Take an example from a research project managed by Guest and Namey:

> Based on a routine monitoring trip for one of our own studies, a potential breach of confidentiality was observed. Local accounting practices at two of our research sites required inclusion of names on receipts for reimbursements given to participants. These practices were followed despite a week-long training of local investigators and field staff that emphasized the importance of not collecting identifying information from study participants. We subsequently addressed the breach by having the accountants discontinue the practice, blacking out names on all receipts, and filing reports with both the in-country and the sponsor's ethics committees. The site then developed alternative documentation strategies for dispersing participant reimbursements. (Guest et al., 2008, p. 192)

This was a moderate breach of confidentiality—certainly the accounting staff should not have ever seen the names of the research participants, but the data collected from those participants remained secure. The ethics committees in question were satisfied with our corrective actions, and the study proceeded—with better understanding of confidentiality protections as a benefit of having discovered the breach. In cases where more serious ethical transgressions have occurred, where, for instance, informed consent has not been properly obtained or documented, an ethics committee may halt the study, require re-consenting of individuals, and/or require that all data collected under the nonstandard informed consent process be tossed out. Though likely painful to all involved, these steps are necessary to ensure the rights of the research participants, the validity of the data, and the integrity of the research enterprise. Transparency, including prompt and honest reporting of problems, is key to the ethical conduct of research.

WORKING INTERNATIONALLY

While the same ethical principles apply to U.S.-based researchers regardless of where they conduct their research, there are additional considerations for those working internationally. First, there are potentially more layers of political difference that can affect the ethics of international research. Among the political issues Woodsong (2008) identifies in field research, perhaps global North–South inequities and research on "hot" political topics are the most relevant here. Global resource inequalities—in terms of human and material resources—can lead to differences in understandings of and priorities ascribed to various research goals, which can affect the ethical conduct of research. Similarly, if you are working on a hot political topic—abortion, for example—the politics and regulations of the countries you work in (including the United States) will likely have an effect on how you can (ethically) implement your research.

Second, the interpretations, valuations, and implementation of the ethical principles of respect for persons, beneficence, and justice are not universal. For instance, the concepts of autonomy and free will vary among cultures, and

> as a consequence, voluntary participation, informed consent, or even the issue of privacy and confidentiality may need additional explanation and even creative accommodation in order for cross-cultural researchers to meet the ethical standards of their own society and simultaneously accommodate the ethical standards of the culture they are studying. (Whiteford & Trotter, 2008, pp. 69–70)

As an example, in many cultures around the world, a woman cannot consent to participate in research (among other things) without the explicit knowledge and approval of her husband or male relative. This runs counter to the (Western) ethical principle of respect for persons, specifically autonomy and self-determination. Whose ethics and values prevail? Woodsong and colleagues (2006) interviewed women in sub-Saharan Africa about this particular dilemma. As one African woman put it, "You have problems because you did not tell your husband properly that you are going to the research study. Hiding this from the husband, it's like it violates her own family because of lies" (Woodsong et al., 2006, p. 11). If insistence on autonomy (and therefore a woman's secrecy or deception) then led to violence in the woman's home, it would come in conflict with the principle of beneficence and "do no harm." In recognition of this ethical conflict, the Scientific and Ethical Review Group of the World Health Organization, though opposed to partners' or spouses' consent to women's research participation, acknowledges that

> In rare circumstances, it may be necessary for researchers to conform to local custom and request partner agreement. An example would be the impossibility of recruiting any research subjects for a study in a particular country without partner agreement and the subsequent impossibility of gaining approval in that country for a new contraceptive drug or device. If failure to conduct the research would result in an inability of people in that country to receive the benefits of the drug or device, this consequence might be judged as sufficiently negative for the common good of the public to outweigh the usual prohibition against partner agreement for the individual subject. (World Health Organization, 2005)

This is just one example of the types of ethical challenges that can arise in international research. There are no easy answers when ethical principles are in conflict—with each other or between cultures. Whiteford and Trotter's ethical problem-solving guide referenced earlier (2008, pp. 98–103) may provide a helpful framework for working through the relevant issues and stakeholder positions.

Local IRBs and/or CABs can also provide important guidance on how best to integrate Western research and research ethics into international contexts. In most cases, research conducted internationally, even if based in the United States, will require some level of local IRB review. Local review presents logistical considerations for research ethics in international research in the preparation, timing, and cost of having a research protocol reviewed in multiple places—and perhaps in multiple languages. And the more sites you have, the greater the logistical burden. Take, for example, a project that one of the authors worked on that involved in-depth interviews and focus groups with service providers, gatekeepers, study participants, and other consumers of HIV prevention and treatment services to gather community perspectives on care options for HIV prevention trial participants (MacQueen et al., 2007). These interviews and focus groups were planned for nine sites in seven countries and required review by no less than 13 IRBs! As Figure 8.2 shows, it took an entire year just to get all of the IRB approvals in place. We began data collection at each site as soon as approval for that site was received, and the data collection itself took no more than 3 months in any given location. Our experience, which has been repeated in several other multisite international projects, underscores the necessity to plan

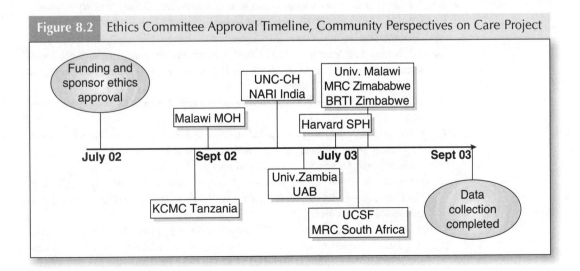

Figure 8.2 Ethics Committee Approval Timeline, Community Perspectives on Care Project

ample time and resources for the work that will need to occur before any data collection takes place.

SUMMING UP

The ethical principles that apply to qualitative research are no different than those that guide any other research with human subjects; the difference is in the nature and scope of harms to participants that are most likely to result from taking part in qualitative research. In studies using participant observation, in-depth interviewing, focus group discussions, or other qualitative data collection techniques, the most salient risks to participants are those related to the principle of respect for persons, particularly issues of informed consent and confidentiality. With this in mind, and foresight about when violations of informed consent or breaches of confidentiality are most likely to occur, you can design your research with appropriate procedures and protections in place to minimize the risk of any harm to participants. In this chapter, we have provided several practical tips for minimizing ethical issues in qualitative research; however, as we stated at the outset, we highly recommend that you complete a research ethics training course prior to designing or conducting any qualitative research. Resources and additional readings are provided below.

REFERENCES

Berg, B. L. (2009). *Qualitative research methods for social sciences* (7th ed.). New York, NY: Pearson.

Green, J., & N. Thorogood. (2009). *Qualitative methods for health research* (2nd ed.). Thousand Oaks, CA: Sage.

Guest, G., Namey, E., & MacQueen, K. M. (2008). A framework for monitoring sociobehavioral research. In G. Guest & K. M. MacQueen (Eds.), *Handbook for team-based qualitative research* (pp. 189–204). Lanham, MD: Altamira.

Howe, K., & Moses, M. (1999). Ethics in educational research. *Review of Research in Education, 24,* 21–60.

Kirsch, I., Jungeblut, A., Jenkins, L., & Kolstad, A. (2002). *Adult literacy in America: A first look at the findings of the National Adult Literacy Survey* (Vol. 201, 3rd ed.). Washington, DC: National Center for Education, U.S. Department of Education.

MacQueen, K. M. (2008). Ethics and team-based qualitative research. In G. Guest & K. M. MacQueen (Eds.), *Handbook for team-based qualitative research* (pp. 21–38). Lanham, MD: Altamira.

MacQueen, K. M., Namey, E., Dzinyemba, W., Patrick-Mtweve, S., Mlingo, M., Morar, N. S. . . . the HPTN 035 Standard of Care Assessment Team. (2007). Community perspectives on care options for HIV prevention trial participants. *AIDS Care, 19*(4), 554–560.

Mack, N., Woodsong, C., MacQueen, K., Guest, G., & Namey, E. (2005). *Qualitative research methods: A data collector's field guide*. Research Triangle Park, NC: Family Health International.

Minkler, M. (2004). Ethical challenges for the "outside" researcher in community-based participatory research. *Health Education and Behavior, 31*(6), 684–697.

National Cancer Institute (NCI). (2011). Checklist for easy to read informed consent documents. Retrieved October 20, 2011, from http://www.cancer.gov/clinicaltrials/patientsafety/simplification-of-informed-consent-docs/page5

National Institutes of Health (NIH). *Belmont report: Ethical principle and guidelines for the protection of human subjects of research (Part B)*. (1979). Retrieved from http://oshr.od.nih.gov/guidelines/belmont/html

Newman, S. D., Andrews, J. O., Magwood, G. S., Jenkins, C., Cox, M. J., & Williamson, D. C. (2011). Community advisory boards in community-based participatory research: A synthesis of best processes. *Preventing Chronic Disease 8*(3), 1–12.

Olson, K. (2011). *Essentials of qualitative interviewing*. Walnut Creek, CA: Left Coast Press.

Ramcharan, P., & Cutcliffe, J. (2001). Judging the ethics of qualitative research: Considering the "ethics as process" model. *Health & Social Care in the Community, 9*, 358–366.

Rivera, R., Borasky, D., Rice, R., & Carayon, F. (2009). *Research ethics training curriculum* (2nd ed.). Research Triangle Park, NC: Family Health International (FHI) 360.

Shaw, I. (2008). Ethics and the practice of qualitative research. *Qualitative Social Work, 7*, 400–414.

Stanford University Research Compliance Office. (2011). Glossary of lay terms for consent forms. Retrieved October 20, 2011, from http://humansubjects.stanford.edu/general/glossary.html

University of Michigan Medical School. (1999). Guidance: Simplification guide to medical terms. Retrieved October 20, 2011, from http://www.med.umich.edu/irbmed/guidance/guide.htm

University of Toronto, Social Sciences and Humanities Research Ethics Board (SSH REB). (2005). *Guidelines for ethical conduct in participant observation*. Retrieved November 25, 2011, from http://www.research.utoronto.ca/ethics/pdf/human/nonspecific/Participant%20Observation%20Guidelines.pdf

U.S. Department of Health and Human Services (HHS). (2009). *Protection of human subjects. Title 45, code of federal regulation, part 46: Revised January 15, 2009.* Retrieved October 11, 2011, from www.hhs.gov/ohrp/hmansubjects/guidance/45cfr46.html

U.S. Department of Health and Human Services (HHS). (2011). *Certificates of confidentiality kiosk.* Retrieved October 11, 2011, from http://grants.nih.gov/grants/policy/coc

Warren, C. A. B., & Karner, T. X. (2010). *Discovering qualitative methods* (2nd ed.). New York, NY: Oxford University Press.

Weijer, C., Goldsand, G., & Emanuel, E. J. (1999). Protecting communities in research: Current guidelines and limits of extrapolation. *Nature Genetics, 23*(3), 275–280.

Whiteford, L. M., & Trotter, R. T., II. (2008). *Ethics for anthropological research and practice*. Long Grove, IL: Waveland Press.

Woodsong, C. (2008). The politics of field research. In G. Guest & K. M. MacQueen (Eds.), *Handbook for team-based qualitative research* (pp. 39–60). Lanham, MD: Altamira.

Woodsong, C., MacQueen, K., Namey, E., Sahay, S., Mlingo, M., & Morrar, N (2008). Women's autonomy and informed consent in international microbicide clinical trials. *Human Research Ethics, 1*(3), 11–26.

World Health Organization (WHO). (2002). *Council for International Organizations of Medical Sciences (CIOMS) and the World Health Organization.* (2002). Geneva, Switzerland: Council for International Organizations of Medical Sciences.

World Health Organization (WHO), (2005). *Special programme of research, development and research training in human reproduction: Guidelines on reproductive health research and partners' agreement* (From the Programme's document Preparing a Project Proposal, Guidelines and Forms, 3rd ed.). Retrieved from http://www.who.int/reproductivehealth/topics/ethics/partners_guide_serg/en/index.html

ADDITIONAL READING

MacQueen, K. M. (2008). Ethics and team-based qualitative research. In G. Guest & K. M. MacQueen (Eds.), *Handbook for team-based qualitative research* (pp. 21–38). Lanham, MD: Altamira.

National Institutes of Health (NIH), Office of Human Subjects Research. (n.d.). Guidelines. (Provides links to the Common Rule, *Belmont Report*, Nuremberg Code, and other guidelines.) Retrieved from http://ohsr.od.nih.gov/guidelines/index.html

Whiteford, L. M., & Trotter, R. T., II. (2008). *Ethics for anthropological research and practice.* Long Grove, IL: Waveland Press.

Online Research Ethics Training Courses

Collaborative Institutional Training Initiative (CITI) (must have participating organization affiliation). https://www.citiprogram.org/Default.asp?

Family Health International (FHI) 360, Research Ethics Training Curriculum (2nd ed.). http://www.fhi360.org/training/en/RETC2/index.html

National Institutes of Health (NIH), Office of Extramural Research, Protecting Human Research Participants. http://phrp.nihtraining.com/users/login.php

EXERCISES

1. Find an online version of the Nuremberg Code (1947), the Helsinki Accord (1964), and the *Belmont Report* (1979). In historical perspective, what concept(s) does each document successively add to the previous?

2. Suppose that you are about to begin a study of underage drinking behaviors on college campuses using in-depth interviews with freshmen. Describe how

each of the three main ethical principles will come into play in your study (respect for persons, beneficence, and justice). What are the risks to participants in this research? How might you mitigate those risks?

3. Read the scenario in the following exercise box and respond to each of the questions. (Answers provided in Appendix 8.1.)

An Ethical Challenge

A Ministry of Health has requested a prevalence and/or behavioral surveillance study for sexually transmitted infection (STI) among commercial sex workers. Participants in this study will be tested for three common STIs and will participate in an interview. Participants will receive a card with a number linking them to their blood sample and will have the option of presenting their cards to get the results of the STI tests. Those with positive results for any of the three infections will be offered free treatment. In addition, all participants will receive a small gift in return for their participation.

The target population consists of brothel-based sex workers who are strictly controlled by the brothel managers. Prior to initiating the research, a researcher meets with the brothel manager to ask permission to conduct the study. During the meeting, the manager states that all of the women working in the brothel will participate in the study.

Questions

1. What steps can the researchers take to ensure that informed consent is freely given by all participants?

2. If a woman chooses not to participate in the study, what can be done to protect her from retaliation by the manager?

3. If you believe that the women will not be able to give voluntary informed consent, what alternatives could you suggest to the Ministry of Health?

Source: Rivera et al. (2009, *Research Ethics Training Curriculum,* 2nd ed., Research Triangle Park, NC: FHI 360.

APPENDIX 8.1   An Ethical Challenge—Respect for Persons

Sexually Transmitted Infections Among Commercial Sex Workers

Suggested responses

- *What steps can the research staff take to ensure that the informed consent is freely given by all participants?*

First, the researcher should work to educate the brothel manager. Informing him that nonparticipation is acceptable might cause him to relax his attitude. In addition, the informed consent process should take place in a private, confidential setting. Women should be reminded repeatedly of the voluntary nature of the research.

- *If a woman chooses not to participate in the study, what can be done to protect her from retaliation by the manager?*

Because the manager might insist that women participate, it will be imperative that nonparticipants are anonymous. Conducting informed consent individually will be important so that peer pressure is reduced. In addition, one might consider treating all of the women as if they had enrolled. (For example, giving nonparticipants thank-you gifts or fake blood sample cards will make it difficult to distinguish the participants from the nonparticipants.)

- *If you believe that the women will not be able to give voluntary informed consent, what alternatives could you suggest to the Ministry of Health?*

If the target population will not be able to consent freely, then you are obligated to change the study or choose a different target population. For example, commercial sex workers who are not brothel-based might not face pressure from a manager that would alter their decision.

Source: Rivera et al. (2009, *Research Ethics Training Curriculum,* 2nd ed., Research Triangle Park, NC: FHI 360).

Index

⑤SAGE research**methods**

The essential online tool for researchers from the world's leading methods publisher

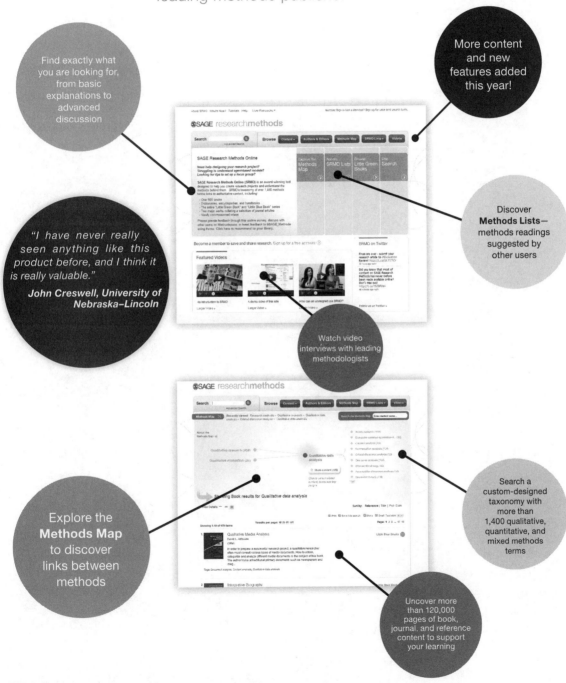

Find exactly what you are looking for, from basic explanations to advanced discussion

More content and new features added this year!

"I have never really seen anything like this product before, and I think it is really valuable."

John Creswell, University of Nebraska–Lincoln

Discover **Methods Lists**— methods readings suggested by other users

Watch video interviews with leading methodologists

Explore the **Methods Map** to discover links between methods

Search a custom-designed taxonomy with more than 1,400 qualitative, quantitative, and mixed methods terms

Uncover more than 120,000 pages of book, journal, and reference content to support your learning

Find out more at
www.sageresearchmethods.com